THE SIEGE OF PETERSBURG

The Battles for the
Weldon Railroad August 1864

John Horn

SB
Savas Beatie
California

© 2015 by John Horn

All rights reserved. No part of this publication may be reproduced, stored in a retrieval system, or transmitted, in any form or by any means, electronic, mechanical, photocopying, recording, or otherwise, without the prior written permission of the publisher.

Library of Congress Cataloging-in-Publication Data

Horn, John, 1951-
The Siege of Petersburg : the battles for the Weldon Railroad, August 1864 / John Horn— First edition.
pages cm
Includes bibliographical references and index.
ISBN 978-1-61121-216-7
1. Petersburg (Va.)—History—Siege, 1864-1865. 2. Wilmington and Weldon Rail Road— History—19th century. 3. Virginia—History—Civil War, 1861-1865—Campaigns. I. Title. II. Title: Battles for the Weldon Railroad, August 1864.
E477.21.H67 2014
975.5'58103—dc23
2014017959

SB

Published by
Savas Beatie LLC
989 Governor Drive, Suite 102
El Dorado Hills, CA 95762

Phone: 916-941-6896
(E-mail) sales@savasbeatie.com

05 04 03 02 01   5 4 3 2 1
First edition, first printing

Savas Beatie titles are available at special discounts for bulk purchases in the United States by corporations, institutions, and other organizations. For more details, please contact Special Sales, P.O. Box 4527, El Dorado Hills, CA 95762, or you may e-mail us at sales@savasbeatie.com, or visit our website at www.savasbeatie.com for additional information.

Proudly published, printed, and warehoused in the United States of America.

Nothing is impossible to men determined to win.
— *Maj. Gen. Henry Heth, C. S. A.*

To Mrs. Helen M. McDonough, my wife's grandmother, born Helen Lee Mulcaha, granddaughter of Thomas Mulcaha, who was born in Ireland around 1826, arrived in Mobile, Alabama in 1856, found employment as a farmhand in Yazoo County, Mississippi by 1860, enlisted in the 12th Mississippi Infantry at Satartia, Mississippi in 1861, married Miss Susan Bacon at Dinwiddie Court House, Virginia on November 29, 1864, was wounded at the Fort Gregg, April 2, 1865, and died in Petersburg, Virginia, Aug. 18, 1908.

Table of Contents

Preface to the First Edition
vii

Preface to the 150th Anniversary Edition / Acknowledgments
vii

Chapter 1: The War at its Crisis
1

Chapter 2: The Second Battle of Deep Bottom,
August 14, 1864
15

Chapter 3: The Second Battle of Deep Bottom,
August 15, 1864
49

Chapter 4: The Second Battle of Deep Bottom,
August 16, 1864
61

Chapter 5: The Second Battle of Deep Bottom,
August 17-21, 1864
105

Chapter 6: The Battle of Globe Tavern,
August 18, 1864
116

Chapter 7: The Battle of Globe Tavern,
August 19, 1864
140

Chapter 8: The Battle of Globe Tavern,
August 20, 1864
178

Chapter 9: The Battle of Globe Tavern,
August 21, 1864
187

Chapter 10: Wrecking the Weldon Railroad,
August 21-24, 1864
211

Table of Contents (continued)

Chapter 11: The Second Battle of Reams Station,
August 25, 1864
227

Chapter 12: The Second Battle of Reams Station,
August 25, 1864:
The Second Confederate Assault
251

Chapter 13: Had Not Success Come Elsewhere
287

Table 1: Federal Strength, July 31, 1864
315

Table 2: Confederate Strength, July-August, 1864
316

Table 3: Casualties
317

Table 4: Combat Efficiency
319

Appendix A: Orders of Battle,
Second Deep Bottom
321

Appendix B: Orders of Battle,
Globe Tavern
330

Appendix C: Orders of Battle,
Second Reams Station
339

Bibliography
345

Index
358

Maps and illustrations have been distributed
throughout the book for the convenience of the reader.

Preface to the First Edition

The battles that took place around Petersurg in August of 1864 have not received the attention that they deserve. Fought during the crisis of morale in the North, they displayed Lieutenant General Ulysses S. Grant at the height of his generalship and the Confederate Army of Northern Virginia at the peak of its qualitative superiority. Grant's Fourth Offensive, which gave rise to the August battles, ranks as the longest and among the two bloodiest of Grant's nine offensives during the Petersburg campaign.

The August battles around Petersburg have suffered neglect because they occurred between the Battle of the Crater and the fall of Atlanta. Yet the Fourth Offensive adhered to the same basic plan that resulted in the Battle of the Crater. The Fourth Offensive also contributed to the fall of Atlanta by preventing the Confederate government from detaching troops from Virginia and sending them to assist in the defense of Atlanta. The fall of Atlanta proved decisive to President Abraham Lincoln's reelection and fatal to the prospect of Southern independence.

The author hopes that this book will heighten interest in the August battles around Petersburg and in the Petersburg campaign as a whole, the longest, bloodiest campaign of the American Civil War.

Preface to the 150th Anniversary Edition

How fortunate to get the opportunity to revise my first book and take advantage of what I have learned since writing it. If only we got a chance to correct all our mistakes. Doubtless, some errors remain, but this edition should provide a richer and more accurate experience for the reader.

Over the years I have reversed course entirely when it comes to footnotes. In the first edition of this book, I footnoted everything. I believe I choked the first edition with footnotes. Since writing that book, though, I have concluded that footnoting everything is unnecessary. Take a look at a history books on other wars—Barbara W. Tuchman's *A Distant Mirror: The Calamitous 14th Century*, or Robert Middlekauff's *The Glorious Cause: The American Revolution, 1763-1789*, or Max Hasting's *Overlord: D-Day & the Battle for Normandy*,[1] for examples. None of them has a note after every sentence. None has a note at the end of every paragraph trying to do the work of a bibliography. In this revised edition, I have footnoted only direct quotations, statistics, and controversial assertions. The footnotes more than suffice for a book of this length. I have written a book, not a brief.

I hope I have enriched the book by including some biographical information about the soldiers involved. Part of the purpose of writing history lies in commemorating deeds such as the troops of both sides performed in August, 1864. The number of soldiers who returned to the ranks after amputations or crippling wounds amazes me.

Petersburg remains the Rodney Dangerfield of Civil War campaigns. It gets no respect. I can never forget the story of the old lady from Petersburg who visited relatives in England and went with them to see Shakespeare's King Richard III. When asked how she enjoyed the play, she said, "I thought it was unfair." Asked to explain that puzzling remark, she replied, "There was all that talk about Norfolk and Richmond, and not a word about Petersburg!"[2]

Acknowledgments

A number of people and institutions deserve recognition for their assistance with this book.

---

1 Barbara W. Tuchman, *A Distant Mirror: The Calamitous 14th Century* (New York: Alfred A. Knopf, 1978); Robert Middlekauff, *The Glorious Cause: The American Revolution, 1763-1789* (New York: Oxford University Press, 1982); Max Hasting, *Overlord: D-Day & the Battle for Normandy*New York: Simon & Schuster, Inc., 1984.

2 James G. Scott and Edward A. Wyatt, *Petersburg's Story: A History* (Petersburg, 1960), 14.

Acknowledgments

Christopher Calkins, former Park Historian at Petersburg National Battlefield, informed me of the opportunity to write this book and made available to me his own research and mapwork on the Battle of Globe Tavern and the Second Battle of Reams Station. Chris also reviewed and commented on my chapters on these battles and drew all the maps for the first edition of the book.

Harold E. Howard, former publisher of the Virginia Civil War Battles and Leaders Series, gave me the opportunity to write the book.

Edwin C. Bearss, former Chief Historian of the United States National Park Service, took time out from his busy schedule to read and comment on my manuscript.

Bryce A. Suderow, at work on his own book on the First and Second Battles of Deep Bottom, generously shared with me his research, map files and insights. He provided me with cited material on each of the battles described in this book, and with almost all of my citations to Confederate newspapers. Bryce also walked the Second Deep Bottom battlefield with me. Diane Svenonius transported Bryce from Washington, D.C. to Richmond that day, accompanied us on our tour of the battlefield, and shared with us her knowledge of its terrain.

Mike Andrus of the staff at Richmond National Battlefield made available to me his research and map files on the Second Battle of Deep Bottom. Mike also reviewed and commented upon my chapters on the Second Battle of Deep Bottom.

Guy R. Swanson, Curator of Manuscripts and Archives at the Museum of the Confederacy, gave me access to the papers of Major General Henry Heth in the Elizabeth S. Brockenbrough Library.

Frances Pollard of the Virginia Historical Society photocopied and mailed to me Major General Cadmus M. Wilcox's report of the Second Battle of Reams Station.

Dr. John T. Hendron of Steger, Illinois, an associate professor of history, read and commented on my manuscript.

Richard A. Shrader, Reference Archivist at the Southern Historical Collection at the University of North Carolina at Chapel Hill, provided a complimentary copy of a Confederate officer's reminiscences.

Steven J. Wright of Philadelphia, Pennsylvania, photocopied and sent me material from the Sessler Collection at the Civil War Library and Museum. Steven also reviewed and commented on my chapters on the Second Battle of Reams Station.

Doris Stack of Chicago took the time to bring a book cited herein twenty miles on a cold day.

Chicago's Newberry Library, where I did the vast preponderance of my research, afforded me a Reader's privileges—most importantly, a carrel. Most of my bibliography sat on the shelves of this library.

The Bedford Park Public Library of Bedford Park, Illinois, eased my task by allowing me to keep out the pertinent volumes of the Official Records for long periods of time.

The staff of the Civil War And American History Research Collection of the Chicago Public Library assisted me in locating illustrations for the book.

The Bremen Historical Society of Tinley Park, Illinois provided the missing ling that made a project that arose from my family's past particularly relevant to my own present by enlightening me as to the identity and history of the company of my township's Civil War soldiers.

Concerning this revised edition, I am particularly grateful to Theodore P. Savas, Managing Director for Savas Beatie LLC, for kindly inviting me to write this new expanded edition of my book, and for all the help provided by Production Director Lee Merideth.

Bryce Suderow of Washington, D.C., an outstanding researcher and an expert on the Deep Bottom battles, again—as with the first edition of this book—generously shared his research and conclusions with me. I could not have written the first edition without his help, much less this edition. Hampton Newsome of Arlington, Virginia, author of his own book on the October portion of the Petersburg Campaign, not only took the trouble to read my manuscript and offer suggestions and insights but provided the maps as well. I cannot thank Hampton enough for his immense contribution. Robert E. L. Krick of Richmond National Battlefield Park kindly read part of my manuscript and offered suggestions. Lt. Col. Henry W. Persons, United States Army (ret.), of Severn, Maryland, generously shared his research on Anderson's Brigade of the Army of Northern Virginia with me. David White of Manassas, Virginia, generously shared his research on Sanders' brigade of the Army of Northern Virginia with me. David Fletcher of Richmond, Virginia generously shared his documents and research on his ancestor, Capt. (later Lt. Col.) Theophilus Gilliam Barham of the 24th Virginia Cavalry. Brett Schulte graciously shared from his trove of material on the Petersburg campaign. Peter Trasskey helped as well. Last but not least, thanks go to my long-suffering wife and law partner, H. Elizabeth Kelley, and our office manager, JoAnn Buckmaster of Griffith, Indiana, as well as JoAnn's assistant, Brooke Sporleder.

John Horn
Tinley Park, IL
July 2014

Chapter 1

The War at its Crisis

At the beginning of August 1864, the fortunes of the United States stood near their low water mark. Those fortunes manifested themselves in the price of gold on the New York Stock Exchange. Traditionally, the price of gold has furnished a pitiless, impartial, inverse index of faith in the established order—the higher the price of gold, the less the faith. On July 11, 1864, as Lt. Gen. Jubal A. Early led a Rebel infantry corps into the suburbs of the Northern capital at Washington, D.C., the price of gold reached its wartime high and the price of a dollar in United States currency reached its wartime low.

The Confederacy had withstood the onslaughts of the two major Union army commands, one launched at the Southern capital in Richmond, Virginia, and the other at the important rail and commercial center in Atlanta, Georgia. The appalling casualties suffered by Federal troops from the beginning of May until the end of July, more than 84,000 in Lt. Gen. Ulysses Simpson Grant's army group alone, seemed in vain.

Grant, general-in-chief of Northern forces, had failed to take Richmond. Gloom and disgust prevailed among his officers and men in the aftermath of the fiasco at the battle of the Crater at Petersburg, Virginia, on July 30.[1]

---

1 For accounts of the Petersburg campaign up to this point, see John Horn, *The Petersburg Campaign: June 1864-April 1865* (Conshohocken PA, 1993), 12-119, and Edwin C. Bearss with

Major General William Tecumseh Sherman had failed to capture Atlanta. In a series of battles, skirmishes and raids lasting from July 20 until August 6, Southerners under Gen. John Bell Hood had halted Sherman's infantry and decimated his cavalry in their efforts to cut the last railroads into Atlanta.

Rear Admiral David G. Farragut's victory in the battle of Mobile Bay on August 5 started the price of gold on a decline it would continue until the end of the month. Though reassuring to the financial community, success at Mobile Bay provided little consolation to the Union electorate for the failures at Richmond and Atlanta.

Public sentiment against the war increased in the North. President of the United States Abraham Lincoln encountered threats of forcible resistance when, on July 18, he called for a draft of 500,000 more men. At the request of Congress, he declared August 4 a day of national fasting, humiliation and prayer.

The Secessionists had not merely frustrated the Federals. The Rebels had taken the offensive. General Robert Edward Lee had detached Early's Corps from the Army of Northern Virginia in early June to march down the Shenandoah Valley and threaten Washington. The move had struck the Northerners a substantial blow. Much as Maj. Gen. Thomas J. "Stonewall" Jackson had done in 1862, Early cleared the Shenandoah of Federal troops, diverted reinforcements from the Unionist command threatening Richmond, and shook the United States War Department's confidence in its general-in-chief's strategy.

Lee wanted more than this. He wanted to raise the siege of Petersburg and drive the Northerners from Richmond's doorstep. The war's heretofore master psychologist pinned his hopes on the effect that Early's threat to the Union capital would have on the command beleaguering Petersburg. Half the railroads supplying Richmond—the Weldon Railroad and the Southside Railroad—had terminals in the Cockade City, a name Petersburg had acquired because an infantry company raised there had worn rosettes, or cockades, in their hats during the War of 1812. The loss of the Cockade City would put the Federals in excellent position to cut Richmond's remaining supply lines and isolate the Confederate capital. As Grant believed in overwhelming numbers, Lee reasoned to his staff, detachment of sufficient force to protect Washington

---

Bryce Suderow, *The Petersburg Campaign: The Eastern Front Battles, June-August, 1864* (El Dorado Hills CA, 2012).

from Early would so reduce Grant's strength that he would withdraw from Petersburg altogether.

Lee's indirect strategy seemed on the verge of even greater success than it had produced in 1862, when it had merely denied reinforcements to the Unionists in front of Richmond. On the night of July 30, after receiving news that Early had crossed the Potomac into Union territory again, Grant sent the following telegram to Maj. Gen. George Gordon Meade, the commander of the Army of the Potomac: "Get all the heavy artillery in the lines about Petersburg moved back to City Point as early as possible." Then the general-in-chief added ominously: "It is by no means improbable the necessity will arise for sending two more corps there."[2] This message indicates exactly how close to success Lee's strategy came. Many on both sides, including knowledgeable observers in high places, expected that Lee would soon march his entire army into Union territory as he had in 1862 and 1863.

Panicky Republican politicians clamored for a new convention and for President Lincoln to step aside for a candidate who could win in the November election. More level-headed Republicans pressured Lincoln to abandon abolition as a stated condition of peace and to insist upon the Union alone as peace's condition. As staunchly Republican a newspaper as the *New York Times* criticized Lincoln for not negotiating with the commissioners whom President of the Confederate States Jefferson Davis had sent to Niagara Falls to take advantage of Northern war weariness by proposing a peace conference. Threatening to split the Republican vote, Maj. Gen. John Charles Fremont, famous as "The Pathfinder" for his western explorations, entered the presidential race as a radical Republican candidate. The Democrats indulged themselves in optimism.

Just as in 1862, Federal Secretary of War Edwin M. Stanton and chief of staff Maj. Gen. Henry W. "Old Brains" Halleck cracked under the strain. In their obsession with Washington's vulnerability, they ordered Maj. Gen. David Hunter, the Union commander in the Shenandoah Valley, back and forth so many times that he soon lost contact with the enemy. The back-biting Halleck criticized Grant for moving south of James River and not keeping his army

---

2 U. S. Grant to Major-General George G. Meade, July 31, 1864, in United States War Department, *The War of the Rebellion: A Compilation of the Official Records of the Union and Confederate Armies*, 128 vols. (Washington, 1880-1901), Series I, vol. 40, pt. 3, 641. Hereafter cited as *OR*. All references are to Series I unless otherwise noted.

group interposed between Richmond and Washington. Halleck also urged Grant to withdraw troops from his front and send them north to enforce the draft against expected resistance, concluding: "Are not the appearances such that we ought to take in sail and prepare the ship for a storm?"[3]

Lincoln and Grant kept their heads. Their resolve accounted for the difference between 1862, when Lee had driven Union forces from the gates of Richmond and carried the war into the North, and 1864, when Lee remained pinned down in defense of his capital. Both the president and his general-in-chief realized the extremity of the South and that the Confederacy's only hope lay in a change of Federal administrations.

As general-in-chief, Grant had the virtue of never losing sight of the overall view. He considered the Northern armies a team, and he wanted them to apply continuous pressure on their respective fronts to prevent the enemy from concentrating against any particular Unionist army. The general-in-chief believed that a withdrawal from James River would insure Sherman's defeat by allowing the Secessionists to shift forces from Virginia to Georgia for a repetition of Chickamauga.

President Lincoln, who had more nerve than any of his advisors, played his part by sustaining Grant against them. The bond between these two men withstood even the tension created by those who thought Grant a stronger presidential candidate than Lincoln and wanted the president to step aside in favor of the general-in-chief.

Before Early's cavalry had burned Chambersburg, Pennsylvania, on July 30, Grant had resisted Lincoln's request to come north in person and rectify the situation in the Shenandoah. The general-in-chief thought that his departure from the Petersburg trenches would signify a loss of faith in the strategy that had taken him south of the James. Early's second incursion into Northern territory created such serious repercussions that during the first week of August Grant finally yielded to the president.

At a conference with Lincoln at Fortress Monroe on July 31, the general-in-chief and the president decided to deal with this crisis—perhaps the crisis of the war—not by abandoning the Siege of Petersburg, but by putting under a single commander the field forces of all four of the Shenandoah's military departments. On August 2, Grant sent to the Shenandoah Maj. Gen.

---

3   H. W. Halleck to Lieut. Gen. U. S. Grant, August 11, 1864, in *OR* 42, pt. 2, 111-2.

Philip H. Sheridan to take command of all the troops in the field there. Grant directed Sheridan to pursue the enemy to the death.

Halleck's quibbling over this order exhausted Lincoln's patience. The president insisted upon Grant's personal presence in the vicinity of Washington not so much to protect the capital as to get the Federal forces in the Shenandoah moving aggressively after Early. Lincoln wanted a general in charge, not a bureaucrat.

Hastening by boat and train to Monocacy Station, Maryland, northwest of Washington, Grant laid the foundation for September's Union victories in the Shenandoah by removing Hunter and placing Sheridan in departmental as well as field command, then reinforcing Sheridan with another cavalry division from the Union army group threatening Richmond, and finally putting Sheridan in charge of a new military division consolidating his own department with three others. For the moment, Sheridan remained untested as an independent commander and uncharacteristically hesitant in the face of exaggerated reports of Early's strength.

Lee quickly perceived that Grant had sent reinforcements to the Shenandoah. The Virginian persisted in his strategy of threatening the Federal capital. To protect Early, Lee on August 6 dispatched to Culpeper Court House Kershaw's division of Anderson's Corps and Fitzhugh Lee's division of cavalry, both under Lt. Gen. Richard H. "Fighting Dick" Anderson, a West Pointer and Mexican War Veteran who had moved up to corps command after a Confederate bullet put out of action the previous corps commander, Lt. Gen. James Longstreet, at the battle of the Wilderness on May 6. Lee ordered Anderson to thwart any enemy move across the Blue Ridge into the Shenandoah by menacing Washington.[4]

---

4 Unaware of the impact of the burning of Chambersburg on the Unionists, an impact which suggested that an army burning its way through Northern territory would furnish the most effective means of relieving Richmond, Lee had already shown by the restrictions he had placed on his soldiers during the previous year's Gettysburg campaign his unreceptiveness to the notion of unleashing terror on enemy civilians as Sheridan and Sherman would soon do in the Shenandoah and the Deep South. The commander of the Army of Northern Virginia preferred what Lincoln's commanders had come to scorn as soft war, to what they had learned to esteem as hard war. Lee had gone so far during the Gettysburg campaign as to post guards at Pennsylvania farms to prevent his troops from pillaging them. He wanted to win the war, but he considered making war on enemy civilians as bad as losing. The idea repelled him, as would the notion of resorting to guerrilla warfare after Appomattox. Field Marshal Viscount Wavell of Cyrenaica and Winchester wrote of Lee, "He was possibly too much of a gentleman for the ungentle business of war." Field-Marshal Bernard Viscount Montgomery of Alamein, *A History*

Federal Pontoon Bridge at Deep Bottom *Library of Congress*

The Southerners also went on the offensive on the Petersburg front. They took steps to eliminate the Federal bridgehead at Deep Bottom. On August 7, Lt. Col. John Clifford Pemberton prepared to implement a plan that he and President Davis had formulated to drive the Unionists from the Deep Bottom bridgehead. Deep Bottom lay where Four Mile Creek emptied into the end of a wide meander of James River, about twelve miles southeast of Richmond as the crow flies. Brig. Gen. Robert Sanford Foster's brigade of the Army of the James had held the bridgehead since June 20. A bluff around forty feet high where mulberries and cherries abounded, Deep Bottom afforded Grant access to the north side of the James from Bermuda Hundred. Whenever he wanted, he could mount a threat to Richmond by reinforcing the bridgehead. Elimination of the Deep Bottom bridgehead would require the Federals to cross James River much farther downstream, significantly reducing the danger to the Confederate capital.

---

of Warfare (Cleveland, 1968), 24. Major General J. F. C. Fuller sheds still more light on Lee in *The Generalship of Ulysses S. Grant* (London, 1929), 228-31, 299-304, 375-81.

Vanquished by Grant at Vicksburg the previous summer, Pemberton served as a lieutenant colonel of artillery in the Department of Richmond because no Confederate unit warranting a higher-ranking commander would serve under the northern-born former lieutenant general. He planned to bring the pontoon bridges linking Deep Bottom with Bermuda Hundred under the fire of enough artillery to force the abandonment of the bridgehead. Heavy artillery at the foot of New Market Heights would enfilade the bridgehead from the north while rifled fieldpieces at Tilghman's Gate created a crossfire.

Despite the importance of opening fire as soon as possible, shortages delayed implementation of Pemberton's plan. They illustrated the immense difference between Northern and Southern industrial capacities. A scarcity of mortars forced Pemberton to supplement the two 10-inch mortars available with four 8-inch howitzers placed with their trails sunk to give the necessary elevation. Positioning the relatively short-ranged howitzers close enough to the pontoon bridges to render the guns effective left them outside the Confederate fortifications at New Market Heights and vulnerable to capture by a sortie from Deep Bottom. A shortage of transportation hampered moving the mortars. Lee's artillerists at Petersburg had a prior claim on the use of the sole serviceable mortar sling cart in the department. Time ticked away on an opportunity for the Secessionists to deny Grant access to the strategy he had employed the previous month and that he would employ in August and September as well—a right cross thrown at Richmond from the bridgehead at Deep Bottom, followed by a left hook delivered on the Petersburg front.

While Pemberton struggled, Grant faced his own challenges. Returning to City Point on August 9, the general-in-chief narrowly escaped death. That morning Brig. Gen. George H. Sharpe, the assistant provost-marshal-general, informed the general-in-chief that spies had infiltrated the Federal supply base at City Point. Grant's army group drew virtually all its sustenance from City Point, a port which had grown into a small city with hundreds of buildings and a wealth of supplies beyond Rebel imagination. Fleets of steamboats, sailing vessels, and barges unloaded at its wharves.

Sharpe, a New York lawyer educated at Yale, proposed a plan to detect and capture the spies. Staff officers present at this meeting included Lt. Col. Horace Porter, Grant's aide-de-camp, the son of a governor of Pennsylvania, and a graduate of Harvard and West Point. Sharpe had just left Grant when, at 11:40 a.m., Porter remembered, "a terrific explosion shook the earth, accompanied by a sound which vividly recalled the Petersburg mine, still fresh in the memory of

Lt. Col. John C. Pemberton, C.S.A. *Library of Congress*

everyone present."⁵ Shells, shot, bullets, timber fragments, body parts and even saddles rained down on the general-in-chief's headquarters in Appomattox Manor. A bullet wounded the hand of Col. Orville E. Babcock, another aide-de-camp and West Point graduate, but the general-in-chief escaped unscathed. A boat loaded with ordnance stores had exploded, destroying the boat and the wharf at which it lay and killing all the laborers aboard as well as

---

5 Horace Porter, *Campaigning with Grant* (New York, 1897), 273.

men and horses near the landing. The blast slew 43 and wounded 126.[6] By all accounts, Grant himself behaved in exemplary fashion.[7]

John Maxwell, a Confederate spy, had built what he called a "horological torpedo"—a time bomb which contained twelve pounds of powder.[8] He and another spy, R. K. Dillard, had entered Federal lines dressed as laborers and headed for the supply base at City Point. Mingling with the workers unloading stores from a boat, the pair placed their torpedo amid the ammunition on the boat and set the clock for half an hour to allow themselves to get far enough away to escape injury or suspicion. They underestimated the enormous blast. The bomb went off after an hour and deafened Dillard but the two spies escaped.

The Federals on James River did not remain idle. On August 10, the commander of the Army of the James, Maj. Gen. Benjamin Franklin Butler, sent a detachment from Bermuda Hundred to begin work on a canal at Dutch Gap, a few miles upriver from Deep Bottom. A lawyer and former governor of Massachusetts known to Southerners as "Beast" because they considered oppressive his occupation of New Orleans, Butler had failed in his mission to capture Richmond before Grant reached James River. Now the Beast intended to open up the James to Union ironclads by digging a new channel. Discovering the excavation, the Rebels prepared to bring Butler's workmen under fire from field artillery and the gunboats of the Confederate Navy's James River Flotilla. The Beast's project would eventually result in today's main ship channel to Richmond—but not until 1865, after its success or failure had ceased to make a difference to the outcome of the war.

Lee continued to send troops from the Petersburg front to menace Washington. On August 11, he appointed Maj. Gen. Wade Hampton III commander of the Cavalry Corps of the Army of Northern Virginia and dispatched Hampton on the 15th with Brig. Gen. Matthew Calbraith Butler's division of horsemen to join Anderson at Culpeper Court House. The

---

6   J. C. Pemberton to James A. Seddon, in OR 42, pt. 2, 1164.

7   One source, based on contemporary hearsay, had Grant alone of those present rushing toward the scene of the explosion. George Agassiz, ed., *Meade's Headquarters, 1863-1865: Letters of Colonel Theodore Lyman from the Wilderness to Appomattox* (Boston, 1922), 217. Another source, a memoir written many years afterward by an eyewitness, had Grant sitting through the incident unperturbed. Porter, *Campaigning with Grant*, 274.

8   Report of John Maxwell, Secret Service, Confederate States, December 16, 1864, in OR 42, pt. 1, 954-5.

appointment of Hampton, a South Carolinian grandee trained in the law and an outstanding leader of cavalry, would pay rich dividends for the Army of Northern Virginia.

Between August 8 and August 11, reports arrived at City Point that several divisions of Lee's army had left the Petersburg front en route to join Early in the Shenandoah or Hood at Atlanta. By August 12, Grant determined that Lee had reinforced Early with two or three divisions of infantry and one of cavalry. To force Lee to recall these troops to the Petersburg front, Grant immediately began to issue directives for another offensive there.

On the morning of August 13, the Rockbridge Battery of light artillery on Signal Hill, Poague's artillery battalion on Proctor's Creek ridge and Confederate rams on James River below Chaffin's Bluff opened a severe cross fire on the Federals at Dutch Gap. The Water Battery at the northern terminus of the Union Bermuda Hundred lines and Federal gunboats near Jones' Neck on the James replied. Firing had almost ceased by noon, and the Confederates had failed to force the Northerners at Dutch gap to stop digging.

At about 3:00 p.m., Pemberton's mortars at the foot of New Market Heights and his howitzers about a half mile closer to the river finally opened fire on the Federal pontoon bridges at Deep Bottom. A section of Parrott rifles at Sweeney's Pottery, where the New Market Road crossed Bailey's Creek, joined in with Pemberton's heavy guns. The Secessionists failed to find the range on the pontoon bridges and soon received the attention of the Union gunboats, which commenced an accurate fire upon the Rebel lines.

On the same day, Grant finally authorized the return of his heavy artillery to the front lines from Broadway Landing, where a subordinate had diverted it on July 30. The Northern general-in-chief also received information that Matthew Butler's division of the Cavalry Corps of the Army of Northern Virginia had departed the Petersburg front for the Shenandoah. A rumor circulated that Lee's entire army, except for Pickett's division, had orders to go north.

In the Bermuda Hundred and Petersburg trenches, the armies roasted during an extraordinary spell of hot and dry weather. George Anson Bruce, a captain in the 13th New Hampshire of Stevens' brigade, Carr's division, in XVIII Corps of the Army of the James, later wrote:

> The summer of 1864 was one of excessive heat. For forty-five days no rain had fallen and a tropical sun, unveiled by a single cloud, beat down upon the earth. Springs and streams had dried up and nowhere was there a green thing visible. The trees were loaded with a coating of dust that obscured their natural coloring and neutralized

everything to a dusty brown. The clayey soil was baked into a hardened mass, but its surface was covered with a find dust that floated in the air like a mist, and, while it somewhat obscured the brightness of the sun's rays, it made the heat more oppressive and harder to bear. The hot and suffocating nights took from sleep its usual refreshment after the hard labors of the day.[9]

Used up in the Overland Campaign and during the opening assaults on Petersburg, the Army of the Potomac lacked the enthusiasm and elan necessary to turn its numerical and positional advantages into victory. Battle casualties of more than 70,000 killed, wounded and missing, as well as detachments, desertion, disease and expiring enlistments, had reduced it from about 120,000 soldiers at the beginning of May to 52,061 at the end of July despite more than 55,000 replacements, most of them poor in quality.[10] The Unionists further reduced the effectiveness of their replacements by employing them in entirely new units rather than integrating them into veteran formations.[11] Meade, the

---

9 George A. Bruce, *The Twentieth Regiment of Massachusetts Volunteer Infantry, 1861-1865* (Boston, 1906), 416. As unlikely as it may seem, this officer of the 13th New Hampshire authored the history of the 20th Massachusetts.

10 Robert U. Johnson and Clarence C. Buel, eds., *Battles and Leaders of the Civil War*, 4 vols. (New York, 1884, 1888), 4:182; Return of Casualties in the Union forces, commanded by Lieut. Gen. Ulysses S. Grant, from the Rapidan to the James River, in OR 36, pt. 1, 188; Return of Casualties in the Union Forces, June 15-30, 1864, ibid., 40, pt. 1, 238; General summary of Casualties in the Union Forces operating against Richmond, VA., July 1-31, 1864, including Deep Bottom (27th-29th), "The Crater" (30th), and along the lines, ibid., 268; H. W. Halleck to Lt. Gen. Ulysses S. Grant, ibid., pt. 2, 47-48; Abstract from return of the Army of the Potomac, Maj. Gen. George G. Meade, U.S. Army, commanding, for the month of July, 1864, ibid., pt. 3, 728. See Table 1: Federal Strength.

11 Pernicious in many other respects, the Bounty And Furlough Act passed by the Confederate Congress in 1861 encouraged enlistments in existing units and further strengthened them with the men who waited for conscription. The Union army, which did not employ conscription until July, 1863, suffered until then from a failure to strengthen existing outfits. Instead, new units formed while old ones dwindled into insignificance. Without the Bounty And Furlough Act and its successors, many Confederate regiments that remained strong to the war's end would have withered away. The constant strengthening of existing formations gave the Southerners an advantage in combat. Conscripts assigned to veteran outfits learned soldiering much more quickly that volunteers who joined green units. Conventional wisdom valued a recruit in an experienced formation as highly as three in a new one. The Bounty and Furlough Act and its successors may have accounted for much of the edge in fighting efficiency that Secessionist soldiers enjoyed over their Unionist counterparts. An Act providing for the granting of bounty and furloughs to privates and non-commissioned officers in the Provisional Army, in OR 5, 1016-7.

Confederate attackers had 92 percent of the combat effectiveness of Union defenders, while Federal soldiers on the offensive had only 42 percent of the combat effectiveness of

Army of the Potomac's leader, in a letter to his wife on July 23, wrote: "The army would hail an honorable peace with delight, and I do believe, if the question was left to those who do the fighting, an honorable peace would be made in a few hours."[12]

Benjamin Butler's smaller Army of the James had suffered a far lower percentage of losses during the months of May, June and July and remained a proportionately more effective fighting force than the Army of the Potomac. More than 13,000 battle casualties, in addition to desertion, disease, and expiring enlistments, had reduced it from about 40,000 men at the beginning of May to 33,816 by the end of July in spite of numerous replacements.[13]

Opposite the Federals, Lee's troops had also endured substantial losses. Detachments, desertion, disease, and about 35,000 battle casualties had reduced the components of Lee's army group at Petersburg from an initial strength of around 100,000 at the beginning of May to almost 56,795 just before Butler's division departed for Culpeper Court House.[14] Lee received too few

---

defending Secessionists. Richard E. Beringer, Herman Hattaway, Archer Jones, and William N. Still, Jr., *Why The South Lost The Civil War* (Athens GA, 1986), 472. The Army of the Potomac attacked at Antietam with 61 percent of the combat effectiveness of the Army of Northern Virginia, while the Army of Northern Virginia on the offensive at Gettysburg had 100 percent of the combat effectiveness of the defending Army of the Potomac. T. N. Dupuy, *The Evolution of Weapons and Warfare* (Indianapolis, 1980), 336.

An interesting discussion of the advantages of reinforcing existing formations occurs in Field Marshal Erich von Manstein's *Lost Victories: The War Memoirs of Hitler's Most Brilliant General* (Novato CA, 1982), 187-8, 268-9, 280. The disproportionately severe losses of newly formed units such as the Union heavy artillery regiments, the Federal equivalents of the hapless Luftwaffe Field Divisions criticized by von Manstein, earned them a category of their own in William F. Fox's *Regimental Losses in the American Civil War, 1861-1865* (Albany NY, 1889), 5-6. On June 18, 1864, at Petersburg, the 1st Maine Heavy Artillery lost more men in a single day than any other regiment in any of the war's actions. Ibid., 451.

12 George Meade, *The Life and Letters of George Gordon Meade, Major-General United States Army*, 2 vols. (New York, 1913), 2:215.

13 Johnson and Buel, eds., *Battles and Leaders of the Civil War*, 4:182; Return of Casualties in the Union Forces, commanded by Maj. Gen. Benjamin F. Butler, U.S. Army (compiled from nominal lists of casualties, returns &c.), May 5-31, 1864, in OR 36, pt. 2, 18; Return of Casualties in the Union Forces, June 15-30, 1864, ibid., 40, pt. 1, 238; ibid., 268; ibid., pt. 2, 47-48; Abstract from returns of the Department of Virginia and North Carolina, Maj. Gen. Benjamin F. Butler, U.S. Army, commanding, for the month of July, 1864, ibid., pt. 3, 737. See Table 1: Federal Strength.

14 Andrew A. Humphreys, *The Virginia Campaign of '64 and '65: the Army of the Potomac and the Army of the James*, 2 vols. (New York, 1963), 1:15-17, 141, 144; Abstract from field return of the Army of Northern Virginia, General Robert E. Lee commanding, for July 10, 1864, in OR 40,

replacements to permit himself the luxury of complaining about anything other than their quantity, but the Secessionist system got the most out of them by integrating them into veteran formations. Lean but healthy from a skimpy yet balanced diet, the Rebels remained in high morale and determined to keep the enemy out of Richmond. On August 6, Dr. Spencer G. Welch, the surgeon of the 13th Regiment South Carolina Volunteers in McGowan's brigade of Wilcox's division, wrote to his wife: "I am willing to do anything to whip out the Yankees."[15]

The Confederates enjoyed no more immunity from internal political strife than did the Federals. A pro-war but anti-Administration faction and an outright peace-at-any-price faction bedeviled the Secessionist government in the same way that their Northern counterparts plagued Lincoln's government. A bitter controversy raged throughout the South over President Davis's removal of Gen. Joseph Eggleston "Joe" Johnston from the command of the army defending Atlanta. The Confederates also suffered from material wants unknown in the North, though prices in Richmond had begun to fall and the value of Confederate currency overseas had begun to rise.

By August 13, Field's division of Anderson's Corps had received orders to prepare to tramp to Culpeper Court House. There it would join General Anderson, Kershaw's division of Anderson's Corps, and Fitzhugh Lee's and Matthew Butler's divisions of the Cavalry Corps. These four divisions would threaten Washington from the southwest. W. H. F. "Rooney" Lee's division of Rebel horsemen appears to have received orders to prepare for a ride to the Shenandoah.[16] With Early's command, it would menace the Federal capital from the west. Five of the Army of Northern Virginia's nine infantry divisions and all of its cavalry would have returned to Northern Virginia. Little would

---

pt. 3, 761; Abstract from tri-monthly return of the Department of Richmond, Lieut. Gen. R. S. Ewell commanding, for July 31, 1864, ibid., 822; Abstract from tri-monthly return of the Department of Richmond, Lieut. Gen. Richard S. Ewell commanding, August 31, 1864, and Abstract from monthly return of the Army of Northern Virginia, General Robert E. Lee, commanding, August 31, 1864, ibid., 42, pt. 2, 1213-4. The components of Lee's army group included the Army of Northern Virginia, the Department of Richmond, and reinforcements from the Department of North Carolina and Southern Virginia and the Department of South Carolina, Georgia and Florida. See Table 2: Confederate Strength.

15 Spencer G. Welch, *A Confederate Surgeon's Letters to his Wife* (New York, 1911), 103.

16 Byrd C. Willis Diary, August 13, 1864, Byrd C. Willis Papers, Virginia State Library, Richmond, Virginia.

remain but for Lee himself to move North before he would shift the seat of war into Union territory and compel Grant to abandon the siege of Petersburg.

Neither Field's foot soldiers nor Rooney Lee's cavalry departed the Petersburg front. Grant beat Lee to the punch and prevented such movements. The Unionist general-in-chief's aggressive leadership would keep the commander of the Army of Northern Virginia from crossing the Potomac in 1864 as he had in each of the two preceding years, or from dispatching forces to assist the Secessionists in Georgia, as he had the previous autumn.

Chapter 2

The Second Battle of Deep Bottom, August 14, 1864

Grant had decided on August 12 to take the offensive. He chose to implement a plan similar to the one that had fallen apart on July 30. That plan had called for Maj. Gen. Winfield S. Hancock to take a force of two divisions of Sheridan's cavalry, as well as Hancock's own II Corps, north of the James to threaten Richmond. The force would cross James River at Deep Bottom. Sheridan and the cavalry would dash around the Confederate right toward the Rebel capital and the Virginia Central Railroad while II Corps pushed toward Chaffin's Bluff on the Secessionist left to prevent the Southerners from cutting off the cavalry. Grant had hoped this would at least draw a large part of Lee's forces away from the Southside, where the general-in-chief intended to follow up with a grand raid on the Petersburg Railroad (commonly called the Weldon Railroad because it connected Petersburg with Weldon, North Carolina). He planned to send four cavalry divisions and an infantry corps to destroy fifteen or twenty miles of track. If Sheridan managed to rip up the Virginia Central north of Richmond, or if he or Hancock captured the capital, so much the better.

In July, Grant had no sooner set the plan in motion than he altered it, dropping the projected attack on the Weldon Railroad to take advantage of the completion of the Petersburg mine. The plan worked well enough that even after the battle of the Crater ended in disaster on the morning of July 30, so many Confederates remained north of the James that at 2:00 p.m. on the same day, Grant changed plan again and ordered the strike on the Weldon Railroad for July 31. By 5:00 p.m., enough Rebels had returned to the Southside that the

Brig. Gen. Francis C. Barlow, Maj. Gen. Winfield Scott Hancock,
Brig. Gen Nelson A. Miles, and Brig. Gen. John Gibbon, U.S.A. *Library of Congress*

general-in-chief again suspended the attack. Grant chose not to lift the suspension after a division of infantry and a division of cavalry departed for Washington that night because of fears for the safety of the capital caused by Early's incursion. Grant's third offensive of the Petersburg campaign came to an end.

In August, Grant again put Hancock in charge of the expedition to the north side of the James. Known as "Hancock the Superb" since the Peninsula Campaign, this thrice wounded West Pointer and hero of Gettysburg stood at the peak of his prestige. This time Hancock had at his disposal three divisions of his own II Corps, two divisions of X Corps under Maj. Gen. David B. Birney, and Brig. Gen. David M. Gregg's cavalry division. The general-in-chief imposed a goal additional to that of laying the foundation for a grand raid on the Weldon Railroad. He had more in mind than drawing a large portion of Lee's forces away from the Southside—Grant wanted to force Lee to recall the troops reportedly sent to Early.

The general-in-chief also added a refinement to the plan. While X Corps crossed the James on the upper Deep Bottom pontoon bridge and Gregg's division crossed on the lower pontoon bridge, II Corps would participate in a ruse. II Corps would march to City Point and there embark upon steamers which would take the corps down the river. Grant hoped this would deceive the Confederates into thinking Washington the destination of the movement. The steamers would reverse course after nightfall, run back up James River to Deep Bottom, throw out gangplanks to the shore, and by 5:00 a.m. disembark the troops, who would then maneuver the lulled Rebels off New Market Heights and push on to the Secessionist capital.

The many branches of Grant's plan would have done Napoleon I proud. If it resulted in the capture of Richmond, it would obtain a result considered decisive of the November election. If it permitted Grant to cut the Virginia Central, it would deny the Confederates an important supply line. If it only drew soldiers north from Petersburg, it would facilitate an advance toward the city that might result in its capture or the cutting of another Rebel supply line, the Weldon Railroad. Threatening even the least of these objectives—the Weldon Railroad—would probably compel Lee to withdraw troops from the Shenandoah.

The preliminaries for Grant's fourth offensive at Petersburg got underway on August 12. II Corps hiked to City Point in the afternoon and bivouacked there that evening. The men and horses plodded the ten miles in excessive heat over dusty roads. Despite frequent halts and a leisurely pace, cases of sunstroke already appeared.

Next day, Hancock issued his orders for the operation. He had formulated them with the benefit of intelligence from Benjamin Butler that the Rebels had fewer than 5,000 soldiers north of James River and southeast of Richmond, exclusive of a small force of reserve militia. Butler based his opinion on a detailed estimate from Lt. John I. Davenport, an Army of the James intelligence officer who reported that three Confederate infantry brigades of the seven recently stationed there had departed, presumably for the Shenandoah Valley.[1]

---

1 Memorandum of John I. Davenport, August 13, 1864, in OR 42, pt. 2, 159-160; Benj. F. Butler to Major General Hancock, August 13, 1864, ibid., 160.

None of the Secessionist infantry north of the James and southeast of Richmond had left. Major General Charles William Field, the Southern commander in this sector, had eight infantry brigades to deploy in the Rebel earthworks stretching from James River to Fussell's Mill on Bailey's Creek, a tributary of Four Mile Creek. Near Dutch Gap on the river, Johnson's Tennessee brigade of the Department of Richmond held Signal Hill. A two-brigade detachment of Wilcox's division under Brig. Gen. James Conner occupied rifle pits in the woods north of the Kingsland Road from Signal Hill eastward to the Deep Bottom Road. Skirmishers of Field's division under Brig. Gen. John Gregg occupied rifle pits from the Deep Bottom Road on Conner's left. Gregg's picket line stretched eastward behind Bailey's Creek to the Long Bridge Road at the foot of New Market Heights, leaving empty the earthworks extending about a mile and a half northeastward to Fussell's Mill. The balance of Field's division, about three quarters of its strength, remained in the breastworks on New Market Heights. From those heights, Brown's battalion of Confederate artillery dominated the approaches from Deep Bottom.

Gary's brigade of cavalry from the Department of Richmond protected the left of Field's infantry. The Hampton Legion of this brigade picketed from James River northward to the Charles City Road while the 24th Virginia Cavalry guarded the extreme Rebel left farther east at Bottom's Bridge. The 7th South Carolina Cavalry remained in camp at a farm about a mile east of Fussell's Mill. Behind Field's right, about two miles upriver from Signal Hill, the 25th Virginia Battalion and the 1st Regiment Virginia Reserves guarded the Secessionist gunners in the vital fortifications at Chaffin's Bluff. All in all, Field had around 12,000 soldiers to face as many as 38,000 foes starting the operation under Hancock's command.[2]

As he had in July, Hancock planned to maneuver the Confederates from their nearly impregnable position atop New Market Heights behind Bailey's Creek by turning the Rebel left flank. His August orders called for David

---

2 Abstract from field return of the Army of Northern Virginia, General Robert E. Lee commanding, for June 10, 1864, in ibid., 40, pt. 3, 761; Abstract from tri-monthly return of the Department of Richmond, Lieut. Gen. R. S. Ewell commanding, for July 31, 1864, ibid., 822; Abstract from tri-monthly return of the Department of Richmond, Lieut. Gen. Richard S. Ewell commanding, August 31, 1864, ibid., 42, pt. 2, 1213; Abstract from return of the Army of the Potomac, Maj. Gen. George G. Meade, U.S. Army, commanding, for the month of July, 1864, ibid., 40, pt. 3, 728; Abstract from returns of the Department of Virginia and North Carolina, Maj. Gen. Benjamin F. Butler, U.S. Army, commanding, for the month of July, 1864, ibid., 737.

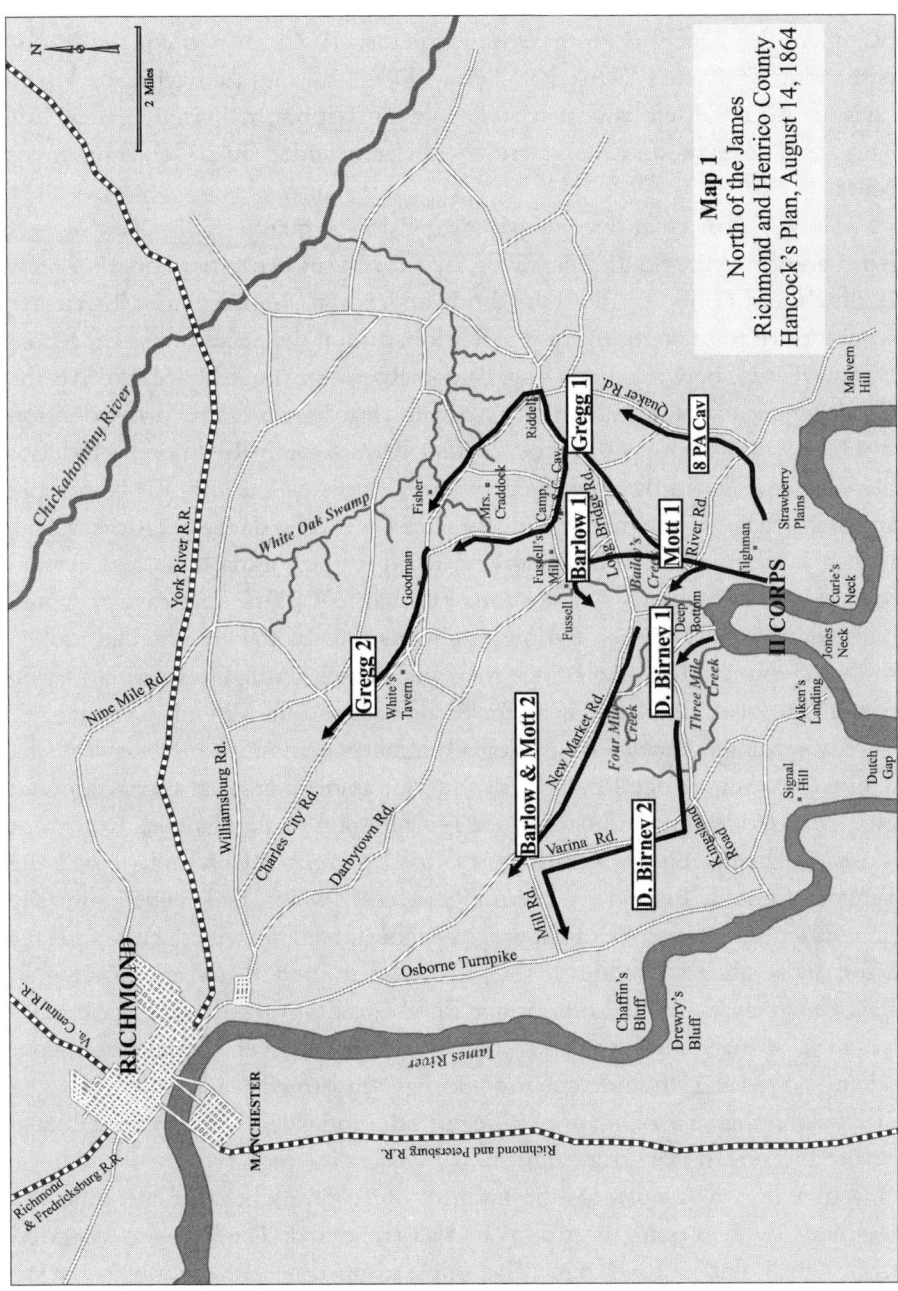

Gregg's cavalry division to cross the James to Strawberry Plains on the lower Deep Bottom pontoon bridge at nightfall. X Corps would cross the upper pontoon bridge at midnight, except for Foster's brigade, which already occupied the Deep Bottom entrenchments. II Corps would finish disembarking at Curle's Neck just below Deep Bottom at daybreak. Mott's division would disembark first, followed by Gibbon's division under Col. Thomas A. Smyth, and then Barlow's division under Brig. Gen. Nelson A. Miles.

The II Corps chief directed Mott's division to march up the New Market Road and drive the Southerners into their fortifications across Bailey's Creek. Barlow's and Gibbon's divisions, both under Maj. Gen. Francis A. Barlow, would move to the right of Mott's division, assault the Secessionist left across Bailey's Creek between the Long Bridge Road and Fussell's Mill, drive the Confederates off New Market Heights, and clear Mott's front. Mott's division would then advance up the New Market Road toward Richmond's Exterior Defense line. David Birney's X Corps would thrust to the left of II Corps and attack the Rebel right behind Four Mile Creek as early as daybreak. If successful, Birney would march up the Kingsland Road to the Varina Road and beyond toward the Secessionist fortifications at Chaffin's Bluff. The cavalry would cover first Mott's and then Barlow's right. As soon as the infantry had broken through between the Long Bridge road and Fussell's Mill, Gregg would swing to the right of II Corps and head for Richmond and the Virginia Central.

Everything depended on Hancock's infantry getting across Bailey's Creek above the Long Bridge Road. Until the foot soldiers crossed there, captured New Market Heights, and opened the New Market Road, Hancock would not loose his cavalry on the Charles City Road to seize Richmond or raid the Virginia Central. Instead of assuming success, which had eluded him the previous month, Hancock might well have considered further concentrating his effort by sending a brigade of Gregg's horse soldiers to seize a crossing of Bailey's Creek above the Long Bridge Road ahead of the infantry. The cavalry would have arrived hours before the foot soldiers. Even if prevented from seizing a crossing, the horsemen could have informed Hancock of what he faced along that axis of advance. Gregg's other brigade of cavalry would have sufficed to screen Hancock's right.

At noon on August 13, the infantry of II Corps began filing onto the steamers. By 7:30 p.m., the troops had all embarked. The steamers departed from City Point at 10:00 p.m. The ships stopped around midnight, having dropped down the James about five miles. Then the fleet reversed course and headed upriver toward Deep Bottom. Having looked forward to seeing Washington again, the soldiers felt disappointed. To make matters worse, the suffocating heat and, in the words of Hancock's senior aide-de-camp, Maj.

William Galbraith Mitchell, a civil engineer who had originally enlisted as a private in the 25th Pennsylvania Infantry, "infernally tormenting" mosquitoes, made sleep or rest impossible.[3] The men of II Corps never forgot that night—or the following day.

The troops of X Corps also spent an unpleasant night on the 13th. That morning they had received orders to prepare to move out early on the morning of August 14. The high command had taken such care to conceal Grant's plan and to make Washington appear the destination of the movement that a rumor developed that X Corps would soon depart for the capital or the Shenandoah. Most of the men looked with approval on the anticipated change of scenery, preferring the wide open spaces of The Valley to the trenches of Deep Bottom and Bermuda Hundred. By the following morning, the depressing truth about their destination had dawned upon them. Sergeant Robert Brady, Jr., a veteran of the 11th Maine in the Deep Bottom bridgehead who had reenlisted in January and survived a shoulder wound at Bermuda Hundred in June, later wrote:

> In the night, a sultry one, with little air stirring anywhere, none at all in the woods, so that we of the picket line were all restless and wakeful from the heat, we could hear the rumble of artillery wagons crossing the bridges from the south shore, and the trampling of a host of cavalry horses as they took the same road. We could not tell by which bridge they were crossing. The sound was evidently deadened by hay that had been strewed over the bridges, but still the dull roar of artillery wheels and the clattering of iron-shod hoofs came clearly to our ears, and then after a time there was a continual screeching of boat whistles, indicating that a large number of steamers were gathering along our river front. What it meant we did not really know, but it seemed to many of us as if our dream of a stirring campaign in the Shenandoah Valley was to remain a dream. Still, some sturdily contended for a time that what we were hearing was but the arrival of a relieving force. But as the artillery rolled, and the horses trampled, and the whistles blew, it became plain to these even that the crossing force was much too large for a mere relieving one. There could be one other meaning—for we knew the signs of the times—and we went to sleep, those that did sleep, with the firm conviction that when we woke it would be to fall into line to learn what sort of soldiers occupied the rebeldom in our immediate front.[4]

---

3   W. G. Mitchell, Copy of daily memoranda taken at headquarters of the Second Army Corps, Army of the Potomac, during the campaign commencing May 3, 1864, with copies of messages, dispatches, &c., ibid., 42, pt. 1, 241.

4   Robert Brady, *The Story of One Regiment: The Eleventh Maine Infantry Volunteers in the War of the Rebellion* (New York, 1896), 237, 422-3.

An unusual amount of straggling prevailed among those brigades which had to cross the James. Believing their immediate destination Bermuda Hundred, where they would embark upon transports, many men unable to endure a march had reported themselves fit for duty. Such soldiers quickly fell out because of exhaustion or the realization of their actual destination, depriving some units of as much as a quarter of their initial strength.[5]

When David Birney's X Corps moved out at sunrise that Saturday morning, it marched toward "rebeldom" and not toward Washington or the Shenandoah. Terry's division took the lead. Forming the right of the division, Foster's brigade plodded up the right bank of Four Mile Creek. Pond's brigade—the Western Brigade—in echelon with its right advanced, formed the division's left. Hawley's brigade remained in reserve. Behind Terry's division tramped a provisional division under Brig. Gen. William Birney, David Birney's older brother. This division consisted of Coan's and Osborn's brigades of William Birney's division of X Corps, and a previously unattached brigade of United States Colored Troops.

At 3:00 a.m., Brig. Gen. Robert S. Foster had ordered his brigade of Terry's division to attack at daybreak. A tinner from Indiana, Foster had enlisted as a private in the 11th Indiana Infantry and worked his way up through the ranks. From his left near the Yarbrough house to his right near Four Mile Creek, his men occupied a line three-quarters of a mile long—a space appropriate for an entire division. Foster had in line of battle, preceded by a heavy skirmish line, the 1st Maryland Cavalry (dismounted), the 10th Connecticut, the 11th Maine, and the 100th New York. The Deep Bottom Road bisected the brigade, running between the 10th Connecticut and the 11th Maine. The right of the 100th New York rested as close to Four Mile Creek as the nature of the ground and the presence of the enemy on the opposite bank would permit—which meant that the brigade often lost contact with the stream. "The ground over which we passed . . . cannot be described," remembered First Lt. George H. Stowits, a former teacher leading Company A of the 100th New York. "Brush, briars, swamp, ravines and pits, are but expressions for the surface of this historic soil."[6] Foster had the 24th Massachusetts in reserve behind the 10th

---

5 Report of Joseph C. Abbott, Seventh New Hampshire Infantry, of operations August 13-20, in *OR* 42, pt. 1, 724.

6 George H. Stowits, *History of the One Hundreth Regiment of New York State Volunteers* (Buffalo, 1870), 283.

Connecticut and the 1st Maryland Cavalry. The 24th Massachusetts had its right on the Deep Bottom Road. Terry deployed the Western Brigade to the left of Foster's brigade between the Yarbrough house and the Ruffin house—a frontage of about a third of a mile.[7] The Western Brigade formed about thirty paces behind the left of Foster's brigade.

From east to west, between Pemberton's howitzers near Four Mile Creek and the Yarbrough house, the pickets of Anderson's, then Law's, and then Bratton's brigades confronted Foster's troops. Skirmishers of Benning's Georgia brigade confronted the Western Brigade. The Rebels west of the Ruffin house—Lane's and McGowan's brigades of Conner's detachment—had no Federals in front of them.

Foster's brigade opened fire at 5:10 a.m. and slowly drove the stubborn Confederate videttes back to the entrenched Rebel picket line just south of the Kingsland Road. There, at about 6:00 a.m., the Unionist advance halted. Terry had spread his men too thinly for them to crack the entrenched Secessionist picket line. For about an hour a firefight raged. A lull followed.

X Corps had not surprised the Southerners. Strewing hay on the Deep Bottom pontoon bridges had failed to deceive the Confederates. They had heard the same sounds as Sergeant Brady and had drawn the same unpleasant conclusion.

One of the Rebel artillerymen on New Market Heights, Sgt. William S. White of the Third Company, Richmond Howitzer Battalion, recalled the anticipated transition from tranquility to hostilities:

> A splendid brass band on our right strikes up that holy hymn of ancient days, "Old Hundred," carrying the mind of many a soldier boy back to the days when he sat under the ministry of some favorite pastor, and many a dimmed and glistening eye looked over the field of battle. Clearly through the calm Sabbath morning's air comes the grand melody of that hymn and as the notes rise higher in praise of that God from whom all blessings flow, they seem to carry a solemn petition to the Throne of Grace for aid in the coming struggle. Hark!—the scene changes. A short distance to our right the sharp ringing notes of the skirmisher's rifle warn us of danger ahead, and men that were but a few moments since religiously thinking of the past now must be heroes in the bloody present and hurry to take up the implements of death.[8]

---

7 Referred to as "Buffin" in some local records.

8 William S. White, *A Diary of the War*, Pamphlet No. 2 in Carlton McCarthy, ed., *Contributions to a History of the Richmond Howitzer Battalion* (Richmond, 1883-1886), 269.

An end had come to the respite north of James River that had begun after the battle of the Crater. Now the Rebels had more to do than spend their pay on the fruit and vegetables that abounded around New Market Heights.

Concerned about his division's lack of progress, Terry at about 7:15 a.m. directed Hawley's brigade—except for the 6th Connecticut—to deploy west of the Ruffin house, to the left of the Western Brigade. Terry ordered the 24th Massachusetts to charge, supported by the rest of his command and by the 6th. With the 10th Connecticut on its left and the 11th Maine on its right, the 24th Massachusetts "rushed forward like lions on their prey," remembered Capt. Adrian Terry, an aide-de-camp to his brother, Maj. Gen. Alfred Howe Terry, the division commander.[9] The 10th Connecticut and the 11th Maine joined the assault. The Western Brigade attacked on the left of Foster's brigade. The 85th Pennsylvania of the Western Brigade found itself behind, and ordered to support, Foster's 1st Maryland Cavalry. The 39th Illinois, the 62nd Ohio and four companies of the 67th Ohio respectively formed the line of the Western Brigade to the left of Foster's brigade.

Foster's troops broke through the entrenched picket line of the 2nd South Carolina Rifles of Bratton's brigade. Wheeling west, some of Foster's men cut off and captured all but one soldier of the left flank company of Bratton's Palmetto Sharpshooters.[10] Foster's brigade and the Western Brigade on its left drove the pickets of Law's, Bratton's and Benning's brigades back to their main works. The Unionists took more than seventy prisoners.[11] Because of the refused left of the Federal formation, many other Secessionist videttes escaped capture.

As the skirmishers of Benning's, Bratton's, and Law's brigades gave way, the pickets to the west, from McGowan's South Carolina brigade, withdrew without much loss because Hawley's brigade did not arrive opposite them in time to advance.[12] The videttes of Anderson's brigade to the east and the 8th

---

9 Letter, Adrian Terry to Isadora Terry, August 26, 1864, Terry Family Papers, Yale University Library, New Haven, Connecticut.

10 Bryce A. Suderow, "Target Richmond: The Civil War North of the James June 21-August 21 1864," Suderow Private Collection, Washington, DC.

11 Report of Lieut. Col. Edward Campbell, Eighty-fifth Pennsylvania Infantry, of operations August 14-20, in OR 42, pt. 1, 698; Richmond *Enquirer*, August 31, 1864, p. 2, col. 2.

12 William S. Dunlop, *Lee's Sharpshooters; or, the Forefront of Battle: A Story of Southern Valor that Never Has Been Told* (Little Rock, 1899), 143-4.

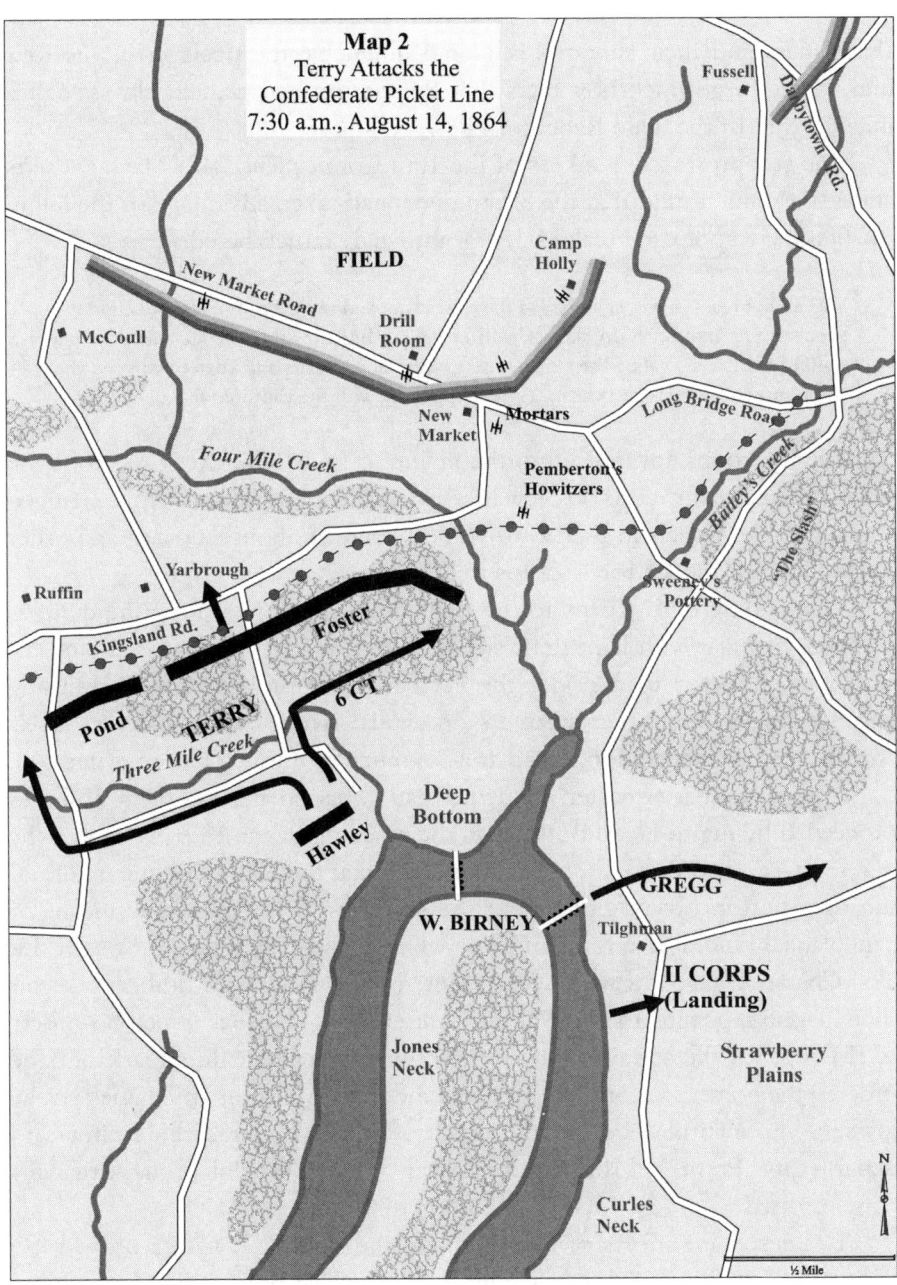

and 59th Georgia, sent out from Anderson's brigade to support those videttes, noticed the Federal breakthrough too late to avoid the loss of twenty-eight soldiers, mostly from the 59th Georgia. The withdrawal of Anderson's skirmishers and their supports rendered untenable the position of the four immobilized eight-inch howitzers that Pemberton had planted almost half a mile in front of the main Rebel trenches.

The self-professed Yankees of the 10th Connecticut, 24th Massachusetts and 11th Maine found that the Southerners had taken advantage of the lull in the fighting to prepare breakfast. Sergeant Brady remembered:

> Our men, breakfastless, snatched at the freshly cooked rations of bread, cooked in the peculiar southern style (in skillets with coals), and at the strips of fat bacon, while waiting for the arrival of their own cooks with baked beans and coffee, satisfied the sharp monitions of their healthy Yankee appetites with the captured food.[13]

Terry's troops advanced into the ravine of Four Mile Creek to probe the Confederate fortifications on New Market Heights. His skirmishers exchanged shots with the Rebels in their earthworks. Then, at about 9:00 a.m., an order arrived from Hancock for X Corps to halt.

The landing of II Corps to the right of X Corps had not gone quite as planned. Familiar with light draft steamers and western rivers, Grant and his staff had neglected to consider the very different problem posed by using ocean-going or large river steamers on a tidal river. Of the sixteen vessels employed in the expedition, some drew as much as thirteen feet of water.

A former quartermaster, Hancock had foreseen this problem and had proceeded by tug to Deep Bottom on the morning of the 13th, as soon as he had received his orders. There he ascertained that the banks and the nature of the river bottom would not permit the steamers to disembark by means of gangplanks. Finding the ruins of three wharves, he sent his chief of staff, Lt. Col. Charles Hale Morgan, a West Pointer, on a barge with timber to repair them. Upon returning to City Point that afternoon, Hancock issued his orders to II Corps for the coming operation. To further facilitate disembarkation, he ordered the horses, wagons, ambulances and artillery to cross the James on the lower pontoon bridge behind the cavalry. He also ordered the steamers to depart City Point at 10:00 p.m. rather than at midnight as originally contemplated.

The desperate efforts of Hancock and the staff of II Corps proved too little, too late. They failed to make up for the lack of preparation at army and army group levels. The fleet arrived at low water, at about 2:30 a.m. Most of the

---

13 Brady, *Eleventh Maine*, 337.

steamers could not run close in enough to shore to disembark the troops over gangplanks and had to disembark over smaller vessels or the makeshift wharves. The solders had difficulty descending from the upper decks of some of the steamers, not adapted to the transportation of troops. One big vessel, carrying 1,200 men from Broady's brigade of Barlow's division, ran aground. Only half of II Corps had landed by 5:00 a.m., when X Corps opened fire. Not until 9:00 a.m. had all but one of the steamers disembarked. The grounded steamer did not disembark her men until almost noon. "Someone should be punished in this matter," fumed Major Mitchell, Hancock's aide-de-camp, who supervised the landing.[14]

At 7:45 a.m., after the last of Mott's II Corps division had landed, its commander, Maj. Gen. Gershom Mott, a Mexican War veteran from New Jersey wounded at Second Bull Run and Chancellorsville, received orders to move out toward the New Market Road crossing of Bailey's Creek. Colonel Francis A. Walker, an Amherst educated lawyer who had suffered a crippled hand at Chancellorsville and who served as Hancock's assistant adjutant general, later wrote: "The rays of the August sun smote the heads of the weary soldiers with blows as palpable as if they had been given with a club."[15] In the intolerable heat, on the dusty roads, sunstroke again began to take its toll. Soon dead and dying men lined the roads. In two small regiments of Mott's division, heat overcame 105 men though only about a mile separated the riverbank from their destination.[16] When the division reached the New Market Road crossing of Bailey's Creek, around 9:30 a.m., Mott found the Confederate position on New Market Heights too formidable to assault. Next in line behind Mott's troops, Barlow's two divisions turned off on a track through a patch of second growth timber called "The Slash" toward the Unionist right and the Secessionist left.

The arrival of II Corps, as the arrival of X Corps, had failed to surprise the Rebels. Corporal John Day Smith, the twice-wounded historian of the 19th Maine in Macy's brigade of Gibbon's division, later summed up the reaction of Union soldiers to the failure of Grant's steamboat scheme to fool the Secessionists:

14 *OR* 42, pt. 1, 241.

15 Francis A. Walker, *History of the Second Army Corps in the Army of the Potomac* (New York, 1886), 572.

16 Ibid.

Well, the men felt a good deal like boys who had stolen around and come up to the old farmer's melon patch from the rear and saw the farmer, with a bulldog and shotgun, calmly looking over the fence into their faces and wearing a smile that was not reassuring.[17]

Meanwhile, Grant arrived with his staff at Curle's Wharf by steamboat and then rode to Hancock's headquarters at Strawberry Plains. There he learned from Hancock that the prisoners taken that morning included soldiers from Field's and Wilcox's divisions, that Lee had thus sent only one infantry division to the Shenandoah, and that therefore Early did not outnumber Sheridan. Grant telegraphed this information to Halleck in Washington and asked him to pass it on to Sheridan. At about noon, after a ride out to survey the lines, Grant re-embarked at Curle's Wharf and steamed upriver to Deep Bottom.

Field, a West Pointer from Kentucky who had suffered wounds at Second Bull Run and in the Wilderness, grasped the threat posed by the heavy columns of Federals anyone on New Market Heights could see slogging toward the Southern left. The fortifications in that direction remained unmanned. The Kentuckian recalled:

> The enemy rightly judged that by getting possession of these abandoned, or rather unoccupied, works at this point, he could, with his large force, probably sweep us before him into the lines surrounding Richmond, as the line upon which we then were was perpendicular to this last line, and the enemy arriving on our left flank would roll us up before we could form line of battle facing him, because our right was at Chaffin's several miles distant.... Fortunately, I was at the moment at my extreme left....[18]

At first Field could not shift soldiers to his left because of the threat posed by X Corps to Chaffin's Bluff and his right. When X Corps had remained inactive while II Corps came closer and closer to his left, Field directed his troops to sidle slowly eastward in the trenches. Brigadier General Martin Witherspoon Gary, a South Carolinian lawyer educated at Harvard, also perceived the danger to the Confederate left and summoned the 7th South Carolina Cavalry to the Darbytown Road crossing of Bailey's Creek and the 24th Virginia Cavalry to Fussell's Mill.

---

17 John D. Smith, *The History of the Nineteenth Regiment of Maine Volunteer Infantry* (Minneapolis, 1909), 224.

18 Charles W. Field, "Campaign of 1864 and 1865, Narrative of Major-General C. W. Field," in *Southern Historical Society Papers* (52 vols.), vol. 14 (1886), 551. Hereafter cited as *SHSP*.

Barlow's two divisions had to go farther than Mott's troops. General Barlow, a twenty-nine year old Harvard educated lawyer, had enlisted as a private in the 12th Regiment, New York State Militia, and had suffered wounds at Antietam and Gettysburg. Hancock had given Barlow the main role in the day's operations because of his aggressiveness, because he had become familiar with the ground opposite the Rebel left in the July operation at Deep Bottom, and to win the major general's star he coveted.

Barlow had acquired a reputation as a strict march disciplinarian. He would whack the backsides of stragglers with the cavalry saber he carried and have a company in skirmish line with fixed bayonets behind his columns to prod them along. This approach proved disastrous in the August heat of Tidewater Virginia. Barlow's units lost about a third of their strength to heat before they ran into the foe.[19] Private Henry Roback had returned to the ranks of Company E, 152nd New York Infantry, in Macy's brigade of Gibbon's division, from a wound inflicted at Petersburg on June 18. He recalled the effect of the first half of his regiment's march:

> We advanced two miles from the river, and came to a deep woods, where we halted. The heat was intense, the foliage was withered, and the air was suffocating. A comrade of Company E started in quest of water, carrying seven canteens. The order came to forward, quick step, march. The 152d was the last in line. The men began to drop from sunstroke, the froth foaming from the mouth, many dying in convulsions. Lieut. D. B. Fitch excused the comrade who carried the double load, his own and the water-bearer's, and just in time to save his life. After resting a few moments, he arose to proceed, when he was called back by Leonard Baldwin, the hospital steward, and assisted him in prying open the jaws of a comrade of the 20th Mass., forcing a potion of medicine down his throat. The comrade coming up with the water, we straightened up our patient and proceeded, counting seven men who had died with the intense heat.[20]

Hancock had intended for Barlow to strike with the greater part of his two divisions by concentrating and not worrying about his flanks, but Barlow dispersed his force by extending from Mott's right. Gibbon's division reached the Long Bridge Road crossing of Bailey's Creek without opposition at about 11:00 a.m. Barlow detached Smyth's brigade of Gibbon's division to protect his

---

19 Suderow, "Target Richmond," Suderow Private Collection.

20 Henry Roback, *The Veteran Volunteers of Herkimer and Otsego Counties in the War of the Rebellion, being a History of the 152d New York Volunteers* (Little Falls NY, 1888), 114.

Barlow's Troops Attack *Library of Congress*

flank. To the right of this brigade, Barlow positioned the brigade-sized 4th Regiment New York Heavy Artillery of his own division. To the right of the 4th, Barlow began dispatching as skirmishers Lynch's brigade of the same division.

Between noon and 1 p.m., on another track about half a mile beyond the Long Bridge Road, Barlow encountered a thin line of Confederate skirmishers, troopers from the 7th South Carolina Cavalry. Their commander, Col. Alexander Cheves Haskell, a graduate of the predecessor of the University of South Carolina, had just deployed his soldiers. He employed a stratagem. Haskell remembered:

> I dismounted my men, except one in every four to handle the horses, put an officer in command of the led horses with instructions to make tracks and kick up dust as much like a Brigade as possible, but to keep out of sight of the enemy and thus delay them as much as he could in their march against Richmond.[21]

Barlow ordered the first unit that arrived, the 2nd New York Heavy Artillery of Lynch's brigade, to clear the track's crossing west of the Darbytown Road and seize the fortifications to the north across Bailey's Creek. The track ran through a cornfield with a wood (and the Darbytown Road) to the right and the ravine of Bailey's Creek to the left. The rest of Lynch's brigade deployed in the trees to the right as skirmishers. The 2nd New York Heavy Artillery entered the cornfield and then shifted left. An orderly from Barlow brought the 2nd's commander, Maj. George Hogg, an order to stop sidling left and advance straight ahead toward the empty earthworks, 900 yards northward across

---

[21] Louise Haskell Daly, *Alexander Cheves Haskell: the portrait of a man* (Norwood MA, 1934), 138-9. Hogg's description of the terrain through which the 2nd New York Heavy Artillery advanced indicates that his unit (and the Irish Brigade soon afterward) attacked along the track west of the Darbytown Road roather than along the Darbytown Road itself.

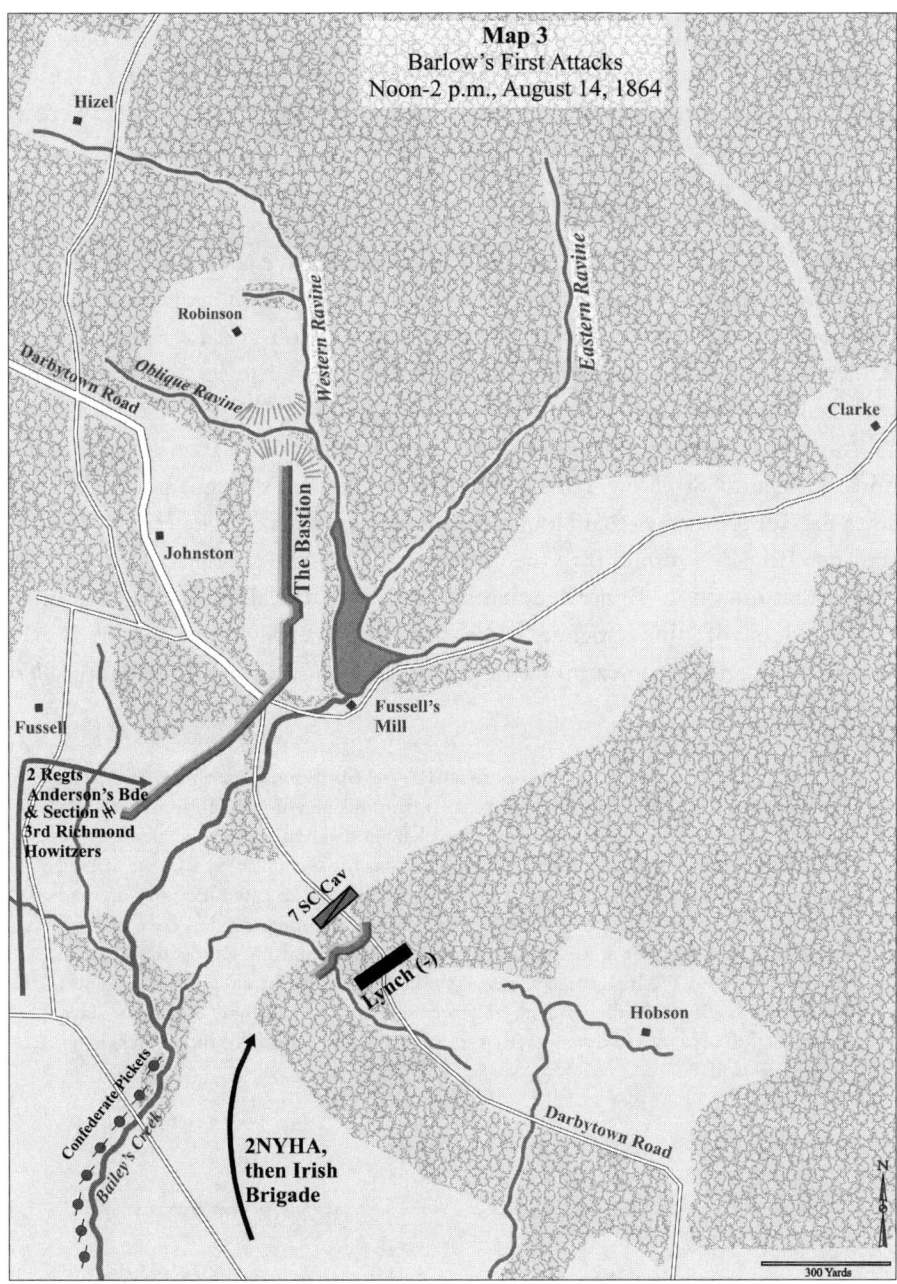

Bailey's Creek. Hogg's left soon came under fire from Confederate skirmishers in the creek's ravine. Another staff officer informed Hogg of Secessionist rifle pits in the trees to the right that would enfilade the 2nd if it kept pushing up the track. Hogg could hear rapid firing in the timber. He veered off to the right and seized some of the rifle pits. A native of New York City, Hogg explained to Barlow shortly afterward: "I was unable to advance farther as the enemy were in strong force and getting artillery into position on his right."[22] Barlow recalled in his official report that Hogg "showed himself utterly unfitted for command, and the regiment did not behave with credit to itself."[23]

With X Corps still inactive, Field had taken decisive action. He dispatched from New Market Heights toward Fussell's Mill the right section of the 3rd Richmond Howitzers under First Lt. Henry C. Carter and two regiments of Anderson's brigade. Meanwhile, the skirmishers on the left of Anderson's brigade neared the Darbytown Road crossing of Bailey's Creek.

Shortly afterword, Barlow ordered the remnant of the Irish Brigade—the 63rd, 69th, and 88th New York—now part of Crandell's New York brigade, to seize the Rebel position that Hogg's men had failed to take. Like Hogg's troops, the Irish Brigade veered off to the right into the woods, taking some more rifle pits in that direction. Barlow remembered in his official report that the once elite solders of this brigade "behaved disgracefully."[24] Captain D. P. Conyngham, an aide-de-camp to the commander of the Irish Brigade, recalled things differently:

> An unusual silence succeeds, and General Barlow, dismounted with his staff, just beneath the crest of the first ridge, started up from his reclining position to ascertain the cause. With a malignant satisfaction, characteristic of a narrow intellect, he suddenly exclaimed, "That damned Irish Brigade has broken at last!" Just as he uttered the words, a mounted officer rode up to the group in time to catch their import, and Adjutant [James J.] Smith, of the 69th, who happened to be the rider, covered with sweat and black with the smoke of battle, promptly and manfully, almost disdainfully, replied, "General, the Irish Brigade has taken the first line of the enemy's works, and I have come back for further orders." The general was so confounded at the sudden contradiction of his spiteful slander, that for a considerable period he did not regain his self-possession."[25]

---

22 Report of Maj. George Hogg, Second New York Heavy Artillery, of operations August 13, 1864, in OR 42, pt. 1, 267.

23 Report of Brig. Gen. Francis C. Barlow, U.S. Army, commanding First Division, of operations August 13-17, 1864, ibid., 248.

24 Ibid.

25 Capt. D. P. Conyngham, *The Irish Brigade and Its Campaigns* (New York, 1867), 473-4.

Firing and falling back, the dismounted South Carolinian horsemen dove into the rifle pits on the west bank of Bailey's Creek and kept up their fire from there. Barlow remembered ruefully: "By this time the enemy had moved troops into that part of the line which I was endeavoring to take, and had brought artillery to bear upon us."[26] Lieutenant Carter's section of the 3rd Richmond Howitzers and the two regiments of Anderson's brigade had arrived and occupied the earthworks by the Fussell farm. Despairing of crossing Bailey's Creek on the track west of the Darbytown Road. Barlow ordered the rest of his division to hoof it farther to the Rebel left.

While II Corps slogged northeastward, to the west Birney's X Corps took cover from Confederate artillery on New Market Heights and from Secessionist sharpshooters in a band of woods along Four Mile Creek. Around 10:00 a.m., David Birney sent Osborn's brigade of William Birney's division toward the junction of the Kingsland and Varina Roads west of Hawley's brigade. The 7th and 9th United States Colored Troops of the Colored Brigade took position in reserve behind Osborn. The rest of X Corps waited for orders in the unbearable heat. Captain James M. Nichols, a graduate of Williams College in Company G of the 48th New York, Perry's Saints (also known as the Fighting Parson's Regiment) in Osborn's brigade, later wrote that, "a most curious effect followed the long exposure to the glaring sun. Many officers as well as non-commissioned officers and privates, succumbed to the heat, and were led or carried to the rear. Some were taken with spasms, and sometimes whole groups fell together. . . ."[27]

The Confederates used this respite to withdraw a section of artillery from the position abandoned by Anderson's brigade as a result of David Birney's morning attack. Pemberton's seacoast howitzers also occupied this untenable position, but Pemberton's guns had no horses, and the Southerners had to leave the howitzers to their fate. On New Market Heights, the Rebel gunners braced themselves for a Federal onslaught. To meet Barlow's threats to his left, Field had almost completely stripped this key position of infantry support. Field himself rode up and down the lines puffing freely on his Meerschaum pipe, his countenance exuding confidence, while his infantry sidled leftward in the earthworks.

---

26 *OR*, vol. 42, pt. 1, 248.

27 James M. Nichols, *Perry's Saints or the Fighting Parson's Regiment in the War of the Rebellion* (Boston, 1886), 254-5.

Maj. Gen. David Bell Birney, U.S.A. *National Archives*

Shortly after noon, Hancock ordered David Birney to shift eastward and attack the enemy fortifications at the foot of New Market Heights. The order became garbled in transmission. Clarification took additional time. Between

2:00 p.m. and 3:00 p.m., Coan's brigade of William Birney's division deployed between Foster's brigade to the right and the Western Brigade to the left. Hawley's brigade remained on the left of the Western Brigade. Osborn's brigade still stood on the left of Hawley. The 7th and 9th United States Colored Troops of William Birney's Colored Brigade remained behind Osborn in reserve. The rest of the Colored Brigade, the 29th Connecticut Colored Infantry and the 8th U.S.C.T. stayed in the entrenchments at Deep Bottom.

Meanwhile, U.S.S. *Agawam* responded to David Birney's request for artillery support. *Agawam*, stationed off Four Mile Creek, turned its 100 pound rifles first on Signal Hill and then on New Market Heights, where Law's brigade of Field's division occupied Camp Holly. George Washington had rested his army at Camp Holly after the British surrender at Yorktown. The position afforded a superb view of James River and *Agawam*. Private William C. Jordan of Company B, 15th Alabama Infantry in Law's brigade remembered:

> A gun boat on James river could plainly be seen about a mile off. I was doing some cooking and would watch the boat, when I could see the smoke flush up, would drop down behind the breastworks. The shells would fly over us, and we would hear the report of piece that was fired from the boat. I could see the flush of smoke before the shell reached us, but the shell would pass over us before we could hear the report of the cannon. As soon as the shells would pass I would get up and go to my cooking again and watch the boat. Soon after a shell struck our breastworks about a hundred yards to our left, knocked the works down, killed and wounded several.[28]

General Grant arrived in the X Corps sector and made his way to the front to see things for himself. About ten yards behind the 1st Connecticut Battery, a badly wounded soldier lay in the middle of the lane and in the sun. Private Edward Griswold of the battery, a farmer before the war, could not leave his post to help, but glancing back he saw a horseman coming up the lane. He recognized the horseman as Grant. As the general-in-chief observed the effect of the battery's shells, he heard the moan of the soldier on whom his horse nearly stepped. Reining in his horse, Grant dismounted and beckoned his orderly. Grant took the soldier by the head, the orderly took the soldier by the feet, and they carried him gently out of the road and placed him in the shade of a tree. The general-in-chief sent his orderly galloping off to return a few minutes later with a hospital squad that carried the wounded man to the rear on a

---

28 William C. Jordan, *Some Events and Incidents During the Civil War* (Montgomery AL, 1909), 90.

stretcher. Private Griswold recalled: "No human being but the orderly and myself saw this kind act of the General who was in command of a million men, and none but soldiers familiar with the scenes of a battlefield can fully appreciate the act."[29]

Finally, at about 3:00 p.m., Grant met with David Birney and General Terry. "We were surprised by a visit from a small quiet looking personage with three stars upon his shoulders who was immediately recognized as General Grant in propria persona," recalled Captain Terry.[30] Accompanied by Birney and the Terry brothers, Grant and some high-ranking staff officers advanced to get a better view of the ground in their front. As General Terry's division advanced under the eyes of the brass, remembered Captain Terry, the Rebels

> immediately treated us to a vigorous shelling, which drove the whole party—Lt. General, Major Generals, Brigadier Generals & their respective staffs to take shelter in an old rifle pit which was very conveniently near but so small as to give very narrow accommodation to the 'illustrious group'. . . . I can boast of having nearly tumbled over Gen. Grant when running for the same shelter.[31]

This view of the Confederate fortifications behind the New Market Road convinced the general-in-chief that X Corps should not assault them.

Sitting in the immediate rear of Foster's brigade on the Kingsland Road, Grant displayed his usual indifference to danger. The soldiers thought the position too exposed for the general-in-chief of the Federal armies, but he calmly puffed on his inevitable cigar and nonchalantly issued orders. "He looked so inward, and distant," Lieutenant Stowits of the 100th New York wrote later, "that a child in the street would hardly dare to ask alms when looking into that face, so blank, but not displeasing."[32]

The orders Grant issued shortly after 3:00 p.m. included instructions for David Birney to cross Four Mile Creek and Bailey's Creek and link up with II Corps to the east. Foster drew this task. He directed the 100th New York to charge to the right, clear the woods of Confederate sharpshooters, and connect with Mott's division of II Corps on the lower bank of Four Mile Creek. The 6th

---

29 Herbert W. Beecher, *History of the First Light Battery Connecticut Volunteers, 1861-1865*, 2 vols. (New York), 2:545-6.

30 Letter, Adrian Terry to Isadora Terry, August 26, 1864, Terry Family Papers.

31 Ibid.

32 Stowits, *One Hundredth New York*, 285.

The Second Battle of Deep Bottom, August 14, 1864

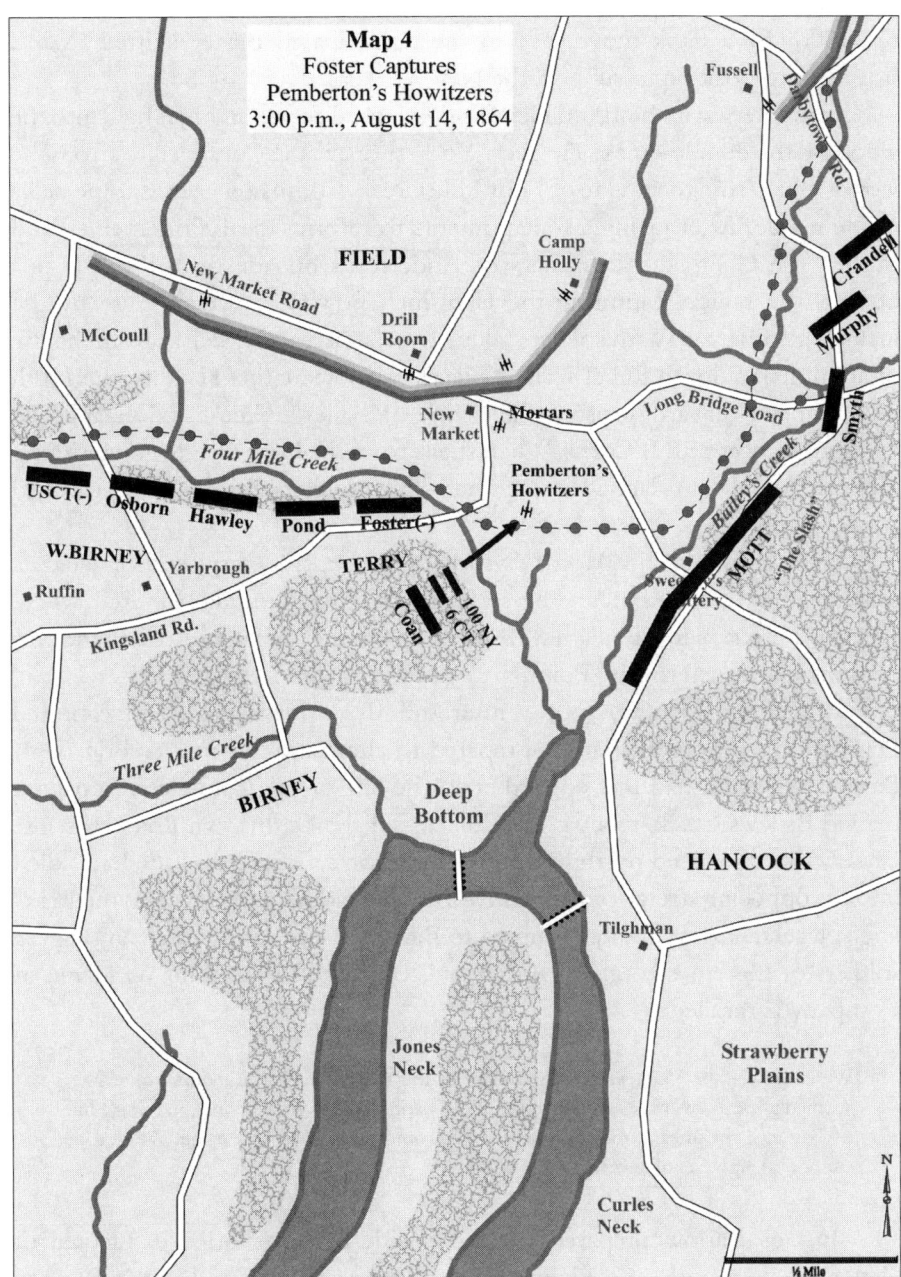

Connecticut of Hawley's brigade got instructions from Terry to support the 100th New York while the rest of the division maintained the connection with the 100th by a flank movement to the right. David Birney shifted Coan's brigade into position to support the New Yorkers.

Soon afterward, the 100th New York attacked across an open field into the woods at the double-quick. The New Yorkers drove the Confederates from the woods and across the ravine of Four Mile Creek. Confusion caused some delay in the ravine. After taking a few moments to reform, the 100th emerged and pushed the Georgian skirmishers of Anderson's brigade from the rifle pits beyond the ravine, capturing the eight-inch howitzers placed there by the luckless Pemberton. With soldiers falling from sunstroke as well as from the fire of about half a dozen Rebel artillery pieces on New Market Heights, the 100th then trudged onward, crossed the ravine of Bailey's Creek, and established communication with II Corps. When shells from the Confederate gunners atop New Market Heights landed among the 100th's soldiers, the regiment scattered in confusion.

After the linkup with Mott's division of II Corps, X Corps consolidated its position and rested. Grant and his staff departed for Bermuda Hundred, where they conferred with Benjamin Butler. Later the general-in-chief and his entourage returned to City Point.

At about 4:00 p.m., shortly after the 100th New York had captured Pemberton's howitzers, Barlow prepared to attack again. Broady's brigade of Barlow's division had moved farther to the left of the Confederate position behind Bailey's Creek, to a wooded hill east of the Darbytown Road crossing. Broady's troops faced northwestward. Anderson's Georgia brigade had sidled into the opposing stretch of the earthworks only moments earlier, and the Rebel line still seemed very thinly occupied to Barlow. Tension mounted among the soldiers of the 9th Georgia of Anderson's brigade. Private John W. Hamil of Company E recalled:

> We could see the Yankees coming out from the river line after line numerous. They seemed to be all over the river bottoms. They kept coming. We had only one single line of Battle. I got uneasy; didn't look like we would be in their way at all. We had no cannon in sight. Yanks were getting close.[33]

Just as Barlow prepared to attack with Broady's brigade, Lieutenant Carter's section of the 3rd Richmond Howitzers opened fire. Captain Richard Corbin, who had journeyed back to Virginia from Paris that spring and found a

---

33 F. M. Hamil, *Memories and Recollections of John W. Hamil* (Chagford AL, 1915), 27.

The Second Battle of Deep Bottom, August 14, 1864

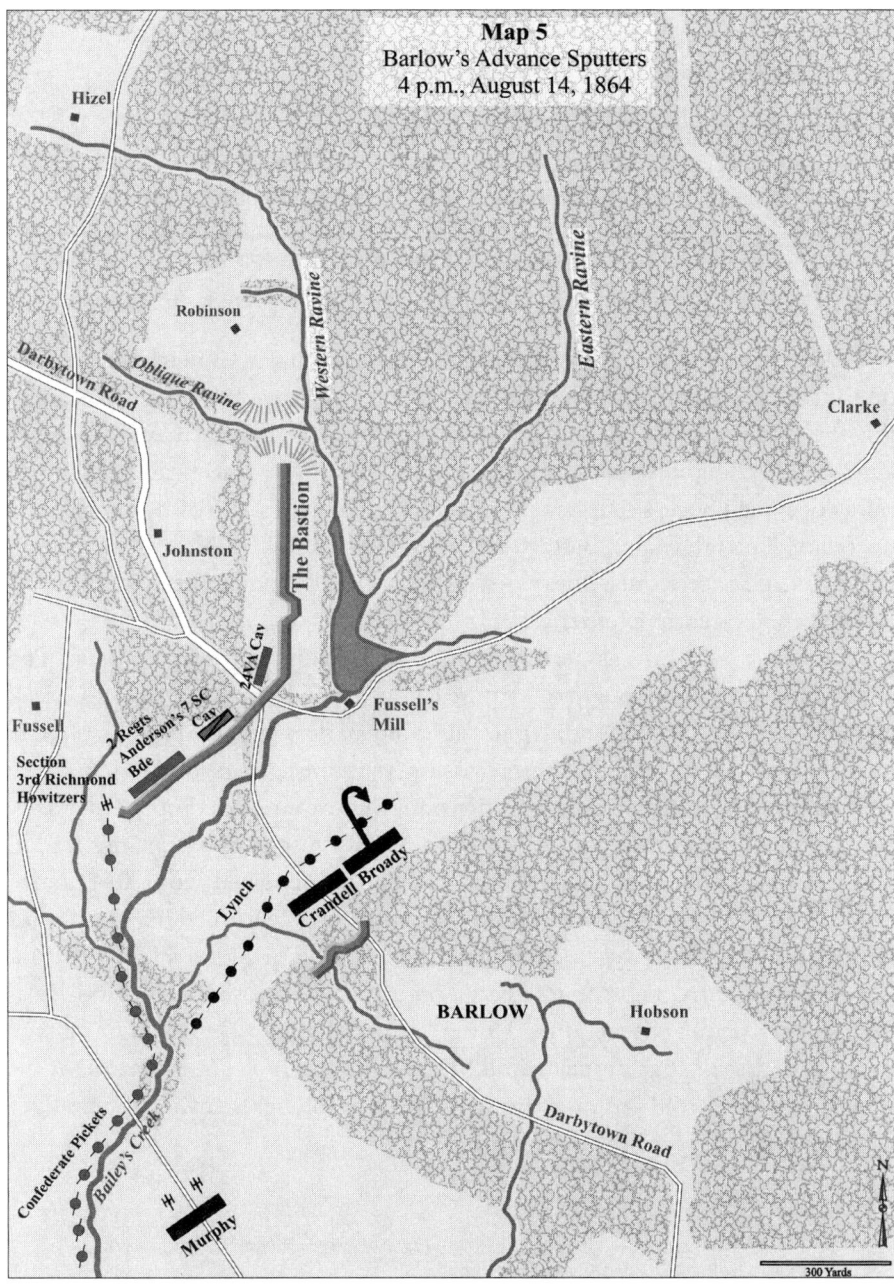

position as an aide-de-camp to Field, remembered that the Federals "rushed towards our position with yells, banners flying and bands playing. . . . The Yankees advanced in four lines of battle, and a magnificent spectacle it was to witness that mighty host bearing down upon our thinly manned breastworks." At about 700 yards,

> two twelve pounders, loaded with canister, blasted away at them. . . . Our fire made wide breaches in their ranks, and after the third discharge the whole line wavered and fluttered like a flag in the wind; another shell exploding in their midst, they broke and fled in every direction without retaining a shadow of their former organization. In their frantic haste to get out of range of our murderous shots they threw away guns, equipments and all their warlike paraphernalia.[34]

Lieutenant Carter and his Rebel artillerists inflicted about eighty casualties on the soldiers of Broady's brigade, who seemed so cowed and demoralized by this fire that Barlow thought it out of the question to employ them in another attack.[35] He ordered Macy's brigade of Gibbon's division to head for the still thinly occupied Secessionist works at Fussell's Mill, a couple of hundred yards upstream. The 6th Maine Battery and a section of the 11th New York Battery replied to the Secessionist gunners with such a shelling that Carter's artillerists thought they faced five batteries.

Barlow made his last effort around 5:30 p.m. at Fussell's Mill. The Confederate works he sought to capture lay across and parallel to Bailey's Creek just below Fussell's mill pond. Up to this point Barlow had used three of his six infantry brigades, all from Barlow's division, piecemeal. Instead of striking now with all three brigades of Gibbon's division, Barlow employed only Macy's.

Colonel George N. Macy of the 20th Massachusetts, the brigade's leader, had lost his left hand at Gettysburg. Having just returned from an absence caused by a Wilderness wound, he led on horseback. He formed his troops into two lines facing northwestward behind a crest. The brigade included the 1st Minnesota Infantry, reduced to a battalion of two companies by its sacrifice at Gettysburg helping save the Union army. Captain James C. Farwell commanded the 1st at Fussell's Mill. Barlow inquired of him the name of his regiment. Farwell told Barlow, who sent the 1st to the right, saying, "If you fight like the Old First all hell won't stop you."[36]

---

34 Richard W. Corbin, *Letters of a Confederate Officer to His Family in Europe During the Last Year of the War of Secession* (Paris, 1913), 62.

35 Suderow, "Target Richmond," Suderow Private Collection.

36 William Lochren, *Narrative of the First Regiment* in Board of Commissioners, *Minnesota in the Civil and Indian Wars*, 2 vols. (St. Paul, 1890), 1:45.

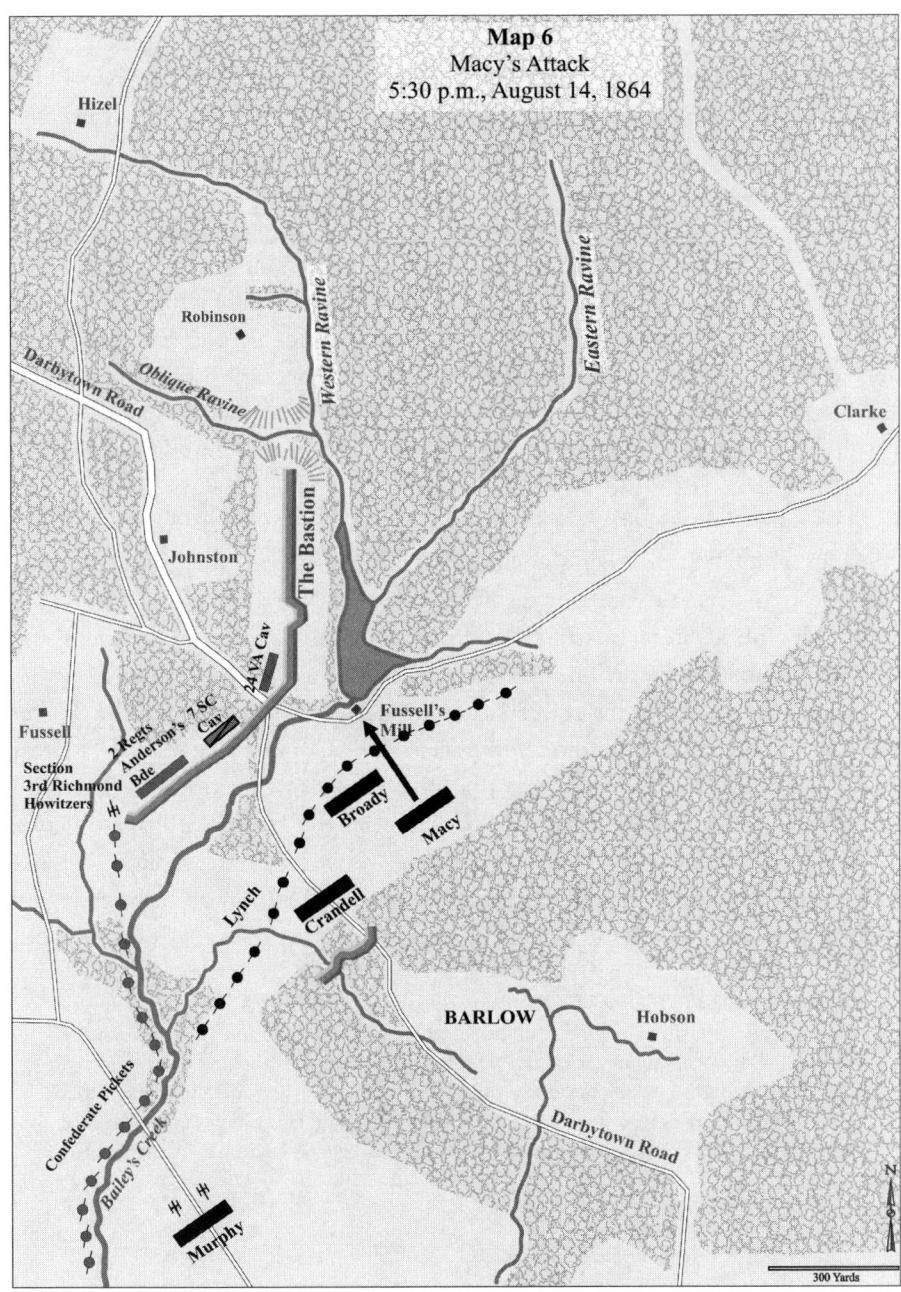

Macy led his brigade of about a thousand men over the crest into a cornfield under a heavy fire. A Rebel bullet wounded his horse. He mounted another. His second mount took a bullet, fell down and rolled over on him, crushing him so severely that Lt. Col. Horace P. Rugg of the 59th New York took command of the brigade. The Federals charged down an open bluff, where they suffered so badly from the carbines of the 24th Virginia Cavalry that Private Roback of the 152nd New York thought the enemy possessed a six shot repeating rifle.

Thick blackberry vines covered the slopes and tripped the Northerners as they ran down into the ravine of Bailey's Creek, making the casualties seem higher. At the bottom of the ravine lay a morass covered by a thicket. The 1st Minnesota in the brigade's first line crossed the ravine on the mill pond dam and seized some empty rifle pits. Gary had ordered the 24th Virginia Cavalry to saddle up and ride for the Charles City Road, where David Gregg's Federal cavalry had appeared, and part of the 24th had withdrawn from the works. The regiment to the left of the 1st Minnesota, the 19th Maine, found a narrow cart road through the thicket and halted about ten or twenty yards from the Rebel rifle pits, which lay up a steep slope. Farther left, the 152nd New York fought its way through what Private Roback recalled as "the entangling meshes of the wait-a-bit vine, a natural obstruction, almost equal to . . . barbed wire" and some of its men made their way up the slope into the rifle pits.[37] On the right of the brigade's second line, a few soldiers of the 7th Michigan penetrated the thicket and planted their colors within a few paces of the Confederate works. The rest of the brigade advanced no farther than the thicket or the cornfield. The 36th Wisconsin in the brigade's second line halted in the cornfield. Private David Coon of the 36th's Company A remembered, "as we lay on the ground a while I picked up a couple ears of corn and ate them raw."[38] The part of the brigade that did not penetrate the ravine's thicket displayed suspect morale. Coon recalled,

> When the line halted and fell back and some took shelter behind some old buildings, I found a good position behind a hog pen where I could load and fire between the boards of the pen, the heads of the rebs being in plain sight behind their works. I would load and fire, taking good aim until I had fired about six or eight times in that way, when an officer who was posted behind an old building just behind me with a lot of men laying low, sent and ordered me to stop as he said there was danger of my

---

37 Roback, *152d New York*, 114.

38 Letter, David Coon, August 16, 1864, David Coon Papers, Elwyn B. Robinson Department of Special Collections, Chester Fritz Library, University of North Dakota, Grand Forks, North Dakota.

shooting our own men, but I knew there was no danger of that. I guess he was afraid that I would draw the reb fire on them.[39]

The Unionists who reached the rifle pits and the top of the slope received a deadly volley from the 24th Virginia Cavalry. Many of the Northerners who survived this volley surrendered. Fire from the Virginians pinned down others. Colonel William Todd Robins of the 24th, a lawyer educated at Virginia Military Institute who had enlisted as a private in the 9th Virginia Cavalry, had left the works pursuant to Gary's order to head for the Charles City Road. Now Robins turned back from the horses in the rear and led a counterattack. A Unionist bullet wounded him beside Capt. Theophilus Gilliam Barham, who took command of the regiment and continued the charge, capturing 60 Unionists.[40] Confederate fire pinned down the rest of the Federals who had penetrated the ravine's thicket. Barlow, having committed only about 2,500 of his 10,000 soldiers, gave up on his attempt to turn the Rebel left.

The personally fearless Barlow unfairly blamed the troops for this failure. Without sleep and on the verge of sunstroke or even death from the heat, they had made an extraordinary effort just to arrive at Fussell's Mill. Furthermore, the soldiers of II Corps had learned from bitter experience to avoid attacking fortifications. Since May 3, Gibbon's division had lost more than seventy-three percent of its initial strength. Many, if not most, of its losses had occurred in assaults upon earthworks similar to those at Fussell's Mill. Sergeant Brady of the 11th Maine in X Corps recalled an incident that occurred during the fighting which illustrated the attitude of the soldiers:

> "Follow me, men, follow me," shouted a general officer riding rapidly to the head of their recoiling column, as if determined to charge the enemy's works, if he must do, alone. For a moment there was a hush, as the men swayed back and forth in the edge of the sheltering woods, but not forward into the storm of lead sweeping the field. Then an Irish voice rang out fiercely, "We'll folly ye to Hell"; then, dropping to a wheedling tone, continued, "But don't ye think 'twud be wiser to go by a longer road, General?" A roar of laughter greeted this Hibernian hit, and half-laughing, half-angry, the discomfited general gave the word to fall back.[41]

39 Letter, David Coon, August 15, 1864, David Coon Papers.

40 Martin W. Gary, "Recommending the Promotion of Capt. T. G Barham," in Compiled Service Record, T. G. Barham, National Archives, Washington, DC; Theophilus G. Barham, *The War Record of T. G. Barham* (Gray VA, 1885), 31-32.

41 Brady, *Eleventh Maine*, 241.

Farther to the Secessionist left, Stedman's brigade of Federal horsemen cleared the Long Bridge Road of the Hampton Legion's pickets and occupied Riddell's shop, at the junction of the Long Bridge Road, the Charles City Road, and the Quaker Road. There Stedman's troopers guarded Hancock's right flank and Gregg's rear. Irwin Gregg's Unionist cavalry brigade succeeded in driving the Hampton Legion from a line of rifle pits constructed in 1862 near Fisher's farm on the Charles City Road. Gregg's brigade took this position by a pincer movement. Saddling up early in the morning, the brigade had ridden by back roads and tracks to within a mile of Goodman's farm, on the Charles City Road. The 1st Maine Cavalry and the 13th Pennsylvania Cavalry trotted along a by-road and got behind the Rebel force at Fisher's farm. At the same time, the 2nd and 8th Pennsylvania Cavalry took the Charles City Road to Fisher's farm to attack the Southerners in front. The Confederates escaped the pincers by retreating north across White Oak Swamp, leaving behind only four prisoners.[42] The 1st Maine Cavalry and the 2nd Pennsylvania Cavalry, mistaking one another for the foe, exchanged shots without inflicting any casualties. Gregg's brigade scouted along the Charles City Road to within half a mile of White's Tavern. Both brigades of Federal horsemen withdrew to Strawberry Plains to feed and water their horses because of a lack of drinkable water along the Charles City Road.

At about 5:00 p.m., Hancock ordered David Birney to demonstrate on the Unionist left to keep the Confederates from concentrating against Barlow's column on the right. Half an hour later, Birney directed Terry to push forward a skirmish line. Terry rearranged his division to face the Rebels with Foster still on the right but Hawley in the center and the Western Brigade on the left. These troops exchanged fire with the Secessionist pickets along the Kingsland Road between Four Mile Creek on the east and the Yarbrough house on the west. Their feeble advance had no effect on the slow shift of Confederate infantry eastward toward Barlow and Fussell's Mill.

At 6:30 p.m., Hancock demanded another demonstration from X Corps. David Birney made the demonstration on his left, employing William Birney's Colored Brigade between the Yarbrough house and the McCoull house. The 7th and 9th United States Colored Troops, joined by a company of the 8th United States Colored Troops, attacked the pickets of Lane's brigade north of

---

42 Report of Bvt. Brig. Gen. J. Irvin Gregg, Sixteenth Pennsylvania Cavalry, commanding Second Brigade, of operations July 30-August 16, 1864, in OR 42, pt. 1, 637.

the Kingsland Road. William Birney's troops charged across a corn field, up a hill, and took some Rebel rifle pits at bayonet point. Some of the African Americans pressed on across the ravine of Four Mile Creek toward the main Confederate entrenchments but suffered a repulse, losing forty-four soldiers.[43] The white Unionists who witnessed the charge expressed admiration, but like all of David Birney's attempts to prevent the Secessionists from sidling to their left, it failed to accomplish its mission.

Night put an end to the fighting and allowed the pinned down soldiers of Macy's brigade to withdraw across Bailey's Creek below Fussell's mill pond. The Northerners had lost about 600 men to enemy action.[44] Foster's brigade,

---

43 Joseph Califf, *Record of the Services of the Seventh Regiment, U.S. Colored Troops from September, 1863, to November, 1866* (Providence, 1878), 34-35; Suderow, "Target Richmond," Suderow Private Collection.

44 For the losses of the Colored Brigade, see note 43, supra. The 28th Massachusetts lost four killed and eleven wounded. Report of Maj. James Fleming, Twenty-eighth Massachusetts Infantry, of operations August 13-20, in *OR* 42, pt. 1, 264. The 2nd New York Heavy Artillery lost four killed, twenty-three wounded, and six missing. Report of Capt. Oscar F. Hulser, Second New York Heavy Artillery, of operations August 13-20, ibid., 266. The 61st New York suffered one man wounded. Report of Maj. James W. Scott, Sixty-first New York Infantry, of operations August 13-20, ibid., 271. The 66th New York lost five wounded. Report of Capt. Albert Gosse, Sixty-sixth New York Infantry, of operations August 13-20, ibid., 279. The 53rd Pennsylvania sustained "a slight loss." Report of Capt. Phillip H. Schreyer, Fifty-third Pennsylvania Infantry, of operations August 13-20, ibid., 281. The 145th Pennsylvania lost several killed and wounded. Report of Capt. James H. Hamlin, One hundred and forty-fifth Pennsylvania Infantry, of operations August 12-25, ibid., 284. The 148th Pennsylvania lost three killed, fourteen wounded, Report of Capt. Alfred A. Rhinehart, One hundred and forty-eighty Pennsylvania Infantry, of operations August 13-20, ibid., 286. Macy's brigade lost twenty-five killed, 127 wounded, 36 missing. Report of Lieut. Col. Horace P. Rugg, Fifty-ninth New York Infantry, commanding First Brigade, of operations August 12-26, ibid., 301. The 8th New York Heavy Artillery lost two men wounded. James M. Hudnut, *Casualties By Battle And By Name In The Eighth New York Heavy Artillery August 22, 1862-June 5, 1865 Together With A Review Of The Service Of The Regiment Fifty Years After Muster-In*, (New York, 1913), 27-28. The 124th New York lost three wounded. Charles H. Weygant, *History of the One Hundred and Twenty-Fourth Regiment, N.Y.S.V.* (Newburgh NY, 1877), 364-5. The 11th Battery, New York Light Artillery suffered one man wounded. Report of Capt. John E. Burton, Eleventh New York Battery, of operations August 12-26, in *OR* 42, pt. 1, 420. The 62nd Ohio lost two killed and two wounded. Report of Lieut. Col. Samuel B. Taylor, Sixty-second Ohio Infantry, of operations August 13-14, ibid., 692; Report of Maj. Francis M. Kahler, Sixty-second Ohio Infantry, of operations August 14-16, ibid., 694. The 85th Pennsylvania lost three killed, ten wounded. Ibid., 698. The 7th Connecticut lost one killed, five wounded. Report of Capt. John Thompson, Seventh Connecticut Infantry, of operations August 13-16, ibid., 710. The 3rd New Hampshire lost "a few" wounded. D. Eldredge, *The Third New Hampshire And All About It* (Boston: 1893), 518. The 10th Connecticut lost six killed, twenty-five wounded. Report of Col. John L. Otis, Tenth Connecticut Infantry, of operations August 14-20, in *OR*, 42, pt. 1, 738. The 11th Maine lost nine killed, forty wounded. Report of Col. Harris M. Plaisted, Eleventh Maine Infantry, of

which had done most of the fighting in David Birney's sector, lost fewer than 150 soldiers.[45] Macy's brigade of Gibbon's division in Barlow's sector had suffered 188 casualties.[46] The Southerners had lost around 200, including about 100 prisoners.[47]

Barlow had severely disappointed his immediate superior. "It was intended that General Barlow should keep the force under his command (nearly 10,000 men) well in hand, and not attempt to develop a line of battle from General Mott's right," Hancock remembered in his official report, which then criticized Barlow for departing from the plan: "It appears however that he extended to the right . . . assaulting near Fussell's Mill with one brigade . . . when I expected him to attack with the greater portion of two divisions." As for Barlow blaming the troops, Hancock could not help but blurt out: "I must say that had they been kept more compact they ought to have broken through the line, then thinly held, by mere weight of numbers."[48] Barlow had failed in his mission, the Federals had thrown away the advantage of surprise, little chance remained of capturing Richmond, and Hancock had made no progress toward a presidential or vice presidential nomination. Hancock seemed to have forgotten the Rebels materializing behind his left on May 6 and routing his corps in the Wilderness. Barlow appeared to recall all too well how the Secessionists had burst out of the

---

operations August 14-16, ibid., 745. The 1st Maryland Cavalry (dismounted) lost two killed, nineteen wounded. Report of Col. Andrew W. Evans, First Maryland Cavalry (dismounted), of operations August 14-20, ibid., 751. The 24th Massachusetts lost two killed, fifteen wounded. Report of Capt. J. Crosby Maker, Twenty-fourth Massachusetts Infantry, of operations August 14, ibid., 754. The 100th New York suffered fewer than thirty casualties. Stowits, *One Hundredth New York*, 286. The other units involved either incurred no losses or did not specify those suffered August 14. The Federals thus lost more than sixty-one killed, 303 wounded, forty-two missing. Suderow, "Target Richmond," Suderow Private Collection.

45 Stowits, *One Hundredth New York*, 286; OR 42, pt. 1, 738, 745, 751, 754.

46 Ibid., 301.

47 U. S. Grant to Major-General Henry Halleck, August 14, 1864, ibid., pt. 2, 167; Suderow, "Target Richmond," Suderow Private Collection. Anderson's brigade lost six killed, four wounded, twenty-five captured. Record Group 109, Compiled Service Records, National Archives. The 1st South Carolina Infantry of Bratton's brigade lost three killed, nineteen wounded. Report of Col. James R. Hagood, First South Carolina Infantry, of operations August 14-December 10, in *OR* 42, pt. 1, 938. Six Confederate artillerists suffered significant wounds, three in the Powhatan Artillery and three in the Third Company Richmond Howitzers. Itinerary of Hardaway's Light Artillery Battalion, August 13-December 31, Ibid., 935.

48 Reports of Maj. Gen. Winfield S. Hancock, U. S. Army, commanding Second Army Corps, of operations August 12-October 28, ibid., 217-8.

woods behind his division's left on June 22 west of the Jerusalem Plank Road and rolled up his command.

Though the day's results had disappointed Hancock, he had already attained all the less ambitious objectives that Grant had set for the operation on the north side of the James. The general-in-chief had forced Lee to recall a portion of the troops dispatched to northern Virginia. The Virginian had cancelled the orders sending Matthew Butler's division to Culpeper Court House and had ordered the division to join Field. Though Lee had sent neither Wilcox's division nor Field's division to Early, as Grant had feared, the Federal thrust from Deep Bottom had prevented Field from executing the marching orders that he had received, and it put any and all reinforcement of Early out of the question. Hancock's efforts drew Rebel forces from the Southside. Lee ordered Sanders' and Wright's brigades of Mahone's division and Rooney Lee's division of cavalry from Petersburg to Field. The foot soldiers of Sanders' and Wright's brigades had pulled out of the fortifications near the Jerusalem Plank Road south of Petersburg around noon and headed for Rice's Turnout north of the Appomattox to board the cars for the Halfway House near Drewry's Bluff.

General Terry, a Yale-educated lawyer from Connecticut, had raised a regiment of soldiers and led them into battle at First Bull Run. Now he basked in the glow of the day's achievements by his division. "The honors belonged to Alfred the whole having been under his immediate supervision and by his troops," his brother Adrian remembered in a letter to his wife. "All the prisoners and guns were taken by his troops."[49]

With the night came a downpour, the first in many days. The troops sought what cover they could find. "We were pleased to see the rain but being in the open field we got drenched to the skin," recalled Quartermaster Sergeant Frederick E. Lockley of the 7th New York Heavy Artillery in Broady's brigade. "I laid my knapsacks against a tree—sat down on it—threw a rubber blanket over my head—and thus fared better than many did. The majority—officers and men—threw themselves on the ground and slept from mere exhaustion—pelted with heavy rain the while."[50] In the heaviest of the rain, the Confederates dined. "We drew a pone of soft baked cornbread to the man and by the time it was divided and in our haversacks it was crumbled till it was

49 Letter, Adrian Terry to Isadora Terry, August 26, 1864, Terry Family Papers.

50 Letters of Aug. 15, 1864, "Letters of Fred Lockley, Union Soldier 1864-65," in *Huntington Library Quarterly*, vol. 16, No. 1, 87.

soft baked corn meal and very coarse at that," recalled Private Hamil of the 9th Georgia in Anderson's brigade.[51] As the rain fell, the thermometer dipped. The night became uncomfortably cool for the sodden soldiery.

While the rank and file sloshed and shivered, Hancock—a master of picketing—established a vidette line stretching from the upper bank of Four Mile Creek all the way out to the cavalry on the Charles City Road. He made dispositions for an attack in the morning. Massing most of the II Corps troops behind this line, he had the men of X Corps shaken from their sleep at 10:00 p.m. and sent on a night march northward beyond Fussell's Mill. David Birney received orders to find and turn the Secessionist left or, failing this, to attack if he could find a suitable place. Hancock and his staff neglected to communicate to Birney the existence of Fussell's mill pond.

About the same time, Wright's and Sanders' brigades exited the cars near Drewry's Bluff, crossed James River to Chaffin's Bluff, and tramped off to join Field. An hour or so later, Field had the soldiers of the Texas Brigade roused and sent to assist the Confederate cavalry out on the Charles City Road.

A morning renewal of the clash of arms seemed imminent.

---

51 Hamil, *Memories and Recollections of John W. Hamil*, 27.

Chapter 3

The Second Battle of Deep Bottom, August 15, 1864

David Birney's X Corps plodded northward toward the Confederate left in two stages, with rain making the hike more difficult. The Federals began hoofing the first stage of this march, which brought them to Strawberry Plains, on the night of August 14. The Unionists tramped the first stage along two routes. Foster's brigade of Terry's division, which had already crossed Four Mile Creek, slogged directly through the position of Mott's II Corps division—the shortest route. The Western Brigade of Terry's division, except for the 39th Illinois, the Yates Phalanx, followed Foster's troops. The rest of X Corps took the long way, crossing the James at the pontoon bridge above Bailey's Creek, trudging along Jones' Neck and then re-crossing the river at the pontoon bridge below Bailey's Creek. Some units began the first stage of the march as early as 10:00 p.m. and finished as early as midnight. Others began as late as 3:00 a.m. and finished as late as daybreak. Along the way, X Corps brought off three of the four howitzers captured by the 100th New York, leaving the fourth because of a lack of transportation. The 29th Connecticut Colored Troops and the 8th United States Colored Troops found themselves detached from the Colored Brigade and garrisoning the entrenchments at Deep Bottom.

A terrible traffic jam developed on Jones' Neck, along the short stretch between the two pontoon bridges. Some units required as many as four hours to cover less than four miles. Second Lieutenant Joseph Califf of Company F,

Jones Neck *Library of Congress*

7th United States Colored Troops, later described the wearisome night-marching as

> moving a few rods at a time and then halting for troops ahead to get out of the way; losing sight of them and hurrying to catch up; straggling out in the darkness, stumbling and groping along the rough road, and all the time the rain coming down in a most provoking, exasperating drizzle.[1]

Dawn on August 15 dripped in even hotter than the previous day. Early in the morning, while X Corps rested on Strawberry Plains to recover from the first stage of its march toward the Rebel left, Irwin Gregg's brigade sent out a squadron on a reconnaissance up the Charles City Road. These troopers rode all the way to White's Tavern. There, according to the brigade's commander, Col. J. Irvin Gregg, a Mexican War veteran, the Federal cavalrymen found the Rebels "in some force."[2] This proved an understatement.

---

1   Califf, *Seventh U. S. Colored Troops*, 35.

2   OR 42, pt. 1, 637.

Gregg had run into Barringer's North Carolina brigade of Rooney Lee's cavalry division, which had arrived from the Southside early that morning. The Tarheels pursued Gregg's reconnoitering squadron back down the Charles City Road. At Fisher's farm, the North Carolinians slammed into the 13th Pennsylvania Cavalry, on picket duty there. The Tarheels drove the 13th across Fisher's Run and back on the 8th Pennsylvania Cavalry. Bringing up artillery, the North Carolinians forced both regiments of Keystoners to retire about two miles to the remainder of Gregg's brigade, which threw up a barricade and stopped the Rebel advance. The dismounted Tarheel cavalry fought so fiercely that the Pennsylvanians thought they faced infantry.

At about 9:00 a.m., X Corps began the second leg of its march. As the soldiers slogged toward Fussell's mill pond, the sun began to take its toll. Fatigued from the night march, soaked in the rain, sick from the heat, prostrated and dying soldiers soon lined the roadsides for the second day in a row. "An army was strewn along the road, under the trees, everywhere, borne down with the power of the sun's rays, and the fatigues of march and exposure," Lieutenant Stowits of the 100th New York in Foster's brigade remembered.[3]

Straggling reached unprecedented proportions. Benjamin Butler had detached about 9,000 men from X Corps to assist Hancock.[4] On August 15, the provost marshal picked up about 3,000 for straggling.[5] Heat prostrated thirty-two men of only four companies in the 67th Ohio, in the Western Brigade of the Terry's division.[6] The 1st Maryland Cavalry (dismounted) in Foster's brigade of the same division suffered thirty cases of sunstroke—while resting.[7] In the fearful heat, soldiers fell out of the ranks by companies at a time. "The army of stragglers soon became larger than the army of operations," recalled Lieutenant Stowits, whose regiment staggered footsore and weary through the straggling host and halted in an open field near the front. "The men were falling to the ground, from heat, foaming at the mouth, shivering like dead

---

3 Stowits, *One Hundredth New York*, 286-7.

4 U. S. Grant to General Meade, August 13, 1864, in OR 42, pt. 2, 141.

5 Ibid., pt. 1, 748.

6 Report of Col. Alvin C. Voris, Sixty-seventh Ohio Infantry, of operations August 14-20, ibid., 696.

7 Ibid., 751.

men, sights to stir any heart."[8] Had the march not halted at around 2:00 p.m., X Corps would have completely disintegrated.

Those of Foster's brigade who completed the march found themselves in reserve, but according to Sergeant Brady of the 11th Maine, these veterans had learned to harbor reservations about the significance of that status:

> "On resarve," said an Irishman of the Second Corps; 'yis, resarved for the heavy foighting,' and his sally became a corps joke; and Foster's brigade found that the 'heavy foighting' was just what it had been reserved for on the 15th.[9]

Terrible marching conditions also prevailed among the Confederates west of Bailey's Creek as they plodded into position to prevent the Unionists from outflanking them north of Fussell's mill pond. The Alabamians of Sanders' brigade and the Georgians of Wright's brigade tramped to the end of the line near the mill pond by 4:00 a.m., and then rested for two hours. Between one third and one half the Southern soldiers who had left Petersburg the day before stumbled into the unfinished earthworks north of the mill pond around 10:00 a.m. General Lee, who had transferred his headquarters to Chaffin's Bluff early that morning, watched anxiously. "Last night's march was one of the worst I ever tried," recalled Master Sergeant William Eppa Fielding of the 9th Alabama in Sanders' brigade. "We are all completely broken down. I feel as if I was 100 years old."[10] Lane's and McGowan's brigades shifted from near James River to Fussell's Mill.

The sound of firing on the Charles City Road distracted David Birney from his mission to turn the left of the Confederate position north of Fussell's mill pond. A Philadelphia lawyer and abolitionist born in Alabama, he worried that if he tried to envelop this position, the Rebel force to his right would take him in reverse as three brigades of Mahone's division to his left had taken him in reverse and routed him on June 22 when in Hancock's absence he led II Corps at the battle of the Jerusalem Plank Road, south of Petersburg. Rather than seek

---

8 Stowits, *One Hundredth New York*, 287.

9 Brady, *Eleventh Maine*, 244. In fact, Foster's brigade did not engage in heavy fighting again until August 16.

10 Faye Acton Axford, *"To Lochaber Na Mair": Southerners View the Civil War, Eyewitness Accounts of Soldiers on the Field of Battle and the Loved Ones They Left Behind Beginning with the War in Virginia and the Occupation of Athens, Alabama, the Sense of the Impermanence of "A Way Of Life" and Ending with an Account of Return to a Modicum of Normalcy a Year after Appomattox* (Athens AL, 1987), 127.

the Secessionist left above Fussell's mill pond, Birney reconnoitered to the sound of the guns on the Charles City Road.

To allow X Corps to recuperate from its night march, Birney needed other troops for this reconnaissance. At about 10:00 a.m., Hancock detached Craig's relatively rested brigade from Mott's division and sent the unit to Birney. The brigade's commander, Col. Calvin A. Craig of the 105th Pennsylvania, a businessman, bore the scars of a slight head wound during the Seven Days Battles, a severe ankle wound at Second Bull Run, a near fatal wound in the face at the Wilderness, and a shell fragment in the shoulder at Petersburg. At Gettysburg, the Rebels had shot three horses from under him. Birney sent Craig's brigade to the right, where the brigade massed behind the Colored Brigade of William Birney's Provisional Division above Fussell's mill pond. Around an hour later, Barlow, who had resumed command of his division, detached its First Brigade under Brig. Gen. Nelson A. Miles, who had resumed command of the brigade. Miles, a former crockery store clerk, had survived multiple wounds since he had used his savings and borrowed money to raise a company of volunteers in the 22nd Massachusetts Infantry, where he received a First Lieutenant's commission. For his heroism at Chancellorsville, he would eventually receive a Medal of Honor. Barlow sent Miles' brigade to David Birney, who dispatched Miles toward the Charles City Road by the Long Bridge Road, a route which did not get the brigade there until the following day.

After massing behind the Colored Brigade, Craig's troops hiked through small but thick pines in the direction of the Charles City Road. At Mrs. Craddock's house they found the skirmish line of the 4th Pennsylvania Cavalry, which had remained in contact with the Confederates since the morning fighting. Here Craig formed his battle line.

The 1st U.S. Sharpshooters deployed in front as skirmishers. From left to right, the battle line consisted of the 105th Pennsylvania, the 1st Massachusetts Heavy Artillery and the 84th Pennsylvania Infantry. Massed in column by division—two companies abreast and several deep—the 5th Michigan Infantry supported the left, the 93rd New York Infantry the center and the 141st Pennsylvania Infantry the right. The 57th Pennsylvania Infantry protected the left flank of the brigade while the cavalry guarded the right.

Craig's brigade encountered skirmishers from Barringer's North Carolina brigade in second growth timber about a mile and a half from the Charles City Road. The Northerners advanced into the woods and drove out the Tarheels. Craig ordered two companies of the 5th Michigan to the left of the 57th Pennsylvania. He also ordered two companies of the 84th Pennsylvania to the

Brig. Gen. William Birney, U.S.A. *National Archives*

1st United States Sharpshooters to connect with the 8th Pennsylvania Cavalry, moving up on the brigade's right. Struggling through first one swamp and then another, Craig's men pushed the increasingly stubborn North Carolinians back to their line of battle. The Unionists then forced the Tarheels to withdraw along the Charles City Road beyond Fisher's Run lest Craig's men cut them off. First Lieutenant Charles Augustus Stevens, a former teacher in Company G of the 1st Sharpshooters who had originally enlisted as a sergeant in the Iron Brigade's 2nd Wisconsin, recalled:

> Owing to the close growth of the young trees it was almost impossible to distinguish the enemy in the Sharpshooters front, they lying close to the ground and after delivering their well-aimed fire, hustling back to farther favorable positions from which to sight on our men as the latter advanced steadily on them—a perilous adventure bravely accomplished.[11]

Chambliss' brigade of Virginia horsemen covered the retreat of Barringer's troopers. The 13th Virginia Cavalry drew picket duty along Fisher's Run. The rest of Chambliss' brigade bivouacked two miles farther back at White's Tavern. On the Federal side of the run, the 2nd and 4th Pennsylvania Cavalry went on picket. Craig's soldiers halted to await further orders.

At about 3:30 p.m., William Birney directed the 7th and 9th United States Colored Troops to pile knapsacks and march. Educated in the law at Yale, this older brother of David Birney had become a professor of English in France, where he had participated in the revolution of 1848. Upon the outbreak of the war, he joined the 1st New Jersey Infantry as a captain and after Chancellorsville began organizing regiments of United States Colored Troops. Against his better judgment, William Birney placed the 7th and 9th under the command of Col. James Shaw, Jr., of the 7th. Shaw, a Rhode Island jeweler capable of organizing and shipping out a regiment in thirty hours, had disappointed Birney during the siege of Charleston.

The 7th and 9th United States Colored Troops had suffered relatively few stragglers during the march from the Kingsland Road to the Unionist right. William Birney dispatched this half-brigade to the right of Osborn's tired brigade of his division with orders to tramp straight through what he considered a narrow strip of woods and attack the Rebel works half a mile distant. Osborn's brigade would plod straight ahead and join the assault as soon as Shaw's men started firing. Terry's division had recovered sufficiently from its night march to stand ready to pitch in farther left. The Federals did not know it,

---

11 C. A. Stevens, *Berdan's United States Sharpshooters in the Army of the Potomac, 1861-1865* (St. Paul, 1892), 482.

but Terry's division faced Fussell's mill pond and William Birney's division faced the weakest point in the Confederate fortifications.

Around 4:00 p.m., Shaw's men slogged three quarters of a mile to their right, into a corn field in front of David Birney's headquarters, which occupied a hill about half a mile northeast of Fussell's mill pond. In the corn field, Shaw's troops formed on the right of Osborn's brigade. "Shaw had nothing before him except a thin line of pickets and a very small force on the works which were little more than rifle pits," remembered William Birney, who chose to remain with Osborn's brigade.

Shaw's soldiers trudged into the woods, alignng on a lane that led to their left. They began groping through the underbrush in search of the Confederate line north of Fussell's mill pond. The lane Shaw's troops followed curved further and further leftward.

Birney waited for Shaw to attack. "The hour passed—there was no sound from Shaw," recalled Birney. "I sent an orderly who reported that Shaw was standing still." Shaw thought his men headed in the wrong direction. Birney rode out to Shaw and ordered him to attack at once. Then Birney rode back to Osborn's brigade. Shaw forged ahead despite his misgivings.

Birney began advancing Osborn's brigade "by regiments, throwing skirmishers in advance to find the Rebel picket line," he remembered. "Instead, they found Shaw's command headed directly back through the underbrush and woods into our line of battle."[12] A firefight broke out between Shaw's troops and Osborn's brigade. Union soldiers killed and wounded one another among the lengthening shadows before they recognized their error and ceased fire. Shaw's regiments returned to the corn field, where they bivouacked. Birney's doubts about Shaw grew. Another chance of outflanking the formidable Confederate New Market Heights fortifications had slipped through Federal fingers.

Practically no time remained for an assault on the Secessionist line before dark, and the dense woods prohibited a night attack—a risky affair in the clearest terrain. David Birney swept under the rug the bungling in his older brother's division, withdrew Craig's troops to the main position of X Corps and

---

12 William Birney, *General William Birney's Answer To Libels Clandestinely Circulated By James Shaw, Jr.* (Washington DC, 1878), 14.

promised Hancock a vigorous attack at daybreak. Union losses for the day probably approached 100 men.[13] The Confederates likely lost half as many.

While the Northerners sought the Rebel line, the Southerners rearranged their dispositions to accommodate the reinforcements that had begun reaching them that morning. Stragglers from Sanders' and Wright's brigades continued to file into the earthworks to the left of Field's division, above Fussell's Mill. The foot soldiers of the Texas Brigade joined the cavalrymen of Gary's brigade and Rooney Lee's division on the Charles City Road.

General Lee made himself conspicuous among his troops on the north side of James River. "Some of the boys say he came over to see what kind of a place *Deep Bottom* was, and how long it would take to *fill it up* at the rate of four guns a week," Sergeant White of the 3rd Richmond Howitzers recorded in his diary, alluding to the four seacoast howitzers captured by the Unionists the previous day and the four 20-pounder Parrott rifles that Hancock had captured on July 27 during the first battle of Deep Bottom.[14]

The Army of Northern Virginia's leader rode up to the portion of the parapet along New Market Heights held by the 5th South Carolina Infantry of Bratton's brigade. Dismounting, Lee passed the regiment's commander, Col. Asbury Coward, and ambled about twenty feet beyond a foundation that afforded some protection from Federal sharpshooters. Born near Charleston, South Carolina, a graduate of The Citadel Military Academy, a co-founder of King's Mountain Military Academy—a preparatory school for The Citadel—Coward had upon the outbreak of hostilities entered the Confederate army as a captain in the adjutant general's department.

"General Lee, the sharpshooters near the battery down there have got the range of this," Coward said. "It would be better for you to stand back near the cornerstone of the house."

Unique in his ability to manage touchy, hot-tempered, honor-jealous Southern superiors and subordinates, Lee administered a typically muted rebuke.

---

13 Report of Col. John Pulford, Fifth Michigan Infantry, commanding Second Brigade, of operations August 14-17, in *OR* 42, pt. 1, 363. William Birney lost thiry or forty soldiers, the Federal cavalry at least a dozen, and the 2nd North Carolina Cavalry twenty-seven. Louis H. Manarin, *Henrico County-Field of Honor*, 2 vols. (Richmond, VA, 2004), 2:490, 492.

14 McCarthy, *Richmond Howitzer Battalion*, 271 (italics in original).

"Well, Colonel, I think two men would be a better target than one," Lee quietly said. "I wish you would go on to that corner. I must see the whole field."

The Virginian strode farther forward, field glass in hand. After looking right and left, Lee turned and strolled back to where he had left his horse. Before he reached his mount, he stopped. Bending over, he picked up an unfledged sparrow from the ground and gently placed it in the fork of a small tree.

"How could he turn from the thoughts of savage war to pity for this infant bird?" the still awestruck Coward wrote many years later. "Here was the fullness of manhood: honor, courage, gentleness. Do you wonder what I saw in him to make me think that he was the greatest man in the world?"[15]

The results of the day's activities, particularly David Birney's concern about his right flank, left Hancock disgusted. "It was my expectation that General Birney would have conducted his operations considerably more to his left, where the enemy's line was supposed to be," remembered Hancock. "Another day thus passed without accomplishing anything commensurate with my wishes."[16] The devastating flank attack of June 22 on the Jerusalem Plank Road seems to have impressed itself far more deeply on David Birney than the flank assault of May 6 that had routed II Corps in the Wilderness had impressed itself on Hancock, the corps commander that day.

That evening Hancock issued a series of orders for August 16. On the extreme Federal right, David Gregg's horsemen and Miles' foot soldiers would reconnoiter and, if possible, attack along the Charles City Road. At the same time, farther left, David Birney's infantrymen would strike westward to turn the Confederate left or attack the Rebel trenches between the Charles City Road and the Darbytown Road. Still farther left, II Corps would demonstrate in front of the enemy fortifications on New Market Heights or attack those earthworks if the foe stripped them to oppose Birney.

Hancock hoped his plans would not go awry for the third day in a row, but he had made a poor plan. Instead of concentrating his troops at the decisive point, with David Birney opposite the thinly manned and scarcely completed Secessionist trenches above Fussell's mill pond, Hancock dispersed his forces in the direction of two other objectives, the practically impregnable New

---

15 Natalie Jenkins Bond and Osman Latrobe Coward, eds., *The South Carolinians: Colonel Asbury Coward's Memoirs* (New York, 1968), 149-150.

16 *OR*, 42, pt. 1, 218.

The Second Battle of Deep Bottom, August 15, 1864

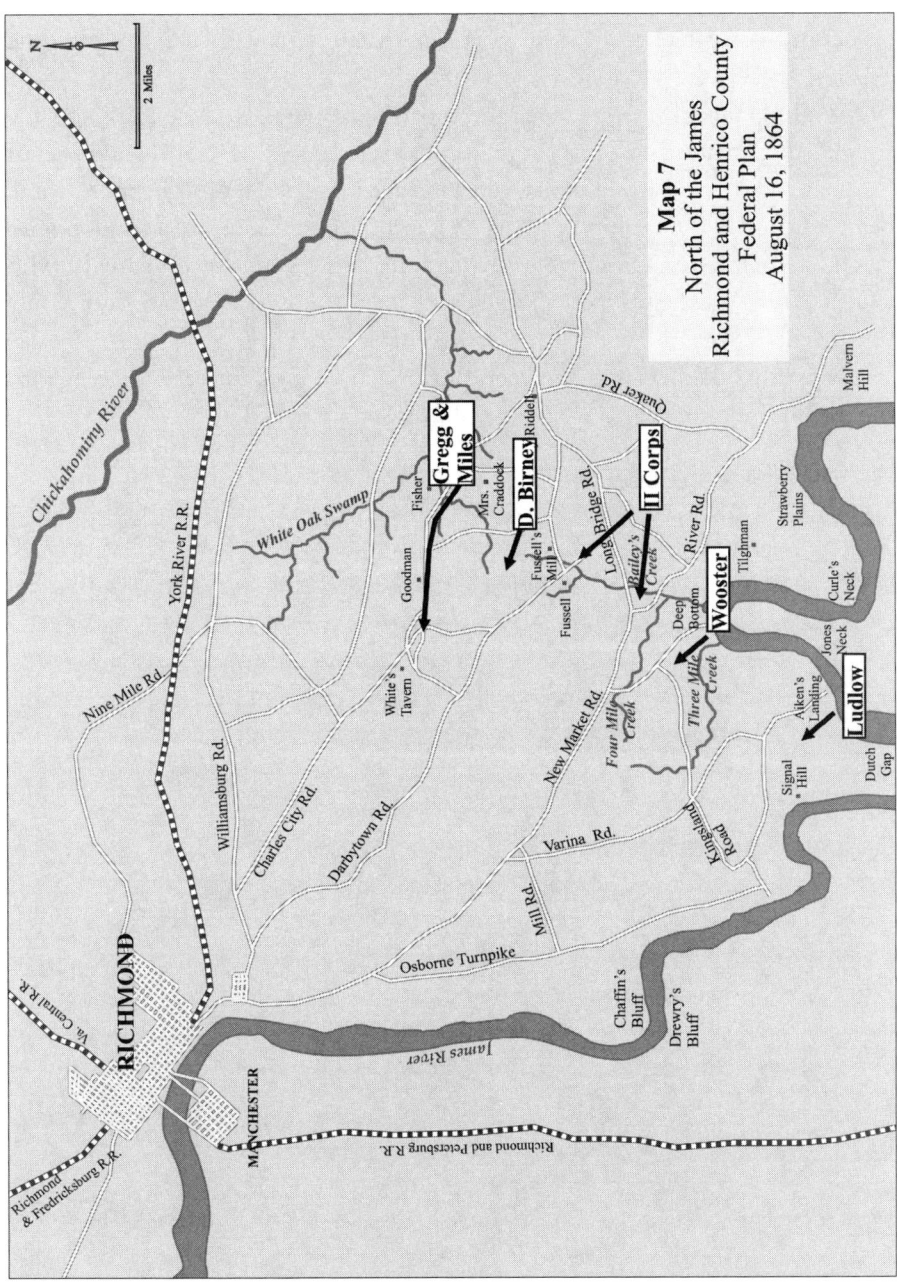

Market Heights fortifications and the easily defended Charles City Road. He and his staff had also put a roadblock of a different type in the path of the plan's execution—they had still failed to communicate to anyone in X Corps the existence of Fussell's mill pond.

While Hancock mapped out the morrow's operations, the rank and file sought such creature comforts as they could scrounge. Company K and part of Company D of the 140th Pennsylvania in Miles' brigade hit the jackpot, "there being a house in the vicinity, with its fruit trees, a corn field, and a sweet potato patch," remembered Orderly Sgt. Benjamin F. Powelson of Company K, who even found "a dry place on which to sleep a little—a stable door, only borrowed."[17]

Few other soldiers around Deep Bottom could look forward to going into combat in the morning so well fed and thoroughly rested.

---

17 B.F. Powelson, *History of Company K of the 140th Regiment Pennsylvania Volunteers (1862-'65)* (Steubenville OH, 1906), 40.

Chapter 4

The Second Battle of Deep Bottom, August 16, 1864

The 16th of August dawned still hotter than the previous day. The heat, lack of water and consequent sunstrokes made an unforgettable impression upon even the more acclimated Southerners. Corporal Joseph B. Polley of Company F, 4th Texas Infantry in the Texas Brigade, the son of one of Texas's "Old Three Hundred" colonists—the Pilgrims of the Lone Star State—remembered:

> The sky was cloudless, the sun had a full head of steam on; not a breath of air was astir in the dense woodlands through which the infantry brigade marched and countermarched, and water was not to be had except at the slow-flowing wells of the few denizens of the section.[1]

At about 6:30 a.m., the infantrymen of Miles' brigade deployed as skirmishers on the left of the Charles City Road at Fisher's farm. Their line consisted of the 26th Michigan, with its right resting on the road, and the 5th New Hampshire, to the left of the 26th Michigan. The 2nd and 4th Pennsylvania Cavalry of Irvin Gregg's brigade deployed as skirmishers on the right of the road.

---

1 Joseph B. Polley, *Hood's Texas Brigade: Its Marches, Its Battles, Its Achievements* (New York, 1910), 250.

The Federals struggled through the underbrush and across the nearly waterless ravine of Fisher's Run. By about 7:00 a.m., they had flanked and driven back the pickets of the 13th Virginia Cavalry stationed on the other side of the ravine. The 16th Pennsylvania Cavalry then charged across the run in column of fours, followed by the 1st Maine Cavalry and the 8th and 13th Pennsylvania Cavalry. The attack routed the Confederate pickets. The Unionists pushed the Rebels back about half a mile into dense woods, where the Secessionists took cover behind barricades. Here, at about 8:00 a.m., Irvin Gregg received a wound in the wrist, and command devolved upon Col. Michael Kerwin of the 13th Pennsylvania Cavalry, a lithographic printer born in Ireland. As the dismounted horsemen continued the advance, Gregg pointed to his wound and said, "Tell the boys to avenge this."[2]

They soon complied with Gregg's request.

Early that morning, Secessionist Brig. Gen. John Randolph Chambliss and his staff rode from his brigade's bivouac near White's Tavern eastward toward Fisher's Run. A graduate of the United States Military Academy, Chambliss left orders that the remainder of the brigade, the 9th and 10th Virginia Cavalry, should follow. The 10th rode forward first. The 9th, unaware of any need for haste, waited while many of its men returned from searching for water. Shortly a courier reached the 9th with an order to move up at a trot.

Accompanied by a member of his staff, Chambliss rode along the front lines in the woods where Irvin Gregg had received his wound. The Rebel horsemen saw a Federal behind a tree and fired upon him. Return fire from soldiers of the 5th New Hampshire separated Chambliss from his staff. The advance of the 16th Pennsylvania Cavalry spotted him on the Charles City Road and called upon him to surrender. He attempted to flee. A volley fatally struck Chambliss in the neck and upper chest. "The general was a small man, neatly dressed, having on a fine, white, well-laundered shirt with coat, hat and pants to match," remembered Maj. William Child, Surgeon of the 5th New Hampshire and a witness to Chambliss' death.[3] The Unionist rank and file immediately began cutting buttons and ornaments off the corpse's uniform. Within moments, Maj. Gen. David McMurtrie Gregg, a friend and classmate of

---

2 Publishing Committee, *A Brief History of the Fourth Veteran Pennsylvania Cavalry* (Pittsburgh, 1891), 98.

3 William Child, *A History of the Fifth Regiment New Hampshire Volunteers in the American Civil War, 1861-1865* (Bristol NH, 1893), 276.

Chambliss from West Point, arrived upon the scene. Recovering from the body a small Testament and, more importantly, a map of the Richmond defenses, Gregg sent the corpse to the rear.

The map retrieved from Chambliss' corpse might have proved decisive if captured the previous day. The Federals had so far made their plans in almost complete ignorance of what lay behind such Confederate lines as the Unionists could locate among the woods and swamps on the north bank of James River. Now, in the heat of action, the Unionists had no time to determine whether they could rely on the map or whether the Secessionists had manufactured it to misinform. The map did not help until weeks after the August fighting had ended.

The 9th Virginia Cavalry had gone less than a mile when the sharp volley that killed Chambliss in the woods to the right made the regiment dismount immediately and form in line at right angles to the road, on the margin of a bottom densely covered with huckleberry bushes. Colonel James Lucius Davis of the 10th Virginia Cavalry, a West Point graduate and cousin of President Davis, assumed command of Chambliss' brigade. The Southern horsemen became embroiled in a brief firefight with the dismounted Federal cavalrymen. The fight lasted until the Northern infantry of Miles' brigade came up and helped turn the flanks of the Virginians, who retreated through the woods and vines at the double-quick for a few hundred yards. The 16th Pennsylvania Cavalry had dismounted during the firefight and the 1st Maine Cavalry took up a position behind the front line, mounted and ready to exploit any Rebel display of disorder.

At the far side of an open field, the Virginians halted and began to erect another barricade. Before they had finished, a courier arrived with an order to keep falling back. The Virginians struggled back through the woods, across another bottom of dense undergrowth and clutching briars. Their division commander, Maj. Gen. William Henry Fitzhugh "Rooney" Lee, the second son of the Army of Northern Virginia's chief and a friend of Henry Adams at Harvard, halted Chambliss' brigade on the crest of the hill beyond, in an open body of large trees. Rooney Lee had already deployed Barringer's North Carolina brigade on the north side of the Charles City Road. He directed the Virginians to the south side. There, with the 10th Virginia Cavalry on the left, the 9th Virginia Cavalry in the center, and the 13th Virginia Cavalry on the right, Chambliss' brigade rested unmolested for more than an hour in the extreme heat. The 2nd Jeb Stuart Horse Artillery unlimbered in support.

David Gregg's advance had arrived within half a mile of White's Tavern. He ordered his horsemen to halt after an advance of three quarters of a mile westward from the bottom where Irvin Gregg had gotten wounded and Chambliss had gotten killed. The Unionist cavalry, now on both sides of the Charles City Road, waited east of White's Tavern until the 26th Michigan and the 5th New Hampshire relieved them. The 2nd New York Heavy Artillery then took the place of the Michiganders and Granite State men on the front line.

News of the Gregg's success on the Charles City Road flew quickly up the Union chain of command. By 10:30 a.m., Grant had perceived that the Union force near White's Tavern threatened the route of retreat toward Richmond of the Confederates farther south, opposite David Birney near Fussell's mill pond. The general-in-chief ordered Butler to demonstrate with his troops at Dutch Gap to threaten the Secessionist retreat route from New Market Heights toward Chaffin's Bluff.

David Gregg's command had advanced about as far westward on the Charles City Road as Gregg had thought possible. He mistook for infantry the dismounted Confederate cavalrymen on the crest east of White's Tavern. Reports arrived of a line of Rebel flankers marching northward toward White's Tavern from Fussell's Mill. Under the circumstances, Miles thought it inadvisable to advance farther westward on the Charles City Road without connecting to David Birney's right. Miles wanted to hold the ground gained and await orders. Shortly after 11:00 a.m., instructions came from Hancock for Miles to close in southward toward Birney if heavy and continuous firing came from Birney's position. Gregg received directions to advance as far westward as possible on the Charles City Road, at least to divert the enemy or at best to force the foe to retreat in front of Birney and II Corps farther south.

At noon, Gregg attempted a maneuver that he thought would compel the retreat of the Secessionists confronting him, despite their artillery support. The 183rd Pennsylvania, deployed as skirmishers, led the way. Using the dense cover to their advantage, the Keystoners quietly crept into the bottom and opened fire. The first volley killed a few Virginians and inspired the battery to limber up and withdraw, but Chambliss' brigade checked the 183rd's advance and repelled the effort to turn the Virginian right. After a short engagement, the Pennsylvanians fell back on the rest of Miles' brigade.

The initiative shifted to Rooney Lee, the Confederate commander on the Charles City Road. Rebel reinforcements arrived. Barringer's North Carolina brigade remained on the north side of the Charles City Road. Chambliss' brigade remained on the road's south side. Gary's brigade joined took position dismounted on the right of Chambliss' Virginians. The 7th Georgia Cavalry, the vanguard of Matthew Butler's division, came under Gary's command. Moving up from near Fussell's Mill, the Texas Brigade filed into place on the right of Gary's troopers. The Texas Brigade and Gary's brigade formed an ad hoc division under Gary's command.

By 12:20 p.m., the situation had changed to the south of Gregg and Rooney Lee. Hancock asked Gregg to cut short his advance westward on the Charles City Road and have Miles connect with Birney's right. By the time Hancock's message arrived, Gregg's position had become too precarious for Gregg to release Miles.

About 1:00 p.m, the Secessionists on the Charles City Road attacked. The first shots caused Miles' infantry to break and fall back, leaving Kerwin's cavalry to bear the brunt of the Southern advance. The 2nd New York Heavy Artillery, which had earned Barlow's censure on August 14, now earned the scorn of the Federal horsemen. Sergeant Edward P. Tobie, Jr., of Company G, 1st Maine Cavalry, a printer from Lewiston, recalled:

> Those who were there will remember how the infantry men (or rather heavy artillery men) ran through the cavalry lines, and long afterwards it was a saying in the regiment that the "heavies got round shouldered going under our horses in their skedaddle."[4]

Kerwin's cavalrymen took up a position on the right of the Charles City Road in a sort of basin. His men could see the Confederates working their way through the woods on the left of the road after Miles' fleeing infantrymen. Among the trees, the right of Chambliss' brigade overlapped the left of Gary's brigade—a situation which led to a fiasco similar to that experienced by William Birney's Northerners the previous day. Gary's men fired into the right of the 9th Virginia Cavalry, wounding several troopers and disordering the 9th's right squadron. The rest of the regiment drove Miles' infantry across an open field and into another wood.

The Federal cavalry on the north side of the Charles City Road fell back to an open field abreast of the timber harboring Miles' infantry on the road's south side. Chambliss' brigade pushed the Unionist foot soldiers out of the trees and exposed the flank of Kerwin's cavalrymen. Fortunately for the Northern

---

4 Edward P. Tobie, *History of the First Maine Cavalry, 1861-1865* (Boston, 1887), 311.

horsemen, the wooded nature of the terrain again caused confusion in the Rebel ranks. After flushing Miles' infantry out of the woods, some soldiers of the 9th Virginia Cavalry saw a group of mounted troopers from the 1st Maine Cavalry on the Charles City Road. The little band of Virginians ran toward the Maine horsemen across the front of the 10th Virginia Cavalry, which had not yet emerged from the woods. The greater part of the 9th and 13th Virginia Cavalry, supposing the pursuers the line of battle, followed them. Though the Mainers got caught in a fierce crossfire as the 10th came up, the Virginians subsequently required a halt to reform their line at right angles to the road.

As the Confederates drove back the first Federal line, which consisted of about half the Union forces, Gregg and Miles formed a second line with their remaining troops about half a mile rearward. This line ran along a crest astride the Charles City Road. The crest afforded a good view of the terrain in front—first the bottom where Chambliss had perished and the 9th Virginia Cavalry had first dismounted earlier that day, then a narrow plateau covered with bushes, and next another bottom. The first Federal line soon passed through the troops on the crest and about half a mile beyond halted to form yet another line on the west bank of Fisher's Run just west of Fisher's farm, under the protection of Unionist artillery.

About 1:30 p.m., the Secessionists resumed their advance. They tramped across the first bottom. About fifty yards beyond, halfway over the plateau, they got a rough reception from the second Federal line. The Virginians recoiled into the bottom they had just crossed with a haste that drew a bitter denunciation from Rooney Lee. Recovering their composure, they returned fire. As the Union right crumbled under pressure from the Rebels on the north side of the Charles City Road, the 13th Virginia Cavalry turned the Federal left, which held a small barricade of fence rails. The 9th Virginia Cavalry then charged directly across the plateau. The Northerners broke and ran, leaving the Southerners to occupy the barricade. There, exhausted and almost out of ammunition, Chambliss' brigade finally received orders to lie down and rest. "The day was the most trying our regiment had ever experienced," remembered Col. Richard Lee Turberville Beale, a University of Virginia educated lawyer in command of the 9th Virginia Cavalry.

> Not one drop of water could be had; the heat was intense, and the wood was dense and tangled. A large force of infantry was in our front with a support of cavalry, itself superior, to our own. Our Brigadier-General, the accomplished, gallant, and loved

Chambliss, had fallen under the volley which led us to dismount and form line on foot in the morning."⁵

The Virginians used the barricade begun by the 13th as a shield from the fire of dismounted Union cavalry on the other side of the Charles City Road. It failed to protect them from another blast of friendly fire.

The Tarheels of Barringer's brigade continued the pursuit down the Charles City Road. The Federals retreated to their next line, on the west bank of Fisher's Run. By about 3:00 p.m., firing had ceased on David Gregg's front. Barringer's troopers did not seem interested in assailing the Unionist position. The Confederate infantry appeared to retire in the direction of Fussell's Mill. Employing his own soldiers to erect breastworks and slash timber, Gregg finally allowed Miles' brigade to tramp off toward David Birney's right. Gregg's cavalrymen stood practically where they had started from early that morning.

* * *

Birney's command, under arms since 3:00 a.m., had begun slogging forward at daybreak. Terry's division led the way on the command's mission to turn the enemy's left or attack his line between the Charles City Road and the Darbytown Road. Terry positioned Foster's brigade behind Hawley's brigade, and the Western Brigade on Hawley's left. In front of this formation, the division commander deployed the 3rd New Hampshire Infantry as skirmishers. Far to Terry's left, II Corps reinforced its picket line and began demonstrating against the Rebels below Fussell's mill pond.

Terry's soldiers began a slow left wheel through the underbrush. The skirmishers gradually drove back their Secessionist opponents. The left wheel came to a halt at the brink of the mill pond. No one had informed Terry of the pond's existence though Barlow had encountered it two days earlier.

By about 9:00 a.m., recovering from this false start, Terry had changed his division's formation. Positioning Foster's brigade on the right of Hawley's to try and force a passage around the head of the mill pond, Terry swung the Western Brigade from left to right and put it behind and in support of Foster's brigade. Foster deployed his brigade with the 10th Connecticut, 24th

---

5 Richard L. T. Beale, *History of the Ninth Virginia Cavalry In The War Between the States* (Richmond, 1899), 140.

Brig. Gen. Alfred H. Terry, U.S.A. *Library of Congress*

Massachusetts and 11th Maine in that order, forming its front line from left to right. The 100th New York supported the left of the front line. The 1st Maryland Cavalry (dismounted) supported the right.

Terry had also received a reinforcement from II Corps—Craig's brigade of Mott's division. Terry assigned this brigade to protect his own division's right. Craig deployed the 1st United States Sharpshooters and the 5th Michigan as skirmishers extending back from the right flank of Foster's brigade. A battle line consisting of the 93rd New York and the 84th, 105th, and 141st Pennsylvania supported Craig's skirmish line. The 57th Pennsylvania and the 1st Massachusetts Heavy Artillery, in column by division, massed behind the battle line.

By about 9:20 a.m., Foster's brigade had encountered Confederate skirmishers on the opposite side of a deep ravine that emptied into Fussell's mill pond—the Eastern Ravine in this battle. After a brief engagement, Foster's men drove the Rebels from their rifle pits, taking about thirty prisoners.[6] The advance prompted Craig to deploy the 1st Massachusetts heavies as flankers on the right of the 5th Michigan.

Reforming, Foster's brigade shortly before 11:00 a.m. drove the Southerners from another line of rifle pits, taking about 40 prisoners.[7] The 11th Maine, ordered by Foster to drive the enemy into his main works and ascertain whether the rest of Foster's soldiers could take those works by assault, rushed onward, accompanied by the 1st Maryland Cavalry and part of Craig's brigade. These Federals reached another deep ravine which also flowed into Fussell's mill pond. This ravine—the Western Ravine in this fight—had sides at this point almost impassably steep. On the opposite side, Sanders' Alabama brigade occupied strong entrenchments protected by a slashing.

The Unionists met with a devastating volley. "The woods fairly rang with the screeching of bullets," recalled Sergeant Brady of the 11th Maine.[8] The Alabamians in the fortifications appeared to waver. Colonel Harris M. Plaisted, the commander of Brady's regiment, remembered that, "the rebel colors were seen to leave the works, and many rebels threw up their caps and arms in token of surrender."[9] Then the 1st Maryland Cavalry suddenly broke and fell obliquely back into the line of the 11th Maine, causing that regiment to retreat as well. The terrible fire also threw Craig's contingent of II Corps into confusion. Foster's and Craig's brigades sought cover. Brady, who sheltered behind a tree with a burly sergeant of the 1st Maryland Cavalry, recalled, "As a glimpse of a dream, I remember that almost at our feet a soldier lay dying from a wound in the throat, the blood flowing in spouting jets as he gasped in his last agonies."[10]

Terry reported the repulse of his reconnaissance to David Birney, who instructed Terry to attack immediately. The division commander organized his troops for the third time that day. First, Terry brought up a fresh brigade to spearhead the assault. He summoned the Western Brigade out from behind

---

6 Report of Capt. George W. Gardner, Twenty-fourth Massachusetts Infantry, of operations August 14-21, in *OR* 42, pt. 1, 755.

7 Ibid., 739; *SHSP*, 14:552.

8 Brady, *Eleventh Maine*, 244.

9 *OR* 42, pt. 1, 747.

10 Brady, *Eleventh Maine*, 244.

Abatis *Library of Congress*

Foster and placed it on Foster's right. The Western Brigade formed about half a mile to the right of Fussell's Mill and approximately 100 yards from the Secessionist earthworks, hidden from sight by the dense woods. Colonel Francis B. Pond of the 62nd Ohio, an Ohio lawyer who had helped raise and organize the 62nd, commanded the Western Brigade that day. He deployed as skirmishers the four companies of the 67th Ohio at his disposal. Behind the skirmish line, from left to right, the 39th Illinois, 62nd Ohio and 85th Pennsylvania formed the brigade's battle line. Every company lined up in two ranks. Each regiment formed a column two companies wide and five deep. The approximately 750 soldiers of the Western Brigade stood ten ranks deep on a front of about 135 yards, including thirty paces separating the adjacent regiments. The 39th Illinois and 62nd Ohio received orders to swing to the left after carrying the Confederate works. The 85th Pennsylvania got instructions to swing to the right.

Next, Terry placed Hawley's brigade behind the right of the Western Brigade, where Hawley's brigade could exploit any opening the Western Brigade created. Hawley's brigade consisted of the 6th and 7th Connecticut and the 3rd and 7th New Hampshire. The commander of the brigade, Col. Joseph Roswell Hawley, a graduate of Hamilton College, had given up the law to become a Connecticut newspaper editor. Terry wanted Hawley's brigade to follow the Western Brigade whether or not it succeeded in taking the Rebel works.

Terry's reorganization of his command took place under a steady fire from the Secessionist fortifications. Hawley's brigade, when it reached its appointed position, got orders to lie down in line of battle. The soldiers immediately began constructing breastworks. Lieutenant E. Lewis Moore, Acting Assistant Adjutant General of Hawley's brigade, who had risen from a private in Company G of the 7th Connecticut because of his clerical skills, remembered that Terry, like Hawley a former colonel of that regiment,

> jokingly told the officers who were on their feet to get the best cover they could against the fire of small arms until we could get orders to move. He himself set the example by shielding his slim figure behind a tree about eight inches through. Most of the officers felt rather slim about that time and dutifully followed the general's example.[11]

While Terry redeployed the Western Brigade and Hawley's brigade to the right of Foster's brigade, Foster conducted a reorganization of his own. The advance to the main Rebel works had so separated the left of the 10th Connecticut from the 100th New York that the Confederates infiltrated the gap between the two Union regiments and took three prisoners.[12] Foster had the two regiments close the gap. Pistol in hand, he walked about behind the 100th New York after the failure of his brigade's attack. The New Yorkers took offense at the display of the sidearm. They felt it implied that their attack had failed because of the feebleness of their effort. They believed the Confederate position impregnable.

The skirmish line of Craig's brigade remained on the right of Terry's division. Craig's battle line remained in support of his skirmishers.

By noon, as David Gregg sent forward the 183rd Pennsylvania on the Charles City Road, Terry's division stood ready to attack for the third time that sweltering day. This time Terry's troops occupied ground in the V between the Eastern and Western Ravines. In support of Terry's foot soldiers, ten cannon of X Corps stood on or near the hill where David Birney had his headquarters, about 800 yards east by southeast of the Rebel earthworks held by Wright's brigade—six 3-inch rifles of Battery D, 1st United States Artillery and four

---

11 Stephen Walkley, comp., *History of the Seventh Connecticut Volunteer Infantry* (Stonington CT, 1905), 161.

12 *OR* 42, pt. 1, 739, 752.

Napoleons of the 4th New Jersey Battery. These guns opened on Wright's brigade to keep down the heads of the Southerners. In the II Corps sector below Fussell's mill pond, the six Napoleons of Battery G, 1st New York Artillery unlimbered on a crest just south of the Darbytown Road and about 400 yards from the enemy, while the four Napoleons of Battery K, 4th United States Artillery unlimbered on a rise around 600 yards from the Secessionist works. The II Corps artillery tore up the Rebel breastworks on both sides of the Darbytown Road and interdicted the road itself.

* * *

Present during the repulse of the 11th Maine and its supporting troops, General Field knew that the Federals threatened the weakest point in his line of defense. A slashing of only about fifty yards protected the Confederate trenches at this place, about half a mile upstream from Fussell's Mill. The Western Ravine ran parallel to the Rebel earthworks near this point, where a small branch slanted through the works from northwest to southeast before it ran into the ravine.[13] The slashing did not extend as far as the Western Ravine. At the edge of a dense forest of oak and pine, the ravine would screen attackers from Secessionist fire beyond the slashing.

Field's command had grown since August 14. Johnson's Tennessee brigade, the 25th Virginia Battalion from the Department of Richmond and newly arrived detachments from Scales' and Thomas' brigades of Wilcox's division held a line stretching from James River to Deep Bottom. Bratton's brigade, Law's brigade, Benning's brigade, and the 7th, 8th, and 59th Georgia of Anderson's brigade, still under Brig. Gen. John Gregg, occupied the trenches from Deep Bottom to Fussell's mill pond.

The ad hoc division of Brig. Gen. John Caldwell Calhoun Sanders, one of the youngest brigadiers in the Confederate army, who had left his studies at the University of Alabama to enlist as a private in the 11th Alabama Infantry, stood behind the breastworks for just over half a mile to the left of Fussell's Mill. Sanders' command consisted of his own Alabama brigade and Wright's brigade

---

13 The branch slanted through the earthworks around fifty yards south of today's marker for the 39th Illinois Veteran Volunteers, which stands about seventy yards east of the Western Ravine on the present day Darbytown Road between Fussell's Ridge Drive on the east and Yahley Mill Road on the west. The Confederate trenches lay approximately twenty yards east of where the marker now stands.

of Georgians, both from Mahone's division. The 8th, 9th 10th and 14th Alabama occupied fortifications on high ground west of Fussell's mill pond and south of a ravine running obliquely from northwest to southeast into the Western Ravine near the head of Fussell's mill pond—the Oblique Ravine in this action. The 11th Alabama formed the left of Sanders' brigade and held about 100 yards of works north of the Oblique Ravine. Wright's Georgia brigade, under Brig. Gen. Victor Jean Baptiste Girardey, stood in the weak stretch of earthworks with the inadequate slashing north of Sanders' Alabamians. The Georgians held about 500 yards of trenches. The Georgian left rested north of the present day Darbytown Road.

Girardey had just received an unprecedented promotion from the rank of captain and the position of assistant adjutant general on the staff of Mahone's division. The promotion had come because of Girardey's meritorious service at the battle of the Crater, less than three weeks earlier, when he had not only conveyed the order to advance but actually led the charge that turned the tide that day. On June 23, he had guided the Florida Brigade of Mahone's division to where the Floridians cut off the Vermont Brigade of VI Corps at the battle of the Jerusalem Plank Road, consigning almost 500 Vermonters to slow starvation in Southern prison camps.

Early in the morning, while Terry felt his way around Fussell's mill pond, Field had moved Conner's provisional division, still composed of Lane's and McGowan's brigades of Wilcox's division, from near Fussell's Mill to the left of Wright's brigade. Under Col. Francis H. Little of the 11th Georgia Infantry, a lawyer educated at the University of Georgia and wounded at Gettysburg, the 9th and 11th Georgia of Anderson's brigade took up a position on the left of Lane's brigade of North Carolinians and on the right of McGowan's brigade of South Carolinians. Despite the reinforcements that Field had received, the extension of his infantry's left to meet Hancock's groping for that flank kept the Secessionist foot soldiers from occupying the breastworks with more than a single rank. The elusive left flank of Field's infantry lay about a mile south of Charles City Road and a mile north of the weak point threatened by Terry's division.

Shortly after Sanders' brigade had repulsed the 11th Maine and its supporting troops, Field dismounted. Tired from having ridden hither and thither since dawn, oppressed by the heat, he and his staff hitched their horses to some nearby bushes and sat down in the corn field of the Robinson farm behind the left of Wright's brigade. Field heard firing and cheering from in front of Wright's brigade about half an hour after the repulse of the first Federal attack. Though Field knew that this meant another Union assault, he felt so sure that it would meet with the same fate as the first that he remained seated.

Field's adjutant general, Maj. Willis F. Jones, a Kentuckian and Field's nephew, got to his feet. With a better field of vision than his commander, Jones suddenly said, very excitedly: "General, they are breaking."

"Well, I knew they would," Field replied, thinking that Jones referred to the Federals.

"But General, it's our men," Jones said.

Jumping up, Field saw what he later called "the most appalling, disheartening sight" in his life. Wright's brigade, immediately in front of Field, and Lane's brigade, on his left, had given way. Disordered squads of both brigades streamed past Field and his staff while the Northerners jumped over the works just vacated "in close pursuit, and cheering like all the world."[14] Field's staff confronted the stampeding Georgians and North Carolinians. "We strove to rally them by entreaties and by menaces, and with pistols drawn we threatened to shoot them if they did not go back; but it was of no avail," remembered Captain Corbin, Field's aide-de-camp. "You might as well try to argue with a flock of affrighted sheep as with a crowd of panic-stricken soldiers."[15]

Mounting his horse, Field dispatched couriers to summon reinforcements from his right while he tried to reach the brigades to his left. The Unionists prevented him, pouring through the gap left by the two brigades that had broken and cutting Field's force in two. Detailed to fill his company's canteens, Private Hamil of the 9th Georgia in Little's detachment recalled the stampede of Lane's brigade:

> The woods seemed to be full of men, some afoot, some on horseback and some Officers and Privates. They said the Yankees had broke our line and our men were routed and the orders were for every one to get inside the breastworks at Richmond just as quick as he could (it was 7 or 8 miles to Richmond). . . . We kept meeting them rushing for the breastworks at Richmond.[16]

---

14 *SHSP*, 14:552-3.

15 Corbin, *Letters of a Confederate Officer*, 59.

16 Hamil, *Memories and Recollections of John W. Hamil*, 28-29.

Field dispatched orders to John Gregg on the Confederate right to send every available man. "At this time not only the day but Richmond seemed to be gone," Field remembered. "I felt that nothing but a miracle could save us."[17]

General Sanders galloped around southwest of the breakthrough rallying the North Carolinians of Lane's brigade and the Georgians of Wright's brigade while steadying his own Alabamians. General Lee and his staff sat their horses on the Darbytown Road west of Sanders' brigade. The army group commander "seemed restless, rode up & down the road, put his hand to his ear to catch the direction, etc., of the sound of strife," recalled Assistant Surgeon Charles William Trueheart of Sanders' 8th Alabama, who had previously served in both the infantry and the artillery.[18]

Sergeant Junius L. Powell of Field's staff had lost his horse to an enemy bullet. Powell ran southward on the Darbytown Road carrying a call from Field for reinforcements. As he passed Lee, Powell shouted news of the penetration in the line. The army group commander dispatched Col. Charles Marshall of his staff to summon help. Then Lee tried to rally his retreating troops.

"My friends, rally, and go back and help your fellow soldiers, drive these people back," he called. "We must drive them back, and retake those works."

The Army of Northern Virginia's leader drafted Surgeon Trueheart, who recalled that Lee, "would make me do rear guard duty sending me hither and thither to halt and turn back men who were running out of the fight. . . ."[19]

Secessionist troops regarded Federals from the Great North West—Ohio, Indiana, Michigan, Illinois, Wisconsin, Iowa, and Minnesota—as especially hard and tenacious fighters.[20] The performance of the Western Brigade of Terry's division bore out this reputation. When the command "Forward!" came, the brigade's troops jumped off in common time with arms at right shoulder shift. The soldiers charged down into the Western Ravine in front of them, which marked the point where the dense woods gave way to the slashing. As soon as the men reached the edge of the slashing, they met with a volley

---

17 *SHSP*, 14:553.

18 Edward B. Williams, ed., *Rebel Brothers: The Civil War Letters of the Truehearts* (College Station, 1995), 111.

19 Ibid.

20 The 85th Pennsylvania's soldiers haled from western Pennsylvania. Luther S. Dickey, *History of the Eighty-fifth Regiment Pennsylvania Volunteer Infantry 1861-1865, Comprising an Authentic Narrative of Casey's Division at the Battle of Seven Pines* (New York: J. C. & W. F. Powers, 1915), 1-5.

from the Georgians of Wright's brigade that almost annihilated the entire front line of each regiment. The troops in front "went down like so many ten-pins," Lt. Col. Edward Campbell of the 85th Pennsylvania remembered.[21] The hail of Southern bullets brought the arms of the Unionists down from right shoulder shift to a trail and sent the colors of the 39th Illinois, the Yates Phalanx, to the ground. The 39th's color sergeant, Pvt. Henry M. Hardenbergh of Company G, the Preacher's Company, had taken a Rebel bullet in the left shoulder.

The soldiers of the Western Brigade staggered, but continued their charge. Though one rank had gone down, nine more remained to pile into the single rank of Georgians. First Lieutenant Norman C. Warner of the 39th's Company E, a War Democrat, literally tore the flag from Hardenbergh, leaving a piece of the banner in Hardenbergh's bloody hands. "Away we went with a regular Western yell, on the full jump, over logs, tree-tops and stumps thrown about in inextricable confusion," recalled Sgt. Maj. Homer A. Plimpton of the Preacher's Company, a teacher who had graduated from Northwestern University. The men crossed the few yards of slashing that separated them from the Confederate works so quickly that the Secessionsts could not deliver another volley.

When the Western Brigade reached the Rebel breastworks, Wright's brigade did not give way. A hand to hand fight began as the Federals attempted to mount the works. A Southern ball shattered Lieutenant Warner's leg. The flag of the Yates Phalanx fell again. Sergeant-Major Plimpton remembered, "Another officer snatched them up and sprang upon the parapets, followed by scores of others, who leaped right over among the "Johnnies," and commenced using the bayonet and clubbed musket."[22] The Western Brigade swept over the parapet into the Confederate works "like a tornado," recalled Colonel Pond, the brigade's commander. "The first time I ever saw this brigade fighting hand to hand, bayonet to bayonet, over breastworks, was that day."[23] Many of the opposing Georgians lacked bayonets though they belonged to a division whose commander levied a fine for this offense.

---

21 OR 42, pt. 1, 699.

22 Charles M. Clark, *The History of the Thirty-Ninth Regiment Illinois Volunteer Veteran Infantry (Yates Phalanx) in the War of the Rebellion, 1861-1865* (Chicago, 1889), 211.

23 Report of Col. Francis B. Pond, Sixty-second Ohio Infantry, commanding First Brigade, of operations August 13-16, in OR 42, pt. 1, 688.

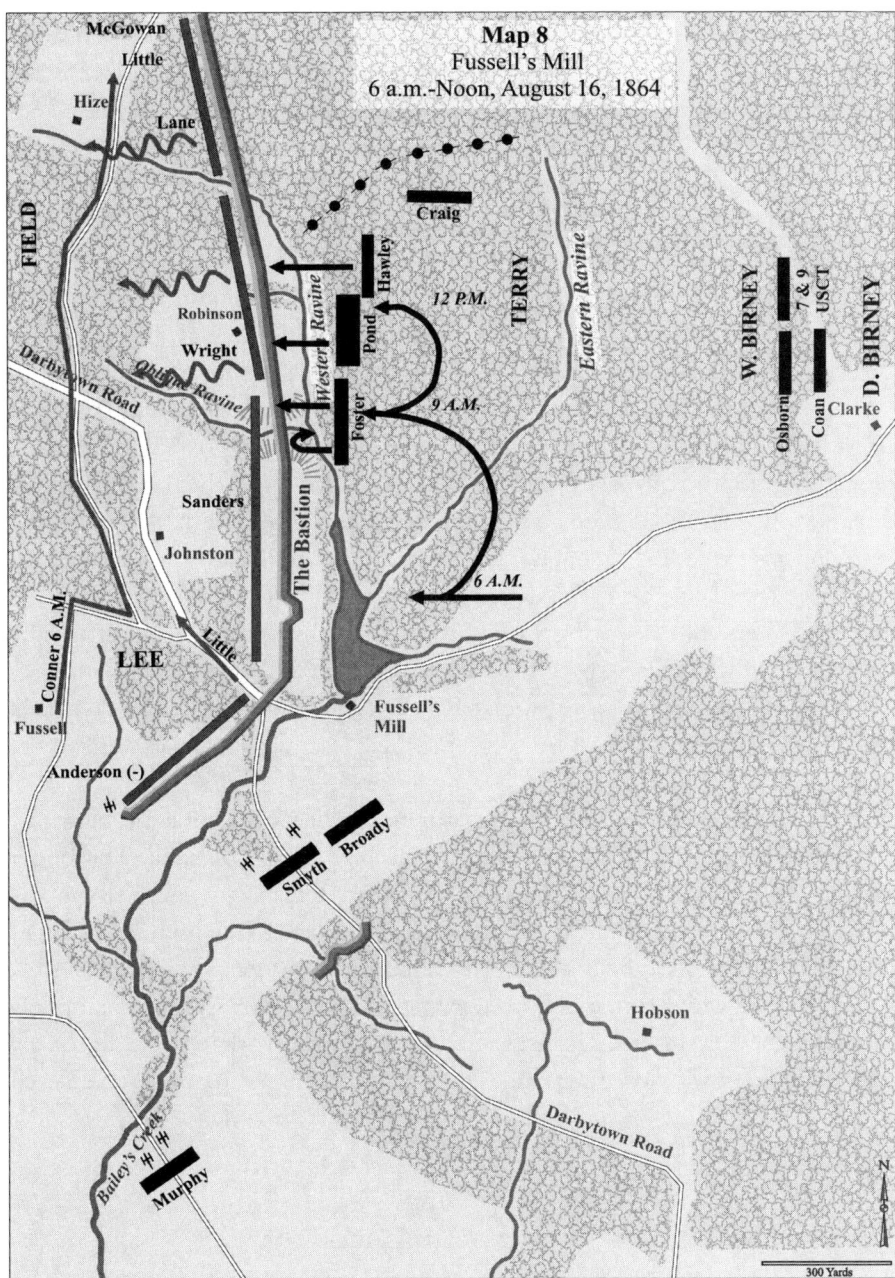

Wright's brigade did not receive any immediate assistance. The Georgians broke between the 2nd Georgia Battalion and the 10th Georgia Battalion. Girardey attempted to rally his soldiers. He seized the colors of the 64th

Georgia just north of the breach in his line. A sharpshooter of the 67th Ohio shot Girardey in the forehead, inflicting a mortal wound. More than 200 Confederates surrendered.[24] Others fled through the Robinson corn field into the woods of the Oblique Ravine, which originated about 300 yards behind the left of Wright's brigade. Corporal John S. Schellenberger of the 85th Pennsylvania's Company B and Pvt. William Edward Leonard of the 85th's Company F captured Confederate banners, earning Medals of Honor. Private A. H. Draper of Company B, 64th Georgia retrieved his regiment's flag from the dying Girardey's grasp and scampered to safety in the rear. Command of Wright's brigade devolved upon Col. William Gibson of the 48th Georgia.

As Wright's brigade disintegrated in surrender and flight, the Western Brigade disintegrated in hot pursuit of the fleeing foe. Most of the Rebels retreated southward. Most of the 39th Illinois headed down the trenches in that direction as ordered. The pursuers from the Yates Phalanx included Hardenbergh, who had picked himself up and rejoined the advance. He and his comrades rolled up the 11th Alabama of Sanders' brigade, taking at least 20 more prisoners and occupying the Confederate earthworks to the mouth of the Oblique Ravine.[25] Hardenbergh, an Indiana native and former clerk in a dry goods store, captured a Secessionist banner from the 10th Alabama after a hand-to-hand fight with its color sergeant which left the Alabamian dead on the field.[26]

The advance of the Yates Phalanx stopped at the Oblique Ravine, halted by Sanders' Alabamians in the trenches on the high southern bank. The better parts of the 62nd and 67th Ohio swung left as ordered and advanced all the way across the Robinson corn field into the Oblique Ravine to the right of the Yates Phalanx. Almost all of the 85th Pennsylvania, against orders, swung left as well. "Nearly crazy with excitement," according to Lieutenant Colonel Campbell, each of these Keystoners, "as fast as he came over the works struck out for the first Rebel he saw, and either made him prisoner, chased him off, or entered

---

24 Ibid.

25 Suderow, "Target Richmond," Suderow Private Collection.

26 Though the 10th Georgia Battalion (if one emphasizes "10th") and the 11th Alabama Regiment (if one emphasizes "Alabama") stood closer to the breakthrough than the 10th Alabama Regiment, Hardenbergh's service record specifically states that he captured the flag of the 10th Alabama Regiment. Henry M. Hardenbergh, Compiled Service Record, Record Group 109, National Archives, Washington, DC.

into combat with him."[27] Campbell and Capt. Rolla O. Phillips of Company D managed to collect only fifty members of the 85th and form them to meet the enemy on the right, who had already begun to advance down the trench toward the Pennsylvanians.

When the Western Brigade charged, on its left charged Foster's brigade. Only the far right of this brigade, the 11th Maine and Companies C, H and E of the 24th Massachusetts, succeeded in getting into the Rebel earthworks above the mouth of the Oblique Ravine. The heavy logs and the tendency of an enemy firing downhill to shoot high reduced casualties among these troops as they advanced. Then the Western Brigade cleared the way for Foster's men by rolling up the 11th Alabama. The 11th Maine and the three companies of the 24th Massachusetts joined the Western Brigade in the stretch of works just north of the Oblique Ravine, and the balance of the 24th Massachusetts took up a line stretching back from where the fortifications crossed the Oblique Ravine, down to the Western Ravine. The sides of both ravines grew impassably steep farther to the Union left and created a bastion—The Bastion in this battle—entrenched high ground from which Sanders' Alabamians enfiladed the works seized by the Federals.[28] The 10th Connecticut, 100th New York and 1st Maryland Cavalry failed to enter The Bastion. Sanders redeployed his troops with the 10th Alabama facing eastward from The Bastion while the rest of his brigade looked roughly northward. The deadly fire of the 10th Alabama pinned down the soldiers of 10th Connecticut, 100th New York and 1st Maryland Cavalry behind the shelter of the Western Ravine's bank. Col. John L. Otis of the 10th Connecticut thought that if other Federals could attack the Secessionists to his left, it would draw off fire enfilading his soldiers and give them a better chance to seize the fortifications in front of them. He passed his idea along to Foster, who forwarded it up the chain of command, but no response came except for the arrival of three companies of the 13th Indiana in Osborn's brigade, which started firing across the ravine at the 10th Alabama. The other regiments of Sanders' brigade held The Bastion and the Oblique Ravine against elements of the Western Brigade and the fragment of Foster's brigade which had made it into the trenches.

---

27 OR 42, pt. 1, 699.

28 Stand where the present day Darbytown Road crosses the Western Ravine, look south, and you will see The Bastion.

While the 7th New Hampshire remained lying down in reserve, the 6th and 7th Connecticut and 3rd New Hampshire of Hawley's brigade tramped forward in support of the Western Brigade shortly after it charged. Hawley's troops drank from the creek in the Western Ravine before assailing the works. First Lieutenant Daniel Eldredge of Company E 3rd New Hampshire Infantry, who had risen from a private because of his clerical skills and nearly lost his left arm as the result of a wound in this battle, recalled the scene that confronted Hawley's men as they emerged from the woods into the slashing:

> It was almost like the rising of a stage curtain. The rebels were being taken prisoners by the first line, its attack having been too furious and precipitate to permit a retreat.... Between the edge of the woods and their works, the ground was rising, very marshy and well filled with fallen trees and other obstructions. Over all of these we clambered and, hastening up the declivity, entered the works and joined the first line in loud huzzas at the victory.[29]

Confederate resistance had begun to crumble by the time Hawley's soldiers reached the Secessionist works. Hawley's troops mopped up the remaining Georgians with their left where they followed the Western Brigade. With their right, which overlapped the Western Brigade, Hawley's men had to capture the breastworks themselves. "Confusion for a few moments followed, the men of both sides fraternizing and exchanging coffee for tobacco, etc.," remembered Elbridge J. Copp, Adjutant of the 3rd New Hampshire.[30] Hawley's troops wasted precious time.

Terry's soldiers had seized the Rebel trenches from the Oblique Ravine on the south to a point about a hundred yards north of where today's Darbytown Road crosses the Western Ravine. Terry tried to expand the breakthrough. After he had brought up the 7th New Hampshire to assist in guarding the breakthrough's right, he shifted the rest of Hawley's brigade southward through the thicket that grew in the branch flowing through the works into the Western Ravine. When the 3rd New Hampshire and 6th and 7th Connecticut had formed line of battle, Terry sent them charging about 300 yards southwestward across the Robinson corn field toward a wooded crest beyond the Oblique Ravine. There Hawley's troops encountered not only fugitives from Wright's

---

29 Eldredge, *Third New Hampshire*, 521.

30 Elbridge J. Copp, *Reminiscences of the War of the Rebellion* (Nashua NH, 1911), 444.

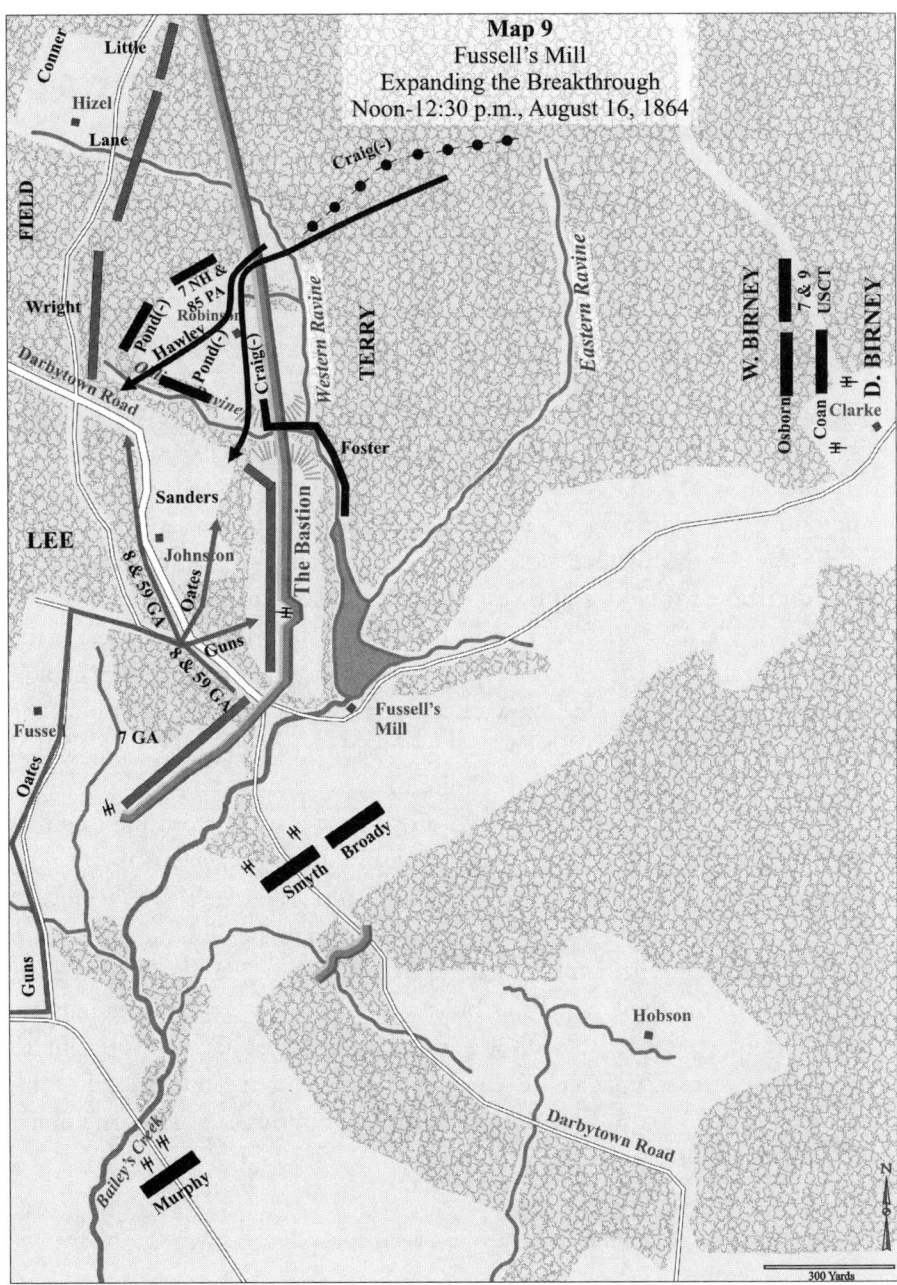

and Lane's brigades, but the first Confederate reinforcements to arrive from the Rebel right.

A member of Field's staff had reached Brig. Gen. George Thomas "Tige" Anderson less than five minutes after the breakthrough. Anderson's Georgians held the line just across the Darbytown Road from Sanders' brigade. "General Anderson, the line is broken just on your left," said the staffer. "You know what to do."[31] The staff officer sped off to Anderson's right. Anderson, a graduate of Emory University and a Mexican War veteran, did indeed know what to do. Leaving his pickets and the 7th Georgia in place, he ordered the 8th and 59th Georgia out of the trenches. These two regiments crossed the Darbytown Road without loss from interdicting fire by the II Corps batteries across Bailey's Creek, which also chewed up the breastworks occupied by Sanders' brigade north of the road. The Georgians double-quicked uphill a quarter mile northward, past fugitives from Wright's and Lane's brigades in the corn field of the Johnson farm, to where the Darbytown Road turned west toward Richmond.[32] There Anderson's troops barred the door to the capital.

The 8th Georgia formed along a rail fence marking the western boundary of the Johnson corn field, southwest of the Robinson farm and in the path of Hawley's brigade. The 59th Georgia hustled toward the fence on the crest to the left of the 8th. If the Federals could get past this fence they might either exploit toward Richmond on the Darbytown Road or flank the Secessionists out of the The Bastion and then out of New Market Heights, opening the New Market Road toward Chaffin's Bluff and Richmond.

Fire from the vanguard of the 59th Georgia as well as from the fugitives from Wright's and Lane's brigades on the crest in front of Hawley's men halted the New Englanders. The 3rd New Hampshire, Hawley's left regiment, changed face to its left and desperately charged through the Oblique Ravine and into the Johnson corn field under a galling crossfire from The Bastion to the left and the crest to the right, as well as bullets from the 8th Georgia dead ahead. Hawley's right regiment, the 7th Connecticut, changed face to its right to confront the 59th Georgia as it massed on the 7th's right flank. Captain John Reed of Company I in the 8th Georgia recalled the appearance of the oncoming 3rd New Hampshire:

---

31 John Reed Memoir, Alabama State Archives, Montgomery, Alabama, 117.

32 The Darbytown Road at that time ran southeast from Richmond approximately along its present course until it reached today's Yahley Mill Road, where the Darbytown Road turned south and roughly followed the Yahley Mill Road across Bailey's Creek below Fussell's Mill to the Long Bridge Road. Cowles, Calvin D., ed., *Atlas to Accompany the Official Records of the Union and Confederate Armies* (New York, 1958), Plates 77, 100.

The enemy was in a field of corn, advancing rapidly, firing as he came, and his huzzas were loud and boastful. . . . The enemy's fire was rapid and precise. Bark, dust and splinter were rising in a cloud from the fence, and many of our men were falling. But they were standing to it. Our fire was beginning to tell.[33]

The soldiers of the 3rd New Hampshire began to lie down. "The lying down was really a confession of weakness," Reed recalled.[34] Anderson's Georgians took heart as their ammunition and that of the Granite Staters, armed with seven shot Spencer rifles, ran low and the firing slowed. The 6th Connecticut, armed with single shot Enfield rifles, advanced to support the 3rd New Hampshire. Hawley's advance had bogged down. Atop The Bastion, a section of Rebel artillery arrived from New Market Heights, unlimbered and began enfilading the Unionists.

Terry tried again to expand the breakthrough. He brought up the uncommitted regiments of Craig's brigade. The division commander formed them into two lines parallel to and facing the Oblique Ravine, almost at right angles to the fortifications. From right to left, the front line consisted of the 93rd New York and the 84th, 141st and 105th Pennsylvania. The 57th Pennsylvania formed the second line. Terry told Craig and his men to "go as far as you can and roll the Rebels right up."[35] Craig led these five regiments through the thicket in the branch running through the works into the Western Ravine. Disordered, Craig's troops reformed in the corn field of the Robinson farm and charged through the corn into the Oblique Ravine under an even more murderous crossfire than Hawley's troops had endured. Craig's soldiers did, as an officer of the 105th Pennsylvania remarked, "roll them up right smart for awhile," clearing the Oblique Ravine of the enemy between the captured trenches and Hawley's left and increasing the bag of prisoners by 103.[36] Veering right to avoid thick timber near the mouth of the Oblique Ravine, the 105th and 141st Pennsylvania penetrated beyond the ravine into the open field of the Johnson farm.

---

33 John Reed Memoir, 118-9.

34 Ibid., 119.

35 Kate M. Scott, *History of the One hundred and Fifth Regiment of Pennsylvania Volunteers* (Philadelphia, 1877), 117-8.

36 Ibid., 118; *OR* 42, pt. 1, 364.

At this moment, a few minutes before 12:30 p.m., the Federal breakthrough above Fussell's mill pond reached its maximum dimensions. The Unionists had moved forward from the breakthrough to form a rough semicircle with the flanks anchored on the captured Confederate trenches. On the extreme left, the 1st Maryland Cavalry, 100th New York, and 10th Connecticut hugged the ground in the Western Ravine below the mouth of the Oblique Ravine. Within the Oblique Ravine, the 24th Massachusetts held a line from its mouth to the captured earthworks. The 11th Maine and a few companies of the 24th Massachusetts held the captured works north of the Oblique Ravine. To the right of the 24th Massachusetts, soldiers of the Western Brigade held the line of the Oblique Ravine. Through the Westerners, the 105th and 141st Pennsylvania of Craig's brigade had advanced into the northeastern corner of the Johnson farm. Farther right, the 57th and 84th Pennsylvania and 93rd New York joined the Westerners in the Oblique Ravine. To the right of Craig's brigade, the 3rd New Hampshire and 6th and 7th Connecticut of Hawley's brigade defended a toe hold on the northwestern corner of the Johnson farm. The New Englanders also occupied the head of the Oblique Ravine. A stray portion of the 39th Illinois guarded the right of Hawley's troops. Fragments of the 62nd Ohio protected the right of the soldiers from the 39th. The troops from the 62nd had their right flank on the left of the 7th New Hampshire, which held a line facing right and at right angles to the fortifications. The line reached back to the fifty soldiers of the 85th Pennsylvania in the trenches defending the right of the breakthrough. The 1st United States Sharpshooters, 5th Michigan, and 1st Massachusetts Heavy Artillery formed a skirmish line that stretched back toward the Eastern Ravine and provided Terry's command with some protection against a Confederate flank attack from the north.

The moment of maximum Federal penetration rapidly passed as the 105th and 141st Pennsylvania ran into the second group of reinforcements from the Rebel right. A detachment of Law's brigade consisting of the 15th and 48th Alabama, under Col. Alexander Allen Lowther of the 15th, arrived less than half an hour after the breakthrough on Sanders' left after covering around a mile at the double-quick from Camp Holly on New Market Heights. Lowther, a Mexican War veteran from Georgia who had suffered a wound at Cold Harbor, quickly suffered another. Command of this detachment passed to Col. William Calvin Oates of the 48th, the former colonel of the 15th. A lawyer in civilian life, Oates had become obsessed with the 15th's failure to capture Little Round Top, where his brother had perished. The Alabamians found themselves nearly opposite the left of Craig's brigade, which seemed almost a mile long, with heavy supports in its rear, moving steadily toward the Alabamians through the Johnson corn field.

Arriving on the battlefield, Oates met Anderson on the Darbytown Road near the south side of the corn field. Informing Oates that some of his Georgians held a piece of woods on the west side of the field, north of the Alabamians, Anderson concluded, "Well, if you think that you can do anything with them, just go tearing at them."[37] Oates went "tearing at" Craig's left as if he had another chance to take Little Round Top. He led his troops to a rail fence at the south edge of the corn field, with the 15th Alabama on the left and the 48th Alabama on the right. Here the Alabamians overlapped the left of Craig's brigade. The 15th exchanged a terrible fire with the Northerners and held the fence at the cost of many casualties. Oates sent the 48th Alabama over the fence to charge the flank of the Federals. The 48th enfiladed the Union line, driving it back about 200 yards but incurring heavy losses. With men falling dead or wounded at every step, the Alabamians pressed onward until they reached a drainage trench on the hillside. Oates ordered his soldiers to sit down in the trench and fire across the Oblique Ravine at Craig's brigade on the opposite slope less than 100 yards away.

A Federal bullet shattered Oates' right arm. Before relinquishing command, he ordered his troops to charge again. The Alabamians ran down into the Oblique Ravine and then up the slope on the opposite side, sending back a stream of prisoners who had lain down in the Oblique Ravine's tall grass to avoid Secessionist fire. When the Alabamians charged, they ran over these Unionists, who threw down their arms and made for the Confederate rear. Enfiladed from its left, the Rebel line halted under Federal fire at the top of the opposite slope, then rolled back down, re-crossed the Oblique Ravine and came to rest in the trench once again.

To Craig and his troops, severe fire seemed to come from every direction—from Sanders' Alabamians on The Bastion to the left, from Oates' Alabamians in front, and from Anderson's Georgians on the right. In the struggle with the Alabamians, as Craig ordered his soldiers to charge, he received a mortal head wound. Command of the brigade passed to Col. John Pulford of the 5th Michigan, a Detroit lawyer who had already earned five red

---

37 William C. Oates, *The War between the Union and the Confederacy and its lost opportunities, with a history of the 15th Alabama regiment* (New York, 1905), 374.

badges—a fractured skull, jaw, and collar bone from a cannon ball at Malvern Hill, a wound at Chancellorsville, two wounds at Gettysburg, and a broken back in the Wilderness that partially disabled his arms. The 105th and 141st Pennsylvania sought shelter with the rest of their brigade in the Oblique Ravine. About half an hour had passed since Terry's breakthrough.

While Oates halted the left of Craig's brigade along the Oblique Ravine just west of The Bastion, more detachments from the Confederate right arrived at the western edge of the Johnson farm. Colonel Coward led the 5th South Carolina of Bratton's brigade into the struggle to the left of Oates' detachment. On Coward's left, Col. Dudley McIver DuBose brought the 15th and 20th Georgia into action. A native of Tennessee, DuBose had graduated from the University of Mississippi and practiced law before joining the 15th Georgia Infantry as a lieutenant after the outbreak of hostilities.

On this blazing day, Coward's and DuBose's men had double-quicked about two miles. "Most of my men had their tongues hanging out of their mouths, like hunting dogs on a hot day," Coward remembered. "The sweat was churning in my boots and my voice had an unnatural tone."[38] He and DuBose led their soldiers forward toward the right of Craig's brigade. Disordered while climbing over a fence, the 5th South Carolina encountered General Lee on Traveler. Coward wanted his men to show up well in front of the army commander.

"Fifth Regiment, Right Dress," the South Carolinian shouted to straighten the line.

"No time for right dress, Colonel," said Lee, removing his hat. "Charge 'em boys with a hearty shout."[39]

With bayonets glistening and flags flying, the troops of Coward and DuBose assaulted the right of Craig's brigade. To the left of Coward's and DuBose's men, the two regiments of Anderson's brigade had replenished their ammunition. Captain Reed remembered how the 8th and 59th Georgia spontaneously charged Hawley's brigade:

> There were swaying movements in our line, something like the waves that run along a rope swung losely between two points when it is shaken at an end. Everybody seemed

---

38 Bond and Latrobe, eds., *The South Carolinians*, 151.

39 Ibid.

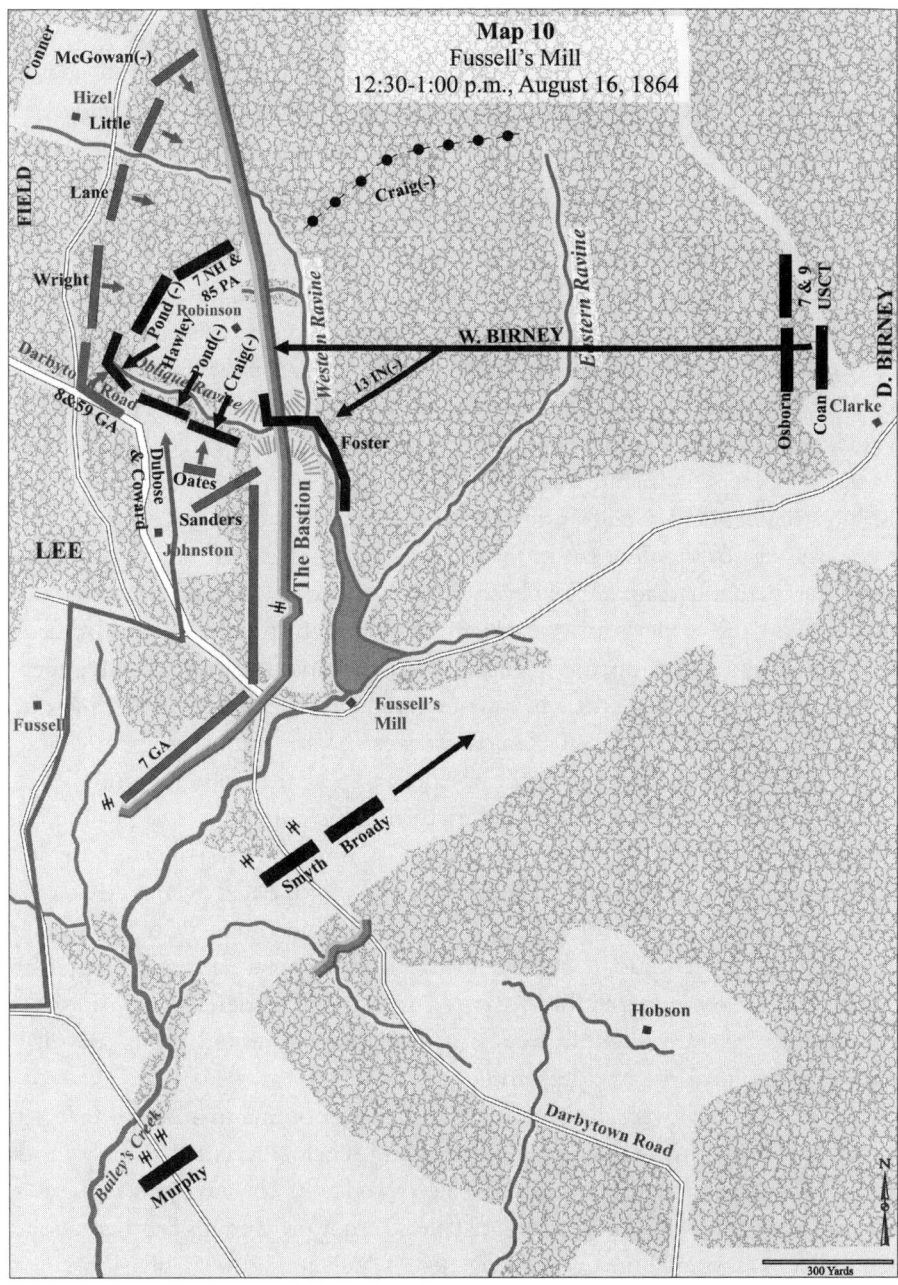

to be tempted forward. Somebody—I believe it was just a private—said in that tone which is always heard by the brave in battle, "Over the fence and charge."[40]

40 John Reed Memoir, 119.

Screaming the Rebel yell, Anderson's and DuBose's Georgians and Coward's South Carolinians dashed through the corn toward the enemy. Instead of rising, steadying their aim, firing, and countercharging the outnumbered 8th and 59th Georgia, Hawley's troops panicked. They loosed a volley from the prone position and skedaddled. Reed recalled that, "as they ran many of them found that while they could outrun us they could not outrun our bullets."[41] The panicked New Englanders streamed back across the Robinson corn field. Colonel Hawley led the retreat, running like a deer. The right of Craig's brigade collapsed under the onslaught of Coward's and DuBose's troops. The left of the brigade withdrew in a more orderly fashion. Except for the 7th Connecticut, which headed for the rear to replenish its ammunition, Hawley's troops reassembled on the northern end of the captured trenches, east of the 7th New Hampshire and 85th Pennsylvania at the northern edge of the Robinson corn field. Craig's brigade also fell back to the captured earthworks, as did the rest of the Federals in the Oblique Ravine west of the works. As the Union units that had advanced beyond the breastworks fell back, they exposed the left flank of Hawley's 7th New Hampshire, which stretched westward from the works along the northern edge of the Robinson farm. This regiment responded by re-crossing the entrenchments and taking a position on a line with them. By 1:00 p.m., the only Unionists west of the captured fortifications occupied the Robinson house or the northern edge of the Robinson corn field.

Overcome with sunstroke, Hawley turned his command over to the 7th New Hampshire's Col. Joseph C. Abbott, a former newspaper editor and former Adjutant General of New Hampshire. Sunstroke also overcame Colonel Pond, and command of the Western Brigade devolved upon Col. Alvin Coe Voris of the 67th Ohio, who had begun the war as a sergeant in the 4th Michigan. The remnants of the Western Brigade took up defensive positions in the fortifications. Ordered to the rear, Craig's brigade retired about 600 yards and reformed near the X Corps artillery.

Terry had deployed all the soldiers under his command and had failed to exploit his breakthrough successfully. Having repeatedly asked David Birney for reinforcements through couriers, Terry rode off to make the request in person. Responding to Terry's personal plea, Birney ordered his brother to send assistance. Osborn's and Coan's brigades of William Birney's division stood massed on a hill near David Birney's headquarters, about half a mile east of the

---

41 Ibid., 120.

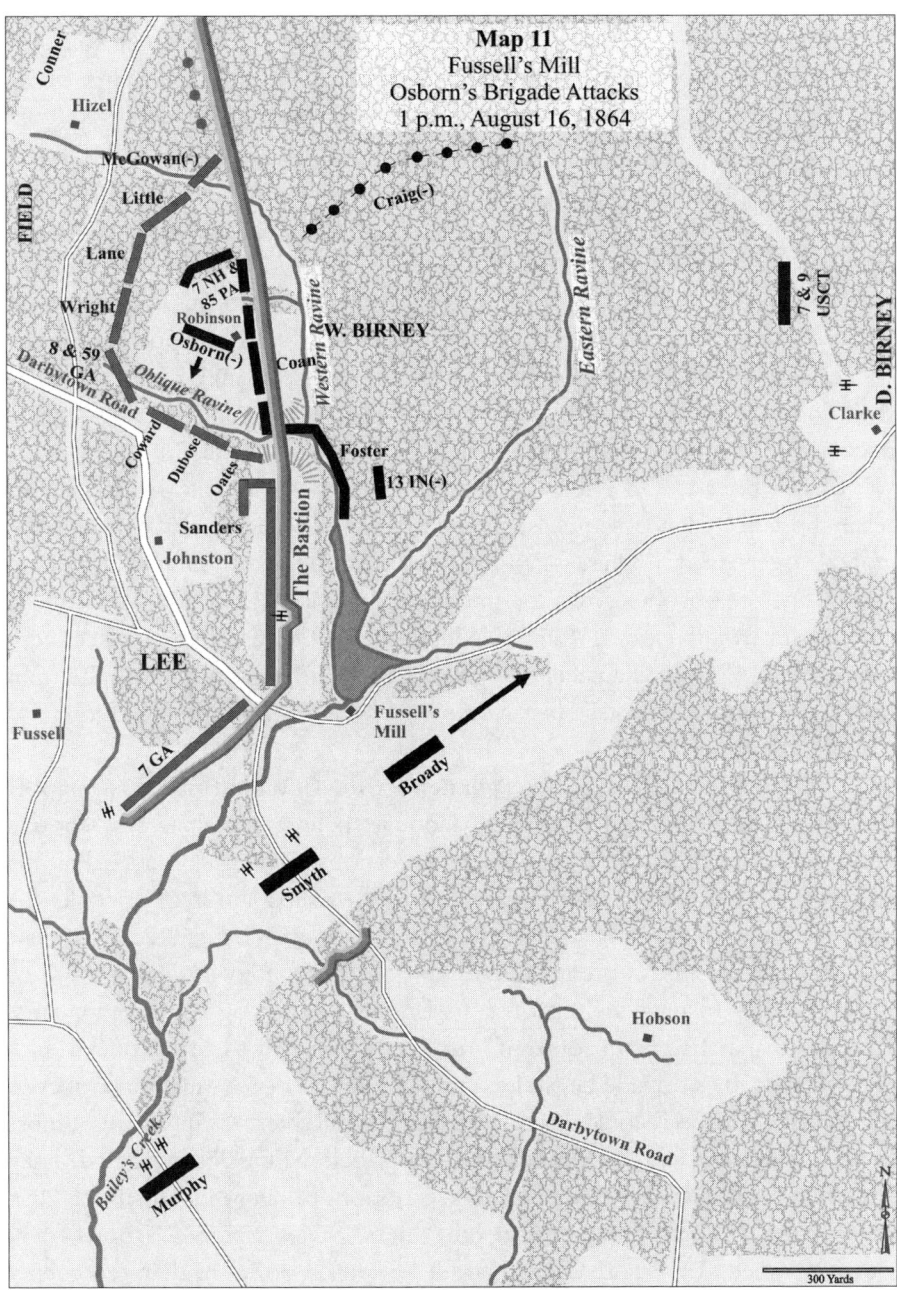

captured Secessionist breastworks. Osborn's brigade held the lead position. A spent bullet had already disabled the brigade's commander, Col. Francis Augustus Osborn of the 24th Massachusetts. Lieutenant Colonel Nathan C.

Johnson of the Iron Hearted Regiment, the 115th New York Infantry, formerly captain of Company I, 93rd New York Infantry, had briefly taken charge of the brigade until he too received a wound. Command of the brigade devolved upon Maj. Ezra L. Walrath of the 115th, a jeweler who had previously served as colonel of the 12th New York Infantry until illness forced him to resign. William Birney ordered Osborn's brigade forward at the double quick to the captured Rebel trenches. Osborn's brigade made this half mile run in heavy marching order and against a stream of disorganized troops from Pond's, Hawley's, and Craig's brigades hastening to the rear. Winded upon arrival, the soldiers of Osborn's brigade formed as best they could among the corpses of their comrades on the reverse side of the Confederate trenches. The brigade occupied the captured works on the right of Foster's brigade.

Coan's brigade had a few more yards to travel than Osborn's brigade to reach the captured works and also advanced at the double quick. "Through the woods, over dead bodies,—Federals and Confederates mingled together, —past lines of prisoners, into the open ground, knapsacks thrown off, full of enthusiasm, away we went," Captain Nichols of the Fighting Parson's Regiment remembered.[42] The exhausted soldiers of Coan's brigade formed by the right into line behind the Secessionist works on the right of the gasping troops of Osborn's brigade.

William Birney left Shaw's detachment of the Colored Brigade to support the X Corps artillery near X Corps' headquarters and accompanied Osborn's and Coan's brigades to the captured fortifications. Having committed all his reserves to Terry's support, David Birney called upon Hancock for reinforcements. Hancock had learned of Birney's success before 12:30 p.m. but had not launched the contemplated assault on the Confederate right south of Fussell's Mill. Instead, in response to Birney's request for reinforcements, Hancock dispatched from south of Fussell's Mill Broady's brigade of Barlow's division. Broady's brigade began its tramp toward Birney about 1:00 p.m. even though the brigade could have attacked the Rebels in its front almost immediately. That left six brigades of II Corps below Fussell's mill pond. They stretched from the mill pond to the Deep Bottom bridgehead, which the 29th Connecticut Colored Infantry and 8th United States Colored Troops of X Corps manned. The six II Corps brigades opposed no more than ten enemy regiments by this time—four from Bratton's brigade, three from Law's brigade,

---

42 Nichols, *Perry's Saints*, 256.

two from Benning's brigade, and Tige Anderson's 7th Georgia—and outnumbered the foe by at least three to one.

The soldiers of Osborn's brigade had not recovered from their run to the captured earthworks when William Birney, with Terry still absent, ordered them to assault The Bastion. Osborn's brigade formed line of battle in the corn field of the Robinson farm south of the thicket in the little branch that flowed through the captured works into the Western Ravine. Instead of employing Coan's men to support Osborn's brigade, Birney marched Coan's troops by the left flank to take the place of Osborn's brigade in the captured trenches on the right of the 11th Maine. First Lieutenant Albert Henry Clay Jewett of Company E, 4th New Hampshire, which occupied the extreme right of Osborn's brigade, reported to William Birney the massing of Rebels in the woods on that flank—soldiers of the 8th and 59th Georgia, DuBose's detachment of Benning's brigade, and the 5th South Carolina shifting northward to link up with the Secessionists on the Federal right.

"Never mind," replied Birney as he ordered Osborn's brigade to charge.

Osborn's brigade dashed southward through the Robinson corn field. Lieutenant Jewett remembered, "Soon we met with a scorching fire, not only from our front but an 'enfilading' fire as it is termed, that is, a sidefire as well as front." [43] A shell fragment wounded Walrath in the side. Command devolved upon Capt. Francis W. Parker of Company E, 4th New Hampshire, a teacher. Parker ordered the 4th New Hampshire to change front and face the sidefire coming from the right. As the 4th executed Parker's orders, a Confederate bullet wounded Parker in the neck. Captain Robert J. Gray of the 9th Maine Infantry took charge. With almost as many men falling from heat as from Secessionist fire, Osborn's brigade disintegrated. The 9th Maine and 4th New Hampshire did not angle as sharply to the south as the 115th New York. They all reached the fence bounding the Robinson farm and found themselves in danger of encirclement. Singing *We'll rally 'round the flag boys*, the surviving soldiers of Osborn's brigade staggered back toward the captured trenches and the Federal rear.

Like Tige Anderson, the Confederate commander isolated to the left of the breakthrough also knew what to do. Brigadier General James Conner, a prosecutor in Charleston, South Carolina, before the beginning of the war, had participated in the bombardment of Fort Sumter and a rifle ball had broken his

---

43 Albert H. C. Jewett, *A Boy Goes to War* (Bloomington IL, 1944), 70.

leg during the Seven Days. He displayed his initiative on August 16 by instantly reacting to the breakthrough. Leaving the sharpshooter battalion of McGowan's brigade to hold the extreme left of the Secessionist line, Conner dispatched the rest of McGowan's brigade as well as Little's two-regiment detachment of Anderson's brigade at the double-quick southward behind the earthworks. Conner's troops hastened about half a mile through the woods, then formed their battle line. McGowan's brigade of South Carolinians advanced on the left, nearest the breastworks. Little's detachment forged ahead on the right of the South Carolinians. Lane's brigade of North Carolinians, having rallied near the bend of the Darbytown Road under its temporary commander, Col. William M. Barbour of the 37th North Carolina, a Maryland lawyer captured at Spotsylvania, pressed forward on the right of Little's Georgians. Conner's battle line muscled its way through the thick, rough woods, halting to redress the smallest irregularities.

The 3rd and 7th New Hampshire, the 6th Connecticut, and the fragment of the 85th Pennsylvania in the captured earthworks opened fire on Conner's men, and the Confederates returned the fire, before either side could see the other in the pine thicket. Despite the musketry, the Southerners continued to press ahead. Conner's battle line ran obliquely to the captured breast works, approaching them more closely with its left than with its right. The extreme left of the Rebel line, the 12th South Carolina of McGowan's brigade, struck the captured fortifications first. Plunging into them at once, this regiment immediately captured a portion of the trenches. Enfilading Union fire from the right quickly forced these South Carolinians to withdraw. Rallying, the 12th assailed the works again, recaptured the same stretch of them, and withdrew from them again under the same enfilading Federal fire from the right. Rallying again on the rest of McGowan's brigade, the 12th kept up the pressure on the foe along with the rest of Conner's command.

A lull occurred in the fight for the captured earthworks. The right section of the Sixth Maine Battery unlimbered on the right of the II Corps line, just east of Fussell's mill pond about 1:45 p.m., in an attempt to silence the Confederate artillery on The Bastion. The Rebel guns slowed but did not cease fire. Field continued to strip his right to retake the fortifications on his left. The soldiers of II Corps could see the Secessionists leaving the works south of Fussell's mill pond. Reports of these movements went up the chain of command to Hancock.

At 1:50 p.m., Hancock prodded Mott's and Gibbon's divisions to attack, but whenever a Unionist regiment advanced it met with a hail of artillery and small arms fire. The prospect of struggling through 1,000 yards of slashing to the formidable Confederate fortifications across Bailey's Creek under such a storm of lead daunted Hancock's subordinates. Hancock abandoned his idea of an assault against the Confederate right, from which so many Secessionists had departed to reinforce their left that the six II Corps brigades between Fussell's Mill and Deep Bottom now faced only half a dozen enemy regiments—three from Bratton's brigade, two from Law's brigade, and one from Benning's brigade—and outnumbered them by about six to one. The afternoon's probes of New Market Heights enabled Mott's men to bring off the last of the seacoast howitzers captured by the 100th New York on August 14—a prize providing little consolation for the failure of II Corps to pierce the attenuated enemy line.

Terry's requests for reinforcements continued to bombard the X Corps chief. At 2:00 p.m, while II Corps balked before New Market Heights, David Birney finally ordered forward the 9th United States Colored Troops of Shaw's detachment, leaving only the 7th United States Colored Troops to guard the guns and headquarters.

Shortly afterward, the last Confederate reinforcements arrived from the Secessionist right: the 7th Georgia of Anderson's brigade, the 4th Alabama of Law's brigade, the 17th Georgia of Benning's brigade and the 2nd South Carolina Rifles of Bratton's brigade. These troops filtered down into the Oblique Ravine with various Rebels knocked loose from their commands.

Lee remained on horseback on the Darbytown Road west of Sanders' Alabama brigade, where the ordnance wagon of Benning's brigade had parked. Surgeon Trueheart of the 8th Alabama recalled:

> General Lee busied himself in rallying and reassuring the troops, who had been driven back. To some he used words of gentlest kindness, praising them for what they had accomplished; others he sternly upbraided and ordered them back into the fight. His presence and words seem to work magical influence on both classes. . . ."[44]

Besides overseeing how Surgeon Trueheart cared for the wounded, Lee made other demands on Trueheart, who recalled, "Time and again he called me up to examine men, who were going to the rear under plea of sickness & wounds. . . ."[45] Lee demanded that each man who passed him on the way to the rear show his wound or return to the front. A tall soldier with his hat pulled

---

44 Williams, ed., *Rebel Brothers*, 111.

45 Ibid.

down over his eyes plodded rearward down the road. Lee blocked the man by wheeling his horse across the soldier's path.

"Why are you sneaking out of the fight?" asked the army commander.[46]

The man raised his hat. An ugly wound marred his forehead.

Lee turned his horse to allow the soldier the pass. The man put his hat back on and continued rearward. The army leader rode after the soldier and in a soft voice told him where he could find some water to bathe his forehead.

David Birney's Federals in the captured trenches found themselves in a cauldron, taking fire from Sanders' brigade on The Bastion to the south, from Oates' men, Coward's troops, and DuBose's soldiers to the southwest, from the 8th and 59th Georgia to the west, from Lane's brigade and Little's detachment to the northwest, and from McGowan's brigade to the north. The Unionists held no more than 1,500 feet of the Rebel trenches. Birney's troops had to expand the hole in the Confederate line. They had to widen the breach until some portion of the trenches provided respite from the relentless cannonballs, shells and minnies. Otherwise, the Federals could not remain and live. "Batteries which were stationed beyond the range of our muskets, in front and flank, redoubled their efforts against us; shells screeched, sputtered, and crashed through the trees, and bounded along the earth; bullets sang and whistled about us, and gave a peculiar thud as they severed human bones and laid low good and brave men," remembered Sgt. Edwin C. Miller of Company C, 11th Maine, in Foster's brigade in the trenches on Unionist left. "Hard-pine trees, seventy and eighty feet high, which stood around the works, were stripped of bark and limbs the entire length, and as completely as could have been done by machinery." No further reinforcements arrived to widen the breach in the Rebel line.

The Northerners could hear cheering as their foes received assistance. Soldiers fell constantly. The troops received orders to shield themselves as best they could. Too often their best proved not good enough. Sergeant Miller recalled taking refuge in a pit:

> Being somewhat exhausted from the heat, I sat down upon the root of a large stump, from which the earth had been removed to build the pit. I had been thus seated only a moment, when a soldier crowded in between myself and the stump. I moved my bigness toward the end which overhung the pit to accommodate him with a seat, which he barely had time to fill before zip came a bullet from the direction of the

46 John Reed Memoir, 127.

cross-fire, which went just deep enough to furrow his face and carry away both eyes. A bounding shot from a battery struck the top of the pit, scattering the earth in a shower, smashing the head of a soldier who was peering over, and nearly tearing to pieces another who stood on the high ground to the rear. The next moment an unexploded shell severed a large limb from a pine tree overhead which leveled three men in the fall.[47]

The fire directed by the Alabamians holding The Bastion enfiladed Birney's soldiers, who closely hugged the earthworks. The foliage along the Oblique Ravine hid the Alabama riflemen from the Unionist troops, who thought the bullets came from sharpshooters in the trees. A staff officer who ordered the 48th New York of Coan's brigade to stand and fire at their invisible foes elicited from Perry's Saints threats that sent him scurrying rearward.

North of the Oblique Ravine, the Secessionists began maneuvering against Federals in the Robinson house, 150 yards west of the captured fortifications, surrounded by trampled corn. Unionist sharpshooters occupied the house. The Southerners charged from two sides and seized the structure. Rebel marksmen employed the structure to pick off Northerners in the captured trenches. The X Corps gunners demolished the building.

The Confederates south of Conner's command crept forward from one bit of cover to another until part of a long crooked line across the Robinson corn field had come within seventy-five yards of the earthworks. Then the Southerners began charging. Captain Reed remembered:

> ... there was no lead or command except the experience of the field and line officers, and the combative, but prudent advancing of the southern volunteers. It is a study for the military critic. Our line looked far more broken and undressed than the militia drill in Georgia Scenes; but that line, so far as I can judge, was exactly what it ought to have been. It was a combination of Indian wariness and English stubbornness. It had antennae throughout, to tell by delicate contact, when to recoil and when to move forward. . . .[48]

The Federals still had some fight in them. "There was nothing intervening to hide so much as a button, save a few straggling corn-stalks on their left," Sergeant Miller of the 11th Maine's Company C recalled of one charge. "Boys, now's our time," big First Sgt. Adoniram J. Fisher of Company E said as his

---

47 Brady, *Eleventh Maine*, 246.

48 John Reed Memoir, 126.

men awaited the order to open fire. After the order finally came, the Federals did not cease fire until they had blasted the Confederates back into the woods.

While awaiting the next charge, the Northerners dissipated the tension by cracking jokes among themselves. Major Henry Ward Camp of the 10th Connecticut, a Yale-educated law student at the time of the war's outbreak, returned to his regiment from a brief trip to the field hospital in response to a summons from one of the wounded. His friend Henry Clay Trumbull, the "fighting chaplain" of the 10th, recalled:

> With thoughtful kindness he brought for us a huge watermelon. It was speedily cut and divided; General Foster very glad to get his share. What could have been more refreshing under fire? Before it was finished, orders were given for our regiment to swing around, fronting the left, and covering the flank, on which an attack was momentarily expected. It was comical enough to see officers forming their men, enforcing their orders with brandished slices of melon, and taking a bite between each command.[49]

The six companies of the 10th Connecticut on the immediate left of the 24th Massachusetts ran out of ammunition. Foster relieved these six companies with 150 men from the 1st Maryland Cavalry and sent to the support of the 24th Massachusetts the four companies of the 10th Connecticut which had not expended all of their bullets. The 100th New York formed the extreme left of David Birney's force.

Soon Foster's troops saw the top of a flag above the Oblique Ravine, not more than fifty yards away. The joking stopped and the Unionists prepared for action again. The banner began to move in a few moments. The whole Rebel line came into sight. The Federals became too excited to maintain fire control. Instead of reserving their fire until the Secessionists had cleared the ravine far enough to ensure their destruction, the Northern soldiers started shooting almost immediately. "The rebel color-bearer was shot dead on the brow of the hill, falling forward upon his staff," Sergeant Miller remembered, "and the line was driven back in less time than it would take to count twenty."[50]

On the other side of the battlefield, the right of Conner's line steadily closed the distance between itself and the captured earthworks. When the right

---

49 H. Clay Trumbull, *The Knightly Soldier, A Biography of Major Henry Ward Camp* (Boston, 1865), 273.

50 Brady, *Eleventh Maine*, 247.

of McGowan's brigade came within twenty yards of the fortifications, the Federals occupying them coolly fired a fearful volley directly into the faces of the Secessionists. The Southerners recoiled several paces in shock and confusion, but continued firing at their adversaries. The Rebels wounded by the volley lay between the two fires. Some of the wounded loudly called upon their comrades to charge. Conner's entire line now approached the works closely enough to deliver a fire that, in combination with the galling enfilade fusillade from The Bastion beyond the Northern left, kept most Unionist heads down and largely suppressed Federal return fire. At about 2:45 p.m., the 9th United States Colored Troops relieved the fifty soldiers of the 85th Pennsylvania at the north end of the captured trenches, opposite Conner's men.

The final Secessionist charge began from far to Conner's right. The Confederates in the Oblique Ravine drove off the 24th Massachusetts and threatened the left of the 11th Maine. That regiment had run so low on ammunition that its men scrounged cartridges from the dead and wounded. With Colonel Plaisted prostrated by sunstroke and Lt. Col. Jonathan A. Hill down with a wound that would cost him his right arm, Capt. Simeon H. Merrill of Company I led the 11th. Cut off from General Foster across the Oblique Ravine to the left, Merrill sought help from Coan's brigade to the right. Lieutenant Colonel William B. Coan of the 48th New York first dispatched the 76th Pennsylvania to the left rear of the 11th Maine and then began to follow with the rest of his brigade. Before the balance of Coan's troops left the trenches, the Rebels boiled out of the Oblique Ravine and outflanked the 100th New York and 1st Maryland Cavalry, which fled. The 76th Pennsylvania dissolved and retreated across the Western Ravine.

The Union line collapsed from left to right, regiment by regiment, brigade by brigade, like the bursting bulkheads of a sinking ship. The Secessionists drove the 24th Massachusetts from its position on the 11th Maine's left rear, then charged the 11th Maine. Private W. A. McClendon of the 15th Alabama recalled:

> Our color bearer, W. I. Defnal, while leading the charge, hat in his right hand and the colors held aloft in his left, had the misfortune of having his left arm cut off at the elbow by a solid shot from the enemy. The colors dropped to the ground, but were still grasped by his hand. Captain Feagan loosed the staff from his hand as it lay on the ground, and carried it in triumph to the breastworks.[51]

---

51 W. A. McClendon, *Recollections of War Times by an Old Veteran while under Stonewall Jackson and Lieutenant General James Longstreet, How I Got in, and How I Got Out* (Montgomery AL, 1909), 215-6.

Rushing into the fortifications, the Southerners rolled up the 11th Maine. As the Confederates uncovered their comrades to the left, those Rebels pitched in as well, one unit after another. The Confederates worked their way northward west of the trenches, inside the trenches, and east of the trenches, threatening the line of retreat of the Federals.

Coan's brigade, assailed front and back, collapsed next. Colonel Galusha Pennypacker of the 97th Pennsylvania, a twenty-two year old printer who had just returned to his command from a wound suffered on May 20, recalled:

> I have seldom been so *close* to the enemy before. Our corps was flanked on the left completely, and driven back. Union and rebel colors waved from the same parapet. The flag of a Virginia regiment and the flag—tattered and torn—of the 97th P. V. were planted not six feet apart. That was hot work, but we brought the flag off in safety.[52]

The Secessionist flood increased its momentum. In the dense woods, the Federal troops in the earthworks had scarcely any warning before they found themselves completely outflanked on the left. With their line of retreat menaced, they had to skedaddle to avoid capture. After the brigades of Foster and Coan had broken, the Western Brigade followed them to the rear. Hawley's brigade on the far right withdrew in a more deliberate fashion pursuant to Terry's orders. As regiment after regiment of Confederates entered the trenches, enthusiasm communicated itself to Conner's command. With a yell, Conner's troops rushed the breastworks and began driving out the Northerners crowded there, taking prisoners and plunder. During the Secessionist counterattack, Lane's brigade lost Colonel Barbour to a leg wound. Colonel William H. A. Spear of the 28th North Carolina took command. The manager of a tannery and an opponent of secession, Spear bore scars from wounds at Chancellorsville and Gettysburg. At about 3:00 p.m., the soldiers of the 9th United States Colored Troops found themselves the only Federal unit remaining in the fortifications. The 9th fell back before the Rebel onslaught. Lieutenant Colonel Samuel Chapman Armstrong of the 9th, the son of missionaries in Hawaii and a graduate of Williams College, wrote about the retreat of his men:

---

52 Isaiah Price, *History of the Ninety-Seventh Regiment Pennsylvania Volunteer Infantry During the War of the Rebellion 1861-1865, With Biographical Sketches of Its Field and Staff and a Complete Service Record of Each Officer and Enlisted Man* (Philadelphia, 1875), 317-8. No Virginia infantry unit operated near this part of the battlefield on August 16, 1864.

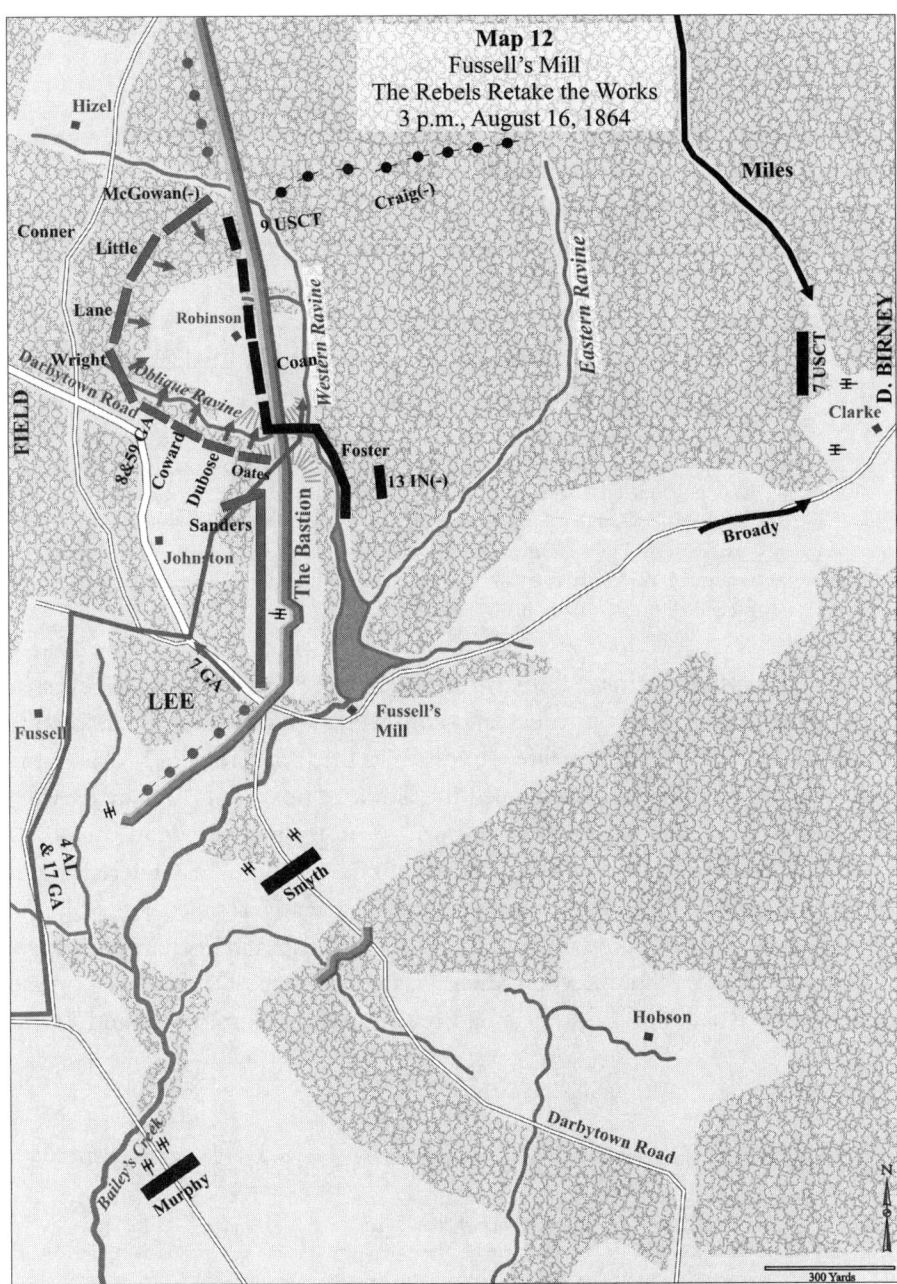

Finally, however, the rebs flanked us on the left and forced us out. Standing there in line we were harassed by an unseen foe hidden in the bushes. It was impossible to hold the position, and I ordered them to walk, and they did so the whole distance, shot at by the unseen enemy as they went, and having to climb over fallen trees and go through rough ground. They got back panting with fatigue and lay down exhausted.[53]

The 9th left a pair of prisoners to the Southerners, but the usual ugliness between Confederate soldiers and United States Colored Troops did not prevail.[54] The Rebels treated their African American prisoners properly and did not massacre them as had the first wave of Southern counter-attackers at the battle of the Crater, little more than two weeks earlier.

General Lee oversaw the pursuit of the Northerners, who began to reassemble behind the Eastern Ravine for another attack. Federal artillery fire did not slacken. Private McClendon recalled:

> . . . we were the recipients of an awful shelling. . . . The ground in our rear was dotted with the killed and wounded Yankees, and they were in direct range of the shells from their friends, and the wounded begged piteously to be removed, but we had no time for that, as we expected that another attack would be made on the works. There was one poor wounded Yankee that lay in our rear that was literally torn to pieces by the explosion of a shell thrown from his friends.[55]

The Secessionists herded their prisoners to the rear under Lee's eyes. A Federal prisoner walked up to Lee and complained that a Confederate private had taken his hat, a matter of life and death in the murderous heat. The army group leader dropped everything, had the Unionist point out the transgressing Southerner, and saw to the hat's return as if its recovery constituted as important a part of Lee's duty as supervision of the fighting. "I wondered at him taking any notice of a prisoner in the midst of battle," recalled Pvt. John E. Davis, a captive from Company E of the 100th New York in Foster's brigade.[56]

Shortly after 3:00 p.m., when Miles' brigade departed David Gregg on the Charles City Road and the Rebels had recaptured the earthworks and David

---

53 Edith Armstrong Talbot, *Samuel Chapman Armstrong, A Biographical Study* (New York, 1904), 113.

54 Augusta (GA) *Daily Constitutionalist*, August 26, 1864, p. 1, col. 2; Savannah (GA) *Republican*, Sept. 1, 1864, p. 1, col. 3. On the other hand, "The Examiner says the negro prisoners got in a fog on their way to the city, and have not been heard of since." Macon (GA) *Daily Telegraph*, August 26, 1864, p. 2, col. 3.

55 McClendon, *Recollections of War Times*, 216.

56 Letter, John E. Davis to Charles Marshall, n.d., *SHSP*, vol. 17 (1889), 242.

Birney's troops had begun to regroup for another attempt on the fortfications, Broady's brigade arrived at X Corps' headquarters.

* * *

David Gregg soon had cause to rue Miles' departure. A section of Federal artillery had unlimbered at the Charles City Road crossing of Fisher's Run. Mounted, the horsemen of Irwin Gregg's brigade stretched away to the right, which left them poorly disposed to meet an attack from the left. Behind them stood a high rail fence. Farther back flowed Fisher's Run, impassable except for the road crossing. In front of Irwin Gregg's brigade lay an abatis, then two hundred yards of open field. Beyond the open field, the brigade's dismounted skirmish line held the edge of the woods.

Shortly after Miles' brigade had departed, the Rebel infantry that had disappeared in the direction of Fussell's Mill returned. The Texas Brigade had done so much marching and countermarching that even among such acclimated veterans, cases of sunstroke appeared. These elite soldiers still had enough fight in them to strike a blow that completely routed the Northerners.

At about 4:00 p.m., supported by artillery, Barringer's brigade of North Carolina cavalry pressed forward north of the Charles City Road while Gary's brigade of horsemen and the foot soldiers of the Texas Brigade hit the poorly guarded Federal left to the road's south. Heat felled many Confederates. The Union artillery replied vigorously at first, but then limbered up and withdrew to a position behind Fisher's Run. The Rebels drove in the Federal skirmishers. "They went through and over the abatis as if it were a grass sward," Colonel Haskell recalled of Gary's command. "They yelled like madmen, and before the fight had well begun they were on top of the works. . . ."[57] The mounted line of Unionists fled.

Gary's troops brought under fire the Charles City Road crossing of Fisher's Run and cut off a substantial number of Northern cavalrymen. Of those cut off, some risked the rifle fire of the Texas Brigade to flee down the road across the run. Many horses returned to Union lines with empty saddles. Other Federal horsemen chose to hazard White Oak Swamp, which bounded the Unionist right. "Of those who plunged into the swamp," remembered Corporal Polley of the 4th Texas, "a few escaped capture, but none a submersion, head and ears, in

---

57 Daly, *Alexander Cheves Haskell*, 140.

the foul-smelling ooze into which they and their steeds sank."[58] The Northerners rallied and reformed on the east bank of Fisher's Run around 4:45 p.m. Opposite the Federals, the troopers of the 9th Virginia Cavalry enthusiastically took picket duty because it stationed them next to free, flowing water.

Miles' brigade reached David Birney too late to prevent the Confederates from retaking the captured earthworks. Birney hoped to attack the Rebel works above Fussell's mill pond again at 5:00 p.m. A reconnaissance indicated that so many Confederates had massed in his front that his troops, even if they could retake the trenches, still could not exploit their capture. At 5:57 p.m., he called off the attack. Miles took command of Broady's and Craig's brigades.

Butler's Federals did not begin their advance until about 6:00 p.m., when Grant discouraged the demonstration and urged caution because of Hancock's standstill. Around 950 men from Dutch Gap under Maj. Benjamin C. Ludlow of Butler's staff took a steamer about three quarters of a mile downriver and debarked at Aiken's Landing. They put to flight the 25th Virginia Battalion and part of Johnson's Tennessee brigade. The Unionists seized Signal Hill. Several miles to the east, Col. William B. Wooster led about 700 soldiers of the 29th Connecticut Colored Troops and 8th United States Colored Troops out from Deep Bottom and drove in the pickets of detachments from Thomas' and Scales' brigades of Wilcox's division north of the Kingsland Road. Brigadier General John Bratton, a doctor and successful planter from South Carolina who had enlisted as a private in Company C, 6th South Carolina Infantry, took command of the Confederate troops in this sector.

As Bratton tried to restore order among the Rebels in this area, General Lee appeared on the way back to his headquarters on Chaffin's Bluff. He visited another portion of Johnson's Tennessee brigade near Four Mile Creek and the New Market Road. The Tennesseans had never seen Lee before. Pointing toward the enemy, the Virginian asked their brigadier, Col. John Madison Hughs of the 25th Tennessee, "how many there was of *those people* over there," recalled Capt. William Henry Harder of Company H in the 23rd Tennessee.[59] Hughs answered that he did not know. Lee ordered Hughs to find out. After a couple of attempts, Hughs ascertained that the Tennesseans opposed a single line of *those people*—Colonel Wooster's African-American soldiers. Lee departed

---

58 Polley, *Hood's Texas Brigade*, 250.

59 William Henry Harder Diary, August 16-17, 1864, Richmond National Battlefield.

for Chaffin's Bluff, where Bratton directed Hugh's troops to protect the vital fortifications. "Those people," the Tennesseans chanted as they marched, "Those people."[60]

Failing to link up with the Federals near Signal Hill, the soldiers of the 29th Connecticut Colored Troops and 8th United States Colored Troops withdrew after dark to Deep Bottom. C.S.S. *Virginia II* and C.S.S. *Richmond* commenced a shelling of the 4th and 6th United States Colored Troops on Signal Hill that lasted all night.

Thus ended the most hotly contested day of fighting at Deep Bottom yet. Private Jordan of the 15th Alabama, who had fought at Little Round Top and Chickamauga, remembered the fight of this day as, "the most terrific battle that I was ever in, in proportion to the time engaged, and the number that participated."[61] General Sanders, wounded at Glendale, Second Bull Run, Antietam, and Gettysburg, a hero of Spotsylvania's Bloody Angle and Petersburg's Crater, "remarked to me the next day that so far as he was concerned it was the severest battle be had passed through," recalled his brother Pvt. William H. Sanders of the 11th Alabama's Company C, the Confederate Guards of Greene County, which the general had originally led. "He was exposed to a more concentrated fire than ever before and for a much longer time."[62] The Northerners had lost one flag and almost 2,000 soldiers, including more than 500 prisoners.[63] The Southerners had lost three flags and about 1,000 men, including about 300 captives.[64]

---

60 Ibid.

61 Jordan, *Some Events and Incidents During the Civil War*, 93.

62 Ronald C. Griffin, *The 11th Alabama Volunteer Regiment in the Civil War* (Jefferson NC, 2008), 204.

63 Return of Casualties in the Union Forces (compiled from nominal lists of casualties, returns, &c.) Deep Bottom, Va., August 13-20, 1864, in OR 42, pt. 1, 116-21. I arrive at my figures by subtracting the Union losses on August 14, 15, and 18. See Chapter 2, note 44; Chapter 3, note 13; and Chapter 5, note 6. Another source indicates the Federals lost 480 captives on August 16. Richmond *Enquirer*, August 18, 1864, p. 1, col. 4. Still another claimed 600 prisoners. Daily (Columbus) *South Carolinian*, August 23, 1864, p. 3, col. 2; Columbus (GA) *Times*, August 24, 1864, p. 1, col. 3; Daily Richmond *Dispatch*, August 19, 1864, p. 1, col. 2.

64 OR 42, pt. 1, 219; J. McEntee to Major-General Humphreys, August 17, 1864, ibid., pt. 2, 245-6; Daily Richmond *Enquirer*, August 31, 1864, p. 2, col. 2; John Beauchamp Jones, *A Rebel War Clerk's Diary at the Confederate States Capital* (2 vols.) (Philadelphia, 1866), 2:267; Suderow, "Target Richmond," Suderow Private Collection. Anderson's brigade lost twelve killed, thirty-two wounded, one missing. Record Group 109, Compiled Service Records, National

Hancock had moved too slowly on August 14. The heat on August 15 had made it impossible for him to transfer substantial forces to his right, where they might have turned the Secessionist left. The failure of Hancock and his staff to inform Terry of the existence of Fussell's mill pond guaranteed that Terry's division would not attack simultaneously with David Gregg on August 16, or before the arrival of Lane's and McGowan's brigades and Little's detachment of Anderson's brigade north of the mill pond, when the Southerners would not have had sufficient forces on their left to counterattack the right of X Corps and the left of David Gregg's force at the same time. The communication breakdown thus eliminated almost any chance of driving the Rebels from the New Market Heights fortifications. Hancock's dispersal of his effort contributed to his failure. Miles', Broady's, and Craig's brigades belonged together, either with the rest of II Corps south of Fussell's mill pond, or with David Birney north of the mill pond, or with David Gregg on the Charles City Road. Whichever of these commands had them would have had a better chance to seize and hold an advantage that could have rendered the New Market Heights-Bailey's Creek earthworks untenable.

Despite the success of the Confederate counterattacks, the Federals had not shed so much blood for nothing. The Union assaults forced Lee to summon Harris' brigade of Mississippi infantry from Mahone's division at Petersburg. Lee also drew from the Howlett line across the mouth of the Bermuda Hundred bottle detachments of Scales' North Carolina and Thomas' Georgia brigades of Wilcox's division and an ad hoc brigade under Lt. Col. Frank Langley of the 1st Virginia Infantry, a Marylander. Langley's detachment consisted of the 11th and 19th Virginia from Pickett's division.

Grant still did not think the time had come to unleash V Corps on the Weldon Railroad. That night he ordered a fleet of steamers to cruise to Deep Bottom and simulate a withdrawal. He hoped this would lure the Secessionists into attacking the supposedly weakened Union forces north of James River.

---

[1] Archives. Law's brigade lost 60. Montgomery (AL) Daily *Mail*, August 26, 1864, p. 2, col. 3. Hood's brigade lost four killed, sixteen wounded, one missing. Harold Simpson, *Hood's Texas Brigade: A Compendium* (Hillsboro, Texas, 1977); Bryce A. Suderow, "Confederate Casualties during the Siege of Petersburg, June 13-August 25, 1864," Bryce A. Suderow Private Collection, Washington, D.C., 44. The 11th Alabama of Sanders' brigade lost two killed, four wounded, and thirty-one captured. Griffin, *11th Alabama*, 204.

Chapter 5

The Second Battle of Deep Bottom, August 17-21, 1864

The Confederates did not take Grant's bait. Little fighting took place north of James River on August 17. Under the shelling by the Rebel rams, the Federals from Dutch Gap had retreated from Signal Hill to Aiken's Landing by early morning, when Johnson's Tennessee brigade reoccupied the prominence and buried the thickly strewn dead. Private John Kennedy Coleman of Company F, 6th South Carolina Infantry, who had just turned eighteen eleven days earlier, remembered how he and his comrades spent August 17 on New Market Heights, which he considered "a very fine position:"

> We can see very distinctly the Enemys skirmish distant - about 1,000 yd You can see their gun boats ascending & decending the James. The gunboats have been annoying us all day by throwing Camp Kittes (as we call them) at us. Our company is supporting a battery of rifed guns they fire with as - much accuracy as we can with our [rifles] Some of our men have been standing by the guns all day watching the shells after they leave the [gun]. We can see them for som moments.[1]

During the day, Grant evaluated his intelligence of Lee's dispositions and correctly determined that nearly all the Secessionist cavalry south of Petersburg had come north of James River along with three brigades of infantry. The

---

[1] Civil War Diary of John Kennedy Coleman, Manuscripts Division, South Caroliniana Library, University of South Carolina, Columbia, South Carolina.

Unionist general-in-chief decided to order the Army of the Potomac's V Corps, under Maj. Gen. Gouverneur K. Warren, to proceed with the planned raid on the Weldon Railroad south of the Cockade City. At 10:15 p.m., Grant notified Halleck of Warren's projected movement and ordered Hancock to take advantage of any opportunity for success on his front.

In the afternoon, the Federal high command determined that no benefit could arise from an advance from Aiken's Landing by Butler's Northerners. Butler's troops accordingly returned to Dutch Gap during the night.

About 4:00 p.m., a truce requested by Hancock went into effect to allow the removal of the wounded and the burial of the dead between the lines above Fussell's mill pond. The truce provided Hancock with the first of the mortifications that he suffered during August, 1864. The Unionists found not a single wounded soldier between the lines. The Southerners had already removed them all. Under the circumstances, the request for a truce amounted to an admission of defeat. Hancock fumed over having admitted defeat for nothing. The admission diminished his outside chance of capturing a spot on the Democratic presidential ticket, whether as the candidate for president or for vice president. Both sides exchanged the dead from within their lines, including the body of General Chambliss. The commander of the Federal picket line, Lieutenant Colonel Armstrong of the 9th United States Colored Troops, remembered:

> We met the rebels half-way between the lines. I saw thousands of them swarming their works, and scores came to meet us, bringing on stretchers the ghastly, horribly mutilated dead whom we had lost in the charge of the day previous. The sight and smell would have made you wild, but we are used to it.[2]

Other Federals experienced anguish besides Hancock—and not only at having lost a fight that at first had seemed won. First Lieutenant Nicholas De Graff of Company D in the 115th New York—the Iron Hearted Regiment—of Osborn's brigade, who had suffered a wound at Chesterfield Court House in May, recalled:

> Col. Plimpton was killed in the charge. A flag of truce was sent in an effort to recover his body by his Regiment. They went to spot where he fell, but could not find it. At last, in a shallow grave, his <u>nude</u> body was with no covering at all, his eyes, ears, mouth and

---

2 Talbot, *Samuel Chapman Armstrong*, 116.

nose still filled with dirt as I saw his remains brought in. They cursed the Rebels [that] had stripped him of uniform, underclothes, boots, leaving only his under shirt. His men as they sadly bore his body away swore eternal vengeance against the scoundrels who did it.[3]

During the truce, President Davis and his entourage rode headlong down the Darbytown Road into its hollow by Bailey's Creek without noticing that they had passed through Confederate lines. They would have entered Federal captivity had not an officer of Sanders' brigade stopped them.

Field spent the day integrating into his position the reinforcements that had just arrived. Langley's provisional brigade from Pickett's division marched and countermarched. The detachments from Thomas' and Scales' brigades of Wilcox's division took position to protect the guns on Chaffin's Bluff. Harris' brigade of Mississippians plodded toward the Rebel left, above Fussell's mill pond. There Brig. Gen. Nathaniel H. Harris took command of the entire detachment from Mahone's division. A lawyer educated at the predecessor of Tulane University, Harris had organized Company C, the Warren Rifles, of the 19th Mississippi Infantry and risen from there. Colonel Joseph M. Jayne of the 48th Mississippi assumed command of Harris' brigade.

On August 18, illness compelled Barlow to relinquish command of his division to Miles. Skirmishing and reconnoitering predominated north of the James until dark, when the Confederates attacked Hancock's right.

Hampton and Lee had conceived an ambitious plan to drive Hancock's force back to the river. The plan called for the Secessionist cavalry to dislodge "those people" on the Charles City Road and then, with the assistance of the Southern infantry, to roll up the entire Union line southward to Deep Bottom. The Rebel horsemen had gotten into position to attack by 11:00 a.m., but a guide's mistake delayed Hampton's arrival at his command post at White Oak bridge. The firing of the cannon assigned to signal the attack did not occur until 5:00 p.m.

As the shadows lengthened, Rooney Lee's division of Confederate cavalry attempted to cross Fisher's Run along the Charles City Road. Butler's division of Secessionist horsemen advanced along the causeways crossing White Oak Swamp toward Riddell's Shop, where the Charles City Road met the Long

---

3 Nicholas De Graff Memoir, *Civil War Times Illustrated Collection*, United States Military History Institute, Carlisle Barracks, Pennsylvania. De Graff refers to Lt. Col. Josiah H. Plimpton of the 3rd New Hampshire in Hawley's brigade.

Bridge Road and the Willis Church Road. The Army of Northern Virginia had assailed the retreating Army of the Potomac around this intersection during the Seven Days, fighting an action known as Glendale or Frayser's Farm.

The frontal attack of Rooney Lee's troopers stalled. Butler's division advanced to Riddell's Shop, forcing David Gregg to communicate with the Federals to his left by means of a wood road. Brigadier General Matthew Calbraith Butler, a pre-war lawyer and politician from South Carolina who had lost a foot at Brandy Station, halted Young's brigade, led by Col. Gilbert Jefferson Wright of Cobb's Georgia Legion, at Riddell's Shop to await a linkup with Rooney Lee's division. Rosser's brigade, under Col. Richard H. Dulany of the 7th Virginia Cavalry, pressed on for a mile and a half farther along the Long Bridge Road. Dulany, the founder of the nation's oldest foxhunting club, led his troopers into the rear of the Unionists opposite the attacking Rebel infantry. The Southern horsemen captured 167 Northerners.[4]

After the Secessionist cavalry had commenced the attack, Field sent forward three brigades of Confederate foot soldiers on his extreme left to feel the Union position, prevent Hancock from reinforcing David Gregg, and assist in rolling up the Federal line. Conner's detachment of Wilcox's division, with Lane's brigade of North Carolinians on the left and McGowan's brigade of South Carolinians on the right, formed the left of Field's ad hoc infantry corps. Harris' detachment of Mahone's division, with Harris' brigade of Mississippians on the left, Wright's brigade of Georgians in the center, and Sanders' Alabama brigade on the right, formed Field's center. The provisional divisions of John Gregg and Bratton formed the Confederate right. Skirmishers of Lane's, McGowan's and Harris' brigades drove in the Federal pickets above Fussell's mill pond, "who came tumbling over the works like sheep," remembered Lieutenant Stowits of the 100th New York in Foster's brigade.[5] A shortfall of friendly artillery fire caused a momentary stampede of the 1st Maryland Cavalry (dismounted) and the 100th New York, two increasingly shaky regiments. Foster quickly reestablished his line with soldiers of the 10th Connecticut. The 10th stood in reserve, deployed in a long open line, ten or

---

4 Edward L. Wells, *Hampton and his Cavalry in '64* (Richmond, 1899), 273; William N. McDonald, *A History of the Laurel Brigade, Originally the Ashby Cavalry of the Army of Northern Virginia and Chew's Battery* (Baltimore, 1907), 268.

5 Stowis, *One Hundredth New York*, 290.

fifteen yards behind the others and savaged by the same friendly artillery fire. Captain Camp of the 10th recalled:

> As the break commenced, our officers rushed among the fugitives, shouted encouragement, entreated, threatened, seized them, and flung them back to the front,—all did our best to turn the tide. I haven't worked so since the Worcester regatta. We were in some degree successful. A dozen looked on hesitatingly while our major flogged an officer, a six-foot skulker, back to the works with the flat of his sword, and concluded to stay there themselves.[6]

The Southern pickets pressed on to the main Union battle line, which the Northerners had fortified with an abatis of scrub oaks. Private David Eldred Holt of Company K in the 16th Mississippi of Harris' brigade remembered, "We laid down at the abatis not over a hundred feet from the Yankee breastworks and kept up such an accurate fire that every Yank who stuck his head up over the breastworks to shoot got it promptly knocked off."[7] No support came up and the Rebel skirmishers found the Northern battle line too strong. After the firefight had gone on for half an hour, the Confederate pickets withdrew in the waning daylight. The Southern effort to roll back the Federals had failed.

Lieutenant Colonel Johnson of the 115th New York in Osborn's brigade commanded the Federal picket line that evening. Lieutenant De Graff of the 115th recalled, "Col. Johnson had sampled his whiskey, and against the judgement of his officers, determined to reestablish that picket line, so issued orders and after dark, he taking he lead, we following, all were warned to greatest care to move without noise and no talking." With Johnson personally leading, his troops arrived where their left had rested. Johnson deployed the men on what he thought the old line. The New Yorkers made considerable progress.

"Halt, who goes there?" someone suddenly sang out on the right.

The New Yorkers realized they had struck the rebel line. Lieutenant De Graff recalled:

---

6 Trumbull, *The Knightly Soldier*, 276-7.

7 Thomas D. Cockrell and Michael B. Ballard, *A Mississippi Rebel in the Army of Northern Virginia: The Civil War Memoirs of Private David Holt* (Baton Rouge, 2001), 198.

Signal Tower *Library of Congress*

they at once shouted surrender, then there was a break and rush for camp each for himself, the Johnnies sending a volley of bullets after us. I with difficulty picking my way through trees that had been cut down by the Johnnies as obstructions to our advance, finally reached camp and to my surprise Col. Johnson was there ahead of me. He was sweaaring and cursing us as cowards, etc and proposed to at once proceed again to establish that picket line. We officers told him no, it could not be done in the darkness, and at once reporting the situation to the Genl in command, he ordered the arrest of Johnson.[8]

So much resentment had developed toward Johnson in the Iron-Hearted Regiment because his transfer in to become lieutenant colonel had thwarted the

---

8   Nicholas De Graff Memoir, *Civil War Times Illustrated Collection.*

ambitions of the unit's home grown officers, that despite suffering another wound he found himself court-martialed for drunkenness—a charge he ultimately beat.[9]

After night fell, Matthew Butler ordered Rosser's brigade back to Riddell's Shop. There Dulany's horsemen formed on the right of Young's brigade, which had waited in vain for the arrival of Rooney Lee's troopers. Later, in a driving rain, Langley's detachment of Pickett's division relieved the Georgians of Wright's brigade near Fussell's Mill. Rooney Lee's division of cavalry and Harris' three-brigade detachment of Mahone's division began departing for Petersburg in response to the request of Gen. Pierre Gustave Toutant "Gus" Beauregard, the Louisianan savior of the Cockade City in May and June, for reinforcements to meet Warren's advance to the Weldon Railroad earlier in the day. Harris' detachment left two-thirds of its strength behind as pickets.

Pursuant to orders from Grant, Hancock contracted his line and dispatched Mott's division to the Petersburg front, where it would take the place of part of IX Corps sent by Meade to reinforce Warren. The departure of Mott's division left Hancock with Gibbon's division on the left, then Barlow's division, then X Corps, and finally David Gregg's cavalry on the right.

By August 19, things had grown so quiet north of James River that the pickets of both sides began exchanging tobacco, coffee and newspapers. Before 10:30 a.m., Grant determined that the Secessionists had begun shifting troops from north of the James to Petersburg. He ordered Hancock to attack with his whole force, screening the rest of his front with a mere skirmish line, if a weak spot appeared in the Rebel dispositions. About 2:00 p.m., pursuant to an order from the general-in-chief, Hancock sent Stedman's brigade of David Gregg's cavalry division to Meade at Petersburg. By the end of the day, Hancock believed he had found a weak spot in the Confederate line below Fussell's Mill. He prepared to attack at daylight the following morning with part of Barlow's division and William Birney's Colored Brigade. Hancock thought this force could carry the Southern earthworks, but he had little hope of holding the trenches or gaining any decisive advantage from their capture. After Hancock had described the situation to Grant, the general-in-chief at 8:00 p.m. that evening suggested the abandonment of the plan, and Hancock followed Grant's recommendation.

---

9   Each side probably lost about 200 soldiers in this picket affair. Wells, *Hampton and his Cavalry in '64*, 273; McDonald, *A History of the Laurel Brigade*, 268.

Early on the morning of August 19, Secessionist troops along the Howlett Line facing Bermuda Hundred detected the movement of Mott's division southward across the James. In response to this shift, and in response to renewed fighting on the Weldon Railroad, Lee ordered Wilcox's division to Petersburg. The Army of Northern Virginia's leader also ordered the ad hoc brigade from Pickett's division to return to the Howlett Line. The withdrawals took place in the rain that night.

No major operations occurred north of James River on August 20. That night, following Grant's orders, Hancock withdrew the remainder of his command. II Corps marched by way of Point of Rocks to the Petersburg front. The cavalry rode to the Petersburg front by way of Broadway Landing. X Corps, which covered the withdrawal, itself withdrew to Bermuda Hundred. The march took place in another miserable downpour in which Lee himself set out for the Cockade City.

At daybreak on August 21, the Rebel pickets found no Federals north of the James except for the garrison of the Deep Bottom bridgehead. Before 10:00 a.m., pursuant to orders from Lee, Field dispatched Anderson's brigade of Georgians to Petersburg. By 4:45 p.m., before Anderson's brigade reached Swift Creek, Lee had reached the Cockade City himself. At that time, he directed Field to send two more infantry brigades to Petersburg, and Field responded by dispatching Law's and Bratton's brigades. At the same time, the Army of Northern Virginia's leader ordered Hampton to the Cockade City along with Butler's division of horsemen.

The second battle of Deep Bottom had ended. Hancock's forces had neither taken Richmond nor cut the Virginia Central Railroad. The threat that they had posed to those objectives had prevented Lee from reinforcing Early with Field's division of infantry and Butler's division of cavalry. The same threat had also driven Lee to reinforce Field not only with a provisional brigade from Pickett's Division on the Howlett Line and detachments from Scales' and Thomas' brigades of Wilcox's division, but with substantial forces from Petersburg—Rooney Lee's division of horse soldiers and a three-brigade detachment from Mahone's infantry division. When the Union V Corps reached the Weldon Railroad on August 18, the Rebels had one brigade of cavalry and fourteen brigades of infantry south of the Appomattox River to oppose two cavalry brigades and twenty-seven infantry brigades.

The Northerners had lost 2,901 soldiers north of the James, including 721 prisoners. X Corps had suffered 1,678 casualties, including 311 captives. II

Corps had lost 964 soldiers, including 321 prisoners. David Gregg's cavalry division had suffered 259 casualties, including 89 captives.[10]

The Southerners had lost around 1,250 soldiers, including about 360 prisoners. Field's division had suffered approximately 315 casualties, including around fifty captives. The detachment of Wilcox's division had lost about 215 soldiers, including approximately thirty-five prisoners. The detachment of Mahone's division had suffered around 415 casualties, including about 250 missing. The losses of the Confederate cavalry approached 300 troopers, including around twenty-five captives.[11]

---

10 Return of Casualties in the Union Forces, Deep Bottom, Va., August 13-20, 1864, in OR vol. 42, pt. 1, 121.

11 Bratton's brigade of Field's division lost at least twelve killed, seventy-eight wounded and twenty missing. Ibid., pt. 1, 938; Columbia Daily *South Carolinian*, August 25, 1864, p. 3, col. 1. Anderson's brigade lost about nineteen killed, forty-nine wounded and twenty-seven missing. Record Group 109, National Archives. Unpublished study of Anderson's Brigade, Private Collection of Henry W. Persons, Jr., Severn, Maryland. The 59th Georgia lost five killed, fourteen wounded, eighteen missing. Macon (GA) Daily *Telegraph*, August 27, 1864, p. 2, col. 3. Law's brigade lost fewer than the 311 killed, wounded, and missing reported by Oates, *The War between the Union and the Confederacy*, 377. The brigade did not lose that many soldiers in the last five months of 1864, when it lost 259. Partial return of casualties in the First Army Corps from August 1 to December 31, in OR 42, pt. 1, 877. The 15th and 48th Alabama fielded only 266 soldiers on August 16. J. Gary Laine and Morris M. Penny, *Law's Alabama Brigade in the War Between the Union and the Confederacy*, (Shippensburg PA, 1996), 295. The brigade in fact lost about eighty at Second Deep Bottom. Suderow, "Target Richmond," Suderow Private Collection; Record Group 109, National Archives. The 15th Alabama lost four killed, thirty-five wounded, one missing. *Richmond Enquirer*, August 26, 1864, p. 2, col. 3-4. Gregg's brigade of Field's division lost about four killed, sixteen wounded and one missing. Suderow, "Confederate Casualties During the Siege of Petersburg, June 13-August 25, 1864," Suderow Private Collection, 44. Benning's brigade lost at least five killed and twenty-three wounded. Ibid., 47; Records Group 109, National Archives.

McGowan's brigade of Wilcox's division lost at least fifteen killed, 103 wounded and eight missing. James F. J. Caldwell, *The History of a Brigade of South Carolinians, Known First as "Gregg's" and Subsequently as "McGowan's" Brigade* (Philadelphia, 1866), 178, 180. Lane's brigade lost at least eight killed, fifty-four wounded and twenty-seven missing. Lane, "History of Lane's N. C. Brigade—Campaign of 1864—Anecdote about Captain G. G. Holland, 28th N. C. Troops," SHSP, 9 (1881), 357.

Sanders' brigade of Mahone's division lost at least eight killed, twenty-one wounded and thirty-eight missing. Richmond *Sentinel*, October 2, 1864, p. 1, col. 6. Wright's brigade lost at least forty-five killed, seventy-four wounded and 211 missing. Macon Daily *Telegraph*, August 31, 1864, p. 2, col. 2; ibid., September 5, 1864, p. 2, col. 5; ibid., September 8, 1864, p; 2, col. 3; Augusta *Chronicle & Sentinel*, October 6, 1864, p. 3, col. 4; Augusta Daily *Constitutionalist*, August. 30, 1864, p. 3, col. 1. The 48th Georgia, which did not report its losses, had one lost in its Company G. Macon *Daily Telegraph*, August 31, 1864, p. 2, col. 2. Harris' brigade lost at least twelve killed, wounded and missing. Richmond *Enquirer*, September 2, 1864, p. 2, col. 3-4.

The battle had used up many of the soldiers engaged on both sides. Captain Corbin, Field's aide-de-camp, wrote in a letter of August 26 to his mother in Europe:

> Last week has been a very fatiguing one to us. For ten days we have not had time to pull off our boots; and as to sleep we have had to nap it, a la grace de Dieu, at one time sleeping in a slushy rifle pit, at another in a shaky morass. This is very rough work, it is true, and well calculated to try the mettle of a Parisian lounger.[12]

Lieutenant Stowits of the 100th New York in Foster's brigade remembered what a week of fighting in hot, wet, vermin-infested woods did to those neither killed, nor wounded nor captured in battle:

> On the arrival of the regiment in camp it was sent on picket. Dirty, sore of foot and stiff in body, we crawled to the picket line. So very warm had it been during the week of active service that the varnish "fried out" from the butt of my pistol at my back, and it was painful to touch the surface of my rubber blanket with my neck, and so pressed was my underclothing, that in removing it, the skin, in spots, came with it.[13]

Gary's cavalry brigade, Benning's and Gregg's brigades of Field's division, Johnson's Tennessee brigade, the 1st Regiment Virginia Reserves, and the 25th

---

Of the four units (including the 7th Georgia Cavalry, detached from Young's brigade of Butler's division) in Gary's brigade of the Department of Richmond, the Hampton Legion and the 7th South Carolina Cavalry lost at least three killed, twenty-two wounded and sixteen missing. Charleston Daily *Courier*, September 6, 1864, p. 1, col. 4; Columbia Daily *South Carolinian*, August 30, 1864, p. 3, col. 2. Gary's brigade probably lost twice as many.

Barringer's brigade of W. H. F. Lee's division lost at least eleven killed, sixty-one wounded and five missing. Richmond *Sentinel*, August 26, 1864, p. 2, col. 2. The brigade may have lost as many as 125 killed, wounded and missing. Walter Clark, ed., *Histories of the Several Regiments and Battalions from North Carolina in the Great War, 1861-'65*, 5 vols. (Goldsboro NC, 1901), 3:619. The losses in two of the three regiments in Chambliss' brigade exceeded thirty-six killed, wounded and missing. Robert K. Krick, *9th Virginia Cavalry* (Lynchburg VA, 1982), 39; Daniel T. Balfour, *13th Virginia Cavalry*, (Lynchburg VA, 1986), 37. The brigade's losses probably approached the number of men lost by Barringer's brigade.

Three of four units in Young's brigade of Butler's division lost at least thirteen wounded. Richmond *Enquirer*, August 27, 1864; Suderow, "Confederate Casualties During the Siege of Petersburg, June 13-August 25, 1864," Suderow Private Collection, 45. Rosser's brigade probably suffered as many casualties as did Young's brigade.

The Confederate artillerists lost at least six wounded. Itinerary of Hardaway's Light Artillery Battalion, August 13-December 31, in OR 42, pt. 1, 935.

See also Chapter 2, note 44; Chapter 3, note 13; and Chapter 4, note 64.

12 Corbin, *Letter of a Confederate Officer*, 62.

13 Stowits, One Hundredth New York, 294-5.

Virginia Battalion stayed on the now nearly silent battlefield, along with Brown's battalion of light artillery. Foster's brigade remained in the Deep Bottom entrenchments. Except for this garrison, X Corps occupied the relatively quiet Bermuda Hundred sector. Opposite X Corps, the ad hoc brigade from Pickett's division returned to help man the Howlett Line. Mott's division held the Petersburg trenches from the Norfolk and Petersburg Railroad to the Strong house. The remainder of the Union and Secessionist troops north of the James, as well as many of their comrades in the Bermuda Hundred lines and south of the Appomattox River, soon tramped toward the Weldon Railroad and more fighting.

Chapter 6

The Battle of Globe Tavern, August 18, 1864

Rain dominated the battle of Globe Tavern almost as completely as heat dominated the second battle of Deep Bottom. The soldiers of both sides ate in the rain, slept in the rain, marched in the rain, entrenched in the rain, fought in the rain, and died in the rain. Mud and flooded passageways hindered their movements. Wet ties hindered the Federals in their destruction of the Weldon Railroad. Wet powder hindered the troops of both sides in their destruction of one another. Chaplain Henry R. Pyne of the 1st New Jersey Cavalry in Stedman's brigade of David Gregg's division recalled:

> The rain, which heretofore during the summer had been withheld to the point of utter drought, now seemed desirous to make up all arrears in the shortest time. All the approaches were flooded with standing water; and the passage of a wagon over the light, porous ground made deep ruts of gradually thickening mud. There seemed no really solid bottom to the soil. Wagon after wagon cut in deeper, until, on a road that three days sunshine would cover with incalculable dust, unloaded wagons sank above the axles, and had to be abandoned until the rains were over.[1]

On the afternoon of August 13, as the soldiers of II Corps boarded the steamers at City Point for their roundabout trip to Deep Bottom, Meade issued

---

1 Henry R. Pyne, *The History of the First New Jersey Cavalry (Sixteenth Regiment, New Jersey Volunteers)* (Trenton NJ, 1871), 280.

orders to Warren on the Petersburg front. The Army of the Potomac's leader directed Warren to prepare its V Corps to move upon short notice. V Corps occupied the extreme left of the Unionist line outside the Cockade City, within earshot of the rail traffic on the Weldon Railroad. "The whistle of the locomotive and the rattling of the trains could be distinctly heard in their passage to and from Petersburg," remembered Chaplain William H. Locke of the 11th Pennsylvania Infantry in Coulter's brigade of Crawford's division of V Corps.[2]

That night, as Hancock's fleet approached Deep Bottom and X Corps and Gregg's cavalrymen plodded across the pontoon bridges, Maj. Gen. Andrew Atkinson Humphreys, Meade's chief of staff, explained to Warren the nature and objectives of the following day's movement north of James River. Humphreys knew Warren and had much in common with him. Like Warren a West Point graduate and civil engineer, Humphreys had preceded Warren as chief topographical engineer of the Army of the Potomac and in that capacity had received assistance from Warren, then the leader of an infantry brigade. Gettysburg had figured prominently in the careers of both officers. Humphreys saw his division wrecked through no fault of his own and afterward agreed to serve as Meade's chief of staff, a position Humphreys had previously declined. Warren, by then the Army of the Potomac's chief topographical engineer, earned a corps command by undertaking on his own initiative the successful defense of Little Round Top, possibly saving the army and the Union.

Humphreys told Warren that if the movement north of the James led to the almost entire abandonment of the Rebel position at Petersburg, Meade would withdraw troops of V and IX corps from the trenches and send them on an operation to take advantage of the situation. The Army of the Potomac held a line extending from the Appomattox River to the Jerusalem Plank Road, with XVIII Corps, detached from the Army of the James, on the right, IX Corps in the center, and V Corps on the left. Kautz's cavalry division from the Army of the James guarded the Army of the Potomac's left flank and rear. Captain Amos M. Judson of Company E, 83rd Pennsylvania Infantry in Gwyn's brigade of Griffin's division of V Corps, recalled, "The army resembled a huge serpent lying coiled around the defenses of Petersburg, with its tail lapped around its

---

2 William H. Locke, *The Story of the Regiment* (Philadelphia, 1868), 357.

Maj. Gen. Andrew A. Humphreys, U.S.A. *Library of Congress*

chief artery of supply, and every now and then tightening its folds and giving the rebellion a more deadly hug."³

Opposite these Federals, four Confederate infantry divisions barred the way into the Cockade City. Johnson's division and Hoke's division of the Department of North Carolina and Southern Virginia, Beauregard's command, held the Secessionist left. Johnson's division had on its left the Appomattox River and on its right Hoke's division. To the right of Hoke's division, Heth's division of Hill's Corps in the Army of Northern Virginia occupied the Rebel trenches. Mahone's division, also of Hill's Corps, defended the Southern fortifications to the right of Heth's division. Dearing's cavalry brigade, part of Beauregard's command, picketed the Weldon Railroad. Rooney Lee's division of horsemen held the extreme right at Reams Station.

On the night of August 14, as X Corps slogged through the rain toward Fussell's mill pond, Meade withdrew V Corps from the Petersburg trenches. V Corps went into reserve while IX and XVIII corps shifted left and stretched to hold the lines that V Corps had vacated. Now XVIII Corps occupied the Union earthworks from the Appomattox to the Crater, and IX Corps defended the Federal trenches from the Crater to the Jerusalem Plank Road.

By the evening of August 16, Northern intelligence officers had located two brigades from Mahone's division north of the James. This meant Lee had withdrawn troops from the Petersburg sector as Grant had hoped. Federal signal officers found indications of other Rebel forces headed from the Cockade City northward. Though unconvinced that the Confederates had weakened their Petersburg position enough that an attack by Warren would result in a material advantage, Meade at 9:20 p.m. ordered Warren to move at 3:00 a.m. the following morning by way of the Strong house and the shortest road. Meade instructed Warren to strike the Weldon Railroad near its intersection with the Vaughan Road, about two miles south of the Cockade City. If the Secessionists held their fortifications in that area weakly, Meade wanted Warren to carry them and occupy the crest behind the Confederate breastworks opposite IX and XVIII corps—the last defensible line between Petersburg and the Federals. Kautz's cavalry division at 9:45 p.m. received orders to guard Warren's left against an attack by Rebel cavalry coming up from Reams Station.

---

3   A. M. Judson, *History of the Eighty-Third Regiment Pennsylvania Volunteers* (Erie PA, 1865), 106.

In issuing these orders, the Army of the Potomac's leader and his chief of staff thought they had anticipated Grant's reaction to Southern movements. Meade and Humphreys had misread the mind of the general-in-chief. Grant did not yet consider the situation ripe for the grand raid on the Weldon Railroad. He wanted the Secessionists to commit still more of their forces to the battle north of James River before he unleashed Warren. At 10:15 p.m., the general-in-chief issued dispatches suspending the planned movement.

By the early afternoon of August 17, Grant had weighed the available intelligence and determined that nearly all the Confederate cavalry south of the Cockade City and also three brigades of infantry from the Petersburg trenches had gone north of the James. Based on the estimate, he unenthusiastically ordered Meade to loose Warren on the Weldon Railroad the following morning. The general-in-chief expected no decisive results under the prevailing circumstances. He ordered this movement in the hope that, with Kautz's aid, Warren might get to the railroad and destroy a few miles of track. Grant also still wanted to force Lee to recall men from the Shenandoah back to Richmond and Petersburg so that Sheridan might advantageously strike the balance of Early's troops.

More optimistic than the general-in-chief, the ordinarily cautious Meade anticipated no difficulty in Warren making a lodgment on the railroad. The Army of the Potomac's leader doubted that the Rebels had men enough available to do more than slow the destruction of the railroad by keeping Warren on the alert by means of threats. At 2:30 p.m., Meade ordered Warren to march at 4:00 a.m. the following morning and try to strike the railroad near Dr. Gurley's house, or as near the Confederate entrenchments as practicable. The army commander told Warren to destroy the railroad as far south as possible and to take advantage of any Southern weakness, but not to assault fortifications. The recent rains had made moving wheeled vehicles through the mud of the roads and fields nearly impossible, and Meade directed Warren to travel light, with only part of V Corps' ambulances and medical wagons. Placing under Warren's orders a brigade of cavalry from Kautz's division, the army leader emphasized his inability to reinforce Warren and warned that V Corps must fend for itself. By 5:45 p.m., the quartermaster at City Point had forwarded to Warren 440 sets of implements for destroying railroad track.

Before 10:00 p.m. that night, Grant had grown more optimistic about Warren's movement. The general-in-chief received intelligence that Mahone's entire division and Johnson's brigade had come north of the James, leaving the force at Petersburg reduced to a mere three divisions. "Warren may find an

The Battle of Globe Tavern, August 18, 1864

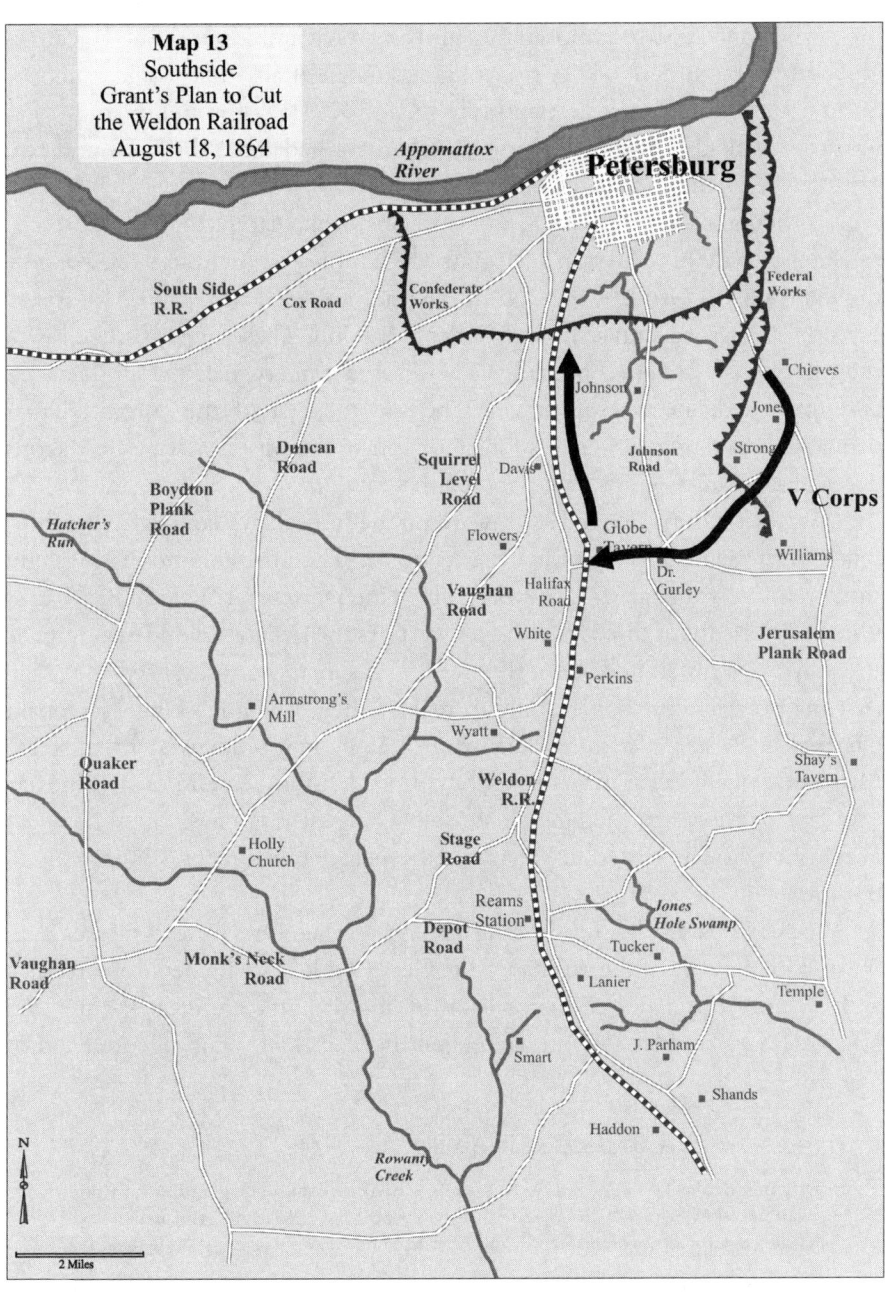

opportunity to do more than I had expected," Grant telegraphed Meade.[4] Forwarding Grant's dispatch to Warren, Meade in his own accompanying message revived and re-imposed the third and most ambitious of the objectives set forth in his orders of the previous night—an attack that would flank the Secessionists out of their line opposite IX and XVIII corps and open the way into the Cockade City. In fact, the Southerners had three divisions and two brigades of infantry in the Petersburg trenches.

At 4:00 a.m. on August 18, as his troops broke camp, Warren expressed satisfaction with his orders in a telegram to Humphreys. An hour later, V Corps moved out with Griffin's division in the lead, followed respectively by Ayres' division, Crawford's division and Cutler's division. These units marched with their previously assigned batteries. The reserve artillery, half the ambulances, and four medicine wagons traveled behind the rest of the corps. Neither ordnance trains, nor battery wagons, nor forage wagons, nor baggage wagons except for spring wagons, encumbered the column.

Warren's troops slogged southward on the Jerusalem Plank Road for three miles from their camp near the Chieves house. Then the column made a right turn on to the Vaughan Wagon Road, which intersected the Weldon Railroad at Globe Tavern about three miles father west. As the Federals plodded along, the excessive heat prostrated about fifty men with sunstroke and caused straggling that temporarily cost some units up to half their strength.[5] First Lieutenant Charles H. Porter, a former clerk from Quincy in Company A of the 39th Massachusetts in Lyle's brigade of Crawford's division, remembered, "The day was one of those exceedingly close, sultry August dog-days, well known to every one who has served in Virginia, extremely debilitating and exhausting to both man and beast."[6]

About 7:00 a.m., the head of the column reached Dr. Gurley's house. Near there, within a mile of the railroad, Brig. Gen. Charles Griffin deployed Tilton's and Gregory's brigades of his division in line of battle. A West Pointer and Mexican War Veteran, Griffin had begun the war as a captain in command of

---

4   U. S. Grant to Major-General Meade, August 17, 1864, in *OR*, vol. 42, pt. 2, 245.

5   Report of Maj. Gen. Gouverneur K. Warren, U.S. Army, commanding Fifth Army Corps, of operations August 18-21, in *OR* 42, pt. 1, 431; Report of Col. J. William Hoffman, Fifty-sixth Pennsylvania Infantry, commanding Third Brigade, of operations August 18-21, in ibid., 483.

6   Charles H. Porter, "Operations Against the Weldon Railroad, August 18, 19, 21, 1864," in *Papers Read before the Military History Society of Massachusetts*, vol. 5 (1906): 247-8.

the West Point Battery—D, 5th United States Artillery—at first Bull Run. Tilton's brigade formed in two lines of battle to the right of the wagon road, with its left on the road. Gregory's brigade formed to the left of the road, with its right on the road. By about 8:20 a.m., Griffin had completed his dispositions. V Corps resumed its advance. The Unionists, who had marched through thick woods all the way from the Jerusalem Plank Road, emerged into a corn field that stretched beyond the Weldon Railroad. The Federals saw the cavalry pickets of Dearing's brigade drawn up across the field and along the railroad. The Rebel horse soldiers fired a volley with their carbines.

"Fix bayonets!" came the order to the Unionist infantry. "Charge!"

The Northerners advanced, yelling, and the first line discharged their muskets as they ran.

"The cavalry did not wait to shake hands with us," remembered Maj. Horatio N. Warren of the 142nd Pennsylvania in the second line of Tilton's brigade.[7] Upon reaching the reserve posts, Tilton's men unsaddled and killed some of the Confederate troopers and captured about twenty more.[8]

Griffin's soldiers reached the railroad at about 9:00 a.m. and cut the telegraph line that ran beside the tracks. The skirmishers screening the battle line advanced about 500 yards west of the railroad and formed a line parallel to the tracks. Parts of Tilton's and Gregory's brigades commenced the destruction of the railroad by tearing up the rails and ties. Soldiers of the 121st Pennsylvania in Tilton's brigade recalled how they dismantled the tracks:

> . . . at the word of command, every man took hold of the rail and lifted the track, ties and all, bodily from the road-bed. While the troops on the right rolled the huge ladder in one direction, those on the left rolled it in the opposite direction, forming an immense screw, until finally it was forced to pieces, when the ties were gathered together in piles short distances apart, and the rails laid crossways on top, and fire applied, and the destruction was complete. The rails becoming red-hot in the middle were taken off and bent round and round a telegraph pole or a tree most convenient, and not a rail left was used again. . . .[9]

---

7 Horatio N. Warren, *The Declarations of Independence and War History, Bull Run to Appomattox*, (Buffalo, 1894), 39.

8 *OR* 42, pt. 1, 429; Report of Lieut. Col. William A. Throop, First Michigan Infantry, commanding First Brigade, of operations August 17-27, in ibid., 460.

9 Survivors Committee, *History of the 121st Regiment Pennsylvania Volunteers* (Philadelphia, 1893), 83.

The more creative souls in V Corps twisted the red hot rails into rough Maltese crosses—the emblem of their corps. When the showers that had made the roads nearly impassable put out the fires and prevented the heating of the rails, the soldiers incorporated the rails and ties into the breastworks they built.

Having attained the first of his objectives, a lodgment on the Weldon Railroad, Warren pursued the second, to extend his hold on the railroad as far as possible toward the enemy's entrenchments. Another part of Tilton's brigade received orders to remain in line of battle, position itself astride the tracks and hike about a third of a mile up the roadbed toward Petersburg. The as yet uncommitted portion of Gregory's brigade began building breastworks. Gwyn's brigade, which reached the railroad soon after the rest of Griffin's division, went into reserve.

Warren's next division, commanded by Brig. Gen. Romeyn Beck Ayres, reached the tracks at about 10:00 a.m. The sunstroke and straggling caused by the terrible heat compelled V Corps to move slowly. Not until nearly 11:00 a.m. had Ayres completed his dispositions for advancing up the railroad toward the Cockade City. A West Pointer who had transferred from the artillery to the infantry because of the more rapid rate of promotion there, Ayres deployed his troops near the Blick house, less than a quarter mile north of where V Corps had first struck the tracks. Hayes' brigade formed a double line of battle across the railroad, with the 12th United States Infantry, the 146th New York—Garrard's Tigers—and part of the 140th New York thrown out as skirmishers. The part of the 140th deployed as skirmishers included the remnant of the 5th New York, uniformed as Zouaves, consolidated with the 140th earlier in the year after the 5th's three years of service ended. Warren had once led the 5th. Hayes' brigade relieved the soldiers of Tilton's brigade who had advanced up the railroad toward Petersburg, and these troops returned to their command and began tearing up track. The Maryland Brigade formed in line protecting Hayes' left flank. Ayres placed the 15th New York Heavy Artillery, which constituted his third brigade, in support of Hayes and the Maryland Brigade. Battery C of the 1st Massachusetts Light Artillery unlimbered its four Napoleons near the Blick house to reply to the fire of a pair of Confederate guns about three quarters of a mile north on the railway.

Shortly before 11:00 a.m., Ayres' troops began trudging up the Weldon Railroad toward the Cockade City. The heat slowed the soldiers. Soon the Federals entered the dense growth of pines and oak that near the railroad formed the northern border of the clearing around Globe Tavern. The clutching underbrush further slowed the troops. At about 1:00 p.m., after an advance of about 1,100 yards under brisk artillery fire, the Unionist skirmishers began to engage a Rebel picket line. Shortly afterward, the rain that had fallen all day began to come down hard.

Warren decided to extend his line to the right until he could turn the Secessionist left flank. He ordered Crawford's division to advance in line of battle and connect its left with the right of Ayres' division, which extended fifty to 100 yards east of the railroad. Brigadier General Samuel W. Crawford, a graduate of the University of Pennsylvania and its medical school, had served as surgeon at Fort Sumter at the time of its bombardment and surrender and afterward transferred to the infantry. He deployed Lyle's brigade as his left, Coulter's brigade as his center, and Hartshorne's brigade on his right. Known as "Seven Shooters" because its men carried the seven shot Spencer rifle, Hartshorne's brigade had the 191st Pennsylvania as skirmishers with the 190th Pennsylvania in support.[10] The 191st Pennsylvania stretched as far east as the Johnson Road. Sending out the 107th Pennsylvania as skirmishers in front of rest of his division, Crawford ordered the 107th forward into the dense, swampy, almost impenetrable thicket to the right of the tracks. The 107th advanced about twenty yards into the woods and then halted for further orders. Discovering that this regiment did not properly cover his front, Crawford replaced it with the 190th Pennsylvania of Hartshorne's brigade, leaving Hartshorne's entire brigade deployed as skirmishers.

While arranging his skirmish line in the pouring rain and under artillery fire from the Confederate cannons near the W. P. Davis house, Crawford dispatched a staff officer to find the right of Ayres' division. The terrain proved so difficult that, when the staff officer returned with the desired information, Crawford began maneuvering his division forward one brigade at a time, from left to right. Lyle's brigade advanced into the woods. Its commander, Col. Peter Lyle of the 90th Pennsylvania, found the underbrush so thick and tangled that he decided to send his brigade forward one regiment at a time, also from left to right. The 16th Maine, on the extreme left of Lyle's brigade, drew the assignment of struggling forward first. As soon as the 16th Maine located Ayres' division, Lyle intended to bring up the 39th Massachusetts on the right

---

10 Report of Brig. Gen. Samuel W. Crawford, U.S. Army, of operations August 18-21, in OR 42, pt. 1, 491; Report of Capt. Henry H. Fish, Ninety-fourth New York Infantry, of operations August 17-September 2, in ibid., 515; Report of Capt. Delos E. Hall, Ninety-seventh New York Infantry, of operations August 18-21, in ibid., 517.

of the 16th, then his own 90th Pennsylvania on the 39th's right. When the 16th Maine arrived at its appointed position, a gap of 150 yards remained between the 16th's left and Ayres' division, which had in the meantime shifted completely west of the railroad.

As Crawford's division inched forward and Ayres' battle line shifted westward, Ayres' skirmishers continued their advance. The Union skirmish line drove the Secessionist pickets back and soon emerged from the northern edge of the belt of woods that formed the northern border of the fields surrounding Globe Tavern. The belt of woods had proven about 500 yards wide. Threatened by this advance, the Confederate battery limbered up and withdrew to a safer position nearer Petersburg. Battery C, 1st Massachusetts limbered up, advanced and unlimbered at the northern edge of the woods. The artillery duel resumed.

Ayres' skirmishers pushed their Rebel counterparts through the Davis corn field and beyond the Davis house toward another belt of woods. The Davis house stood where the Vaughan Road slanted off southwestwardly toward Dinwiddie Court House from the Halifax Road, which ran parallel to the railroad. The Union skirmishers halted short of the woods beyond the Davis house, waiting for their battle line to arrive within supporting distance. The battle line of Hayes' brigade halted about thirty yards back from the northern edge of the woods between the Davis house and Globe Tavern. The Maryland Brigade stopped about seventy yards back from Hayes' left. The 16th Maine of Lyle's brigade arrived abreast of Hayes' right. Lyle brought up the 39th Massachusetts on the right of the 16th, then the 90th Pennsylvania on the 39th's right as planned. The gap of 150 yards remained between the 16th's left and Hayes' right. Warren wanted Crawford's division adjacent to, extending eastward from the right of, and advancing with Ayres' division. Crawford's failure to close up left Ayres' right inadequately protected.

At about 2:00 p.m., the skirmishers of Ayres' division resumed their advance. They crawled with arms at trail toward the woods north of the Davis corn field. Bullets sang over their heads, clipping off the tops of the stalks. Two Southern battle lines rose fifty yards in front of them. The skirmishers heard the eerie ululation of the Rebel yell. The Confederates blasted the skirmishers with a volley. Then the Secessionists charged.

* * *

Throughout the morning, Brig. Gen. James Dearing had forwarded reports of the progress of the Federal column to Beauregard. Dearing, who had led his

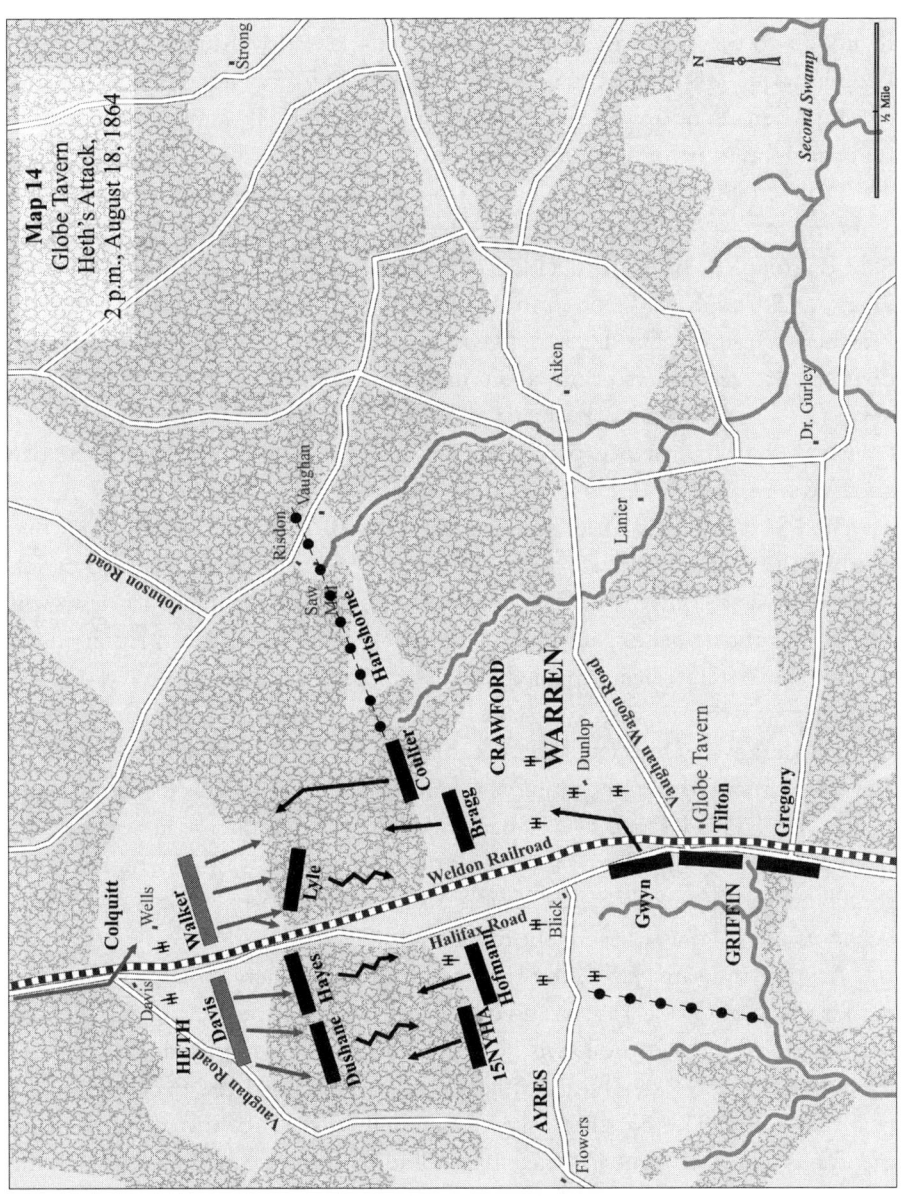

Map 14
Globe Tavern
Heth's Attack,
2 p.m., August 18, 1864

West Point class until he resigned just short of graduation in 1861, had entered Confederate service as an artillerist and then transferred to the cavalry. Beauregard commanded at Petersburg in the absence of Lee, who remained north of the James. Around 10:00 a.m., the Louisianan received from Dearing a report that Union infantry and cavalry had driven in Dearing's pickets and reserve in front of Globe Tavern just as he prepared to lead another of his regiments to that location. Beauregard immediately forwarded this message to Lee's headquarters at Chaffin's Bluff with a request for cavalry reinforcements.

Just before noon, the Louisianan got another dispatch from Dearing reporting the Northerners advancing on the railroad and the Vaughan Road. This movement threatened all the Confederate supply lines south of the Appomattox—the Weldon Railroad, the Boydton Plank Road, and the South Side Railroad. Beauregard decided to commit half of his reserve to support Dearing. Through Lt. Gen. Ambrose P. Hill, the commander of the Army of Northern Virginia's Third Corps, Davis' brigade and Walker's brigade of Heth's division received orders to move out under the command of Maj. Gen. Henry Heth. A Virginian and a graduate of West Point who went by the name of "Harry," Heth had helped precipitate the battle of Gettysburg, where he had suffered a head wound. Davis' brigade, stationed a mile behind the front line, marched at two thirds of its strength. One third of its soldiers, detailed that morning, remained at their work. Because the departure of Heth's force left Beauregard with only two brigades in reserve, he ordered Heth to return his brigades to their positions at Petersburg that evening. The four Napoleons of the Letcher Artillery accompanied Heth's troops.

Soon afterward, displaying the boldness which had characterized his brilliant defense of the Cockade City during the initial Federal onslaught in June, Beauregard ordered Colquitt's Georgia brigade of Hoke's division to join Heth's men. This left the Louisianan with only four regiments in reserve, one from each of the brigades of Johnson's division, in case of a Federal attack on the Petersburg trenches by the Union XI or XVIII Corps. Colquitt's brigade began its march toward Heth shortly after 1:00 p.m.

Around the same time, the Union skirmishers emerged from the belt of woods north of Globe Tavern and drove Dearing's troopers through the Davis corn field and beyond the Davis house. This advance compelled the retreat of the section of the Petersburg Artillery that had harassed the Federals for the past two hours. The Northern skirmishers halted short of the woods beyond the Davis house to wait for their battle line to catch up with them. Dearing mistakenly thought that his force of about 500 cavalrymen had checked the Unionists, and he underestimated Federal strength as only a few regiments of infantry and one or two of cavalry.

As the Federal skirmishers marked time near the Davis house, Heth's soldiers completed their march of about three miles. As soon as the Confederate infantry came within sight of the Northerners, the Rebels formed line of battle. The brigade of Brig. Gen. Joseph Robert Davis, a nephew of

President Davis, formed west of the railroad, with its left resting on the tracks. Walker's brigade, under the command of Col. Robert Murphy Mayo, a graduate of Virginia Military Institute, formed east of Davis' brigade, with its right on the tracks. Heth put out skirmishers, who relieved Dearing's troopers. Then Heth ordered an attack.

* * *

The Secessionists charged the skirmishers of Ayres' division "with dash and spirit, at double-quick," remembered Adjutant Charles M. Cooke of the 55th North Carolina in the center of Davis' brigade west of the railroad.[11] The Union skirmishers panicked and fled without firing a shot. The Southerners drove the Federal skirmishers through the Davis corn field into the belt of woods between the corn field and Globe Tavern. Red-pantalooned Zouaves scampered through the lines of the 16th Maine in Lyle's brigade east of the tracks. The Rebels then struck the battle line of Hayes' brigade, thirty yards deep into the woods and just west of the railroad. Davis' troops took advantage of the seventy yard gap between the left of Hayes' brigade and the right of the Maryland Brigade. Walker's soldiers infiltrated the 150 yard gap between Hayes' right and the 16th Maine of Lyle's brigade. Hayes' men turned tail and fled to the rear edge of the woods.

Beyond the left of Hayes' brigade, Davis' Mississippians and North Carolinians muscled their way forty yards through the thick brush until they met the Maryland Brigade. Crouching unseen behind hastily erected breastworks around fifty yards away from Davis' Confederates, the Marylanders stood and fired a volley that to Adjutant Cooke in the 55th North Carolina seemed, "a veritable sheet of flame" in the twilight of the woods. Stunned, the center of Davis' brigade momentarily fell back about fifty yards.[12]

The Maryland Brigade had no sooner repulsed the Rebels in front of them than they found themselves outflanked. The retreat of Hayes' brigade on the Maryland Brigade's right widened the gap between Ayres' and Crawford's divisions. The left of Davis' brigade curled around the right flank of the Marylanders. Colonel Nathan T. Dushane of the 1st Maryland Infantry, the commander of the Maryland Brigade, had nothing to protect his left flank but

---

11 Clark, *North Carolina Regiments*, 3:309.

12 Ibid., 310.

Federal Zouave *Library of Congress*

skirmishers. The far right of Davis' brigade drove in the skirmishers and enfiladed the left of the Maryland Brigade's battle line. Rallying, the center of Davis' brigade resumed its charge. Dushane ordered his soldiers to retreat. The density of the woods and the proximity of the Rebels turned retreat into rout.

Every member of the color guard of the 1st Maryland took a bullet, including seven color bearers who fell one after another. Lieutenant Colonel John W. Wilson of the 1st, a Mexican War veteran, remembered, "At no time in my life could I have shed tears more freely than when I saw the men fall around my colors as fast as I could count one, two, and three."[13] The colors, presented to the regiment by loyal Marylanders who lived in California, held special significance for the 1st's soldiers, who knew them as the "California Flag."[14] After the last of their appointed bearers fell, Second Lt. William Taylor of Company C seized the beloved banner and carried it to safety. The collapse of the Maryland Brigade endangered Battery C, 1st Massachusetts Light Artillery and forced the gunners to draw their guns rearward by hand.

East of the railroad, Walker's brigade also took advantage of the gap created by the retreat of Hayes' brigade. The 16th Maine briefly held its ground, but soon Walker's troops worked their way around the 16th's left flank and into its rear. Discovering this, the soldiers from Maine fell back along with the 39th

---

13 Charles Camper and J. W. Kirkley, comps., *Historical Record of the First Regiment Maryland Infantry* (Washington DC, 1871), 169.

14 Ibid., 213-6, 240.

Massachusetts and the 90th Pennsylvania. The withdrawal turned into a skedaddle.

Gutshot, Col. Charles L. Pierson of the 39th Massachusetts fell to his knees from shock. Second Lieutenant Henry A. Seaverns of Company K, the regiment's left company, rushed up and reported, "Everything is swept away from the left." Pierson ordered Seaverns to go out and investigate. Seaverns got wounded and did not return. Pierson staggered over to Company K and instructed its commander, Capt. Willard C. Kinsley, to go out and investigate. Kinsley did not return. Pierson limped out to investigate himself. Meeting a "secession soldier," Pierson commanded, "Drop that gun and come in here." The secession soldier obeyed, not understanding that Pierson lacked the strength to compel him to do anything. Pierson learned from the Southerner that his comrades had slipped behind the 39th's left flank. The direction from which the bullets came confirmed this.

"Fours, right about, forward on the left company," shouted Pierson. "March!"

Exhausted by loss of blood, he then collapsed.

Second Lieutenant John H. Dusseault, a former carver in the 39th's Company H, recalled what followed:

> Just as I rose, a bullet struck me in the right side, broke the eighth rib and entered the lower lobe of the lung. I was taken off the field, along with the Colonel, to the field hospital just back of us. Sergeant [Elbridge] Bradshaw . . . and Private [George N. B.] Thomas, both of Company H, were leading me and while thus supporting me, the latter was shot in the wrist, in consequence of which, hesitating a moment, he was captured.[15]

After retreating about 150 yards southeastwardly, which widened the gap between the divisions of Ayres and Crawford still more, Lyle's remaining troops encountered the left of Coulter's brigade. Under the command of Col. Richard Coulter of the 11th Pennsylvania, a Mexican War Veteran and pre-war lawyer wounded at Gettysburg and Spotsylvania, this brigade had by now tramped into the woods north of the Globe Tavern clearing. Coulter had not completely recovered from his Spotsylvania wound. Upon meeting the fugitives from Lyle's brigade, Coulter relinquished command to Col. Charles Wheelock of the

---

15 Alfred S. Roe, *The Thirty-Ninth Regiment Massachusetts Volunteers 1862-1865* (Worcester MA, 1914), 246-7. Colonel Pierson survived his seemingly mortal wound.

97th New York, the Conkling Rifles, a former produce dealer wounded at Gettysburg. Wheelock immediately shook out three companies of the 97th as skirmishers and deployed his brigade into line extending to the right, with the 88th Pennsylvania—the Cameron Light Guards—faced to the right on the right flank. Lyle's soldiers reformed on Coulter's left. Lyle's three leftmost regiments, the 16th Maine, 39th Massachusetts and 90th Pennsylvania, formed on the left of the 104th New York of their brigade.

Ayres reacted rapidly to the sound of heavy firing and committed his divisional reserve, the 15th New York Heavy Artillery, which formed near the rear edge of the woods north of the Globe Tavern clearing. Hayes' brigade reformed on the 15th's right. The Marylanders, after disentangling themselves from the woods, rallied on the left of the heavies. Heth's attack had driven Ayres' division back almost half a mile and seemed to threaten the entire Federal position on the railroad. Ayres asked Warren for reinforcements.

Warren responded as quickly to the unmistakable sound of battle as Ayres. The V Corps chief dispatched reinforcements to Ayres before his request for reinforcements arrived. Warren ordered Brig. Gen. Lysander Cutler, commander of the corps' Fourth Division, to send Hofmann's brigade to the aid of Ayres' division. Half of this brigade's soldiers had fallen out during the morning's march, but most of the stragglers had reported during the two hours that the brigade had spent resting near Globe Tavern.

Hofmann's brigade marched to the edge of the woods north of the tavern. There Col. J. William Hofmann of the 56th Pennsylvania, a former clothing manufacturer, deployed his troops in line of battle, with their left on the railroad. He sent the 147th New York forward as skirmishers. Upon the brigade's detachment from Cutler's division, the body of the brigade shifted to the west of the tracks, leaving the 147th New York to the east. The body of the brigade relieved the Maryland Brigade and halted the advance of Davis' Confederates. The 147th New York plodded forward through the forest until it met Walker's brigade. Then the New Yorkers fired almost blindly at the Secessionists in woods and brush that limited visibility to less than twenty yards.

Warren also called upon the commander of his artillery brigade, Col. Charles Shields Wainwright, for support. Wainwright, a New York farmer, brought six batteries into position in a line running from just west of the Blick house to east of the railroad. As Ayres' soldiers emerged from the woods, twenty-four guns opened fire. They soon silenced the Letcher Artillery, which had unlimbered near the Davis House, and they slowed the advance of Heth's troops.

When Ayres' request for reinforcements reached Warren, the V Corps leader directed Cutler to send the other of his two brigades to cover the interval between Ayres and Crawford. Cutler, a Milwaukee businessman who had begun the war as colonel of the 6th Wisconsin, complied and dispatched Bragg's brigade. As the main body of Hofmann's brigade shifted west of the tracks, Bragg's brigade—which included the remnant of the Iron Brigade—took its place behind the 147th New York. Brigadier General Edward Stuyvesant Bragg, a lawyer from Wisconsin, had nominated Stephen A. Douglas for President of the United States at the Democratic National Convention in Charleston, South Carolina in 1860. Upon the outbreak of war, Bragg entered the Union army as a captain in the 6th Wisconsin Infantry, and he carried the scars of wounds suffered at Chancellorsville. He sent forward his old regiment to join the 147th New York as skirmishers while he entrenched his main line. The 6th Wisconsin advanced until it joined the 147th New York and came under the command of the 147th's Lt. Col. George Harney.

Ayres now had Hayes' brigade on the railroad, with the 15th New York Heavy Artillery to the left of Hayes' brigade, Hofmann's brigade on the left of the heavies, and the Maryland Brigade on Hofmann's left, curving to the rear. To the right of the roadbed, Ayres had Bragg's brigade behind a skirmish line composed of the 147th New York and the 6th Wisconsin. To the right of Bragg's brigade stood Crawford's division.

Warren also summoned Gwyn's brigade of Griffin's division out of reserve and into the fight east of the tracks. Gwyn's brigade, led by Col. James Gwyn of the 118th Pennsylvania, an Irish immigrant who had worked as a store clerk before joining the army as a captain in the 23rd Pennsylvania, formed line of battle and tramped off to the support of Crawford's division. Mindful of Meade's admonition that V Corps must fend for itself, Warren left the rest of Griffin's division in reserve to look out for flank attacks.

The V Corps chief then rode into the struggle on Whitey, his bay horse. Whitey made a good target for a Secessionist sharpshooter, who shot the animal between the eyes. Horse and rider both went down. Warren survived unhurt. Whitey survived miraculously—the bullet had ricocheted off his thick skull instead of penetrating it.

Outnumbered in manpower by at least three to one and in artillery support by no less than four to one, Heth's soldiers came to a halt about 2:30 p.m. The Confederates had pushed Ayres' troops back from the edge of the woods north of the Davis house to the northern edge of the clearing around Globe Tavern, a distance of about 700 yards. The Rebels had taken two lines of hastily constructed breastworks. They had also recaptured Rev. Thomas B. Flowers' house, which stood near the Vaughan Road almost due west of the Blick house and which Union cavalry had occupied around 11:00 a.m. "The enemy was found to be in much stronger force than was at first supposed," Heth recalled, "and the two brigades had done all that could be expected of them."[16] A static firefight with the Federals continued.

The crisis had passed before Gwyn's brigade engaged the Secessionists. Gwyn received orders to shift left of the railroad and build breastworks. Griffin placed Gwyn's troops on the extreme left of his division. With Tilton's brigade on its right, Gregory's brigade in the center, and Gwyn's brigade on the left, Griffin's division stretched from the left of the Maryland Brigade to a point about a mile south of the Blick house.

By about 4:00 p.m., Warren had reorganized his corps. He resumed his advance toward Petersburg over the ground lost to Heth's attack. Though both Ayres and Crawford received instructions to advance, Ayres—west of the railroad—had almost all his men entrench. Not until shortly before dark did he attempt to head toward Petersburg, and then he sent forward only a skirmish line formed of the 76th New York and the 157th Pennsylvania under Lt. Col. John E. Cook of the 76th, a carpenter. Under a heavy picket fire from Davis' brigade, this detachment from Hofmann's brigade found it impossible to advance farther than halfway through the woods to the Davis cornfield, its objective.

East of the railroad, the advance of the Unionists took the form of a slow left wheel to outflank the foe. Skirmishing all the way, Harney's ad hoc brigade from Cutler's division on the left and Crawford's division on the right slowly drove Walker's brigade back from two lines of hastily constructed rifle pits. "To advance my line was a matter of the greatest difficulty," Crawford later wrote. "So dense and tangled was the undergrowth, and so interspersed with swamps, than it was almost impossible to keep up the connection or to see beyond twenty or thirty feet."[17] Lyle's brigade did not advance with the rest of Crawford's division. Coulter's brigade veered left toward the railroad behind Hartshorne's brigade—still deployed as skirmishers. Coulter's brigade lost contact with the 191st Pennsylvania of Hartshorne's brigade and reeled from a

---

16 Henry Heth, "Report of December 7th, 1864," Heth Papers, Eleanor S. Brockenbrough Library, Museum of the Confederacy, Richmond, Virginia.

17 OR 42, pt. 1, 492.

point blank volley received when its soldiers unsuspectingly stumbled upon Confederate entrenchments on the north edge of the Davis corn field around 100 yards beyond the right of Harney's men. As night came on, a picket line from Lyle's brigade relieved Harney's troops. Crawford's division entrenched.

Shortly before Wheelock reached the Secessionist works, the Georgians of Colquitt's brigade finally arrived from Petersburg. The Georgians formed line of battle behind Walker's brigade. Heth did not employ Colquitt's brigade to renew the afternoon's attack. Keeping the Georgians in reserve represented the better course in the face of a foe of superior strength, which Heth recognized by this time from the prisoners taken earlier—they came from three divisions of V Corps, which still had four uncommitted brigades of infantry. The engagement of Colquitt's brigade would almost certainly have failed to push the Unionists from the tracks. The Federals captured a number of Colquitt's pickets.

While Crawford advanced, Wainwright rearranged his batteries. He ordered the four Napoleons of the 15th Battery, New York Light Artillery 100 yards farther to the west of the Blick house and the four Napoleons of Battery H, 1st New York Light Artillery west of the Halifax Road in order that these batteries might fire to the north or west. To the right and rear of the easternmost battery of the line of six that crossed the railroad, Wainwright emplaced four more batteries along the Halifax Road facing east. The artillerists employed their spades to throw up lunettes and began scrounging lumber to build gun platforms.

Having decided to hold his position, Warren ordered all obstructions thrown down between the tracks and the Vaughan Road to the west. He directed Ayres to slash all the timber in his front. Ayres went Warren one better and on his own initiative ordered a deep ditch dug across the roadbed and the Halifax Road. Warren instructed Crawford to make himself as strong as possible and hold his position until morning. Then he would receive Bragg's brigade to replace the videttes of the 3rd New York Cavalry who connected along the Vaughan Wagon Road east of the tracks with the pickets of IX Corps. The IX Corps skirmishers had advanced from their previously refused position to shorten the gap between themselves and V Corps, but the horsemen patrolled too far in Crawford's right rear for his safety.

Crawford sent the 88th Pennsylvania of Coulter's brigade to the 191st Pennsylvania of Hartshorne's brigade. The left wing of the 88th relieved part of the 191st and the right wing extended the skirmish line farther east. Crawford would need to make himself strong indeed, because the day's maneuvers had left his troops in a position that just asked for trouble. From left to right,

Warren's line ran northeastward across the railroad, past the Johnson Road, and all the way to the east side of the eastern V of the W formed by the southern end of the Johnson farm. There it rested in the air, vulnerable to a thrust from Petersburg.[18] The V Corps leader thought that only a very large Secessionist force could succeed in driving him from his present position. Not having experienced three Confederate brigades rolling up three Federal divisions as had David Birney at the Jerusalem Plank Road in June, Warren did not imagine how much damage a smaller Southern force could do to a command in as awkward a posture as V Corps.

Despite Meade's admonition that V Corps must fend for itself, he and Grant had every intention of reinforcing Warren. At 10:30 p.m. on August 17, while informing Hancock of Warren's orders for August 18, Grant had told Hancock that Warren's movement might lead to a withdrawal of troops from Hancock's front. At 10:30 a.m. on August 18, before receiving any word whatsoever of Warren's progress, the general-in-chief telegraphed Hancock that if he could spare a division and still hold his position, he should send one to Meade that night. Hancock replied that he would send Mott's division. Shortly after noon, Grant wired Meade that after withdrawing from the north side of the James, Hancock would go to Warren's support. Between 6:00 p.m. and 7:15 p.m., the general-in-chief informed the Army of the Potomac's leader that Hancock would not bring his entire corps but would dispatch a single division. At 8:20 p.m., Mott received instructions to report to Meade.

Because the distance involved precluded Mott's arrival at Warren's position before noon on August 19 in any state other than complete exhaustion, at 7:40 p.m. Grant suggested that Meade use Mott's division of about 5,000 men to relieve an equivalent number of troops from IX Corps and then use those troops to reinforce Warren. The Army of the Potomac's commander immediately began to implement the general-in-chief's recommendation.

---

18 Sketch, in OR 42, pt. 1, 433. This map represents Warren's position on the evening of August 18, 1864. G. K. Warren to Major-General Humphreys, August 18, 1864, in ibid., pt. 2, 276. Observe how far eastward the Federal line extends and how it angles generally northeastward and then northeast by north at the right (eastern) terminus. This last stretch looks like the eastern leg of the western V of the W formed by the southern boundary of the Johnson farm. About half a mile separated Warren's right from the IX Corps pickets, and around one and three quarters of a mile separated it from the Petersburg fortifications. See also the sketch of this area in Records Group 77, Office of the Chief of Engineers, National Archives, Washington, D. C.

Mott's division could not reach IX Corps before morning. Meade and Humphreys on their own initiative figured out a way to send reinforcements to Warren sooner. At 9:50 p.m., Meade ordered Maj. Gen. Edward Otho Cresap Ord, Sherman's roommate at West Point and the commander of XVIII Corps, to send his reserve of 1,500 soldiers to IX Corps. Major General John Grubb Parke, another West Pointer and the commander of IX Corps, would use Ord's reserve to relieve the 1,000 to 1,200 men of Willcox's division of IX Corps. Willcox's division would depart for Warren's position at 3:00 a.m. and would arrive around daybreak. Potter's and White's divisions of IX Corps would leave to join Warren as soon as Mott's division relieved them. Though the V Corps chief had used less than half the cavalry instructed to report to him, at 8:00 p.m. Kautz received directions to put another cavalry regiment at Warren's disposal.

The Confederate high command also hastened forces to the Weldon Railroad. By 7:00 p.m., Beauregard had received Heth's account of the battle. Heth reported driving the Federals about a mile from the Davis house and taking about 200 prisoners from three divisions of V Corps.[19] He believed that, if reinforced, he could drive the Northerners from the roadbed. The Louisianan forwarded to Lee Heth's report and request for reinforcements with the comment, "He has already all I can spare, three brigades of infantry, which must return to vicinity of lines during the night."[20] In fact, Heth's two brigades remained near the Davis house. Only Colquitt's Brigade returned to Petersburg. Held in reserve in case of a seemingly imminent attack on the eastern approaches of the Cockade City by IX and XVIII corps, Colquitt's Georgians did not get much rest.

Upon receipt of Beauregard's message, Lee did not follow up the late afternoon's attack north of James River. That evening the Virginian ordered back to Petersburg Rooney Lee's division of cavalry and Harris' three-brigade detachment of Mahone's division. As early as June 19, just after the repulse of Grant's initial assaults on Petersburg, Lee had written off the Weldon Railroad as indefensible because the dilapidated tracks lay too close to enemy lines. He urged the Confederate government to prepare the South Side Railroad and the Richmond and Danville Railroad to carry the supplies necessary to compensate for the Weldon road's loss. He also stoutly defended the Virginia Central

---

19 Columbus (GA) *Times*, August 26, 1864, p. 2, col. 3; Daily (Columbia) *South Carolinian*, August 23, 1864, p. 3, col. 2.

20 G. T. Beauregard to General Robert E. Lee, August 18, 1864, in ibid., pt. 2, 1187.

Railroad. Lee did not intend to abandon the vulnerable Weldon roadbed without a fight. If he did not succeed in driving the Unionists from the right-of-way, he planned to make them pay as dear a price as possible for cutting this supply line. From June 21 to June 23, during the battle of the Jerusalem Plank Road, the run down railway had served as bait to lure Federal foot soldiers out in the open where his forces routed and decimated them.[21]

The damage inflicted on the South Side and the Richmond and Danville railroads by Unionist cavalrymen during the Wilson-Kautz Raid at the end of June complicated matters. It gave the Rebels more incentive to fight for the Weldon Railroad's right-of-way. With the South Side and the Richmond and Danville roads still not fully repaired in mid-August, the Secessionists needed every ounce of supplies they could haul over the Weldon road's decaying ties and poorly tempered rails. Lee could not just coolly dangle the railway as bait in front of the Federals. He had to give a full measure of devotion to keeping it running. "It is touching a tiger's cubs to get on that road," wrote Lt. Col. Theodore Lyman III, the Masschusetts-born, Harvard educated, headquarters archivist of Meade's staff on the following day in regard to Heth's August 18 attack. "They will not stand it."[22]

In the fields, scrubs and swamps along the Weldon Railroad, firing died out by midnight. The Federals had lost about 936 soldiers, including more than 150 prisoners.[23] Secessionist killed, wounded and missing totaled approximately 350, including around fifty captives.[24] The tangled terrain must have made the troops of both sides feel as if they had refought the Wilderness with heat and rain adding to their misery. Some may have realized that fighting the Wilderness again in the torrid August showers had at least one blessing: the underbrush did not catch fire and cremate the wounded as it had in cooler, dryer May.

---

21 Some have called the battle of the Jerusalem Plank Road the First Battle of the Weldon Railroad, and the August fighting the Second Battle of the Weldon Railroad.

22 Agassiz, *Meade's Headquarters*, 217.

23 OR 42, pt. 1, 429; ibid., pt. 2, 1187; Heth, "Report of December 7th, 1864," Heth Papers. Another source reports 158 prisoners. Columbus (GA) *Times*, August 24, 1864, p. 1, col. 3.

24 Daily (Columbia) *South Carolinian*, August 23, 1864, p. 3, col. 2; Charleston *Mercury*, August 23, 1864, p. 1, col. 1. The number of wounded reached about 200, high in proportion to the number of killed. Petersburg Daily *Register*, August 19, 1864, p. 2, col. 3. Davis' brigade lost 219 killed or wounded. Ibid., August 22, 1864, p. 2, col. 3. Dearing's brigade lost about twenty troopers as prisoners. OR 42, pt. 1, 460; Report of Maj. George W. Jones, One Hundred and fiftieth Pennsylvania Infantry, of operations August 18-21, in ibid., 465. Heth lost about thirty prisoners. Richmond *Whig*, August 20, 1864, p. 1, col. 1.

As on the first day of battle north of the James, Grant had attained his less ambitions objectives on the first day of this action. His forces had gained a lodgment on the Weldon Railroad. They had entrenched as closely as practicable to Petersburg, even if that meant not very closely at all. Davis' and Walker's brigades had permitted the eleven brigades of Federal infantry, tired, unfamiliar with the territory, and touchy about their flanks, to approach no nearer.

That the movement north of the James had drawn away from the Cockade City three brigades of Confederate infantry and two brigades of Secessionist cavalry had proven truly fortunate for the Unionists. The qualitative superiority of the Army of Northern Virginia over the Army of the Potomac had reached the point where Warren needed at least seven brigades of Federal infantry with overwhelming artillery support to stop the less disciplined half of Heth's Division.[25] A five-brigade attack by the Southerners on August 18—the whole of Heth's Division and Colquitt's Brigade—might well have driven V Corps from the railroad. The Southerners could spare no more than the three brigades sent.

On the following day, the Rebels trying to drive the Northerners from the roadbed would have to contend with more than just V Corps thanks to Meade and Humphreys. Warren would no longer have the element of surprise working to keep down the number of Secessionists opposing him. Both sides had entered into a race to strengthen their forces on the railroad, with the tracks themselves as the prize.

---

25 H. E. Peyton to General S. Cooper, September 22, 1864, in *OR* 42, pt. 2, 1275. Whatever the state of their discipline, the 2nd and 11th Mississippi had exceptional combat records extending back to First Bull Run. Dunbar Rowland, *Military History of Mississippi, 1803-1898* (Nashville, 1908), 44-49, 54-57. As for Archer's and Field's brigades, the components of Walker's brigade, they had belonged to the famous Light Division in its heyday.

Chapter 7

The Battle of Globe Tavern, August 19, 1864

Warren wanted no surprises on August 19. He knew that his right flank hung in the air and invited Confederate attack. Instead of refusing and fortifying his right flank as he had his left, he elected to provide himself with warning of the approach of a Rebel force from his right by stretching a picket line from his right to the IX Corps videttes near the Secessionist fortifications about half a mile west of the Jerusalem Plank Road.

At about 2:00 a.m., Warren took his first step in connecting a picket line with IX Corps. He instructed Bragg's small brigade of about 760 soldiers to report to Crawford. Bragg and his troops reached Crawford's division about an hour later. Crawford directed Bragg to shift to Crawford's right flank and take position there until further orders came. Captain Walter T. Chester, an engineer on Crawford's staff, conducted Bragg's soldiers toward their assigned position. Neither Bragg, nor Crawford, nor Chester, had the benefit of the map Warren had drawn for Meade the previous evening.

Well to the east, the troops from XVIII Corps arrived behind Willcox's division of IX Corps as directed by Meade and Humphreys shortly after 2:00 a.m. The relief and assembly of Willcox's division took place under a heavy fire from Confederate artillery and sharpshooters. At about 3:30 a.m., the order to march came from Brig. Gen. Orlando Bolivar Willcox, a West Pointer who had served in the Mexican and the Third Seminole Wars before resigning in 1857 to practice law. Wounded and captured at First Bull Run, he eventually received a

Medal of Honor for his service there. His division tramped off to join V Corps on the Weldon Railroad. Willcox's division would constitute the reserve at Warren's disposal to deal with penetration of the picket line between the right of V Corps and the left of IX Corps.

Warren did not neglect other vulnerable points. At daybreak, to guard the left rear of V Corps, Col. Samuel Perkins Spear's brigade of Kautz's cavalry division trotted southward down the Weldon Railroad from Globe Tavern. His horsemen drove the Secessionist cavalry videttes to within a mile of Reams Station. Spear, a veteran of the Mexican and Seminole Wars, halted and picketed all the roads between that point and Globe Tavern coming in from the west.

Bragg's brigade reached at daybreak the extreme right of Crawford's division on the southeastern edge of the Johnson farm, near a fork in a lane running southward along the east edge of the farm. From the fork, one track continued southward toward the Vaughan farmstead, while another led southeastward in the direction of the Strong house. The pickets of the 88th Pennsylvania extended along the southeastern edge of the Johnson farm to about 100 yards north of the fork, where the 88th formed the extreme right of Crawford's skirmish line. To relieve the 88th Pennsylvania, Bragg deployed the 1st Battalion New York Sharpshooters and part of the 7th Indiana. Bragg slightly refused the right of his skirmishers, who stood along the track that ran southeastward toward the Strong house. The left of Bragg's picket line connected with the right of Hartshorne's brigade. The line's right hung in the air, unconnected with IX Corps videttes farther east. Bragg entrenched the remainder of his brigade at the fork in the road about 100 yards behind his picket line.

Around the same time, Crawford redeployed the two brigades of his division that remained in line of battle. Lyle's brigade relieved Coulter's brigade on the front line near the railroad. Coulter's brigade shifted to the right of Lyle's brigade and began entrenching.

At 7:00 a.m., Captain Chester conducted to Bragg's headquarters Capt. Emmor B. Cope from Warren's staff. Cope brought verbal orders for Bragg that gave rise to misunderstandings about the placement of Bragg's picket line. Like Crawford, Bragg, and Chester, Cope lacked a copy of the map Warren had drawn for Meade the evening before.

Warren wanted Bragg to push out a line of skirmishers by the flank a few degrees north of east from the right of Crawford's line until the pickets met the Rebels. The V Corps leader then wanted the skirmishers to fall back a short distance and push on by the flank as closely as possible to the Confederates until the pickets made contact with the videttes of IX Corps west of the Chieves house and the Jerusalem Plank Road.

Instead of communicating those orders directly to Bragg, Cope conveyed them to Chester. Communication broke down. Cope failed to make clear exactly where Warren wanted Bragg to establish the skirmish line. Warren wanted Bragg's picket line to connect with IX Corps about three quarters of a mile north of the Strong house. This line would have stretched from the right of Crawford's line a few degrees north of east and would have detected any Secessionist force moving around Crawford's right and into his rear. Two o'clock on a clock face represented the angle Warren desired.

In the presence of Cope and Bragg, Chester interpreted what Cope said to mean that Warren merely wanted Bragg to deploy his brigade along the shortest line to connect with the pickets of IX Corps. Cope replied uncertainly. Chester indicated that Bragg ought to connect with IX Corps near the Jones house, about three quarters of a mile northeast of the Strong house. This line would have extended southeast by east from the right of Crawford's line and would have permitted a Rebel force to march into Crawford's right rear before encountering Bragg's pickets. Four o'clock on a clock face represented the angle Chester had in mind.

After listening to this confusing colloquy, Bragg threw up his hands and said, "Well, we will do it."[1] He sent First Lt. James P. Mead, his Commissary of Musters, eastward to find the near end of the IX Corps line. Soon Mead located the pickets of IX Corps on a lane passing the Aiken house, nearly a mile and a half behind Bragg's refused right. The lane ran from the Dunlop house near the railroad eastward to the Jerusalem Plank Road north of the Vaughan Wagon Road. Bragg deployed his troops along the track running southward from the fork behind the right of his skirmish line until he established contact with the IX Corps skirmishers. He dared not post his pickets on the track running southeastward from the fork lest he leave in the forest behind the track an undetected enemy force. After a ride over to the IX Corps line as far as the Strong house, Bragg determined that he should place his right there. A line from Crawford's right to the Strong house would stretch southeastward and would allow a force of Confederates to thrust undetected even farther into Crawford's

---

1 Reports of Brig. Gen. Edward S. Bragg, U.S. Army, commanding First Brigade, of operations August 18-21, in OR 42, pt. 1, 539.

right rear than a line with its right at the Jones house. The angle Bragg decided upon represented five o'clock on a clock face. He would place his right three quarters of a mile south of where Warren wanted it to rest. A dripping, dense, tangled thicket filled the distance between Bragg's right and the Strong house.

At about the same time as Cope reached Bragg, Mott's division of II Corps began arriving behind IX Corps. Mott's rain-soaked, exhausted soldiers had crossed James River at 10:00 p.m., paused on Jones Neck, resumed their march at 1:00 a.m., and crossed the Appomattox at 3:00 a.m. They reached the Petersburg front at 7:00 a.m. Mott's troops began relieving White's and Potter's divisions of IX Corps at 11:00 a.m. Waist-deep water in the covered ways compelled the soldiers to expose themselves to enemy fire during this relief operation and delayed it considerably. Not until 2:00 p.m. did Mott's troops complete the relief of the IX Corps division commanded by Brig. Gen. Julius White, a lawyer who had begun the war as colonel of the 37th Illinois Infantry. Assembling around divisional headquarters near the Jones house, White's division did not march until 3:00 p.m.

Returning to the right of his brigade at about 8:00 a.m., Bragg ordered a left half-wheel, guiding his right by the front of the IX Corps line. "This increment was attended with great difficulty," Bragg remembered. "The nature of the wood, the pelting storm, and the extended line encumbered and seriously embarrassed the whole operation."[2] The 9th Battery, Massachusetts Light Artillery near Globe Tavern shelled the woods on the right to dislodge Rebel skirmishers, and this also hindered Bragg's deployment. The right of Bragg's line floundered toward the Strong house very slowly.

At about 7:30 a.m., having marched by way of Dr. Gurley's house, Willcox's division of IX Corps reached Globe Tavern. Warren did not employ the tired soldiers of this division as imaginatively as Meade and Humphreys had used the reserve of XVIII Corps earlier that morning. The V Corps leader declined to order Wilcox's exhausted troops to relieve Griffin's division, half again as big and much fresher. Warren feared an attack from his left as well as from his right, but Griffin's division would have furnished a stronger, less fatigued reserve to meet either contingency. Defending behind a picket line as long as Warren's required as large and rested a reserve as possible.

The V Corps chief directed Willcox's men to bivouac in the field to the east of Globe Tavern. Willcox deployed his division in two lines in the field, placing

2 Ibid., 535.

the first line about 500 yards behind, and nearly parallel to, the right of Coulter's brigade. Hartranft's brigade formed the first line, Humphrey's brigade the second. Willcox sent staff officers to ascertain the positions of, and routes to, the various divisions of V Corps. His troops drew rations in the pouring rain. Commissary Sergeant Lewis Crater of Company F, 50th Pennsylvania Infantry in Humphrey's brigade recalled:

> Some of us were sent after wood, while others commenced building fires, and our Regimental Commissary Sergeant issued a ration of salt mackerel, which caused considerable amusement among the men. Instead of putting them in pans, as we did at home, we threw them into holes filled with rain water, to soak.[3]

Before 8:50 a.m., Grant had decided that Hancock, by detaining a large force of Rebels north of James River, made the Federal force at Petersburg as strong as if he had his troops there. The general-in-chief declined to order any more of Hancock's men to follow Mott's division south of the James. Noting the sensitivity of the Confederates to thrusts toward Chaffin's Bluff, Grant determined to threaten as much of the enemy front as possible as the best way to force the Southerners to withdraw reinforcements sent to Early in the Shenandoah.

By 9:00 a.m., in front of Warren, the pickets in front of Hayes and Lyle had advanced. In front of Lyle's brigade, the 190th Pennsylvania discovered that the Secessionists had pulled back. Hayes' brigade pushed forward to the southern edge of the Davis corn field, recovering a number of Federal wounded who reported the Confederates feeling their way toward the Union left.

Shortly before 10:15 a.m., Warren learned from Crawford that Bragg had established contact with the IX Corps pickets a quarter of a mile northeast of the Aiken house. This placed Bragg's brigade at an angle represented by six o'clock on a clock face. Cope had not yet returned, but a discussion between Warren and another member of his staff convinced the V Corps commander that Crawford had not established the picket line where Warren had intended. At 10:15 a.m., Warren sent Crawford a written message that Bragg's skirmishers should stretch northeastward, not southward, from the extreme right of Hartshorne's brigade.

---

3 Lewis Crater, *History of the Fiftieth Regiment, Penna. Vet. Vols., 1861-1865* (Reading PA, 1884), 70.

Mistakenly satisfied about Bragg's compliance with Warren's orders by an 8:00 a.m. ride along the IX Corps line to the Strong house, Crawford did not act upon Warren's message until around noon. Crawford and a member of his staff rode up the line held in the morning by IX Corps, which soldiers of Mott's II Corps division had already relieved, in search of the right of Bragg's picket line. Crawford departed for his left without finding the junction of Bragg's right with the II Corps vidette line, but the staff officer located it at about 2:30 p.m. in the woods opposite the Strong house, where Bragg's skirmishers had just arrived after struggling for hours through the thick underbrush and dense timber—about three quarters of a mile south of where Warren wanted Bragg's right.

Shortly after noon, Meade rode out with some members of his staff toward Warren's headquarters. "It was raining steadily, and we went slop, slop along," recalled Lieutenant Colonel Lyman.[4] Near the Chieves house, Meade and his staff encountered a sodden brigade of Potter's IX Corps division. The army leader prodded along these rain-soaked soldiers in case Warren should need them. Meade then rode along the Vaughan Wagon Road past the Aiken house to the headquarters of V Corps at Globe Tavern.

According to Lyman, the flaw in Warren's position cried out for rectification. Lyman remembered,

> It could scarcely fail to strike me that, while the left flank was well protected, the right was 'in the air,' having nothing in connection with it but the picket line. However, as I am not a military man, I thought no more of it. The enemy *did* think a good deal of it.[5]

At about 1:00 p.m., Mahone's division advanced a strong skirmish line through the Johnson corn field and into the woods, striking the right of the 190th Pennsylvania and the front of the 191st Pennsylvania. After a short struggle, the Seven Shooters forced the Confederates to withdraw.

Around an hour later, on the left of Warren's line, Ayres rearranged his division. The Maryland Brigade stretched northward from near the Blick house to the fringe of the Davis corn field. To the right of the Maryland Brigade, Hofmann's brigade stretched eastward, followed by the 15th New York heavies, and then Hayes' brigade. The 12th and 14th United States Infantry of

---

4   Agassiz, *Meade's Headquarters*, 219.

5   Ibid.

Hayes' brigade found themselves on the front line to the east of the railroad. The 14th had its left on the roadbed and its right on the 12th. The rest of Hayes' brigade remained west of the railway. Lyle's and Coulter's brigades of Crawford's division shifted about 200 yards eastward. Hartshorne's Seven Shooters conformed, shortening their front by around 200 yards but still occupying a skirmish line connected with Bragg's left. The V Corps artillerymen made their gun platforms large and comfortable.

Bragg's left remained near the fork in the road on the southeast side of the Johnson farm. As soon as Bragg had reestablished the right of his line near the Strong house, at 2:30 p.m., he returned to his headquarters. There he met Maj. Washington A. Roebling, Warren's brother-in-law and an engineer on the corps commander's staff who would one day build the Brooklyn Bridge. Roebling wanted Bragg to advance his left northward across the Johnson corn field. Bragg thought it impossible to do this without bringing on an engagement with the Secessionists, but he rode to his left to reconnoiter.

At 3:30 p.m., Meade started riding back to his own headquarters by the same way that he had come. "Both going and coming I quite expected to see the picket line tumbling in on top of us," Lyman wrote.[6] As the army leader and his staffers rode past the Aiken house a few minutes later, they heard a number of what Lyman called "dropping shots" to their left—the north.[7]

While Bragg established his right near the Strong house, Warren received word that the Southerners had begun massing in front of Hayes' and Lyle's brigades. At 3:45 p.m., Warren notified Griffin and Willcox of this and ordered them to put their commands in readiness to move to the front.

Crawford returned toward his left along the rear of his line. When behind the 19th Indiana of Bragg's brigade, Crawford met soldiers from that regiment on the road along which Bragg had strung his pickets that morning before ordering them into the thickets. Asked why they had left the front, the men of the 19th told Crawford that the Rebels had driven them back and asked him if he had heard the firing. Crawford, who had not heard any firing, ordered the second lieutenant in charge to reform his line, return to his position, and reestablish his connections to his right and his left. The division commander also ordered Bragg to send a portion of the 6th Wisconsin, his reserve regiment,

---

6 Ibid., 219-220.

7 Ibid., 220.

to support the 19th Indiana's line. Crawford then continued his ride down the rear of his division.

At about the same time, near the Strong house, the commander of Bragg's easternmost regiment, the 7th Wisconsin, reported that the Confederates had broken Bragg's line to the 7th's left. The 7th's commander expected an attack at any time.

As Meade and his staff reached the Jerusalem Plank Road, and Warren prepared for an attack on the front of Ayres' division, and Crawford reached the center of his division, and Bragg examined his line's connection with Hartshorne's brigade, heavy firing erupted on the left center of Bragg's line.

One of the war's most chaotic, desperate struggles had begun.

* * *

The Alabamians, Georgians and Mississippians of Harris' detachment of Mahone's division crossed the James on the pontoon bridge at Drewry's Bluff and began arriving at Petersburg at 4:00 a.m. They staggered into their old places in the line near the Branch house. The three brigades of this detachment left two-thirds of their strength on picket duty north of James River. The soldiers who reached Petersburg proved unfit for anything but sleep after their all night trek in the rain. Even in this state, they furnished a reserve that permitted Beauregard to commit more troops to attack the Federals on the Weldon Railroad than he had committed on the previous day.

By 8:00 a.m., Beauregard knew that the Northerners whom Heth had stopped on the previous evening had not withdrawn from the railway, but had begun fortifying, and from the prisoners taken the Louisianan knew that Heth had faced at least three divisions. Beauregard decided that he would try to dislodge the Unionists with four brigades of infantry, as well as the division of cavalry that Lee had promised to send him. The Louisianan believed that a stronger force of infantry would make the result more certain.

Before 9:20 a.m., disturbing information from a captured Federal captain reached Beauregard. The captain said that Grant had sent V Corps to break the Weldon Railroad to draw enough Rebels from the Petersburg trenches that another blow might crack that Secessionist line. If Beauregard committed too many of his soldiers to strike Warren, the Unionists might storm the Cockade City's fortifications. Despite this information, the daring Louisianan committed a fifth brigade of infantry to the attack on the Weldon Railroad.

Maj. Gen. William Mahone, C.S.A.
National Archives

On the afternoon of the previous day, Maj. Gen. William Mahone had proposed a plan of attack to Capt. Richard Henry Toler Adams, Lt. Gen. Ambrose Powell Hill's acting assistant adjutant and inspector general, who had enlisted as a private in the 11th Virginia Infantry in 1861. "I knew every foot of the ground around Petersburg," Mahone remembered.[8] The thirty-seven year old native of Virginia's Southampton County, terminus of the Jerusalem Plank Road, had surveyed the vicinity of the Cockade City for the Norfolk and Petersburg Railroad several years earlier. A dyspeptic who always kept a cow and chickens near his tent, and a pastry cook at his headquarters, Mahone had served as a brigade commander distinguished more for discipline than for battlefield prowess from late 1861 until his elevation to division command on May 6, 1864. Command of Anderson's division devolved upon Mahone as its senior brigadier general when Lee chose "Fighting Dick" Anderson to command Longstreet's Corps after Lt. Gen. James A. Longstreet's debilitating wound at the battle of the Wilderness.

Mahone quickly distinguished himself as a division commander after Lee's army reached Petersburg. On June 22, with three brigades of his division, Mahone routed all three divisions of the once elite Union II Corps near the Johnson farm, capturing almost 1,800 prisoners, nine flags, and four guns. On June 23, his division bagged almost 500 prisoners from the Vermont Brigade of the Northern VI Corps engaged in wrecking the Weldon Railroad near Dr. Gurley's house. On June 29, two of Mahone's brigades participated in the capture of about 1,000 Federal cavalrymen at the first battle of Reams Station. On July 30, three of his brigades took about 1,000 prisoners and a dozen

---

8 Smith, *Nineteenth Maine*, 209-10.

banners, and recaptured four guns, in the counterattack that drove the Unionists from the Crater. By August of 1864, if not earlier, the Northerners had come to consider Mahone Lee's most effective division commander.

As the horse artillery accompanying Dearing's cavalry brigade sounded the arrival of V Corps on the Weldon Railroad on the previous day, Mahone had pointed out to Adams that the Federals could not possibly have covered the heavily timbered space between Warren's right and the termination of the main Union line near Secessionist Fort Sedgwick on the Jerusalem Plank Road. Mahone proposed to sneak a column of attack southward up the ravine west of his headquarters at the Branch house on the Dimmock Line—the heavy fortifications that Confederate engineers had constructed around Petersburg in 1862. The Virginian had utilized the same route to slip his forces through enemy lines for his June 22 surprise attack on II Corps. The ravine would keep the Rebel column out of view of the Federals until the column reached the wood skirting the field east of the Johnson house. Mahone expected to encounter a Unionist picket line in the woods south of the field, and he intended to plunge through the Northern videttes into the right rear of Warren's position on the Weldon Railroad. After explaining the proposed movement to Adams, Mahone rode out to Heth's line on the railway.

Before noon on August 19, Mahone's suggestion had made its way up the chain of command through Hill to Beauregard. The Louisianan decided to employ Hill's plan of attack, which incorporated Mahone's suggestion. Hill's plan called for Heth to attack down the railroad with Davis' and Walker's brigades as soon as Mahone struck the right rear of V Corps. Sending two brigades from Hoke's Division to Mahone, Beauregard ordered Mahone to take one of his own brigades as well to make up the attacking force. Heth's soldiers would pin down the Federals in front while Mahone's troops scooped up the Unionists from the rear.

"Old Porte," as Sgt. John F. Sale of the 12th Virginia in Mahone's former brigade called him because of his poshly appointed headquarters, disliked Beauregard's arrangement.[9] The cantankerous native of Southampton County did not hesitate to voice his disapproval. "I suggested that as troops always fought better under their own commander than under a stranger," Mahone

---

9 John F. Sale Diary, May 25, 1864, John F. Sale Papers, Virginia State Library, Richmond, Virginia. Sergeant Sale belonged to the Norfolk Juniors, Company H, 12th Virginia Infantry, Weisiger's brigade.

recalled, "and both commander and troops generally did their best when accustomed to each other, it would be best for General Hoke to take charge of the attacking force."[10] This suggestion fell on deaf ears. Old Porte also strenuously urged the use of more than three brigades for the flanking movement, but Beauregard could not spare a larger force. Shortly after noon, Colquitt's and Clingman's brigades arrived at Mahone's headquarters. Old Porte had already quietly withdrawn from the trenches the Virginians of his former brigade, now under the command of Brig. Gen. David A. Weisiger, a Petersburg wholesaler severely wounded at Second Bull Run.

After the column formed, Mahone's men entered the ravine. They marched southward toward the Johnson house with Colquitt's Georgians leading, Clingman's North Carolinians following and Weisiger's Virginians bringing up the rear. According to Lt. Col. William H. Stewart of the 61st Virginia, a twice wounded veteran from Norfolk, the column snaked along "during a rain storm, which made marching through the bushes very disagreeable, but our soldiers pressed on, hastily gathering and eating ripe whortleberries, that were plentiful along the route."[11] Old Porte's troops entered the woods southeast of the Johnson house and hurried onward until they pierced the Union picket line anticipated by Mahone.[12] The Southerners penetrated the skirmish line of Bragg's 19th Indiana. The penetration gave rise to the "dropping shots" heard by Meade and his staff as they passed the Aiken house. Had Mahone swung a

---

10 George S. Bernard, "The Weldon Railroad Fight: General Mahone's Brilliant Move," in Hampton Newsome, John Horn and John G. Selby, eds., *Civil War Talks: Further Reminiscences Of George S. Bernard & His Fellow Veterans* (Charlottesville VA, 2012), 264.

11 Ibid., 277.

12 None of the sources cited by Edwin C. Bearss with Bryce Suderow in *The Petersburg Campaign: The Eastern Front Battles, June–August 1864*, 276, n. 124, support their assertion that Hartshorne's brigade no longer occupied a skirmish line. (They cite Report of Col. Charles Wheelock, Ninety-seventh New York Infantry, commanding Second Brigade, of operations July 30-August 30, in OR 42, pt. 1, 510; ibid., 515; ibid., 517; Report of Capt. Benjamin F. Haines, Eleventh Pennsylvania Infantry, of operations August 18-21, in ibid., 518; and Report of Maj. Henry J. Sheafer, One hundred and seventh Pennsylvania Infantry, of operations August 18-21, in ibid., 522.) Neither Warren nor Crawford describes Hartshorne's brigade as anything but a skirmish line after late on August 18. Ibid., 429, 492-3. At most, the part of the 191st Pennsylvania of Hartshorne's brigade relieved by the left wing of the 88th Pennsylvania of Coulter's brigade, or the equivalent, around 100 men, stood in anything other than a skirmish formation—and that part almost certainly stood in support of Hartshorne's picket line. I made the same error myself in the first edition of this book.

The Battle of Globe Tavern, August 19, 1864

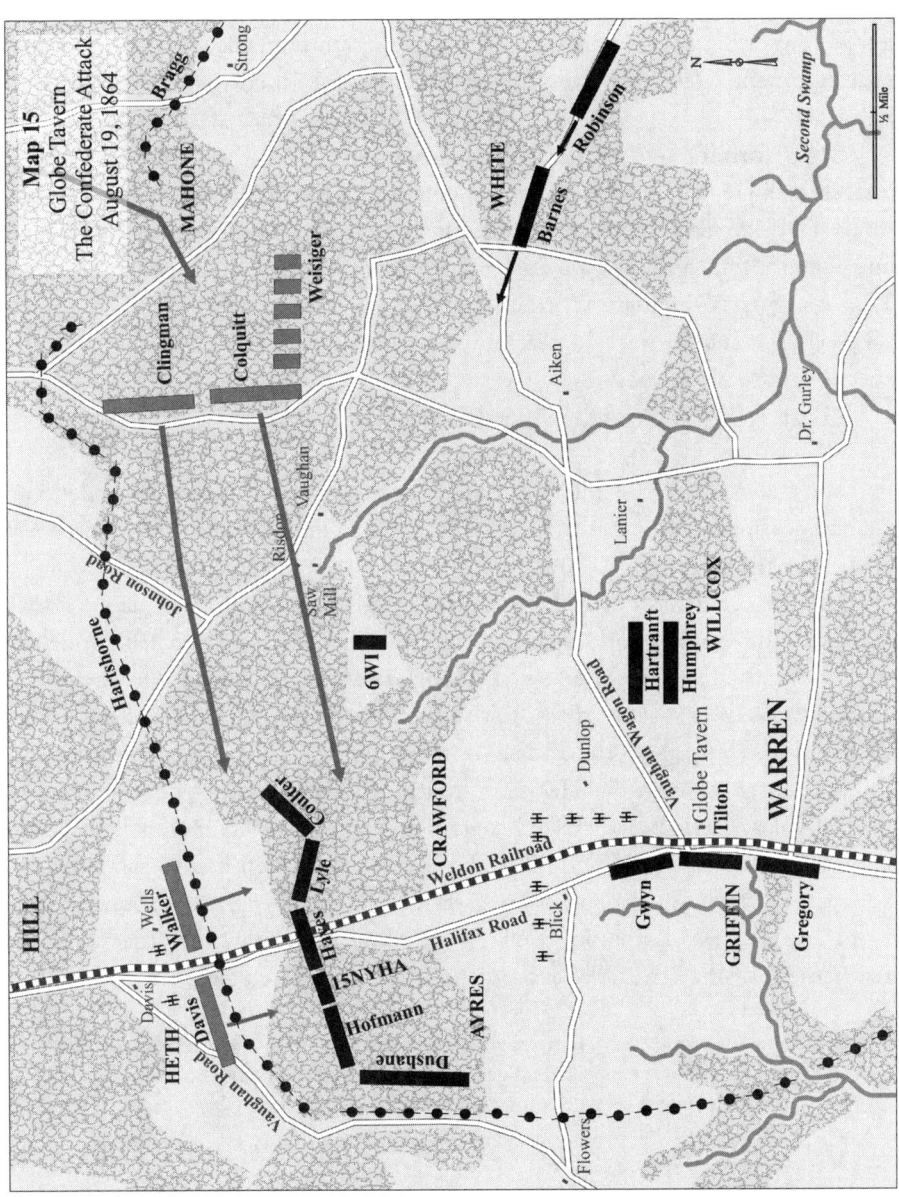

Map 15
Globe Tavern
The Confederate Attack
August 19, 1864

quarter mile wider to his left, he might have taken prisoner the commander of the Army of the Potomac.

The Secessionists did not return the shots fired at the attacking column. As soon as Mahone adjudged his force in the right rear of the Federal battle line facing Heth's troops, Old Porte formed line of battle with Colquitt on the left, Clingman on the right and Weisiger in column of regiments behind Colquitt's left. Mahone apprehended that any counterattack from Unionist reinforcements sent over from the Jerusalem Plank Road would emerge from his left.

After forming his battle line, Mahone called his three brigadiers to a conference. He explained to them the location of Globe Tavern. He told them that a steady advance would bring the attacking force into the rear of the Federal line facing Heth and straight into Warren's headquarters. Brigadier General Thomas Lanier Clingman, a former United States Senator from North Carolina, asked what would protect the rear of the attacking force from an advance of the enemy on the plank road.

"That is my look-out, General," replied Old Porte. "Your duty is in front."[13]

Mahone told the brigadiers to pay no attention to the fire of any vidette or picket line, but to hold their fire until they reached the works and the main body of the Northerners.

Late in the afternoon, Mahone's force advanced and soon came under shellfire. The Confederates again struck the skirmishers of the 19th Indiana, this time as the Hoosiers tried to reestablish Bragg's picket line. Because of the dense brush, the 19th's soldiers first sighted the Rebels at a distance of about twenty yards. Surprised, the Indianans drew the fire of the Secessionist front line. Breaking through the Hoosiers, Mahone's troops then encountered the 24th Michigan, which had shifted to its right from the 19th Indiana's left. The soldiers from Michigan briefly plugged the gap, but then had to fall back for want of support. Clingman's men, swarming to their right, surrounded and captured the 1st Battalion New York Sharpshooters and the adjacent detachment of the 7th Indiana. Soldiers of the 24th Michigan remembered:

> Every man then took care of himself, and there was a lively foot race amid shower after shower of bullets, as the men had no desire to visit Georgia and other Southern prison pens. A volume might be written on the narrow and often laughable escapes of the men at this time.[14]

The 24th Michigan fled southwestward toward the Aiken house. On Bragg's right, the 7th Wisconsin and the portion of the 19th Indiana east of the

---

13 Newsome, Horn, and Selby, eds., *Civil War Talks*, 265.

14 O. B. Curtis, *History of the Twenty-Fourth Michigan, of the Iron Brigade, Known as the Detroit and Wayne County Regiment* (Detroit, 1891), 271.

Secessionist penetration fell back to the Union works near the Strong house. The gunfire did not rise to alarming proportions until the Southerners had reached the left center of Bragg's line and Bragg, pursuant to Crawford's orders, brought up his reserve regiment, his own 6th Wisconsin, seventy-four strong. The 6th fought as it had in the heyday of the Iron Brigade. As the Rebels hiked westward along the base of the L-shaped Vaughan cornfield, capturing the simmering pork and beans of Bragg's pickets near the Vaughan house, the 6th made the Confederates pause to reform twice before the vastly outnumbered men in black hats had to retreat to avoid encirclement.

While Colquitt's Georgians drove the old Iron Brigade, Clingman's North Carolinians began rolling up Hartshorne's Seven Shooters. Within minutes, the Tarheels surrounded the 191st and then most of the 190th Pennsylvania. After a brief but sharp fight, the Seven Shooters destroyed their repeating rifles by breaking their stocks against trees and surrendered. The North Carolinians captured about three quarters of these Keystoners. Those who escaped took the nearly suicidal risk of running through the gap in the Confederate lines. Private Mike Coleman of Company C, 190th Pennsylvania remembered that he "heard men call 'Halt! Halt!' on every side; but he looked neither to the right nor left, and went ahead" to survival.[15]

Hearing the gunfire of Mahone's attack, Heth ordered Davis' and Walker's brigades into action. Davis' brigade advanced on the west side of the roadbed, Walker's brigade mostly on the east side. Each amounted to little more than a skirmish line. Davis' brigade covered the fronts of Hofmann's brigade and the brigade-sized 15th New York heavies. Walker's brigade stretched to oppose Hayes' and Lyle's brigades. Colonel William Steptoe Christian of the 55th Virginia, a doctor wounded at Glendale and Chancellorsville and captured at Gettysburg, had taken command of Walker's brigade after illness sidelined Colonel Mayo.

Heth also had at his disposal eight guns from three batteries of Pegram's Battalion. Heth had posted two of the guns east of the railroad and the six others west of the tracks near the Davis house. As soon as Heth's guns opened fire, Wainwright's gunners near the Blick house batteries replied and gave Heth

---

15 R. E. M'Bride, *In the Ranks from the Wilderness to Appomattox Court House* (Cincinatti, 1881), 118-9.

and the Rebel artillerists a severe shelling. "I was never before or after, subjected to such a terrible fire of artillery," Heth remembered.[16]

Driving the Federal pickets before them, Heth's foot soldiers entered the woods south of the Davis corn field. West of the railroad, Davis' skirmishers pushed the Unionist pickets of Hofmann and the 15th New York heavies from three successive lines of rifle pits and back on the main Federal position. There the attenuated Confederate line suffered a repulse. The 55th North Carolina lost its colors to Pvt. James T. Jennings of Company K of the 56th Pennsylvania. Jennings later received a Medal of Honor for this exploit.

Along the tracks and eastward, Christian's skirmishers pursued the enemy pickets of Hayes' and Lyle's brigades back to the main Union works, behind a slashing thirty yards wide with the trees felled with their tops toward the Secessionists. A firefight began between Christian's soldiers and the Federals. The Union soldiers had also heard the gunfire to the east that preceded Christian's attack, and the Federals grew increasingly apprehensive as the musketry on their right grew in volume.

North Carolinians and Georgians from Mahone's detachment began penetrating into the rear of Coulter's brigade. Some of the Tarheels surprised the three right companies of the 94th New York, the most easterly regiment of Coulter's brigade. The soldiers of these three companies, mostly new recruits, panicked when Clingman's troops opened fire on them. The three companies surrendered without any effort to repulse the attack. According to Pvt. John D. Vautier of the adjacent 88th Pennsylvania's Company I, who carried the scar of a Cold Harbor wound, the first intimation the men of his regiment had of the menace behind them came from the unexpected appearance

> of a squad of Confederate, led by a hatless and excited officer, coming directly through the woods that every man in the 88th was fully convinced was the rear. They were immediately halted and ordered to surrender, but decidedly objected, explaining that we were the ones to surrender, as they had us surrounded; this story was not credited, and, taking the officer's sword, Sergeant John Wallace, with an escort, proceeded with the prisoners back through the woods, where they ran into a moving column of the enemy, and were in turn captured and run Dixieward without further ceremony.[17]

---

16 James L. Morrison, ed., *The Memoirs of Henry Heth* (Westport CT, 1974), 190-1.

17 John D. Vautier, *History of the 88th Pennsylvania Volunteers in the War for the Union, 1861-1865* (Philadelphia, 1894), 197.

Wainwright's batteries soon silenced the Confederate guns at the Davis house. Moments later, Bragg's pickets tumbled in upon the butchers of V Corps as they slaughtered cattle near the northern edge of the Globe Tavern clearing. Though Warren and Wainwright rode northward from Globe Tavern to the Dunlop house, neither could see the Rebels who had flushed Bragg's troops. The belt of woods where Warren had stationed Crawford's division hid the westward progress of Mahone's detachment from the view of any of the Northerners in the Globe Tavern clearing as long as the Southerners remained in the trees.

Finally, around 500 yards east of the railroad, the extreme left of Colquitt's brigade emerged from the edge of the timber north of Globe Tavern. Wainwright hesitated to fire on the approximately 200 Georgians visible with their battle flag because few of Crawford's soldiers had retreated from the woods. Then Wainwright recalled that during the previous night, Warren had instructed his infantry to retire by the flanks if unable to hold their advanced position, 600 yards in front of Wainwright's batteries. This method of withdrawal would unmask Wainwright's guns. Wainwright therefore concluded that the Rebels must have driven Crawford's troops to the left and out of the line of fire. After the Secessionists had swept about 300 yards closer, within 400 yards of his batteries, Wainwright opened fire.

Others blasted away on their own initiative. Behind the 9th Massachusetts Battery, that former artillerist General Griffin saw the Georgians and rode up to the gunners.

"See those Rebs?" he said. "Fire on them,—shell, case, solid shot, anything; ricochet them in, give it to them!"[18]

The gunners let fly as fast as they could load.

The Georgians Wainwright could see immediately fell back toward the east, but Crawford's soldiers had not retired by the flanks as planned. Many of Wainwright's shells fell among them. Crawford had stationed himself near the junction of the left of Coulter's brigade with Lyle's right. When the shells began striking the works of Crawford's division from the rear, the division commander decided to implement Warren's orders of the previous night. Crawford dispatched a staff officer with directions for Colonel Wheelock to march Coulter's brigade by the left flank and leave the works. This just added to

---

18 Levi W. Baker, *History of the Ninth Mass. Battery Recruited July, 1862; Mustered in Aug. 10, 1862; Mustered out June 9, 1865, at the Close of the Rebellion* (South Framingham MA, 1888), 139-40.

the panic among the troops caused by reports that the enemy had gotten into their rear. The men of the 97th New York, the brigade's extreme left regiment, complied with Crawford's instruction before Wheelock could reach them and countermand the order. As the Conkling Rifles headed for the Globe Tavern clearing, the New Yorkers ran into the Secessionist battle line in the woods and lost about 100 soldiers.[19]

Aware of the Rebels in the rear and not pinned down by Confederates to the front, Wheelock halted the rest of his brigade and ordered his troops to leap over the works and lie down on the front side to avoid the shells. A stray group of Southerners appeared in the rear that had now become Wheelock's front. The Rebels ordered Wheelock to surrender. His soldiers drove off the Secessionists and recaptured thirteen of their comrades. Wheelock ordered his right to form and cut off the enemy. His troops captured only a few more of the Confederates in woods where visibility did not exceed fifty yards. Wheelock pulled all his men back into the works. Private Vautier recalled that between Wainwright's fire and that of the foe,

> it appeared as if Crawford's division would be wiped out,—a veritable case of between the devil and the deep sea; but the Confederates, sweeping across our rear, quickly disappeared, capturing in their erratic course a large number of the 5th Corps who were so unlucky as to be in their way.[20]

This large unlucky number included the better part of Lyle's brigade on Wheelock's left. Wainwright's hesitation to open fire on Colquitt's left allowed the Georgian's right to advance all the way to the Weldon Railroad. Pinned down by Walker's brigade in their front, Lyle's soldiers did not fare as well as Wheelock's troops. When first shells and then bullets suddenly began whizzing at them from behind, Lyle's exhausted and rain-soaked men panicked. Lieutenant Porter of the 39th Massachusetts in Lyle's brigade remembered:

> All was now confusion. Without leaders, the men were completely demoralized. In these dark and dismal woods, dismayed by the fire of our own guns . . . the men made but a short resistance. The enemy, quick to perceive that large captures could be made,

---

19 OR pt. 1, 510.

20 Vautier, *88th Pennsylvania*, 197-8.

rushed upon the troops and, finding them without formation, but with every man looking out for himself, captured them without much difficulty. . . .[21]

Half of Lyle's troops surrendered on the spot. The other half bolted for the second line of Federal works in the Globe Tavern clearing. These soldiers thrashed their way through the thorny vines and slashing branches in the midst of the downpour. Friendly fire from Wainwright's batteries killed and wounded some of them. Colquitt's front line intercepted and captured almost all of them. First Sergeant George E. Fowle of Company K, 39th Massachusetts, a former carpenter, recalled:

> I started back with the rest and came across a canteen with the string cut; picking it up, I took a drink and filled my own canteen, but when this was done, I found myself alone, but I followed along in the direction which the others had gone. I came to a cartpath, where I saw some of our men with a few Johnnies on the other side of the path. The bushes separating us were so thick and low that I had to spread them apart with my hands to get through, and when I did and straightened up, with my gun in my hand, I found myself looking into a rebel gun barrel. . . . I was told to throw down the gun, which I did and walked across the road. . . . There were so many prisoners that we were in all sorts of position, one, two and three deep. . . .[22]

Like a few other members of his regiment, Fowle had the good fortune to escape later in the prevailing confusion.

Not in the line of fire of Wainwright's guns, Hayes' brigade did not suffer the unnerving effect of shells striking from the rear. Ordered by Brig. Gen. Joseph Hayes, a Harvard graduate who had returned to duty after a Wilderness head wound, to hold their lines at all costs, the 12th and 14th Regiments United States Infantry—highly trained professional soldiers from the pre-war army—remained in their works east of the railroad until Lyle's troops fled. Second Lieutenant J. Chester White, commander of the 14th United States Infantry on the railroad, and Second Lieutenant August Thieman, commander of the 12th United States Infantry to the 14th's right, then independently ordered their soldiers to fall back, "deeming it folly to remain longer."[23] Major James M. Culpepper, in command of the 6th Georgia, at the head of about fifty

---

21 Porter, "Operations Against the Weldon Railroad," 257.

22 Roe, *Thirty-ninth Massachusetts*, 250-1.

23 Report of Lieut. J. Chester White, Tenth U.S. Infantry, commanding Fourteenth U.S. Infantry, of operations August 19, in OR 42, pt. 1, 479.

of his troops, had already reached the rear of Hayes' brigade. Culpepper and his men captured almost all of the 10th, 11th, 12th, 14th and 17th United States Infantry. Sergeant Richard H. Powell of Company C, 6th Georgia, captured General Hayes himself along with his Assistant Adjutant General, Lt. George K. Brady, when Hayes tried to reach his troops east of the railway upon hearing they faced encirclement. Command of the brigade devolved upon Col. Frederick Winthrop of the 5th New York Veteran Volunteer Infantry, a banker who had begun the war as a private.

The Georgians failed to bring off all these Regulars as prisoners. Discovering the weakness of their captors, the Regulars tried to turn the tables and capture the vastly outnumbered Georgian guards. Lieutenant Thieman succeeded in cutting his way through with the colors of the 12th United States Infantry. Sergeant Ovila Cayer of the 14th's Company A earned himself a Medal of Honor when, in command of his regiment after the death, wounding, or capture of all its officers, he saved the regimental flag by putting it under the shirt of a private and sending him to the rear. Sergeant Cayer could not save himself. Major Culpepper managed to escape with his soldiers, three stands of colors, and about 250 prisoners, including Lieutenant White and Sergeant Cayer. Too closely pressed to bring off Capt. Samuel S. Newbury of the 12th United States Infantry as a prisoner, a Georgian officer put a pistol to the Regular's breast and mortally wounded him.

"I had Regulars—what were known as the Regular Division before I went into the battle of Gettysburg," remembered Ayres. "I left one half of them there, and buried the rest in the Wilderness."[24] Ayres memory had failed him. Many of his regulars lay along the Weldon Railroad, or, as a result of entering captivity there, in the cemeteries of Southern prison camps. Politics had precluded employing the spit and polish Regulars as non-commissioned officers among the state troops who formed the bulk of the Federal army. The professionals might have brought consistency to the haphazardly trained volunteers. Instead, the administration squandered this elite force by using it as cannon fodder.

West of the railroad, Ayres reorganized to prevent the Rebels from enveloping the rest of his division. The remainder of Hayes' brigade abandoned its breastworks and retreated about 700 yards to the cover of the artillery. The

---

24 Proceedings, Findings and Opinions of the [Warren] Court of Inquiry (Washington, DC: Government Printing Office, 1883), 389.

15th New York heavies shifted to maintain their connection with Hayes's brigade in its new position and with Hofmann's brigade, which did not move.

In the woods east of the railroad and north of Globe Tavern, chaos prevailed. Colquitt's Georgians and Clingman's North Carolinians had disintegrated in the thick brush under the weight of captives from the brigades of Bragg, Hartshorne, Coulter, Lyle and Hayes. Stragglers, fugitives and small bands of Confederates shepherding big groups of Federal prisoners floundered through the trees and swamps in the midst of the rain and the shells. Second Lieutenant A. A. McKethan of Company B in the 51st North Carolina of Clingman's brigade, wounded on June 17 remembered:

> This was a regular woods scramble, it being impossible to preserve anything like a line of battle on account of the density of the woods; the result was that we captured a large number of prisoners, and suffered considerable loss ourselves, some of our men being captured and recaptured several times.[25]

Captain M. C. House of Clingman's 8th North Carolina found himself captured and recaptured three times. During House's second captivity, a Union officer wrote down his address and handed it to the Tarheel. The Northerner said he would assist House if the North Carolinian wrote him from prison. "I lost the address," recalled House.[26]

"The men of both sides were now pretty well mixed up in the woods," remembered Second Lieutenant Dusseault of Lyle's 39th Massachusetts, a former carver hit in the lung the previous day. "Whichever squad was the larger would capture the other."[27]

While a prisoner of the 18th North Carolina with about 300 other soldiers of Lyle's brigade, Pvt. Solomon J. Hottenstine of Company C, 107th Pennsylvania, rallied his comrades, obtained the surrender of their guard, seized the colors of the Tarheels and brought them, along with the North Carolinian color bearer, within Union lines. Hottenstine later received a Medal of Honor for this feat. Colonel Lyle, to avoid capture, abandoned his horse. Lyle emerged from the woods with a command the size of a color guard.

---

25 Clark, *North Carolina Regiments*, 3:213.

26 "Capt. M. C. House, Company H, Eighth North Carolina Regiment, writes. . . ." *Confederate Veteran*, vol. 7 (1899): 217.

27 Roe, *Thirty-Ninth Massachusetts*, 248.

Rank had no privileges. "The rebels passed freely around me on every side," General Crawford recalled, "and I was in their hands but escaped almost immediately."[28]

Lieutenant Porter remembered:

> The men of the 3d Division, such of them as had not been captured, every man being for himself, turned in all directions for escape. The experience of the individual was about the experience of the whole. Now dodging behind trees, running now east, then turning west, those of this fated division that were left finally got the true direction and came out at the edge of the clearing looking towards our artillery.[29]

As Colquitt's Georgians and Clingman's Tarheels emerged from the woods into the Davis corn field herding more than their own number of prisoners up the Halifax Road toward Petersburg, the captured Federals narrowly escaped the fire of the two Confederate guns stationed on the east side of the railroad. Thinking so large an array of men in blue necessarily represented an attacking party, the artillerists prepared to open fire. A timely disclosure of the actual state of affairs prevented a misguided slaughter of the captives.

Wheelock wisely waited until the Secessionists had departed from his rear before he retreated to avoid Wainwright's shells. Cautiously, Wheelock's three remaining regiments picked their way back to the Globe Tavern clearing. During his brigade's withdrawal, it captured about sixty Southerners and liberated many Northern prisoners.[30] When Wheelock's troops emerged from the woods, Wainwright realized what had happened and ceased fire on Crawford's works. Warren ordered Griffin to make two of his brigades available. Griffin dispatched Gwyn's and Tilton's brigades from the breastworks west of the railway. The two brigades formed, marched up the Halifax Road, and massed in line of battle behind Ayres' division. Gregory's brigade extended to the right and left to occupy the vacated works.

Not until after the sound of musketry had arisen from the direction of Bragg's picket line, Bragg's pickets had tumbled in on the V Corps butchers, Colquitt's left had emerged from the trees, and Wainwright had opened fire, did Warren finally order forward Willcox's division of IX Corps. Willcox directed

---

28 *OR* 42, pt. 1, 494.

29 Porter, "Operations Against the Weldon Railroad," 259.

30 Roe, *Thirty-Ninth Massachusetts*, 252; Isaac Hall, *History of the Ninety-Seventh Regiment New York Volunteers ("Conkling rifles") in the War for the Union* (Utica NY, 1890), 219.

his First Brigade, under Brig. Gen. John F. Hartranft, to support Crawford. Hartranft had so distinguished himself at First Bull Run that he would ultimately receive a Medal of Honor for his service there. His 1,100 man brigade began with its left about 400 yards due east of Globe Tavern and advanced in the direction of the Confederate attack, which seemed 700 or 800 yards to the northeast. Hartranft's brigade encountered a line of Colquitt's troops at a distance of 150 yards near the northeast corner of the Globe Tavern clearing, where Wainwright's guns had driven the Georgians. The Georgian line extended into the corn field from the eastern edge of the woods and had a full view of the clearing. Hartranft's brigade had its left four regiments in the corn field and its right three regiments screened by a copse of woods to the east. While the regiments in the corn field engaged the Georgians, the regiments to the east advanced, met some Georgians advancing, and took fifty or sixty prisoners.[31] The Federals on the left drove the Georgians out of the corn field and into the timber at the northern edge of the clearing. Hartranft's troops advanced seventy-five to a hundred yards. The Georgians rallied in a smaller adjacent clearing and countercharged. Both battle lines blazed away at one another at a distance of about seventy-five yards for a few moments before the Georgians withdrew again.

Willcox's Second Brigade, under Col. William Humphrey, advanced in support of Hartranft's brigade. Starting out behind Hartranft, Humphrey veered far enough to his left to uncover his front and then received orders to advance again. This maneuver brought his line into contact with a force of Rebels coming out of the woods at the northern edge of the Globe Tavern clearing. Halting and opening fire at once, Humphrey's soldiers blasted the Confederates back into the woods.

Pursuant to orders from Warren to shift to the left toward Ayres' division, Willcox dispatched Humphrey in that direction. Humphrey received instructions to form his brigade in two lines, sidle farther left, charge into the woods, and recapture the works along the railroad abandoned by Ayres' troops.

Slowed by roads rendered exceedingly bad by the pouring rain, White's division of IX Corps approached from the east along the Vaughan Wagon Road. Shortly after passing the Aiken house, White heard musketry to his right and front. Dispatching a staff officer to Warren for instructions, White sent his

---

31 Report of Brig. Gen. John F. Hartranft, U.S. Army, commanding First Brigade, of operations August 19-21, in *OR* 42, pt. 1, 593.

soldiers at the double-quick in the direction of the firing. The gunfire seemed to approach rapidly. White formed his First Brigade, under Lt. Col. Joseph H. Barnes of the 29th Massachusetts, into line with its right resting on the Johnson Road, a short distance east of the Globe Tavern clearing. The staff officer sent to Warren had returned with orders for White to connect his left with the right flank of Willcox's division. Trying to accomplish this end, White marched Barnes' brigade by the left flank into the position vacated by Hartranft's soldiers. Barnes' left rested in the Lanier corn field while his right remained in the woods. Then White deployed his Second Brigade, under Lt. Col. Gilbert P. Robinson of the 3rd Maryland Infantry, on the right of Barnes' brigade. Robinson posted the 179th New York as skirmishers on his right flank stretching rearward. White led on horseback, waving his light felt hat. He called upon his troops to remember Campbell's Station and Knoxville, victories gained by IX Corps the previous autumn. His soldiers cheered.

While the IX Corps men entered the fray, Mahone reached an old saw mill in a small open field near the Risdon house, about a quarter mile west of the Vaughan farm. Swollen by rainwater, a branch ran southwardly past the saw mill. Old Porte thought the decisive moment of the battle had arrived. Colquitt's and Clingman's brigades had practically wiped out three Federal brigades and mauled two more. Globe Tavern stood in view less than half a mile away. Mahone thought that an advance the rest of the way to the tavern would bag the entire Unionist force on the Weldon Railroad. Lieutenant Colonel Stewart of the 61st Virginia in Weisiger's brigade recalled:

> . . . [W]e had now arrived at that point in the enterprise when its consummation was capable of completeness. So perfect had been the surprise, three brigades might possibly have done the work, certainly five would have effected it. . . .[32]

Old Porte at first glance found only Weisiger's brigade available for the delivery of the *coup de grace*. Mahone's attempts to scrounge up support for Weisiger's brigade accomplished little. First the Virginian met litter-bearers carrying off Clingman, who had incurred a wound that would cost him a leg and had relinquished command to Col. Hector McKethan of the 51st North Carolina, wounded himself on June 17. Mahone could not see any of McKethan's troops. Then the Virginian observed Brig. Gen. Alfred Holt

---

32 William H. Stewart, *A Pair of Blankets: War-Time History In Letters To The Young People Of The South* (New York, 1911), 172.

Colquitt on the fringe of the small clearing. Mahone rode over to Colquitt, a Princeton graduate, lawyer, and Mexican War veteran. Old Porte asked the Georgian what had happened to the rest of his brigade. Colquitt pointed to a small body of about 150 of his men. "These are all I have left," he said.[33]

The indomitable Mahone did not give up. He sent two staff officers and a courier to contact Hill, who had remained with Heth. Old Porte wanted Hill to order Heth to extend his left, connect with Weisiger's right and press the enemy immediately in Heth's front. Mahone does not appear to have realized that this would have thinned Heth's two brigades to ineffectiveness—they already covered a front of almost two divisions.

One after the other, the two staff officers took a short road to the right. The second, Capt. William Norborne Starke, Hill's Assistant Adjutant General, who had studied at the University of Virginia, followed the customary short distance behind the first, Capt. R. P. Duncan, Mahone's Assistant Adjutant General, an attorney who had also studied at the University of Virginia. This road took them over the ground that Mahone's force had just crossed. Though by this time most of Clingman's and Colquitt's soldiers bringing off the Unionist prisoners had reentered the Confederate lines to the north, many stragglers and fugitives of both sides still roamed the woods. A squad of Northern fugitives captured Duncan. Starke saw his colleague captured, rallied a few Southern stragglers, and in turn captured the Federals, thus releasing Duncan. Moments later, another group of Unionists captured this whole party and took it with them through the rear of Weisiger's brigade toward Federal lines. Old Porte observed this, put himself at the head of a group of his soldiers and rushed on the Northerners. Mahone captured them and freed the Rebel staffers and stragglers.

Still under artillery fire from the front and left, Old Porte directed Weisiger's brigade to form and charge the enemy's works to the left, by Globe Tavern. Mahone's courier returned. The courier, Pvt. Robert Randolph Henry, formerly of the 12th Virginia Infantry's Company E, the Petersburg Riflemen, had taken a cart path farther east than the route taken by the staff officers. Henry quickly got lost in the dense thicket almost impossible to penetrate on horseback. Soon he reached the clearing around the Lanier house. No more than 150 yards away he saw two limbered batteries of Northern artillery, followed by infantry and a train of ambulances—the head of White's division of

---

33 Newsome, Horn, and Selby, eds., *Civil War Talks*, 266.

IX Corps, floundering westward from the Jerusalem Plank Road to the rescue of V Corps. Turning back to avoid capture, Henry retreated to a sharp turn in the path about 100 yards from where he had left Mahone. At the turn, Henry found himself face to face with two Federal horsemen, one of them Col. William Ross Hartshorne, wounded and captured during the Seven Days. Drawing a revolver captured at the Crater and not in working order, Henry bluffed the bewildered Unionists into surrendering and delivered them to Old Porte. Mahone dispatched Colquitt's remaining Georgians to reinforce Weisiger and set out himself to find Hill.

Weisiger's Virginians double-quicked toward the Federal battery shelling them. The "Kid Glove Boys," as one of their members had called them for their spit and polish during their march through Richmond to Seven Pines in 1862, hastened to another branch a quarter mile beyond the Risdon saw mill, into ground cleared of Georgians by Hartranft's brigade.[34] Weisiger halted when he saw Hartranft's brigade ahead in the northeast corner of the Globe Tavern clearing. The Virginian did not want to walk into a trap. Weisiger's former regiment, the 12th Virginia, called the Petersburg Regiment because six of its ten companies haled from the Cockade City, faced west and formed the brigade's right.[35] Also facing west on the left of the 12th stood the 41st Virginia, the deceased General Chambliss' first regiment, then the 61st Virginia, followed by the 16th Virginia, and finally the 6th Virginia. The troops stood in the branch up to their knees in the cold water.

The Virginians shifted southward 100 or 200 yards along the branch and then eastward as it curved around an elbow. Their line came to form a lopsided U. The 12th and the right of the 41st, a total of fifteen companies, still faced west. The left of the 41st and Company A of the 61st in the elbow, a total of six companies, faced south in a thicket of burnt pines. The rest of the 61st, together with the 16th (which had just eight companies instead of the usual ten) and the 6th, a total of twenty-seven companies, bent around to face east. Only about 75 yards separated the backs of the Virginians at the tips of their formation.

---

34 Letter. Alexander Whitworth Archer to George S. Bernard, November 29, 1893, George S. Bernard Papers, Southern Historical Collection, Wilson Library, University of North Carolina at Chapel Hill, Chapel Hill, North Carolina.

35 Letter, William Mahone to Francis H. Smith, May 8, 1861, William Mahone Papers, Preston Library, Virginia Military Institute, Lexington, Virginia; Letter, James E. Whitehorne to Sister, June 9, 1861, James E. Whitehorne Papers, Virginia State Library, Richmond, Virginia.

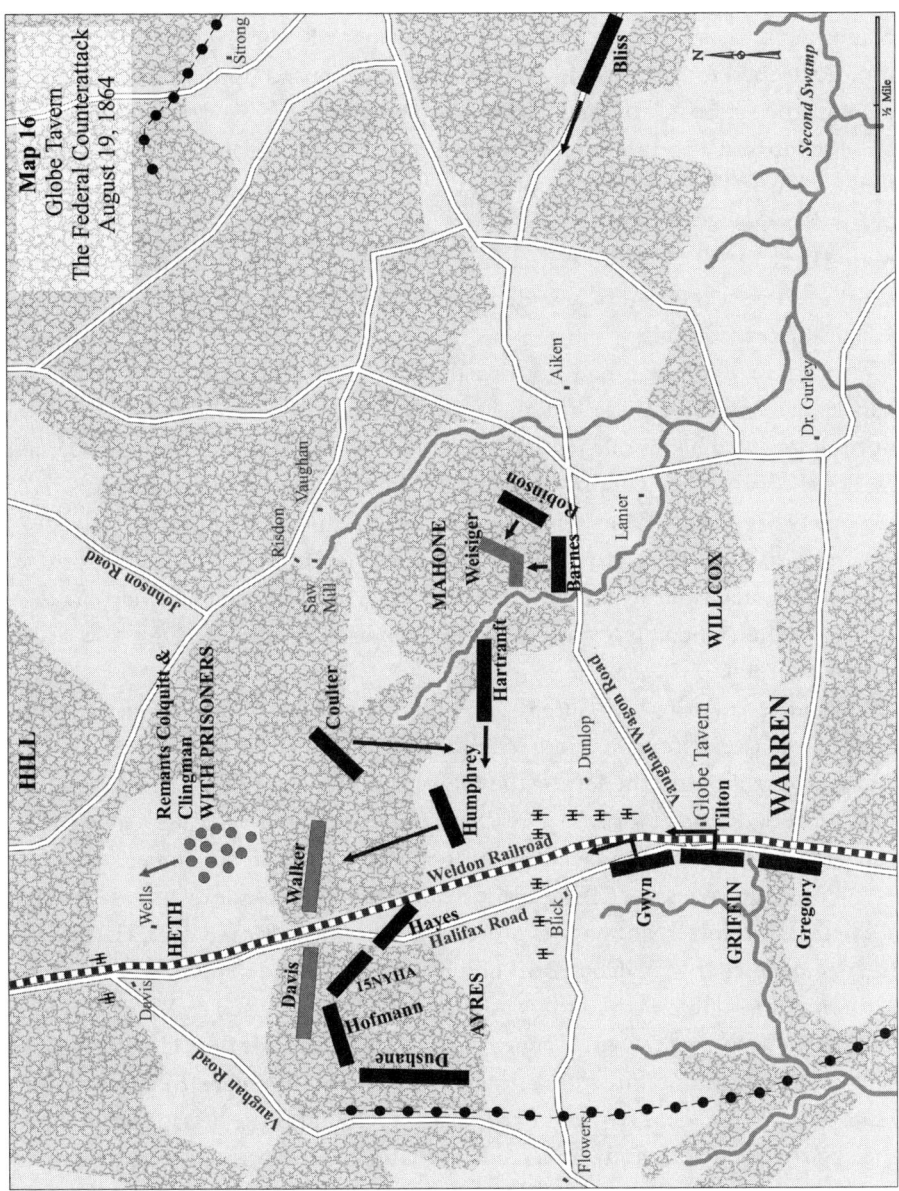

A hundred yards behind the 12th stood a body of second growth pines. On the west and south banks of the branch lay slightly rising ground. The Petersburg Regiment and the left of the 41st Virginia could see Hartranft's line of battle not more than 150 yards to their right and front, facing north. First

Sergeant Thomas Emmet Richardson of Company K, the Archer Rifles, an iron molder, leaped to the west side of the ditch and started up the slope.

"Come on boys," he said. "They are Yankees! Let's charge 'em."[36]

Richardson's comrades doubted that the soldiers in front of them belonged to the enemy. The Virginians thought the troops ahead too quiet for Unionists, given that they must have known of the presence of Weisiger's brigade in their rear. The 12th Virginia did not charge. A group of Colquitt's Georgians filed southward past the Petersburg Regiment. Weisiger put the Georgians on the left of the 6th Virginia.

Hartranft's soldiers had no idea that Weisiger's brigade stood poised to attack them from behind. "Much of the fighting was in thick woods and we never knew which was our front or rear until attacked, as the Johnnies seemed to come from all directions," recalled Orderly Sergeant Howard Aston of Company F, 13th Ohio Cavalry (dismounted) in Hartranft's brigade.[37] Discharged from the 97th Ohio Infantry in March, 1863, for heart disease, Aston had reenlisted in the 5th Independent Battalion Ohio Cavalry in July, 1863, and then when his term of enlistment expired, in the 13th Ohio Cavalry in February, 1864.

Minutes later the 12th Virginia and the right of the 41st received orders to about face. These troops crept back to the edge of the pines east of the branch and took position on the left of the Georgians. The line of Weisiger's brigade had morphed into a rough J. Six companies faced south and more than forty-two bent around to face east. None faced Hartranft's Federals.

Now that Weisiger's Virginians had turned their backs on Hartranft's soldiers, Hartranft might have captured the Kid Glove Boys with a charge into their unprotected rear if he had known that his brigade stood behind them. Orders from Willcox spared the Virginians this fate. Advised by Warren that he still expected the main Confederate effort to come west of the railroad, Willcox sent Hartranft in that direction and away from the Virginians to connect with Humphrey's brigade. Hartranft's troops sidled left about a brigade front along the edge of the woods and connected with Humphrey's brigade, which plodded into the woods without connection to its left and opened a gap between its right

---

36 Newsome, Horn, and Selby, eds., *Civil War Talks*, 271.

37 Howard Aston, *History and Roster of the Fourth and Fifth Independent Battalions and Thirteenth Regiment Ohio Cavalry Volunteers Their Battles Skirmishes Rosters of the Dead etc.* (Columbus OH, 1902), 81.

and Hartranft's brigade. Before Hartranft's brigade could advance on Humphrey's right, fighting broke out again near the northeastern corner of the Globe Tavern clearing. Warren dispatched Hartranft's brigade to White's assistance.

Hardly had the 12th Virginia and the right of the 41st taken position on the left of the Georgians in Weisiger's formation when White's division received orders to advance. Robinson's brigade of White's division appeared in the pines about 150 yards east of the 12th Virginia and the right of the 41st and immediately opened fire. The Kid Glove Boys lay down and returned fire. Through the gloom they could see nothing but the flash of the foe's rifles, occasionally a man's figure.

Barnes' brigade of White's division started shooting from the south. Weisiger's force took bullets not only from its front, but from its right flank. Barnes' brigade struggled with the Georgians from Colquitt's brigade as well as the part of Weisiger's brigade on the southern fringe of the Globe Tavern clearing. Robinson's brigade continued blasting away from the east. Despite the unnerving Federal crossfire, the Secessionists remained full of fight. They repeatedly charged the Unionists through the dense underbrush. Veterans of the 35th Massachusetts in Barnes' brigade recalled:

> Kneeling in the mud, the word was, "Fire, and give them hell!" and at it we went, firing and loading as rapidly as nimble fingers could. The only command of the officers was, "Fire low, men, fire low!" and the carnage was deadly.
>
> As soon as our line of fire became distinct, the artillery in rear opened, throwing shells so closely to our heads that the boys asserted they cut the tops of the corn stalks....[38]

Officers picked up the rifles of the wounded and added to the hail of bullets.

General White posted the 57th Massachusetts of Barnes' brigade in an exposed and unsupported position. First Sergeant Edward F. Potter of Company K, discharged for disability from the 10th Massachusetts before he joined the 57th, took up his position as left general guide. Before the 57th could form line, the Confederates charged and drove the regiment back. Potter remained at his post amid a shower of bullets that killed the right general guide.

---

38 Committee of the Regimental Association, *History of the Thirty-Fifth Regiment Massachusetts Volunteers, 1862-1865* (Boston, 1884), 285-6.

White rode up and exclaimed to First Lt. Albert Doty, the regimental commander that day: "What the hell is that damned fool doing out there? Who in hell is he?"

"That, sir, is my left general guide, posted by your order, which he obeys," replied Doty. A student at Williams College when hostilities commenced, Doty had enlisted in a New York regiment and then, upon the expiration of his enlistment, in the 57th Massachusetts.

"Doesn't that darned fool know enough when to come in?" asked White.

"That man always obeys orders and will stand there until shot, unless relieved by proper authority."

"Well, relieve him mighty quick."[39]

Doty complied with White's order and spared Potter a wound, captivity, or death.

Most of the Virginians lost their bayonets in these charges, which rendered them liable for a fine in Mahone's division. Casualties mounted fast. For at least twelve feet on each side of the 12th Virginia's colors, every man of the color guard fell killed or wounded except Color Sgt. William Crawford Smith of Company B, the Petersburg Old Grays, a builder who had returned to Petersburg from Tennessee to enlist in 1861 and had suffered wounds at Crampton's Gap and in the Wilderness, and Pvt. Henry Van Leuvenigh "Birdie" Bird of Company C, the Petersburg New Grays, a clerk in a dry goods store sufficiently educated to quote medieval French in his letters to his sweetheart back in the Cockade City.

Things looked bleak for Weisiger's command. Ammunition ran low. The Rebels lay down, determined to wait until the enemy closed with them, and then to use the butts of their muskets on the Northerners. "We had all made up our minds not to be captured as we knew well enough that Mahone men neither asked nor gave quarter," Bird recalled.[40] Less than three weeks earlier, at the battle of the Crater, the Mahone men had given the African-Americans of IX Corps no quarter until Old Porte had sickened of the slaughter.

White's division did not charge but poured in a devastating fire from eighty yards away. White's soldiers seemed to surround the Virginians and Georgians

---

39 John Anderson, *The Fifty-Seventh Regiment of Massachusetts Volunteers in the War of the Rebellion, Army of the Potomac* (Boston, 1896), 407-8.

40 Letter, Bird to Randolph, August 20, 1864, Henry Van Leuvenigh Bird Letters, Bird Family Papers, Virginia Historical Society, Richmond, Virginia.

completely. Color Sergeant Smith stripped the colors of the Petersburg Regiment from the staff and hid them in a haversack to save them from capture. Weisiger recognized the danger. Standing on the left of his line, he gave his horse to his Adjutant, Capt. Hugh Ritchie Smith, the color bearer's brother, and dispatched Captain Smith to inform Mahone that the Federals threatened to surround Weisiger's force. On the way, Smith met Henry, who carried an order from Mahone to withdraw. Unable to obtain reinforcements, satisfied that Colquitt's Georgians and Clingman's North Carolinians had brought off their prisoners, Mahone wanted the remainder of his troops to retreat.

The firing of the Federals slowed. Weisiger took advantage of this lull. He directed his troops to fall back about seventy-five to a hundred yards to a smaller clearing. On the formation's left, the 12th Virginia had to withdraw only a few paces. Near the bottom of the J formed by Weisiger's brigade and the group of Georgians from Colquitt's brigade, Col. Virginius Groner of the 61st had farther to withdraw and far more difficulty covering the ground. A courier who had carried the order to fire on Fort Sumter, he had suffered wounds at Chancellorsville and Spotsylvania. That very day he had returned from the furlough for his Spotsylvania wound, though still on crutches, to lead his regiment into action. To deal with the marshy ground, he reversed the crutches, putting the pointed ends under his arms and the cushioned ends on the ground. The Mahone men and the Georgians who followed them reformed their lines. Bliss' brigade of Potter's IX Corps division arrived at the Aiken house, relieving the 179th New York of Robinson's brigade.

The firing briefly returned to its former pitch as White's soldiers converged on Weisiger's force. Both battle lines blazed away at one another at a distance of about seventy-five yards for a few moments before the Secessionists withdrew another 200 yards and broke contact with the foe. Mahone arrived without reinforcements and repeated his order to Weisiger to retreat. Their troops began marching briskly northward out of the Union vise. "It was 'no time to swap jack knives,'" remembered Private Bird.[41] Weisiger's troops retreated to the Johnson farm. Some Georgians and some members of the 41st Virginia's right remained behind in the confusion, and the Federals took about sixty of them prisoner.[42] A captain captured by the 29th Massachusetts had fought that

---

41 Ibid.

42 Report of Brig. Gen. Julius White, U.S. Army, commanding First Division, of operations August 19-20, in OR 42, pt. 1, 550.

regiment at Big Bethel in 1861. The Southerners also left behind their dead and badly wounded as well as 516 stand of small arms, about 200 of Confederate issue.[43] A Rebel flag of truce to inform the attendants left behind with the wounded to surrender delayed Unionist pursuit. Contrary to Bird's fears, the IX Corps soldiers treated the Mahone men with every courtesy.

Ordered back to the right in support of White's division, Hartranft's brigade hiked along the edge of the woods until its right arrived about seventy-five yards from White's left. White's soldiers did not appear to require any assistance. Hartranft's troops prepared to advance into the trees north of the Globe Tavern clearing. Crawford's division reformed with the right of the remnant of Coulter's brigade at the Dunlop house, about 100 yards to the left of Hartranft's brigade. Crawford placed Lyle's survivors to the left of Coulter's remnant. Scarcely a third of the strength with which Crawford's division had begun the day remained. Even Coulter's brigade had lost half its soldiers. Crawford did not even mention Hartshorne's brigade. It no longer existed.

Near the railway, Humphrey's brigade advanced cautiously until it approached the works occupied by the thin line of Walker's brigade. Humphrey ordered a charge at the double-quick. Without halting to fire, his Federals surprised Walker's troops and threw the Rebels into a panic. Humphrey's troops took the breastworks, the colors of the 47th Virginia, and 100 prisoners. Sergeant Charles E. Brown of Company C, 50th Pennsylvania, received a Medal of Honor for capturing the colors.

About an hour later, toward dusk, elements of V corps plodded up and retook the empty works on both sides of Humphrey's brigade. To Humphrey's left, the remnant of Hayes' brigade occupied the rifle-pits that it had abandoned a few hours earlier. Several hundred yards to Humphrey's rear, Gwyn's brigade of Griffin's division returned to its former position. Tilton's brigade remained with its left on the railroad in support of Ayres' division. The remnant of Crawford's division occupied the works on the right of Humphrey's brigade. Hartranft's brigade tramped forward on the right of Crawford's division. Bliss' brigade advanced from the Aiken house. The failure of White's division to advance opened up a potentially dangerous gap between Hartranft and Bliss. White's division did not advance and close the gap until night had fallen.

About ten minutes after the survivors of V Corps and Hartranft's brigade joined Humphrey's soldiers in the works, Heth's troops began feeling the

---

43 Ibid.

Federal position. Twice the Confederates probed the Union line. Twice the Unionists drove off the Rebels. By the end of the second Southern push, Hayes' brigade had grown so tired that Colonel Winthrop called for reinforcements. Drawing upon the reserve provided by Tilton's brigade, Ayres sent the 187th Pennsylvania. The Keystoners took position on the right of the 5th New York and assisted in seeing off a third and last Secessionist thrust, again relieving from danger Battery C, 1st Massachusetts Light Artillery. By 8:30 p.m., quiet reigned. The remainder of Tilton's brigade came up and took over from Hayes' brigade the line that it held to the right of the railroad. The 140th and 146th New York of Hayes' brigade still held the front line to the left of the roadbed.

West of the railroad and south of Globe Tavern, Dearing's cavalry probed Spear's vidette line. Spear learned from a prisoner that a Rebel cavalry brigade occupied the Vaughan Road in his front. Strengthening his outposts, Spear prepared for a reconnaissance in force at daylight.

Hill directed Colquitt's and Clingman's disorganized troops back to their original camps as rallying points. He ordered Weisiger's brigade inside the Petersburg lines. The Virginians occupied once more their old position on the Wilcox farm. Private George Smith Bernard of the Petersburg Riflemen, a lawyer educated at the University of Virginia who had rejoined the 12th Virginia in 1862 after receiving a discharge for illness the previous year, described his regiment and brigade as "pretty well fagged out after the evening's expedition."[44] Morale remained high. "What our Div. can't do—*can't be done*," remembered Private Bird.[45] Later he added, "I feel much better satisfied when our Division is engaged because I know that it is in good hands and will go farther and do more than any other division."[46]

Leaving Heth's two brigades on the Weldon Railroad, Hill instructed Rooney Lee to head down to the Davis house at 3:00 a.m. Hill thought that this would put the Confederates in position to push the Federals in the morning if Hill could obtain more troops. "The indications are that the enemy are leaving," Hill wrote to Beauregard at 10:00 p.m. Hill expressed regret that the weakness of his force prevented him from following up on the severe blow he knew that he had struck.

---

44 George S. Bernard Papers, Southern Historical Collection.

45 Letter, Bird to Randolph, August 20, 1864, Bird Family Papers.

46 Letter, Bird to Randolph, September 8, 1864, Bird Family Papers.

Warren did not realize the extent of the damage that had befallen his corps. His dispatches to Meade that night unintentionally misled the Army of the Potomac's leader about the condition of the Union forces on the Weldon Railroad. Though Warren mentioned that he had lost very considerably in prisoners, Meade had no reason to expect that the number of prisoners would prove extraordinary—practically a whole division. Meade focused primarily on Warren's report of repulsing the Rebels and regaining the position. The affair appeared an unequivocal victory. As a result, the commander of the Army of the Potomac declined Grant's suggestion that Meade send Mott's division of II Corps to Warren. Meade even began prodding Warren to attack the Secessionists in the morning, before they could draw reinforcements from north of James River. Warren, whose awareness that something awful had happened to his troops grew with each moment, hedged: "I have given orders to advance at daylight in every direction and will govern my movement according to the developments under your sanction where it is practicable."[47]

The Northern forces under Warren on the Weldon Railroad had lost about 3,000 men, including an astonishing 2,700 prisoners in addition to seven flags.[48] The Southerners had lost fewer than 600 soldiers, including around 300 prisoners.[49] "We did not do but little fighting: we got badly scattered,"

---

47 *OR* 42, pt. 2, 310.

48 Ibid., pt. 1, 430; Reports of Lieut. Gen. Ambrose P. Hill, C.S. Army, commanding Third Army Corps, of operations August 19-25, in ibid., 940.

49 "No return has yet been made of our losses, but it is not believed that they will exceed 600 men." From P. W. A., the correspondent of the Savannah *Republican* in Macon *Daily Telegraph*, August 27, 1864, p. 2, col. 4.
   Davis' brigade of Heth's division lost 63 killed, wounded and missing on August 19. Petersburg *Daily Register*, August 22, 1864, p. 2, col. 3; ibid., August 25, 1864, p. 1, col 6.
   The 55th Virginia of Walker's brigade of Heth's division lost two killed, thirteen wounded and one missing on August 18 and 19, and the 40th Virginia lost three killed, fifteen wounded and one missing on those days. Richmond *Enquirer*, September 2, 1864, p. 2, col. 3-4. The 47th Virginia lost one killed, eight wounded and seven missing on August 19. Richmond *Examiner*, September 7, 1864, p. 1, col. 4. The 2nd Maryland Battalion lost five killed, thirty-five wounded and thirty-eight missing during the battle of Globe Tavern, but it lost most of its prisoners during a picket affair on August 20. Richmond *Examiner*, Aug. 24, 1864, p. 1, col. 4; W. W. Goldsborough, The *Maryland Line in the Confederate Army, 1861-1865* (Baltimore, 1900), 183-4. Walker's brigade also contained the 22nd Virginia Battalion, the 1st, 7th and 14th Tennessee, and the 13th Alabama, which probably lost proportionately on August 19.
   The 6th Virginia of Weisiger's brigade lost three wounded and six missing. Richmond *Daily Dispatch*, August 24, 1864, p. 1, col. 2. The 12th Virginia lost six killed, twenty-seven wounded and four missing for a total of thirty-seven of ninety-four carried into action, and the 41st Virginia lost five killed, twelve wounded, and eighteen missing. Petersburg *Daily Register*,

remembered Capt. Washington L. Dunn of the 27th Georgia in Colquitt's brigade. "I do not think there were many killed on either side."[50] Outnumbered by at least fifteen brigades to five in infantry, and even more disproportionately in artillery, the Confederates had performed one of the war's most amazing feats of arms despite their failure to attain their objective—knocking the Unionists off the Weldon Railroad.

Until the end of his life, Mahone believed that with two or three more brigades of infantry at his disposal, he would have bagged the entire V Corps and driven the Federals off the railway. "With the force of a division at his command no doubt he would have captured Warren and all of his people and repossessed the Weldon Railroad," remembered Lieutenant Colonel Stewart.[51] Beauregard's enemies in the administration joined in the criticism of the Louisianan for attacking with insufficient force. Lee came to the defense of Beauregard and ascribed the failure to the scarcity of troops. The facts justified Lee. Two days later the personification of audacity itself would dare leave no fewer troops in the Petersburg fortifications than Beauregard had on August 18 and 19.

Against the five Rebel brigades involved, the Federal counterattack did not even employ all of Warren's reserves. Only a single regiment of Griffin's

---

August 22, 1864, p. 2, col. 2-3. The 16th Virginia lost twenty-one killed, and twenty-two wounded. Richmond *Enquirer*, September 2, 1864, p. 2, col. 3-4. The 61st Virginia lost about seventy-seven killed, wounded and missing of fewer than 200 men carried into action. Stewart, *A Pair of Blankets*, 175; Charles R. McAlpine, "Sketch of Company I, 61st Virginia Infantry, Mahone's brigade, C. S. A." in *SHSP*, vol. 24 (1896), 103. George S. Bernard put the brigade's loss at 187 out of more than 500 muskets carried into action. George S. Bernard Papers, Southern Historical Collection.

Company B, 2nd Georgia, of Colquitt's Brigade, lost one killed, two wounded and eight missing on August 19. Macon *Daily Telegraph*, August 26, 1864, p. 2, col. 2. Company C, 6th Georgia, lost one killed and one prisoner. Wendell D. Croom, *The War History of Company 'C', (Beauregard Volunteers) Sixth Georgia Regiment, (Infantry)* (Fort Valley GA, 1879), 26. The 23rd Georgia lost six wounded out of 250 rifles. *Southern Watchman* (Athens, GA), September 7, 1864, p. 2, col. 3. The 27th Georgia suffered 57 casualties on August 18 and 19. Washington L. Dunn Diary, August 20, 1864, United Daughters of the Confederacy Collection, Georgia Department of Archives and History, Atlanta, Georgia.

Bragg claimed to have taken fifty-seven prisoners. OR 42, pt. 1, 536. White reported taking sixty prisoners. Ibid., 550. Hartranft claimed fifty or sixty prisoners. Ibid., 593. Humphrey reported 100 prisoners. Ibid., 595. Coulter's brigade may have taken as many as sixty prisoners. Hall, *Ninety-seventh New York*, 220.

50 Washington L. Dunn Diary, August 19, 1864.

51 Stewart, *A Pair of Blankets*, 175.

three-brigade division became engaged on August 19, and Bliss' brigade of Potter's division arrived just as Mahone began to withdraw. Given the damage Mahone did with a mere three brigades, he would have required at least two more to have had a decent chance of accomplishing his mission. Four more would have had a much better likelihood of doing the job. Beauregard could not give Mahone such a force because the Louisianan did not have the troops to spare.

Grant and Meade shared much of the responsibility for the disaster on the Union side. Sherman had not captured Atlanta, which left it up to Grant and Meade to seize Richmond. They had ordered Warren to maintain his hold on the railroad at all hazards, to extend to connect with IX Corps if practicable, and to push the enemy back nearer his own lines. "These were too many conditions to impose upon him on ground of the character he was operating in," Humphreys recalled. "Informed of the general object he was to accomplish, everything else as far as possible should have been left to his judgement." The requirement that V Corps entrench as close up to the Confederate works as possible had contributed most to the catastrophe, concluded Humphreys:

> The necessity of remaining stationary, even a single day, in a dense wood like that in which the greater part of General Warren's troops were posted, subjects a command to having some part of it taken in flank or rear, broken, thrown into confusion, and many of them captured. [52]

Some of the responsibility for the disaster rested upon Warren. If initially he had specified in writing the desired location of Bragg's line, or supplied his subordinates with the map such as the one drawn for Meade on the evening of August 18, the V Corps chief would have eliminated the possibility of the misunderstanding that arose. Properly positioned, recalled Lt. Col. William H. Powell of the 11th United States Infantry in Hayes' brigade, Bragg's soldiers might have given Crawford and Ayres more "time to prepare to meet the emergencies of the occasion" and prevented the catastrophe.[53]

The Unionist reaction to the piercing of Bragg's skirmish line east of the Vaughan farm suggests that the source of trouble lay more in the quickness and

---

52 Andrew A. Humphreys, *The Virginia Campaign of '64 and '65: the Army of the Potomac and the Army of the James,* (New York: 1963), 276, note 1.

53 William H. Powell, *The Fifth Army Corps (Army of the Potomac) A Record of Operations during the Civil War in the United States of American, 1861-1865* (New York, 1896), 716n.

strength of the response to a penetration of the picket line than in the position of the pickets. Nobody but Lyman seems to have noticed the breaking of Bragg's vidette line. Crawford eventually reacted, but Bragg had just seventy-four members of the 6th Wisconsin to close the gap—an impossible task. Colonel Wheelock had a theoretical chance to turn to face Mahone's oncoming battle array because no Confederates tied down Coulter's brigade from in front. Infantry attacks to the right and left and cannon fire from the rear kept that chance in the realm of the theoretical.

Warren reacted far too slowly to the Confederate breakthrough. Had he committed Willcox's division when Bragg's pickets disrupted the V Corps butchers, he might have spared Coulter's, Lyle's and Hayes' brigades their ordeals. Had the V Corps leader ordered Willcox to advance when Colquitt's Georgians emerged from the woods north of the Globe Tavern clearing, he might have averted disaster for Lyle and Hayes. Instead, Warren's dilatory response helped maximize the damage inflicted by Colquitt's and Clingman's brigades. If Mahone had dispatched Weisiger's brigade along the same axis, Old Porte might have devastated not only Crawford's division but Ayres' division as well.

The V Corps chief also failed to create sufficient reserves. He had at hand to deal with Mahone's attack only Willcox's exhausted, depleted division. Warren had that reserve as the result of the efforts of Meade and Humphreys, not his own. Everyone else in Warren's command, except for the seventy-four men of the 6th Wisconsin, stood on a skirmish line or occupied breastworks. The V Corps leader forewent the opportunity to increase the size of his reserve by relieving Griffin's more than 3,000 men in three brigades with Willcox's smaller, tired division. Warren needed as large and rested a reserve as possible to defend the enormous perimeter demarcated by his prodigious picket line, which he had posted so far afield that none charged with supporting it could hear its fire—making defense practically impossible. Griffin's division remained in its works because the enemy's movement led the V Corps chief to expect an attack on his left instead of his right.

Lyman's comments suggested that Warren ought to have refused, entrenched and slashed on his right as he had on his left, employing Bragg's brigade in line of battle behind Hartshorne's pickets and at right angles to Coulter's brigade. Then Bragg's troops would have protected Crawford's right as Dushane's brigade protected the left of Ayres' division—by entrenching a return. Humphreys ratified Lyman's assessment on October 1, 1864, when Warren's corps again held a position where its right failed to connect with the main body of the Army of the Potomac. Humphreys directed Warren to refuse his right. This thwarted an attempt by Heth to repeat Mahone's flanking maneuver of August 19.[54]

Refusing his right on August 19 could not have guaranteed that Warren would avoid the disaster which occurred that day. A refused left on June 22 had not saved David Birney and II Corps from a similar rout at Mahone's hands—Old Porte simply overlapped Birney's left and then rolled up II Corps. A refused right on August 19 just represented what Brig. Gen. Edward Porter Alexander would have called "the safest game" in the situation that Grant and Meade had put Warren that day.[55] Mahone might well have overlapped a refused right on August 19—he attacked in the same formation as on June 22, with his former brigade (Weisiger's) in reserve and available to outflank the foe. The refused Federal right of October 1 may have withstood A. P. Hill's assault of that day because he and Heth failed to fnd the weak spot farther east where only a picket line connected Warren to the rest of the Army of the Potomac. Humphreys probably hit the nail on the head about August 19 when he wrote that Grant ought to have allowed Warren to stay out of the woods north of Globe Tavern and fight his own battle—something the V Corps commander would soon do quite successfully.

Crawford and Bragg also shared responsibility for the fiasco. Bragg did as little as possible, anchoring his right at the Strong house, three quarters of a mile south of where Warren desired it. Crawford acquiesced in Bragg's recalcitrance rather than insist that the skirmish line angle northeast as ordered.

Meade and Humphreys may have saved V Corps by the way they shifted the reserve of XVIII Corps to free Wilcox's division of IX Corps to reach Warren many hours before relief by Mott's division of II Corps would have permitted. Otherwise, Willcox's division would not have arrived before the division of General White. Willcox's division may not have provided much of a reserve, but without it Warren would have had virtually no reserve. Without Hartranft's brigade in its path, Weisiger's force might well have charged all the way to Globe Tavern before Griffin pulled Tilton's and Gwyn's brigades out of the breastworks west of the railroad. No one can predict the effect of enemy

---

54 Richard J. Sommers, *Richmond Redeemed: The Siege at Petersburg* (Garden City NY, 1981), 315; Horn, *The Petersburg Campaign*, 166.

55 Gary Gallagher, ed., *Fighting for the Confederacy: The Personal Recollections of General Edward Porter Alexander* (Chapel Hill, 1989), 276.

soldiers popping up unexpectedly in the rear. Few have the sang-froid of a Wheelock.

On the night of August 19, it seemed to Lieutenant Porter of Lyle's 39th Massachusetts—unaware of Beauregard's mistaken critics and the disappointed Mahone—that "all was joy" among the Southerners in Petersburg.[56] Little joy existed among the Federals, though they remained in possession of the railway and technically qualified as victors—Pyrrhic victors. Even Lee's Miserables could win a war of attrition if they inflicted five casualties for every one they suffered as they had this day. The 50th Pennsylvania of Humphrey's brigade lay in pits full of water that night to avoid Rebel fire. To the right of Humphrey's brigade, according to Porter, "But few slept that night, and the weary hours rolled on and it seemed as if daylight would never come to bring relief to the suspense and dread that hung over the command that night."[57] Farther right, Captain Isaac Hall of Company A, 97th New York, recalled, "The ground was low and somewhat swampy, a drizzling rain set in, and to keep themselves out of the water, many cut small poles and lay upon them during the night."[58] The 35th Massachusetts of White's division, still farther right, occupied higher ground and according to its veterans enjoyed a measure of luxury mixed with the overall misery:

> Upon corn-stalk beds, the men got such sleep as the care of watching and the dripping rain allowed. During the night all was still except the groans and cries of the Confederate wounded in the dark forest, who had to wait until daylight before they could be moved.[59]

Of the rank and file, perhaps only the Federal artillerymen slept well—on their big, comfortable gun platforms.

The decisive day of the battle neared.

---

56 Porter, "Operations Against the Weldon Railroad," 259.

57 Ibid.

58 Price, *Ninety-seventh New York*, 220.

59 Committee, *Thirty-Fifth Massachusetts*, 287.

Chapter 8

The Battle of Globe Tavern, August 20, 1864

 fighting took place on August 20, and for that very reason this day proved decisive for the battle of Globe Tavern.

On the night of August 19, Gus Beauregard and Hill began to organize another attack for the next day. Things went wrong almost immediately.

At 9:00 p.m., Brig. Gen. Johnson Hagood received orders to turn over command of his brigade of Hoke's division to the senior officer present and report to Hill. The Third Corps leader directed Hagood, a graduate of The Citadel and a member of the South Carolina bar, to take command of a brigade of Maj. Gen. Bushrod Johnson's division near the Lead Works, where the Halifax Road and the Weldon Railroad passed southward through the fortifications of Petersburg, and prepare to participate in the renewal of the fight on August 20.

General Johnson, whose division held the line between the Appomattox and Hoke's division, habitually kept one regiment from each of his four brigades resting behind his lines. Instead of sending an established brigade to the rendezvous near the Lead Works, Johnson sent the four individual regiments in reserve at that time. Johnson's regiments began arriving at about 11:30 p.m, and Hagood required until 3:00 a.m. on August 20 to organize the four regiments into the semblance of a brigade. Haphazardly appointing an acting staff, Hagood learned only the names of his staff officers and of his regimental commanders. Darkness prevented him from learning their faces.

Gen. Pierre Gustave Toutant Beauregard, C.S.A. *Library of Congress*

After imposing this minimal degree of organization, Hagood reported to Hill. The South Carolinian found the lieutenant general asleep in his nearby ambulance. Hagood remembered, "When General Hill learned the heterogenous character of the brigade sent him, he, much to Hagood's relief, declined to receive it, and directed the regiments returned to their division."[1]

---

1   Johnson Hagood, *Memoirs of the War of Secession* (Columbia SC, 1909), 288-9.

Hill's rejection of this provisional brigade contrasted with Field's acceptance of a similarly constituted brigade from Pickett's division on the evening of the 16th north of James River, but Hill needed soldiers capable of an attack whereas Field required troops capable only of defense—universally acknowledged as an easier task. By not using the force at hand, Hill gave the Federals another day to dig in and erect breastworks, which would make evicting them from the Weldon Road much more difficult—if not impossible.

Once a soldier dug in, it became very hard to remove him from his position. Attacks against earthworks rarely succeeded. The storming of the Bloody Angle at Spotsylvania on May 12, 1864, had resulted from a freakish chain of events that included the withdrawal of supporting Confederate artillery and a mist that hid the approaching Unionists. The breach in Girardey's line on August 16 above Fussell's mill pond had occurred where only fifty yards of slashing protected the Confederate fortifications, filled with only a single rank of troops.[2]

After Hagood's abortive mission to Hill, the Secessionist effort to concentrate for another attack on the railroad continued to go awry. Rooney Lee's division of horsemen, ordered to leave Petersburg for the Davis house, ended up north of the Appomattox at Swift Creek.

Shortly after dawn, the Southerners began felling timber beyond the Vaughan Road to prepare artillery placements. Before 8:15 a.m., Beauregard and Hill knew that, contrary to the expectations of the previous night, the Unionists had not only remained on the railroad, but had continued to fortify. The morning passed without any further Southern efforts to make the necessary arrangements to dislodge Warren on August 20. The last soldiers of Harris' detachment of Mahone's division arrived from north of James River and filed into the Dimmock line near the Branch house south of Petersburg.

---

2 One could say of Civil War fortifications, as the Wehrmacht's Maj. Gen. F. W. von Mellenthin, a former staff officer of Field Marshal Erwin Rommel, said of Soviet bridgeheads: "If a bridgehead is forming, or an advanced position is being established by the Russians, attack, attack at once, attack strongly. Hesitation will always be fatal. A delay of an hour may mean frustration, a delay of a few hours does mean frustration, a delay of a day may mean a major catastrophe. Even if there is no more than one infantry platoon and one single tank available, attack! Attack when the Russians are still above ground, when they can still be seen and tackled, when they have had no time as yet to organize their defense, when there are no heavy weapons available. A few hours later will be too late. Delay means disaster: resolute energetic and immediate action means success." Maj. Gen. F. W. von Mellenthin, *Panzer Battles: A Study of the Employment of Armor in the Second World War* (New York, 1971), 223.

"The journey was disagreeable as twas rainy & muddy," remembered Master Sergeant Fielding of the 9th Alabama in Sanders' brigade.[3]

Warren utilized the respite afforded him by the Confederate failure to attack on August 20 to consolidate his position on the Weldon Railroad. The V Corps chief began by straightening the northern stretch of his line. First, Warren advanced Potter's division of IX Corps half a mile north from the Aiken house. Next, at about 9:05 a.m., Potter's right linked up with the detachment of Bragg's brigade—the 7th Wisconsin and part of the 19th Indiana—to the right of Mahone's breakthrough on the previous afternoon. Since Bragg's brigade connected with Mott's division of II Corps, Warren had closed the gap where Mahone had penetrated the previous day. At the same time, White's division of IX Corps advanced to fill in the opening between his division's left and Willcox's right occasioned as Willcox's division advanced into contact with Rebel skirmishers.

West of the roadbed, Ayres consolidated the remnant of Hayes' brigade with the 15th New York heavies. This force relieved Tilton's troops, who returned to their place in Griffin's line. The pickets of Ayres' division found Confederate skirmishers still occupying part of the Federal works abandoned on the previous day. The Unionist videttes began skirmishing with their Secessionist counterparts. In a small, vicious, hand-to-hand affair, the pickets of Ayres' division, including the 1st Maryland, recaptured the works abandoned during the day before and took prisoner about thirty rebels of the 2nd Maryland Battalion in Walker's brigade.[4]

By 9:10 a.m., Meade had begun to prod Warren to attack. If the army leader had wanted to find a way to lose his grip on the Weldon road, he could scarcely have chosen a better course than to send V Corps floundering forward through unfamiliar woods and swamps that would expose it to Confederate ambushes. Warren wisely stuck to his decision to adopt a defensive posture. Though he still did not know the full extent of the catastrophe that had befallen his soldiers the previous day, he realized that his command lacked the capacity to deliver a successful attack. Convinced that he could not hold a line across the area

---

3 Axford, *"To Lochaber Na Mair,"* 129.

4 Charles Camper and J. W. Kirkley, *Historical Record of the First Regiment Maryland Infantry, with an Appendix containing a Register of the Officers and Enlisted Men, Biographies of Deceased Officers, etc., War of the Rebellion* (Washington, 1871), 171; Goldsborough, *The Maryland Line*, 182-5; OR 42, pt. 1, 489.

between his right and Mott's II Corps division without reinforcements, the V Corps chief determined to select a position suitable for artillery defense and keep his infantry in reserve to meet a Secessionist advance from any direction. By 10:00 a.m., Warren's engineers had begun marking out a line that ran along a crest which roughly paralleled the Vaughan Wagon Road from the Lanier house west to the Dunlop house closer to the railroad, and then south to Globe Tavern, which stood next to the roadbed. The V Corps chief elected to defend more or less along the lines that Lyman had kept to himself the previous afternoon.

Before the engineers had finished their work, Gregg's First Brigade, under Col. William Stedman of the 6th Ohio Cavalry, arrived at Warren's headquarters. The all night ride from north of the James in the rain had exhausted Stedman's troopers.

Shortly after noon, the divisions of IX Corps and, on their left, the remnants of Crawford's division of V Corps, left their pickets in place and withdrew into reserve positions behind Wainwright's guns. The Confederates may have already run out of time to drive the Unionists from the Weldon Railroad.

At 1:30 p.m. and 1:45 p.m., Lee exhorted Beauregard to make a concentrated effort to dislodge the Northerners, rather than piecemeal attacks as on the preceding days. The army group leader, like the Louisianan and Hill, failed to grasp the urgency of the situation. If a piecemeal attack on August 20 inflicted as much damage on "those people" as the piecemeal attacks of August 18 and August 19, the Southerners could count themselves most fortunate. "Piecemeal" described the attacks of August 18 and 19 unfairly because Beauregard and Hill had employed every man they could safely spare from the trenches.

Later that afternoon, the Louisianan abandoned the attempt to attack the Federal position on the Weldon Railroad on August 20 and started preparing for an assault the following day. Too late, Gus began shifting troops around. He used units exhausted by the fighting on August 19 to relieve relatively fresh soldiers in the trenches. Weisiger's brigade of Mahone's division relieved Finegan's brigade of the same division. Clingman's brigade of Hoke's division relieved Hagood's brigade of Hoke's division. Colquitt's brigade of Hoke's division relieved Ransom's brigade of Johnson's division. Davis' and Walker's brigades of Heth's division relieved Cooke's and MacRae's brigades of Heth's Division. The Louisianan called up the Petersburg militia, the City Battalion and rear echelon men of all types—even clerks and musicians—and sent them along with every straggler the provost guards could scrape up to relieve Harris', Sanders' and Wright's brigades of Mahone's division. Finegan's, Harris', Sanders', Wright's and Hagood's brigades tramped toward the vicinity of the Lead Works. Ransom's brigade hiked to a position near the Davis farm while Cooke's and MacRae's brigades plodded toward the same destination.

The southern high command could have issued all these orders the previous evening, but a strange lethargy had come over Lee, Beauregard, and Hill. The Secessionist leaders wanted to make the enemy pay a high price for the indefensible, dilapidated Weldon Railroad, but they moved with little sense of urgency to strike the foe before he fortified. They failed their soldiers by not moving faster.

Some of the Southern brigades coming out of the trenches did not arrive in much better shape than their relief. Debilitating service in the earthworks had rendered Hagood's brigade sickly and feeble. "They tired badly in the short evening march," Hagood recalled. He asked Hill to excuse the brigade from participation in the next day's attack, if possible. The condition of the brigade quickly improved, remembered Hagood:

> . . . The change from the cramped and noisesome trench to the freedom of the bivouack, and the call upon the men for action, instead of endurance, aroused their spirits wonderfully. And although it rained all night, the fires of the brushwood crackled merrily, and there was once more heard the light laugh, and ready joke, and the busy hum of voices as the men prepared their suppers or smoked their pipes stretched at length before the exhilarating blaze.[5]

During the afternoon, Warren shifted Bragg's brigade west of the railroad. Bragg's troops demolished the Federal works along the Vaughan Road. They dug in along a line parallel to and about a quarter mile west of the railroad, from the left of Wainwright's row of guns to a little ravine.

The Confederates constantly demonstrated. The Northerners could see Secessionist infantry marching down the Halifax and Vaughan Roads. The Unionists could hear the Rebels felling timber beyond the Vaughan Road. All this alerted Warren to the possibility of an assault on his left during the late afternoon, but the day ended without a Rebel attack.

By 7:00 p.m., Beauregard had withdrawn from the Petersburg trenches every available man he could spare for the following day's attack. That night,

---

5 Hagood, *Memoirs of the War of Secession*, 289-90.

pursuant to Lee's orders, the Louisianan called upon Maj. Gen. Cadmus M. Wilcox for a further brigade. Wilcox, a West Point graduate and Mexican War veteran, sent Scales' brigade and a detachment of Thomas brigade to the Lead Works. Lane's and McGowan's brigades of Wilcox's division arrived from north of James River and filed into the Cockade City fortifications. Lee planned to call on Field for more reinforcements as soon as Hancock, as expected, left Field's front.

Beauregard and Hill entrusted the planning of the following day's attack to Mahone. In formulating his plan, Old Porte relied upon intelligence provided by one of the few men alive who might have known the ground around Petersburg as well as or better than did Mahone himself.

Private Roger Atkinson Pryor had the blood of several old Petersburg families in his veins. A newspaper editor and politician before the war, he had served the Confederacy as a brigadier general in the Confederate States Army until August of 1863. Deprived of troops to command by the breaking up of his brigade so that its regiments might serve more effectively under other leadership, Pryor resigned his commission to remain in the field. He enlisted as a private and a scout in the Rebel cavalry.

Pryor had spent much of August 20 reconnoitering the woods in front of Warren's left. To study the Federal position, Pryor climbed a tall tree. From this perch, Ayres' left appeared unguarded. The tree did not afford a view of Griffin's division behind Ayres' left, and Pryor failed to reconnoiter farther. Satisfied that the Union left hung in the air, he returned to report this misinformation to Mahone.

Old Porte accepted Pryor's account at face value. Without reconnoitering further, Mahone took for himself the most important role in the attack. While Heth drove straight down the railroad near the Davis house again with two infantry brigades and a third in reserve, Mahone would march down the Vaughan Road from the Lead Works with six infantry brigades and part of a seventh, strike the Federals from the left and rear, and finally drive them from the Weldon Railroad. This time the Confederates would employ what Lee considered a sufficient force—not three infantry brigades, as on August 18, not five infantry brigades, as on August 19, but nine full infantry brigade and a portion of a tenth. Lee and Beauregard could have mounted this attack on August 20. They had to do no more for it than issue the appropriate orders on the evening of August 19.

Before dark, a 200-man working party from the Quartermaster's Department at City Point reached Warren's headquarters. Pursuant to orders from Meade, the V Corps chief put these men to work burning ties and twisting rails. As the wreckers worked their way southward on the Weldon Railroad, Stedman's brigade of horsemen escorted them. Spear's cavalry brigade, 700 strong, felt toward Reams Station on the railway, about five miles south of Globe Tavern.

After nightfall, Ayres put his soldiers to work slashing timber and throwing down their breastworks west of the railroad in preparation for a withdrawal similar to that conducted earlier by the infantry east of the roadbed. At about 8:00 p.m., Warren sent Hofmann's brigade to join Bragg's troops and reconstituted Cutler's division of V Corps. Cutler deployed Hofmann's soldiers on Bragg's left. Hofmann's brigade occupied a crest that stretched southward from the Blick house and ran parallel to and about a quarter of a mile west of the railroad. Lieutenant Colonel Harney of the 147th New York in Hofmann's brigade recalled:

> Through the night, cold and rainy, the men labored faithfully, and the morning dawned upon a formidable line of breastworks, stoutly made and tastefully finished. These works were erected under peculiar disadvantages. The night was very dark, with frequent showers, which kept the clothing of the men saturated with water during the entire night, this rendering labor very difficult, and added to this, the men were almost broken down from the effect of the excessive fatigue of the three days previous. For the erection of these works, under the circumstances, I think the One hundred and forty-seventh is entitled to as much credit as if it had fought and won a great battle.[6]

By fortifying so thoroughly, Warren's troops had very nearly assured that they would win any further battle they might fight on the Weldon Railroad. They may have worked in miserable conditions, but they knew that cold and fatigue beat Andersonville.

By 2:00 a.m., Ayres' soldiers had finished slashing timber and demolishing their breastworks. Leaving his pickets in place, Ayres withdrew the remainder of his troops about 700 yards. This took them out of the pines and placed them on the crest of a gentle slope in the large open field north of Globe Tavern, with Hayes' brigade and the 15th New York heavies on the right and the Maryland Brigade on the left. The exhausted soldiers began throwing up another line of earthworks. In front of those works, the Federals constructed abatis and stretched trip wires just above the ground.

---

6 Report of Lieut. Col. George Harney, One hundred and forty-seventh New York Infantry, of operations August 18-21, in *OR* 42, pt. 1, 488.

Fortifying on the Weldon Railroad *Library of Congress*

By dawn the Unionists had demolished their old works, which ran along the southern edge of the Davis corn field and then southwardly between the Vaughan and Halifax Roads. In place of these works, the Northerners left a picket line with orders to weaken the Rebels before they reached the main line hundreds of yards in the rear.

Warren had conducted a tactical withdrawal similar to that employed by Beauregard on the night of June 17 during the initial assaults on Petersburg. When the Secessionists attacked on August 21, the V Corps leader would have in store for them a surprise as unpleasant as the Federals had encountered on June 18. The activities of Warren's soldiers during the day rendered obsolete any useful intelligence gleaned by Pryor's inadequate reconnaissance. In the morning, the Confederates would implement an attack plan that bore little relation to reality.

Chapter 9

The Battle of Globe Tavern, August 21, 1864

At 2:00 a.m. on August 21, Mahone's officers roused the troops of his command for the third Confederate attack in four days. His force began tramping out from the vicinity of the Lead Works at about 3:30 a.m. Rain continued to fall as his soldiers marched first southwestwardly along the Squirrel Level Road and then southeastwardly along the Vaughan Wagon Road. Mud and standing water slowed the trek. Near Poplar Spring Church, halfway between the Squirrel Level Road and the Vaughan Road, Old Porte ordered Hagood's brigade to halt by the roadside and go into reserve. By this time, the rain had stopped and given way to the fog of early morning. Fatigued by the march, Hagood's soldiers lay down and rested. The other brigades slogged along the Vaughan Wagon Road toward the Vaughan Road, where Mahone deployed them.

Finegan's Florida brigade and Sander's Alabama brigade formed line of battle to the left of the Vaughan Wagon Road. Sanders' brigade deployed with its right on the road, Finegan's brigade with its right on the Alabamians. Harris' Mississippi brigade, under Col. Joseph McAfee Jayne of the 48th Mississippi because of Harris' illness, deployed as a flank guard behind the left of and at a right angle to the Floridians. Wright's Georgia and Scales' North Carolina brigades and the detachment from Thomas' Georgia brigade formed to the right of the Vaughan Wagon Road.

Before 9:00 a.m., Mahone had finished deploying. At about the same time, the fog gave way to sunshine. Skirmishing began almost immediately as Old

Porte sent his soldiers forward through the tangled woods and gallberry swamps to drive in the Federal pickets on the western face of Warren's position.

The guns of Pegram's battalion opened fire, twelve blasting away from the Flowers house on the Vaughan Road and eight shooting from near the Davis house at the junction of the Vaughan Road with the Weldon Railroad and the Halifax Road. A few long-range Confederate guns in the Petersburg lines to the northeast also opened fire. The Rebel artillerists put the Unionists under what Wainwright later called "a very ugly cross-fire."[1] The open ground around Globe Tavern afforded no cover, and some Northerners amused themselves by dodging cannon balls or watching skulkers cower. The Southern gunners drove Hayes' brigade, on the railroad, and Crawford's division, east of the railroad, to the outer side of their earthworks. West of the roadbed, a Secessionist cannon ball decapitated Colonel Dushane and left the Maryland Brigade under the command of Col. Samuel Graham of the Purnell Legion, a prominent Maryland lawyer. The converging fire of the Rebel guns soon silenced the 15th Battery, New York Light Artillery. This battery occupied the angle where the line of Bragg's brigade, which faced west, joined the Maryland Brigade's works, which faced north.

When Mahone's battle line, which faced northeast, emerged from the woods just east of the Vaughan Road, the Secessionists did not find what Pryor had led Old Porte to expect but the remnants of the earthworks that Bragg's brigade had razed during the previous night. Hill and Mahone had planned the attack with the now demolished works as their objective. The fog had prevented the Third Corps leader and his subordinate from detecting the change in the Federal dispositions. For the first time, Hill and Mahone saw the new Unionist position to the east across a corn field several hundred yards wide. Rather than withdraw into the woods and formulate a new plan of attack, they elected to launch their main force across a much longer stretch of open ground than they had anticipated.

Sending a courier to Hagood directing the South Carolinian to bring up his brigade on the Rebel right to outflank the Northerners, Mahone briefly paused to realign his force. The razed Federal line ran parallel to the Vaughan Road, from southwest to northeast. The Secessionist battle line faced northeast to enfilade the razed Union line. The Confederates partially executed a right wheel

---

1 Report of Bvt. Brig. Gen. Charles S. Wainwright, First New York Light Artillery, commanding Artillery Brigade, of operations August 18-21, in *OR* 42, pt. 1, 541.

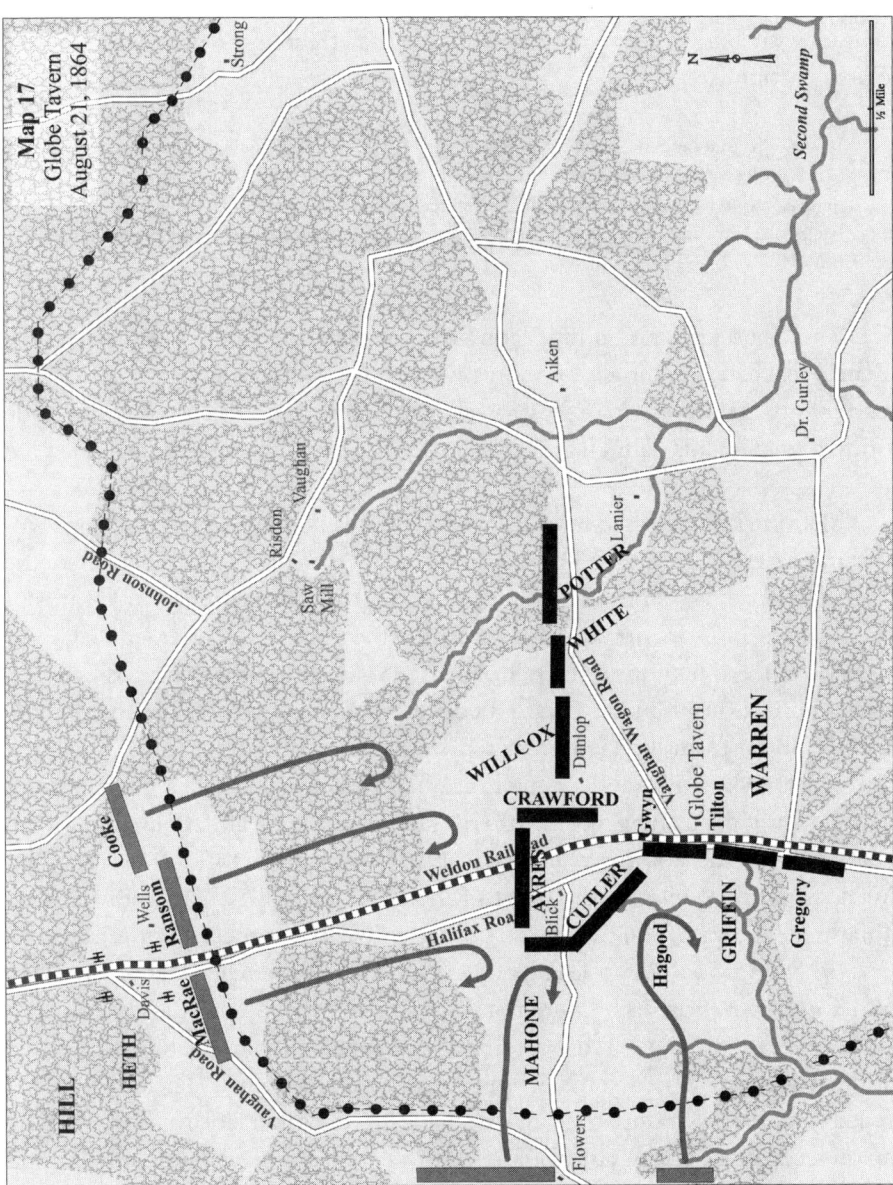

in an attempt to parallel the newly sighted enemy earthworks, which ran north and south. Mahone's line of battle then resumed its advance.

The 15th Battery, New York Light Artillery remained silent because of the casualties inflicted by the Confederate barrage. The battery's commander begged Bragg for crews, which Bragg's brigade furnished. The Federals had to hold or they would lose their guns. Artillerists of the Third Massachusetts

Battery with Griffin's division remembered the effect of the heavy rains on the marshy ground:

> It was Virginia land without any bottom, and it was very difficult to move batteries. Our whole battery was sunk to the hubs in the road near the line of battle. It could neither move forward nor back. Orders were given to commanders if obliged to move back to spike their guns, as it would be impossible to move as from every discharge they sank deeper in the soil.[2]

The Southerners continued onward through the open field. When the Rebels reached a point about 500 yards west of the Unionist works, the 15th Battery opened up on the Secessionists with grape and canister. Mahone rode off to a rendezvous with Hagood's brigade. Hill oversaw the attack of the main force.

Mahone's courier had reached Hagood as the sound of firing on Hagood's left increased in volume. The courier guided the South Carolinians to the Vaughan Road by a short cut, then up the Vaughan Road to within 600 yards of the Flowers' house. Turning across a field to the right, the courier led Hagood's Brigade in the direction of the railroad. The South Carolinians passed between Rebel guns firing blindly toward Federals rendered invisible by intervening woods. Shells from the vigorously replying Unionist batteries frequently burst in the field, which Hagood's brigade crossed at the double-quick. As the South Carolinians jogged along, the Northern shells took their toll. "A file of four men was killed in the company just in front of the Edisto Rifles," recalled Sgt. William Valmore Izlar of the Edisto Rifles, Company G, 25th South Carolina Infantry, "and all of the troops in rear had to pass over these poor fellows."[3]

When Hagood's brigade reached the far edge of the field, Mahone rode up and took over from the courier. Old Porte led the South Carolinians into position along the edge of the wood and facing the railroad. The brigade formed at the woods' edge, fifty yards behind the swamp of a branch. The Federals had felled trees in the swamp, forming an abatis. On the other side of the branch lay an unoccupied clearing at the foot of a little hill that screened everything beyond it from sight.

---

2   Committee, *History of the Fifth Massachusetts Battery. Organized October 3, 1861, Mustered Out June 12, 1865* (Boston, 1902), 905.

3   William V. Izlar, *A Sketch of the War Record of the Edisto Rifles, 1861-1865* (Columbia SC, 1914), 81.

"Now," Mahone said to Hagood, "you are upon the flank and rear of the enemy. I have five brigades fighting them in front and they are driving them. I want you to go in and press them all you can."

Thinking Hagood stood behind the Unionist left as the brigades of Colquitt, Clingman and Weisiger had behind the Federal right on August 19th, Mahone pointed to the branch.

"When you have crossed the branch swamp," he added, "you will come upon a clearing in which some 300 yards further is the enemy's line and they are not entrenched."[4]

Old Porte urged Hagood to attack promptly, and the South Carolinian immediately gave the order to advance.

To Hagood's left, Hill's battle line pressed forward. Bragg's brigade, reinforced by the 4th and 7th Maryland, prepared to deliver a devastating volley. When Hill's troops arrived within musket range, little more than a fizzle initially greeted them. The constant rain had wet the powder of Bragg's soldiers. A member of the Sauk County Riflemen—Company A, 6th Wisconsin —remembered:

> It was a continuous snapping of caps with here and there a p-i-s-h until the exploding caps had dried the powder sufficiently to burn and generate gas enough to blow the ball out of the gun. The enemy continued to advance and it began to look like a bayonet fight for a finish. Finally the charges began to explode and eject the ball. . . .[5]

The delay only made the Federal fire deadlier when it finally came. "The fire poured on our ranks was most severe of the war," Capt. W. L. Fagan of Company K in the 8th Alabama of Sanders' brigade recalled.[6] While twenty-four year old General Sanders advanced on foot with his brigade, a bullet pierced both of his thighs and severed the femoral arteries. Without falling, this hero of the battles of the Crater and Second Deep Bottom said quietly, "Take me back."[7] Removed a short distance to the rear, he asked those

---

4   Hagood, *Memoirs of the War of Secession*, 290-1.

5   Phillip Cheek and Mair Pointon, *History of the Sauk County Riflemen Known as Company 'A', Sixth Wisconsin Veteran Volunteer Infantry, 1861-1865* (Madison, 1909), 134.

6   Fortin, Maurice S., ed. "Colonel Hilary A. Herbert's History of the Eighth Alabama volunteer regiment, C.S.A.," *Alabama Historical Quarterly*, vol. 39 (1977), 174.

7   Evans. Clement, ed., *Confederate Military History*, (11 Volumes) (Atlanta, 1899), vol. 7 ("Alabama"), 444.

carrying him to lay him down. A few minutes later he breathed his last and Lee's army lost another promising brigadier.

As a result of the adjustment made while crossing the Vaughan Road, Hill's line marched toward the Union fortifications at nearly the same angle that the Vaughan Road made in relation to the Federal earthworks. The left of the Confederate line neared those works first. Finegan's brigade, disease-wracked and depleted by desertion, no more than 800 strong, charged to within 100 yards of the Unionist breastworks before breaking. After trying in vain to reform, the Florida Brigade fell back in confusion and disorder. The Secessionists to the right of the Vaughan Wagon Road tramped steadily through the corn field to within fifty feet of Hofmann's brigade before they broke.

Harris' brigade, which had rapidly formed line of battle and advanced at the double-quick to the support of the Floridians, passed through and over Finegan's soldiers as they retired. The Mississippians then charged. The left regiments of the brigade, the 12th and 16th Mississippi, struggled to within thirty yards of the works of Bragg's brigade. Harris' brigade received no assistance. The panic of the Florida Brigade had spread to the other brigades of the assault column, and their soldiers headed for the woods west of the Vaughan Road. A Southern battery attempted to unlimber near the Flowers house, but the fire of the Federal batteries drove the Rebel artillerymen away. The Federal fire became unbearable for the regiments on Harris' left. Many of the soldiers in these regiments sought cover in the ditch which drained the meadow over which they had charged. Veterans of the 24th Michigan in Bragg's brigade recalled:

> ... the enemy charged in good style. They were allowed to come up pretty close, when a general rattle of musketry and artillery cut them in pieces. Some concealed themselves in a ditch near by, and it being death to advance or retreat, they dropped their guns and, waving their hats or anything they had in token of surrender, rushed pell-mell over the Union works as if Satan would get the last man. Our men took them by the hand in many instances and helped them over the works.[8]

Lieutenant Colonel Albert M. Edwards of the 24th Michigan, who had endured ten months of captivity after First Bull Run, asked a captured and wounded colonel to what troops he belonged.

---

8 Curtis, *Twenty-Fourth Michigan*, 273.

"The troops that have whipped you so often—Mahone's Division—but they did not do much of that thing to-day," replied Col. Samuel B. Thomas of the 12th Mississippi, whose regiment had lost a flag.[9] Harris' brigade, which had left 900 soldiers on picket duty north of James River, lost at least 254 of the 450 troops that it took into action on the Weldon Railroad.[10] Bragg's soldiers captured banners from the 12th and 16th Mississippi.[11] Corporal Horace A. Ellis of Company A in the 7th Wisconsin in Bragg's brigade earned a Medal of Honor for capturing the flag of the 16th Mississippi. The survivors of Hill's attack force hastened back into the woods west of the Vaughan Road. There they rallied.

No sooner had Bragg's brigade repelled Hill's assault from the west than the Maryland Brigade and Hayes' brigade had to fight off part of Harry Heth's attack from the north. Heth commanded a force consisting of Cooke's and MacRae's North Carolina brigades of his own division and Ransom's North Carolina brigade of Johnson's division. On the previous afternoon, Ransom's brigade had relieved Walker's brigade on the left of the railroad and pushed forward pickets to the southern fringe of the Davis corn field. Cooke's and MacRae's brigades, each a crack unit, had not reported to Heth until after midnight. MacRae's brigade relieved Davis' brigade on the right of the railway. Heth kept Cooke's brigade in reserve east of the roadbed to protect the left flank of the attacking force.

At dawn on August 21, Brig. Gen. William MacRae deployed his brigade in line of battle and advanced his sharpshooters to clear his front. After a sharp skirmish, his marksmen drove the pickets of the Purnell Legion and the 146th New York through the Davis corn field and back to the belt of woods north of the Globe Tavern clearing. East of the railroad, the battle line of Ransom's brigade marched down and formed on its picket line.

When Mahone's artillery opened, Heth directed his own guns to fire. Heth's infantry took cover. Colonel William J. Martin of the 11th North Carolina in MacRae's brigade and Capt. Edward R. Outlaw of the 11th's Company C recalled: "We lay between our batteries…and theirs during the artillery duel which opened the ball, and came in for some pretty severe

---

9 Ibid.

10 Report of Capt. James Hays, C. S. Army, Assistant Inspector General, Harris' Brigade, Anderson's Division, of operations August 21, in *OR* 42, pt. 1, 939.

11 Ibid., 431; Curtis, *Twenty-Fourth Michigan*, 273.

shelling."¹² As soon as Mahone's infantry advanced, Heth sent forward his foot soldiers. MacRae's brigade struggled forward into the thick undergrowth of pine and oak to the west of the railroad. East of the roadbed, Lt. Col. John L. Harris of the 24th North Carolina led Ransom's brigade into the dense, swampy almost impenetrable thicket that had retarded the progress of Warren's Federals on August 18.

MacRae's Tarheels encountered the Unionist pickets along the razed line of breastworks at the northern edge of the woods. The North Carolinian battle line drove through the pines and oaks, mauling the Purnell Legion. At the southern edge of the trees, MacRae's troops stormed another lightly held line of demolished Federal earthworks. As the hapless Maryland pickets ran for the main Union line and safety, they fell prey to the trip wires that they and their comrades had strung during the previous night. Soldiers of the 146th New York in the main line of works remembered

> Suddenly a number of men fell flat on their faces and we thought that they had been hit by the enemy's fire. To our surprise, they hurriedly scrambled to their feet again and continued towards us. A few steps more and again they plunged to the ground. It dawned upon us then what was the cause of their strange behavior. They had tripped over the telegraph wires stretched about a foot high along the ground. The men, too, realized what was the matter and they carefully picked their way the rest of the distance, being greeted with laughter as they approached. They, however, were in no mood to enjoy the merriment.¹³

MacRae's crack soldiers rushed for the main line of Federal fortifications. Canister from four Northern batteries drove MacRae's battle line back into the woods, though some of his skirmishers made it to the cover of a ravine close to the main Unionist breastworks. Describing the corn field between the timber and the works occupied by the Maryland Brigade, soldiers of the 118th Pennsylvania, the Corn Exchange Regiment, in Gwyn's brigade of Griffin's division farther left, recalled: "The corn-stalks were cut off by the bullets as if by a knife."¹⁴ While MacRae's battle line tried to reform, word arrived to halt. The

---

12 Clark, *North Carolina Regiments*, 1:599.

13 Mary G. Brainard, *Campaigns of the One Hundred and Forty-sixth Regiment New York State Volunteers, Also Known as Halleck's Infantry, the Fifth Oneida, and Garrard's Tigers* (New York, 1915), 241.

14 Survivors' Association, *History of the Corn Exchange Regiment, the 118th Pennsylvania Volunteers* (2 vols.) (Philadelphia, 1885), 2:502.

Federal gunners blasted the timber with solid shot as the Tarheels hugged the ground, awaiting the signal of Mahone's success before they rushed the main Union fortifications. Mahone's attack had failed before MacRae's brigade, with more distance to cover, tougher terrain to negotiate, and stronger resistance to overcome, had reached the southern edge of the woods. Captain Louis G. Young, Assistant Adjutant General of MacRae's brigade, remembered that the brigade, "found itself alone in front of the works, too weak to go on and too near to retreat."[15] The sniping of the Tarheel skirmishers and sharpshooters annoyed the Federal gunners, and Colonel Winthrop of Hayes' brigade assigned the remnants of the 5th and 140th New York to maintain a scattering fire upon the North Carolinians.

East of the railway, the five regiments of Ransom's brigade strode forward across the Davis corn field by company front, with intervals corresponding to regimental strength. At the northern edge of the woods, each regiment formed line on its right company. With Cooke's brigade in echelon behind it and to its left, Ransom's brigade resumed the advance in line of battle through a swamp and came to a level pine road. There the Tarheels halted and reformed their lines. A narrow road ran through the trees toward the Union line.

The artillerists of both sides exchanged shells above the heads of the soldiers of Ransom's brigade as the North Carolinians drove the Federal skirmishers back upon the razed works of Crawford's division. Despite the demolition of Crawford's breastworks, the abatis in front of those fortifications remained. The criss-crossed tree trunks and sharpened limbs that had impeded the advance of Walker's brigade on August 19 now hindered the advance of Ransom's brigade. To reach the Union works, some of the Tarheels had to remove the timber and fashion a passageway for themselves. Others, according to Capt. William H. S. Burgwyn of Company B, 35th North Carolina Infantry, "had to pick their way through the interlaced timbers and advance without regard to company or regimental formations."[16] The Federals kept up a galling fire.

Once through the abatis, the North Carolinians reformed and again advanced under the same fire. Captain Robert D. Graham of Company D, 56th North Carolina, in Ransom's brigade, remembered that the brigade's line of

---

15 Clark, *North Carolina Regiments*, 4:564.

16 Clark, *North Carolina Regiments*, 2:625.

battle, "under the severe punishment it is receiving at short range, staggers and writhes like a monster serpent, mortally wounded, and as if about to snap at every vertebrae."

The foe kept up the same galling fire.

"On with the yell, boys," shouted a beardless youth in the 56th, "on with the yell."

Captain Graham recalled, "The old Fifty-sixth, in the center, responds with a will and volume that the Comanche tribe might have envied; the deadly aim of the enemy is diverted at random, and the fusillade slackens perceptibly, while the brigade, like a human tornado, rushes over their line."[17]

General Lee, who had arrived in Petersburg from Chaffin's Bluff to oversee the attack, witnessed this charge. According to Captain Young of the 35th North Carolina, the advance evoked from the army leader the compliment that "he had often heard of men straggling to the rear, but he had never before seen men straggle to the attack."[18]

After taking the razed line of works just south of the Davis corn field, Ransom's brigade reformed again and rushed forward to the next Union line, along the southern edge of the woods. The Federals had dismantled this line during the previous night and their pickets did not reoccupy it as they fled from the Tarheels. The North Carolinians soon encountered the direct fire of the Northern artillery, posted on elevated ground across the Globe Tavern clearing. Besides Federal shell and canister, shortfalls of friendly fire also struck the Tarheels. The Unionist guns broke up the battle lines of the brigade before they emerged from the trees. More difficult terrain, more formidable fortifications and more resistance had delayed the progress of Ransom's brigade so much that the Federals considered its attack separate from that of MacRae's brigade.

Reforming at the edge of the woods, Ransom's brigade continued its advance through another abatis of trees felled with their tops facing the Southerners. The North Carolinians became so entangled in the fallen trees that they could make no headway whatsoever. Private William A. Day in Company I of the 49th North Carolina in Ransom's brigade recalled:

> John Landen, the color bearer of the 49th, was up in the tree tops with the flag in one hand and fighting his way through the limbs with the other. The enemy opened on our

17 Ibid., 3:377-8.

18 Ibid., 2:625.

left with all their artillery, double-shotted with grape and canister, giving us an enfilading fire which mangled our men terribly. Seeing that we would all be uselessly slaughtered in that death trap, [Lieutenant] Colonel [James T.] Davis shouted to us to fall back to the other line; but in the din of shouts, crashing tree tops, and bursting shells only about half the regiment heard the order and fell back, while the other half were still trying to get back through the pines. [Assistant] Adjt. [Lieutenant] J. H. Sherrill, of the 49th, ran back, found Landen with the flag, and, collecting the men as best he could in the storm of grapeshot, brought them back to the line. To make bad matters worse, we had a battery of artillery in a field half a mile off on our right which, mistaking our retreat for a charge of the enemy, opened all their guns on us, killing and wounding a number of our own men who had escaped death in the battle.[19]

Ransom's brigade failed to get within 300 yards of the main Federal works on the Vaughan Wagon Road. A direct fire of canister and a cross-fire of case-shot from twenty-six guns drove most of the Tarheels back into the woods. Some skirmishers from Ransom's brigade hid in a ditch and tried to pick off the Union gunners.

While Ransom's Tarheels reformed for yet another charge and Cooke's brigade braced for an expected counterstroke on its left, orders arrived to halt any further attacks on account of the failure of Mahone's assault. The assault on Cooke's left failed to materialize. The main bodies of MacRae's and Ransom's brigades withdrew to the first line of captured Federal works, leaving many North Carolinians pinned down in front of the main Union line. Colonel Martin and Captain Outlaw of the 11th North Carolina in MacRae's brigade, who hugged the earth in front of the Federal fortifications, remembered: "If Warren had known how few we were in his front, and had sent out an adequate force, he might have captured the most of these two brigades, isolated as we were."[20] A Northern counterthrust resulted in the capture of at least sixty-five prisoners, mostly from Ransom's brigade.[21] Private George W. Reed of Company E, 11th Pennsylvania in Wheelock's brigade of Crawford's division captured the flag of the 24th North Carolina in Ransom's brigade, earning himself a Medal of Honor.

About half a mile to the south, Hagood's troops made their way across the swamp. Crossing the morass considerably disordered the line of the brigade.

---

19 W. A. Day, "Life Among Bullets—In The Rifle Pits," *Confederate Veteran*, vol. 29 (1921), 216.

20 Clark, *North Carolina Regiments*, 1:599.

21 Alan Nevins, ed. *A Diary of Battle: The Personal Journals of Colonel Charles S. Wainwright, 1861-1865* (New York, 1962), 454-55.

On the other side, the soldiers found themselves in the clearing under the little hill which blocked their view. Some Federal pickets had noticed the advance of the brigade and had begun to fire in its direction. Hagood immediately pushed skirmishers up the hill for reconnaissance and protection from enemy attack while he and his staff reformed the brigade's line of battle. He reformed the brigade in a matter of minutes, not knowing that the other Confederate thrusts had met with bloody repulses at the hands of the Unionists.

A rider passed who had in front of him across his horse the body of Sanders. A report came back to Hagood from the skirmishers that the Federals occupied rifle pits only a short distance ahead, thus confirming Mahone's statement. Hagood dismounted and placed himself in front of his brigade's center to steady his soldiers and stifle excitement. He cautioned his troops to move only at a quick step until he gave the order to charge. The South Carolinian directed his brigade to advance. He marched backward in front of the line for a short distance as if on a drill. Then he halted below the crest of the hill. The line passed. He followed with his staff behind the right of the 21st South Carolina. This regiment had the 25th South Carolina on its left and the brigade's other three regiments on its right.

Captain Judson of the 83rd Pennsylvania of Gwyn's brigade of Griffith's division recalled how Hagood's brigade first appeared to the Federals: "They advanced in the most splendid order through the cornfield which lay before them, and their heads could be just seen above the tall corn, with their red battle flag moving over it."[22] Soon after Hagood's brigade became visible ascending the hill, the Unionists in the rifle pits opened fire upon the South Carolinians. Without loosing a shot in reply, Hagood's troops hastened forward steadily at quick time with arms at right shoulder shift. As the South Carolinians neared the line of rifle pits, the Northern pickets bolted and fled. The Rebel yell rose from the ranks of Hagood's brigade, and its soldiers spontaneously broke into double-quick time in pursuit.

Hagood perceived that the Federal line amounted only to an entrenched picket line, though so heavy as to have deceived his skirmishers into thinking it a line of battle. He observed a strongly entrenched line 250 yards beyond, crowded with men and guns. This line stretched right and left as far as the brigadier could see. Nowhere could he detect Mahone's force, now already back under cover in the woods west of the Vaughan Road. Hagood's brigade headed

---

22 Judson, *Eighty-Third Pennsylvania*, 107.

at an oblique angle toward the line of Griffin's division, an infantry parapet five feet high behind a ditch eight or ten feet wide with artillery at intervals. Immediately to the right of where the South Carolinians would strike the line, a small bastioned work for field artillery thrust forward. The oblique angle of approach subjected Hagood's troops to a flank fire from Cutler's division to the left, besides the unavoidable flank fire from the artillery bastion to the right.

Hagood saw at a glance the hopelessness of the assault. Stopping, he shouted again and again for his command to halt, but the roar of artillery and the crash of musketry drowned out his voice. His troops strode forward, he remembered, "with the steady tramp of the double-quick."[23] Dressing on their colors, they neither broke ranks nor stopped to fire. The brigade marched with its line almost perpendicular to the 3rd Delaware of Hofmann's brigade. Refused at a forty-five degree angle, the 3rd Delaware formed the left of Cutler's division.

When Hagood saw that his efforts to save his troops from certain destruction had failed, he felt obliged to share their fate. With his orderly, Pvt. J. Dwight Stoney, and two members of his staff, Capt. P. K. Moloney, Assistant Adjutant General, and Lt. Ben Martin, an aide-de-camp, Hagood followed the advancing line. Before they had plodded fifty yards, Martin fell with a leg wound. A few steps farther, Moloney went down with a mortal head wound. Seconds later, Stoney suffered a shoulder wound but plodded onward.

The 21st and 25th South Carolina on the brigade's left struck the works first because of the oblique direction of the advance. While they struggled in vain to penetrate the abatis in front of Hofmann's breastworks, the other three regiments tramped ahead. They halted in the thick bushes of the ravine to the left of, and about 150 yards behind, Hofmann's brigade. This ravine ran between the line of Cutler's division and the line of Griffin's division, which stood in echelon about 300 yards behind Cutler's left. Seventy-five to 100 yards separated the two sections into which Hagood's brigade had broken.

Federal fire had so fearfully cut up the South Carolinians that their assault seemed to have no chance of success, where their only hope of safety appeared to lie. Some of Hagood's troops held up their hands and the butts of their muskets. Others ran to the rear and escaped. The Unionists thought that Hagood's troops had surrendered. Captain Dennis B. Dailey, Provost Marshal of Cutler's division, galloped out of a sally port. He seized the colors of the 11th

23 Hagood, *Memoirs of the War of Secession*, 291-2.

South Carolina on the left of the portion of Hagood's brigade in the ravine. Dailey demanded the surrender of the brigade. Parleying began around him and led to confusion. Some of Hagood's soldiers surrendered, but the Northerners did not take them into custody. Other South Carolinians refused to surrender, but stopped fighting. Still others continued to fight. The Federals pushed out from the right and left a thin line behind Hagood's brigade and encircled the South Carolinians.

Hagood called to his soldiers and told them to shoot the Union captain and then withdraw. They either did not hear him or, bewildered by the surrender of part of their number, failed to obey. "It was a critical moment and demanded instant and decided action," Hagood recalled. "In a few minutes the disposition to surrender would have spread and the whole brigade would have been lost."[24] Under fire from the 3rd Delaware, scarcely thirty yards distant, Hagood dashed from one fragment of his brigade to the other. Approaching Captain Dailey, Hagood demanded the colors of the 11th and declared Dailey free to go back within Federal lines. Hagood stood on the ground near Dailey and extended his hand to receive the colors. Dailey began arguing with Hagood. The captain pointed out the hopelessness of further struggle and gestured toward the line of Northerners behind Hagood's brigade.

"The battle seemed to halt," Sergeant Izlar of the 25th South Carolina remembered. "Firing had practically ceased on both sides, and both armies stood in breathless expectancy awaiting the issue of the momentous parley between these two brave, determined men."[25]

Hagood cut Dailey short and demanded a categorical reply to his demand for the 11th South Carolina's colors.

"Yes or no," said Hagood.

Dailey raised his head proudly.

"No," he said.

Hagood drew his revolver and shot Dailey. The captain reeled from the saddle on one side. Hagood seized the bridle and mounted from the other. Orderly Stoney snatched the 11th's banner as it fell from Dailey's hands. Hagood recalled:

---

24 Ibid., 294.

25 Izlar, *Edisto Rifles*, 84-85.

There was no thought of surrender now. The yell from the brigade following the act and ringing out above the noise of battle told their commander that they were once more in hand and would go now wherever ordered—whether to the front or rear.[26]

Waving his hat over his head, Hagood shouted to his soldiers to face about and follow him out of the encirclement. He led all who could run against the still thin line behind the brigade, passing over many of their comrades who had fallen during the advance. "This line melted before our charge," he recalled.[27] Until now, the surrounding Federals had largely held their fire—in part out of bewilderment and in part out of fear of hitting their own comrades. After the South Carolinians broke through the line blocking their retreat, the Union fire intensified severely. Many of Hagood's troops fell before the remnant of his brigade reached shelter in the valley of the branch. Upon its margin, after Hagood had ridden about 200 yards, a shell fragment mortally wounded the horse he had seized from Dailey. The horse struggled as it fell. The dying animal kicked in the head Second Lt. William J. Taylor of Company G, 7th South Carolina Battalion, who had recently returned to his command despite an unhealed wound from Second Drewry's Bluff in May. The kick rendered Taylor so confused that one of his soldiers had to lead him from the field.

Hagood's brigade suffered on August 21 the envelopment that had threatened Weisiger's Virginia brigade on August 19. The South Carolinians lost 449 of the 740 officers and men who went into action. "It was a heartrending sight to look along the line of the brigade, as it mustered in the Vaughn road after the action," Hagood recalled. "It was now shrunk to the proportions of a small battalion."[28] As he moved about among the pitiful remnant of his once magnificent brigade, Hagood's eyes welled up with tears. For a while he kept a line of skirmishers as near as possible to the Federal breastworks while the stretcher bearers removed the wounded. Many wounded crawled within the line and thus escaped captivity.

The misfortune of Hagood's brigade proved the gain of the opposing Unionists. Private Fred C. Anderson of Company A in the 18th Massachusetts of Gwyn's brigade won a Medal of Honor for capturing the flag of the 27th

---

26 Hagood, *Memoirs of the War of Secession*, 295. Hagood later assisted Dailey, whom the South Carolinian assumed he had killed, with a postwar pension application. Ibid., 279n.

27 Ibid., 295.

28 Ibid., 299.

South Carolina as well as its bearer. First Sergeant John Shilling of Company H, 3rd Delaware, a native of England, earned a Medal of Honor for capturing another South Carolina banner.

Colonel Wainwright, the commander of the V Corps artillery that had contributed so much to the catastrophe on August 19, patted himself on the back. He remembered:

> Thus ended a battle in which the artillery on our side bore a more prominent part than in any other action of this campaign. Our lines being formed entirely in open ground, though within short range of the surrounding woods, afforded the very best opportunity possible for an effective artillery fire, which was so well employed that the infantry had comparably little opportunity to take part in the fight. Particular instructions had been given the day before that in firing into the woods only solid shot should be used, and fired at so low an elevation as to strike the ground at the edge of the woods and enter on the ricochet. The appearance of the woods and the enemy's dead left there gave ample testimony to the excellence of this practice.[29]

The Rebels did not consider the battle over yet. Undaunted by the repulse of the concentric attack based on the inadequate reconnaissance of the previous day's Union line, Hill and Mahone immediately began looking for a weak point in the new Federal position. Shortly before noon, they sent Barringer's brigade of Tarheel horsemen on a reconnaissance in force about a mile south of Globe Tavern, beyond Warren's left—a move they ought to have made earlier that morning if not the previous afternoon.

Barringer's cavalrymen trotted along the road from Poplar Spring Church to White's farm on the Weldon Railroad. East of the Vaughan Road, Barringer put in the 3rd and 5th North Carolina Cavalry to charge. The Federal skirmishers resisted sharply, but the Tarheels started the Unionist videttes and carried their entrenched picket line. The North Carolinians swept everything before them. Arriving within a few yards of the railroad, they met "the deadliest and heaviest single discharge we had ever known" coming from a breastwork near the railway, recalled Maj. John M. Galloway of the 5th North Carolina.[30]

The volley came from the 121st, 143rd and 187th Pennsylvania of Tilton's brigade of Griffin's division, the 1st Massachusetts Cavalry and a battalion of the 10th New York Cavalry of Stedman's brigade, and the 11th Battery,

---

29 OR 42, pt. 1, 542-3.

30 Clark, *North Carolina Regiments*, 3:540, 619-20.

Massachusetts Light Artillery. These units had just rushed down from the vicinity of Globe Tavern and thrown up the earthworks. "By this time the troops had become so accustomed to throwing up works as soon as a halt was made that one of the natural consequences of a halt was the erection, in a remarkably short space of time, of a line of breastworks," veterans of the 121st Pennsylvania remembered.[31]

The North Carolinians fell back under heavy fire but still in order. The Federals took the offensive and sought to envelop the Tarheels as their comrades had enveloped Hagood's brigade. The 1st New Jersey Cavalry hurried up through flooded fields, dismounted and threatened Barringer's right. Other Union formations threatened Barringer's left. The 1st and 2nd North Carolina Cavalry took position on each flank of the retiring Tarheel regiments and checked the Northerners.

After this reconnaissance, Mahone encountered Lee near the Davis house. Old Porte told the army leader that if given two fresh brigades, he would guarantee to drive the Federals from the Weldon Railroad. Lee sent for Anderson's, Bratton's and Law's brigades of Field's division from north of James River.

The Unionist high command continued to move up reinforcements to secure Warren's position on the Weldon road. Shortly after 11:00 a.m., Ferrero's division of IX Corps received orders to reinforce Warren. At about the same time, Barlow's and Gibbon's divisions of II Corps, making coffee near the Deserted House, got word to join Warren in case of an emergency. The two divisions had reached the Deserted House at daybreak after an all night hike. Hundreds had fallen out during the march. Orderly Sergeant Powelson of Company K, 140th Pennsylvania, in Miles' brigade, wrote: "We, of K, well remember the never-to-be-forgotten tramp, tramp all the night of the 20th, through darkness, rain and mud; awful and yet laughable, when men got lost, when hats, shoes, caps, etc., disappeared, as the boys stumbled on in brush and darkness."[32] At 11:30 a.m., the soldiers of Barlow's and Gibbon's divisions plodded toward the Strong house, where they again encamped for a few hours. They staggered in behind Warren's position at 3:00 p.m. in terrible condition. Lieutenant Colonel Lyman of Meade's staff remembered:

---

31 Survivors' Association, *History of the 121st Regiment Pennsylvania Volunteers* (Philadelphia, 1893), 84.

32 Powelson, *History of Company K, 140th Pennsylvania*, 40.

The long, rapid marches of this Corps have given it the name of "Hancock's cavalry." When a halt was ordered, one soldier said to the next: "O Jim, what er we a-stoppin for?" "The Staff is getting fresh hosses!" replied James.[33]

Irvin Gregg's cavalry brigade had ridden along the nearly impassable roads since 6:00 p.m. the previous evening in its journey to the Weldon Railroad from Deep Bottom. These horse soldiers reached Prince George Court House at daylight. After a pause there, they pushed on to McCann's house on the Jerusalem Plank Road, where they arrived at 4:45 p.m. After another rest, they rode the remainder of the way to Dr. Gurley's house by 10:00 p.m.

Anderson's brigade of Field's division arrived at Petersburg in the afternoon, but it became apparent that the Confederate transportation system could not deliver Bratton's and Law's brigades from north of James River in time for another attempt to retake the Weldon Railroad that day. Around nightfall, Lee called off the attack, withdrew from Warren's front and conceded the loss of the railway to "those people." The day's operations had cost the Rebels about 1,400 soldiers, including approximately 525 prisoners.[34] The

---

33 Agassiz, *Meade's Headquarters*, 221.

34 In Heth's command east of the railroad, Cooke's brigade lost seven killed, fifty-two wounded and three missing. Raleigh *Daily Confederate*, August 26, 1864, p. 2, col. 4. Ransom's brigade lost twenty-four killed, 159 wounded and sixty-two missing. Richmond *Examiner*, August 31, 1864, p. 2, col. 5. The 56th North Carolina lost 71, Ransom's brigade 240. The Weekly *Catawba Journal*, August 30, 1864, p. 2, col. 2.

In Heth's command west of the railroad, which consisted entirely of MacRae's brigade, the 26th North Carolina lost six killed and twenty wounded. Raleigh *Daily Confederate*, August 27, 1864, p. 2, col. 5-6. The 44th North Carolina lost seven killed and twenty-one wounded. Ibid, p. 2, col. 5. The 47th North Carolina lost four killed and twenty-two wounded. Ibid., August 30, 1864, p. 2, col. 5. The 11th and 52nd North Carolina of the brigade probably suffered losses consistent with the aforesaid three regiments, giving the brigade a loss of about 130.

In Mahone's command north of the Vaughan Wagon Road, Harris' brigade lost at least 254 killed, wounded, and missing, and may have lost as many as eleven killed, 108 wounded and 151 missing. *OR* 42, pt. 1, 939. The 2nd, 5th and 8th Florida of Finegan's brigade lost four killed, eighteen wounded, and one missing. Richmond *Enquierer*, September 2, 1864, p. 2, col. 3-4. Losses in the 9th, 10th and 11th Florida approximately equaled those in the other half of Finegan's brigade, leaving the entire brigade with a loss of around fifty soldiers. Fred L. Robertson, comp., *Soldiers of Florida in the Seminole Indian, Civil, and Spanish-American Wars* (Live Oak FL, 1903), 207-44. Sanders' brigade lost three killed, thirty-seven wounded and one missing. *The Sentinel*, Richmond, October 29, 1864, p. 1, col. 6. The 11th Alabama suffered three killed, ten wounded, two captured. Griffin, *11th Alabama*, 207-8.

In Mahone's command south of the Vaughan Wagon Road, Wright's brigade, Scales' brigade and the detachment of Thomas' brigade each probably suffered fewer casualties than Sanders' brigade. They probably lost 100 men among them.

Federals had lost around 302 troops, mostly captive pickets.[35] During the entire battle of Globe Tavern, the Confederates had lost approximately 2,400 soldiers, including about 800 prisoners.[36] The losses of the Army of the Potomac amounted to at least 4,279, including no fewer than 2,879 prisoners.[37] August 21's repulse had raised the level of Northern victory from the Pyrrhic to the merely costly.

In a letter to President Davis written the next day, Lee summed up the battle of Globe Tavern, enumerated the considerations leading him to abandon the effort to dislodge the Northerners and set forth his understanding of Grant's strategy. The Virginian thought Grant had given up on taking Richmond by storm and instead intended to compel the evacuation of the Confederate capital by cutting off its supplies. Lee's letter began:

> The enemy availed himself of the withdrawal of troops from Petersburg to the north side of James River, to take a position on the Weldon Railroad. He was twice attacked on his first approach to the road, and worsted both times, but the attacking force was too small to drive him off.

The Virginian omitted that only three brigades of his infantry had withdrawn from Petersburg to the north side of the James. Lee then wrote, "Before the troops could be brought back from north of the James River, he had strengthened his position so much, that the effort made yesterday to

---

Hagood's brigade lost fourteen killed, 125 wounded and 309 missing. List of casualties in Hagood's Brigade on August 21, 1864, in an attack on enemy's work near Petersburg, in *OR* 42, pt. 1, 937.

35 Ibid., 431

36 "Our casualties in the affair of Sunday, the 21st, have been greatly exaggerated. Hagood's brigade suffered most, both in prisoners and killed and wounded; but our entire loss on Friday [August 19] and Sunday [August 21] does not exceed 1,500." From P. W. A., correspondent of the Savannah *Republican* in Macon *Daily Telegraph*, Sept. 3, 1864, p. 2, col. 2. The casualty figures available for August 19 and August 21 prove 1,500 a low estimate of Confederate casualties on August 19 and August 21. The Secessionists lost a total of around 2,000 those days.
  For Confederate losses on August 18, see note 24 to Chapter 6.
  For Confederate losses on August 19, see note 49 to Chapter 7.
  For Confederate losses on August 20, see note 4 to Chapter 8.
  For Confederate losses on August 21, see note 34 to Chapter 9.

37 Return of Casualties in the Union Forces, Weldon Railroad, VA. (or Globe Tavern, Yellow House, and Blick's Station), August 18-21, 1864, in *OR* 42, pt. 1, 128; Reports of casualties of Fifth Army Corps and in First and Third Divisions, Ninth Corps, for the 18th, 19th, 20th, and 21st of August, 1864, ibid., 432.

dislodge him was unsuccessful. . . ." He overlooked that the three infantry brigades had begun returning to the Cockade City from north of James River on the morning of August 19 and had all completed their journey back by the morning of the next day. The high command had the same number of foot soldiers available for an attack south of the James on the morning of the 20th as on the morning of the 21st. The Federals strengthened their position during that interval while the Southern high command arranged a set-piece attack at the leisurely pace of a wheezing, sputtering Confederate ironclad.

Lee then engaged in an analysis of costs and benefits that brooked no dispute, writing that dislodging the enemy "could not be accomplished even with additional troops, without a greater sacrifice of life than we can afford to make, or than the advantages of success would compensate for. . . ." Likewise, none could argue that the Southerners could ever render the rails invulnerable to Northern depredations. The Virginian explained,

> The proximity of the enemy and his superiority of numbers rendered it possible for him to break the road at any time, and even if we could drive him from the position he now holds, we could not prevent him from returning to it or to some other point, as our strength is inadequate to guard the whole road. . . .[38]

With the South Side Railroad and the Richmond and Danville Railroad still not repaired from the damage that the Wilson-Kautz Raid had done, the loss of the indefensible Weldon Railroad came at a bad time for the Confederates. They had exhausted their corn reserves in Richmond. As a result, the long anticipated loss of the Weldon road seriously constricted Lee's supply. The Army of Northern Virginia's leader soon had to cut rations by at least a quarter and perhaps as much as from a half pound of bacon and a pound and a half of corn meal per day to a quarter pound of bacon and half a pound of corn meal per day. Previously occasional shipments of sugar and coffee stopped altogether. As time went on, meat became even scarcer. Civilians suffered worse than did soldiers as the price of commodities on the Richmond market skyrocketed.

Though Lee did not contemplate abandoning Petersburg and Richmond, six lean weeks loomed ahead before the harvest would replenish the exhausted corn reserves. Soon after the Northerners cut the Weldon Railroad, the

---

38 Clifford Dowdey and Louis Manarin, eds., *The Wartime Papers of R. E. Lee* (Boston, 1961), 842.

Virginian dispatched wagon trains to haul supplies along a thirty mile route from Stony Creek to the Cockade City to minimize the damage caused by the railroad's loss. The wagon trains traveled from Stony Creek to Dinwiddie Court House on the Flat Foot Road, and then from Dinwiddie Court House to Petersburg on the Boydton Plank Road.

Lee never felt that he had enough soldiers. He did not miss an opportunity to trumpet how effectively Grant had utilized the Federal superiority in numbers. On August 23, the Army of Northern Virginia's leader recommended to James A. Seddon, the Confederate Secretary of War, "that all details of arms bearing men be revoked, except in cases of absolute necessity." Lee declared that "the time has arrived in my opinion when no man should be excused from service, except for the purposes of doing work absolutely necessary for the support of the army." He finished by warning: "Without some increase of strength, I cannot see how we are to escape the natural military consequences of the enemy's numerical superiority."[39]

In Lee's eyes, the loss of the Weldon Railroad amounted to just such a consequence.

He perceived a silver lining to the cloud that arose from the demise of the Weldon road. The Federals had incurred casualties out of all proportion to the military advantage gained. Long lists of killed, wounded and missing could only affect Northern morale adversely. Severing the Weldon Railroad did not amount to a success of the magnitude that the Lincoln administration required to sell the electorate on four more years. Around the time Lee wrote, Lincoln began to take steps to prepare for an orderly transition to the next administration in the increasingly likely event of his losing the November election.

By cutting the Weldon Railroad, Grant attained one of his less ambitious objectives in launching his Fourth Offensive. The general-in-chief sought to push his advantage to the utmost. The relentless Grant characteristically responded to the morning's attack on Warren by directing Meade to threaten the Rebel lines east of Petersburg by opening fire, which Meade did with XVIII Corps and Mott's II Corps division. The bloody repulse of the morning's Confederate assault at the Weldon Railroad did not satisfy Grant and Meade. They wanted Warren to assume the offensive and annihilate the defeated Secessionists. The V Corps chief, the proverbial man on the ground, aware of

---

39 R. E. Lee to Secretary of War, August 23, 1864, in *OR* 42, pt. 2, 1199-1200.

Maj. Gen. Gouverneur K. Warren, U.S.A. *Library of Congress*

the piteous condition of the troops under his command, wisely contented himself with preparing to meet further Southern attempts to recapture the railroad. For Grant and Meade, Warren's failure to counterattack robbed the day's victory of its sweetness.

The general-in-chief and the Army of the Potomac's leader did not repose the same confidence in Warren as they did in Hancock or Sheridan. They gave the II Corps chief and the commander of the Shenandoah departments the benefit of the doubt, which they did not give the V Corps leader. Whenever Hancock or Sheridan declined to attack, Grant and Meade believed that the II Corps commander or the chief of the Shenandoah departments had good reason for his decision. If Warren declined to attack, Grant and Meade ascribed the decision of the leader of V Corps to a lack of aggression. They resented such decisions by Warren even when events proved him right—as they did on August 21 when, left to his own devices, he won a significant victory.

Grant and Meade wanted subordinates who leaned toward the aggressive. That lent credibility to any decision such a subordinate made to call off an attack. Unlike Hancock and Sheridan, Warren did not fill this bill. Years later, Grant wrote of the V Corps chief:

> He could see every danger at a glance before he had encountered it. He would not only make preparations to meet the danger which might occur, but he would inform his commanding officer what others should do while he was executing his move.[40]

Warren ought to have sought employment elsewhere. He did not fit in within Grant's army group. The bad fit only generated friction that increased the ill will of his superiors. The V Corps leader lacked either the social antennae to perceive this growing animosity or the sense to understand the enormous damage his dissatisfied superiors could—and ultimately would—do to his career. Meade resented Warren's decision to call off a planned attack during the Mine Run Campaign of the previous autumn, even though the commander of the Army of the Potomac conceded the correctness of the decision. Meade had seriously considered sacking Warren in June. Grant would invite Sheridan to sack Warren the following spring, and Sheridan would take Grant up on the invitation after Warren had won for Sheridan the battle of Five Forks. On August 21, Grant prodded Warren to attack until the V Corps chief in none too

---

40 Grant, *Personal Memoirs of U. S. Grant*, 604.

subtle a fashion suggested that Grant put in charge of any such operation Major General Parke, the commander of IX Corps, who ranked Warren and had arrived on the field. Backing down, Grant added the incident to his list of grievances against Warren and looked for an opportunity to strike the enemy elsewhere.

The general-in-chief thought that he had found such an opportunity. On the previous day, Benjamin Butler had detected a weakness in the Bermuda Hundred lines opposite Port Walthall because of the departure of Langley's detachment of Pickett's division and the detachments from Scales' and Thomas' brigades of Wilcox's division. The commander of the Army of the James proposed using David Birney's X Corps to exploit the weakness when it returned from north of James River. At 1:00 p. m. on August 21, Grant ordered Butler to make a reconnaissance with X Corps on the following morning, to take the Rebel line if possible and, if not successful, to relieve the disease-wracked XVIII Corps and put it on high ground in reserve. More than two months in the trenches, malaria from the corps' previous assignment in the swamps of the southeastern coast, and the recent heavy rains had increased the sick from seven percent of XVIII Corps to between seventeen and twenty percent. Butler directed David Birney to feint near Ware Bottom Church and strike between Bake House Creek and the Appomattox River.

Chapter 10

Wrecking the Weldon Railroad, August 21-24, 1864

During the latter half of the first week of the offensive, the Federals had torn up the Weldon Railroad primarily to fortify their position along the tracks. The railway's destruction began in earnest after the failure of the Southern assault of August 21. Grant wanted to wreck the Weldon road as far south as possible.

About noon, Colonel Spear rode westward from Globe Tavern with three regiments of horsemen. By 1:00 p.m., he had reached the Vaughan Road and found that the Rebels had withdrawn even their outer pickets. Spear pushed on to Wyatt's house, farther southwest on the Church Road. There he found Rooney Lee's division of cavalry. Picketing every point strongly, Spear skirmished with the advance posts of the Secessionists. Late in the afternoon, Spear's troopers drove a seventy-man Confederate detachment from Reams Station. The Unionists destroyed two big water tanks, some pumps and a large storehouse, then tore down the telegraph wires for two miles to the south while in pursuit of the fleeing Rebels.

By nightfall, the 200-man working party from the Quartermaster's Department had destroyed the track for a mile and a half south of Globe Tavern since reaching Warren the previous evening. Stedman's cavalry brigade still guarded the working party. According to Chaplain Pyne of the 1st New Jersey Cavalry, the wreckers employed in their destruction of the Weldon Railroad, a machine patented for that purpose; but the road was in such bad condition that the machine could not add seriously to its worthlessness. The ties were so rotten, the rails so poorly tempered, that there was no purchase afforded for the instrument, no sufficient resistance to call forth its powers.[1]

Shortly after midnight, David Birney detected the return of the Secessionists from north of James River. At 1:30 a.m. on August 22, Grant suspended the X Corps attack that Benjamin Butler had prepared for later that day on the Bermuda Hundred front. The general-in-chief ordered Butler to hold X Corps ready for another day or two in case Union operations south of Petersburg induced the Confederates to weaken their Bermuda Hundred trenches again.

South of the James, Meade worried that the Rebels withdrawn from Warren's front during the previous night might assault the thin line of the sickly XVIII Corps, which Grant wanted to relieve. During the morning, V Corps pickets allayed Meade's fears by locating the Secessionists about a mile back from the previous day's position.

At about noon, Meade sent Barlow's II Corps division—still led by General Miles—to assist the working party in tearing up the tracks south of Globe Tavern and to assist Gregg's cavalrymen in covering the party. Placed under Gregg's command, Spears received orders to attack the Southerners. During the afternoon, Spears' brigade engaged a small force of Confederate cavalry on the Church Road near Wyatt's house. In a fight about forty-five minutes long, the Federal horsemen drove the Rebels cross country toward Petersburg. The Secessionists found refuge by burning a bridge over a branch of Arthur Swamp.

By 6:00 p.m., Barlow's division and the working party had wrecked the railroad to within one and a half miles of Reams Station. Gregg's cavalrymen rode into Reams Station at dark and found no opposition there, though they learned of the proximity of a brigade of Confederate cavalry—Chambliss' brigade, encamped at Tabernacle Church, six miles southwest of Reams Station.

That night a very heavy rain fell. The rain left the country roads impassable for artillery and wagons. Only the main roads remained capable of bearing traffic. On the morning of August 23, the same day on which Lincoln began preparing for the possible loss of the November election, Meade perceived that the condition of the roads posed serious problems for large-scale troop

---

1 Pyne, *First New Jersey Cavalry*, 288.

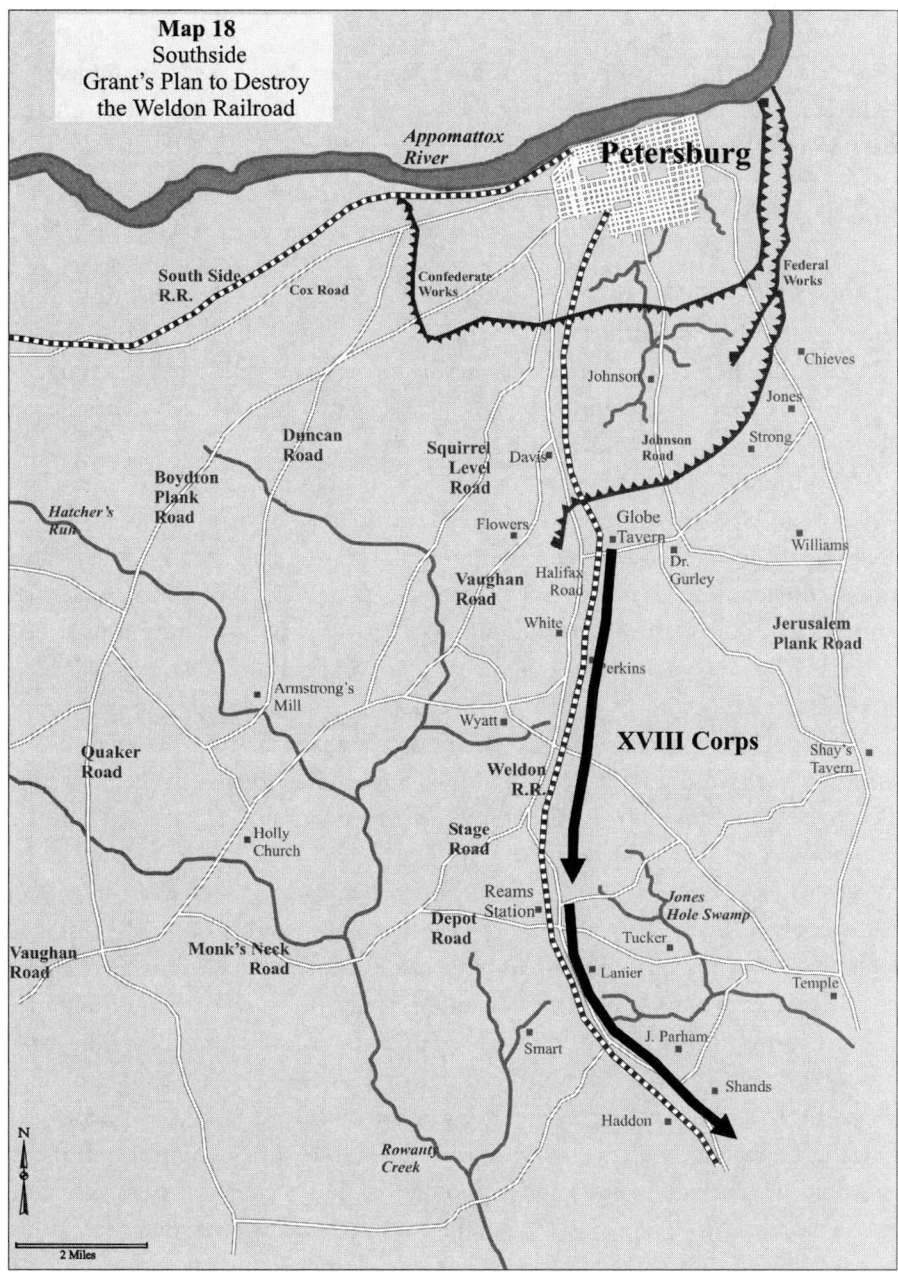

movements. Supplying any large force at a distance from the main army would prove difficult, if not impossible. Wagons, cannon, limber chests and caissons could make no progress in the mud.

Before 10:45 a.m., Grant learned for the first time of the actual proportions of the disaster that V Corps had suffered on August 19. He had the unpleasant experience of discerning them not from Warren or Meade, but from the Richmond newspapers. Queried by the general-in-chief about the accuracy of the Southern reports, the Army of the Potomac's leader had to admit that the official returns of V Corps tended to confirm Rebel claims of 2,700 prisoners.

About the same time, Gregg dispatched Spears' tired brigade of cavalry to Miles, who sent Spear on a reconnaissance west of Reams Station reinforced by the regiment-sized Companies A and H from the 4th New York Heavy Artillery. The horsemen and the heavies drove the cavalry pickets of Barringer's North Carolina brigade almost all the way back to Monk's Neck Bridge on Rowanty Creek before withdrawing.

At around 11:00 a.m., Barlow returned to the command of his division and Miles returned to the command of his brigade. Barlow directed Miles to occupy Reams Station. Miles gave this assignment to the 81st and 183rd Pennsylvania under the command of Colonel James C. Lynch of the 183rd, who had commanded Miles' brigade while Miles commanded Barlow's division. Lynch occupied Reams Station without meeting any opposition. The rest of Miles' brigade arrived before 1:00 p.m. Miles' troops began tearing up the railroad.

Back at City Point, shortly before noon, Grant instructed Butler to use X Corps to relieve XVIII Corps. The general-in-chief then travelled to Fort Powhatan, downriver from City Point, arriving before 2:15 p.m. There he conceived the plan of sending XVIII Corps and the cavalry to wreck the Weldon Railroad all the way down to Hicksford, part of modern Emporia on the Meherrin River, as soon as the roads dried. This would double the distance to Petersburg from the railhead and increase the inconvenience to the Rebels.

Before 2:00 p.m., Companies G and M of the 4th New York heavies under Capt. Gardner L. Morrison relieved Companies A and H of their duty with Spear's brigade. Near Monk's Neck Bridge on Rowanty Creek, about two miles west of Reams Station, Spear's videttes again drove in the pickets of Barringer's brigade of Rooney Lee's cavalry division, this time just as Matthew Butler's division, which had crossed the Appomattox that morning, began relieving those pickets. An engagement began that went on so long that Sergeant Tobie of the 1st Maine Cavalry in Irvin Gregg's brigade called the action the "fight by moonlight."[2] The Rebels knew the action as "Gravelly Run."[3]

---

2 Tobie, *First Maine Cavalry*, 313.

3 U. R. Brooks, *Butler and His Cavalry in the War of Secession 1861-1865* (Columbia, SC), 284.

Butler encountered Spear's pickets just east of Monk's Neck Bridge and drove the Federals back. The Virginians of Rosser's brigade—the Laurel Brigade—still under Dulany's command, deployed in woods on the Stage Road, which ran northeast from the bridge. They formed Butler's left. The 11th Virginia Cavalry dismounted on the left of the Stage Road, the 7th Virginia Cavalry on the right. Part of the 12th Virginia Cavalry dismounted and plodded forward as skirmishers. The rest of the 12th Virginia Cavalry remained mounted along with the 35th Battalion Virginia Cavalry, the Comanches. The First Squadron of the Comanches joined Butler, who had ridden to the right with Dunovant's South Carolina brigade. The South Carolinians formed Butler's right, dismounting on the Depot Road in an open field. The Depot Road diverged from the Stage Road about a mile northeast of Monk's Neck Bridge and ran east by southeast to Reams Station.

Along the Stage Road, the Laurel Brigade drove the mounted Federal pickets back through the woods to a corn field. The dismounted Virginians could see a line of breastworks occupied by infantry about 500 yards across the field, which gently sloped downward from the Laurel Brigade. The 7th and 11th Virginia Cavalry lay down behind a dilapidated rail fence on the crest at the edge of the woods.

After the passage of what seemed half an hour to the Virginians, a body of Federals that looked as big as a brigade advanced. The apparent brigade actually consisted of two companies of the 4th New York heavies. One, Company M, menaced the left flank of the 11th Virginia. The other, Company G, charged the rail fence. Spear had ordered this advance, promising that he would support the heavies with his whole brigade, though he counseled Captain Morrison not to get too ambitious—the cavalry brigade, armed with sixteen shooters, had run low on ammunition.

"A charge up a hill through a field of tall corn made a very lively experience, the Johnnies' bullets whistling through the stalks at a great rate, and in the most discouraging manner," recalled First Lt. William B. Knower of Company G of the 4th New York heavies.[4] The bullets whistled faster as the Federals neared the fence. "A withering fire met them, but they fell flat on the ground and, partly concealed by the grass, poured volley after volley into the thin lines of the dismounted men," remembered Capt. William N. McDonald, Ordnance

---

4 Hyland C. Kirk, *Heavy Guns and Light of the 4th New York Heavy Artillery* (New York, 1890), 335.

Maj. Gen. Wade Hampton, C.S.A. *National Archives*

Officer of the Laurel Brigade.[5] The Virginians fell back through the trees to where they had initially deployed. The New Yorkers followed and continued the firefight with the Virginians. The heavies became apprehensive as they

---

5   William N. McDonald, *A History of the Laurel Brigade Originally the Ashby Cavalry of the Army of Northern Virginia and Chew's Battery* (Baltimore), 270.

waited for support from Spear. The company-sized regiments of Virginia cavalry looked bigger and bigger to the regiment-sized companies of New Yorkers as time passed.

Unnoticed by the heavies, Spear deployed his brigade on the Depot Road, to their left. Dunovant's brigade advanced along the Depot Road through the open field in which the South Carolinians had deployed. The brigade entered the woods on the other side of the field without first throwing out a skirmish line. In the timber, the dismounted South Carolinians met with a heavy fire from the concealed troopers of Spear's brigade. Dunovant's soldiers received orders to lie down, but a prone position did not make the fire much less galling.

Spear suddenly seized the initiative and sent forward several mounted squadrons to charge Dunovant's line. "Their cavalry came rushing on us as if just risen from the earth," recalled Pvt. Charles M. Calhoun of Company C in the 6th South Carolina Cavalry, the Dixie Rangers.[6] Dunovant's brigade fled before the horsemen of the aggressive Spear.

The Federals smote the routed South Carolinians with pistol and sabre. The panic spread to the Laurel Brigade. Some Virginian field officers began counseling retreat. The hard-fighting Spear might have driven the Virginians and South Carolinians back across Rowanty Creek but for the steadiness of Matthew Butler. Though encircled by Unionists at one point, the one-legged division commander kept his head with hand to hand fighting going on all around him. He rallied his troops after they had retreated about 100 yards. Then, committing his reserves, he led a counterinteraction. Spear, who had received no support from David Gregg or Barlow other than the two companies of heavies, reluctantly retreated. Butler reestablished the Southern picket line and quickly removed the dead and wounded from the battlefield.

While Spear struggled with Butler, Gregg arrived at Reams Station. About an hour after Butler's troopers had driven off Spear and reestablished the Rebel picket line, Gregg sent the 2nd and 16th Pennsylvania Cavalry out on the Depot Road to investigate the reports of an engagement about a mile and a half to the west. The two Keystoner regiments soon encountered the Confederate pickets and drove them in on Butler's main body. Butler in turn pushed the Federals over a hill and back toward Reams Station. Gregg reinforced his advance force until he had committed eight of his nine available regiments. He kept in reserve

---

6   Charles M. Calhoun, *Liberty dethroned. A Concise History of Some of the Most Startling Events Before, During, and Since the Civil War* (Greenwood SC, 1903), 138.

his ninth regiment to guard his flanks and plug any gap that developed. The Unionists brought the Rebels to a halt about a mile west of the railroad. Along that line, the Federals would rise up, fire, and drop down as quickly as possible. "Shooting was brisk, and bullets did everlastingly hum there," remembered Sergeant Tobie.[7] David Gregg had no difficulty supplying his troopers with all the ammunition they wanted.

By this time, the rest of Barlow's division had joined Miles' brigade at Reams Station. Barlow's soldiers had wrecked the railway all the way there despite the rain, which repeatedly put out the fires of destruction. The Southern cavalry continued to press David Gregg's line vigorously and long after dark, when the "fight by moonlight" acquired its name.

"Each side improvised breastworks of rails, logs, rocks, and such material of defense as old soldiers of both sides understand how to provide without the instructions of engineers or technical advice," recalled Pvt. Ulysses Robert Brooks of Company B, the Edgefield Rangers, in the 6th South Carolina Cavalry.[8] The soldiers could aim only by the flash of the enemy's guns. At times they would remain quiet for perhaps a quarter of an hour. Then firing would start on both sides, "that would make the woods ring, sometimes by volleys and sometimes scattering," remembered Tobie. "When the rebs fired by volley we could see their whole line in the flash." Then shooting would die down and all would go quiet again. Both sides would listen intently to catch the least sound of any attempt of the other side to sneak up in the dark. Several times the Secessionists tried to surprise his regiment under cover of darkness, recalled Tobie,

> and once succeeded in almost reaching the line in what may be called a silent charge, but their coming was made known, either by some one of their number firing a shot too soon, or by some exclamation, and each time the boys rose up and poured such a rapid fire into the foe that they were only too glad to get back to their lines, and they finally gave up the attempt, having made nothing by it.[9]

---

7   Tobie, *First Maine Cavalry*, 314.

8   Brooks, *Butler and His Cavalry*, 285.

9   Tobie, *First Maine Cavalry*, 313.

At about 9:00 p.m., Butler withdrew his tired troops. The Federals had lost around 130 soldiers.[10] The Confederates had lost 136.[11]

In reaction to the fight by moonlight, Meade ordered the Unionists at Reams Station reinforced with Gibbon's division of II Corps and four batteries of artillery. Dispatching Gibbon's division gave the assignment of wrecking the railroad down to Hicksford to II Corps instead of XVIII Corps as Grant had contemplated. For II Corps, the assignment may have proven the straw that broke the camel's back. "Used up" described both II Corps and XVIII Corps, but II Corps had arrived at that condition by marching and fighting. XVIII Corps merited the description because of illness and a long stay in the trenches in close proximity to the enemy. The way Hagood's brigade had revived upon leaving its earthworks two days earlier suggested that troops apparently debilitated by service in the trenches might recover much more quickly than soldiers fatigued by marching and fighting. XVIII Corps may not have had any more soldiers than Barlow's and Gibbon's divisions of II Corps and if given the assignment it might not have fared any better at Reams Station than those divisions of II Corps, but employing yet again those once elite II Corps formations represented poor personnel management.[12] II Corps wound up used twice during the offensive, V Corps once, IX Corps once, X Corps once, but XVIII Corps not at all. Had Meade followed Grant's directives, each of the army group's infantry corps would have fought just once.

---

10 The 4th New York Heavy Artillery suffered four killed, six wounded, two missing, three sunstruck. Report of Capt. John B. Vande Wiele, Fourth New York Heavy Artillery, of operations August 22-26, in *OR* 42, pt. 1, 269-70. Spear's brigade lost eight killed, thirty-two wounded. S. P. Spear to Lieut. Col. F. T. Locke, August 23, 1864, ibid., pt. 2, 427. David Gregg did not think his loss in killed and wounded would exceed seventy-five. D. McM. Gregg to Major-General Humphreys, August 23, 1864, ibid., 436.

11 Wells, *Hampton and His Cavalry in '64*, 277.

12 *OR* 42, pt. 1, 228; Military Order of the Loyal Legion of the United States, Commandery of the State of Illinois, "Military Essays and Recollections" (3 vols.), 3:128. Ord asserted that he had about 10,000 infantry fit for duty in XVIII Corps on August 21. E. O. C. Ord to Col. J. W. Shaffer, August 21, 1864, in *OR* 42, pt. 2, 385-6. At the end of August, XVIII Corps had 9,179 officers and men present for duty in its three divisions. Abstract from returns of the Department of Virginia and North Carolina, Maj. Gen. Benjamin F. Butler, U.S. Army, commanding, for the month of August, 1864, ibid., 618. II Corps, despite the losses of Second Deep Bottom and Second Reams Station, had present for duty in its three divisions 13,233. Abstract from return of the Army of the Potomac, Maj. Gen. George G. Meade, U.S. Army, commanding, for the month of August, 1864, ibid., 611.

Meade also sent Hancock to take command at Reams Station. Named after Lt. Gen. Winfield Scott, Hancock headed down into Dinwiddie County, Scott's birthplace, with Gibbon's division and the four batteries. Under Maj. Gen. John Gibbon, a West Pointer and former commander of the Iron Brigade who had just returned from a personal leave of absence, the Second Division of II Corps slogged southward on the Jerusalem Plank Road followed by the artillery. The column turned off toward Reams Station at Shay's Tavern. Trees felled by the Rebels slowed progress, as did a battery that got stuck in dry quicksand. Gibbon's troops and the guns did not begin occupying the works at Reams Station until 3:00 a.m. on August 24. By 10:00 a.m., all the components of Gibbon's column had arrived. Hancock's command at Reams Station consisted of 6,000 to 6,500 infantry and about 2,000 cavalry, with sixteen guns.[13]

VI Corps had begun the earthworks at Reams Station at the end of June, just after First Reams Station, a rout of Federal cavalry retreating from the Wilson-Kautz Raid on the South Side Railroad and the Richmond and Danville Railroad. Rain had washed down the sides of the works. Stagnant water stood in the ditch that ran along the inside of the fortifications. They began at the edge of Jones Hole Swamp, about half a mile northeast of Oak Grove Church and the burnt railroad station, and they ran southwestward to the railway. This stretch of earthworks—the northern return—had embrasures for guns and stood high enough to protect the gunners. Behind this return ran the road to Shay's Tavern. South of and parallel to this road, a small branch ran from near the church to Jones Hole Swamp.

This northern return resumend west of the tracks. At a blunt angle—the northwest angle—scarcely five yards west of the railway, the works turned southwest by south for about 700 yards. The fortifications gradually diverged from the roadbed, which ran south by southwest from the northern passage through the works to the Depot Road. There the railroad began turning gently to a south by southeasterly direction, and the southern end of the western face of the earthworks rested about forty-five yards west of the tracks.

In approximately the center of the western face of the works, an opening about ten yards wide existed for the Depot Road. North of this road, the railway ran through a cut as deep as thirteen feet. South of the road, the railroad sat on an embankment up to six feet high. The cut and the embankment made it difficult to reinforce the troops in the works west of the roadbed or supply them

---

13 Ibid., pt. 1, 228; see notes 54-57 to chapter 12.

with ammunition and also rendered withdrawal difficult. Private John D. Billings of the 10th Battery, Massachusetts Light Artillery later described the works immediately south of the Depot Road as, "a mere rifle-pit not more than three feet in height, and of frail structure, being built of fence-rails within, and these were slightly banked with sods and loose earth."[14] The earthworks here could not protect artillerymen as they loaded and fired. About halfway south from the Depot Road to the acute angle where the works bent back to and terminated at the railroad, a traverse ran at approximately right angles to the earthworks. South of the traverse, the fortifications afforded gunners more protection than did the works immediately to the north, though not as much as did the works in the northern return.

Morning illuminated a pleasant change of scenery for the soldiers of Gibbon's division and the four batteries. Instead of the battle-scarred landscape around Petersburg, the troops found themselves in a veritable garden of earthly delights. Private Billings remembered:

By daylight we found ourselves in the midst of a country which had not been much desolated by the march of war. Through this we passed cheerily along amid apple-trees laden with fruit, and cornfields whose ears were just ready for roasting.[15]

The landscape did not bear this visage long. The funeral pyres of the railroad soon began consuming the countryside. Corporal William D. Robinson of Company C in the 4th New York heavies recalled:

Brigade after brigade of the First and Second Divisions of the Second Corps would pass each other, form a line along the track, take hold of the uncovered ends of the ties, all lift at once, and throw rails and ties over on the opposite side. Cavalry had preceded us, and not only acted as skirmishers, but pulled the spikes which hold the rails to the ties. After throwing them over, we would place the ties alternately in a heap until we had twenty or twenty-four piled up. We laid the rails on top of all. Then we took the fence-rails, boards, and posts, and split and broke them into small pieces and thrust them between the ties, and set the whole on fire. The heat would make the centre of the rails red hot, and they would bend of their own weight until the ends touched the ground. While the fire was heating the rails we went into the cornfields on each side of

---

14 John D. Billings, *The History of the Tenth Massachusetts Battery of Light Artillery in the War of the Rebellion Formerly of the Third Corps and Afterward of Hancock's Second Corps, Army of the Potomac. 1862-1865*, (Boston, 1881), 241.

15 Ibid., 240.

us, and pulled armfuls of green corn, which was in its prime, and roasted it in the fire…
We continued doing this all day—tearing up, firing, and roasting.[16]

The Federals did not confine themselves to roasting corn. Union foragers returned with chickens, pigs and sheep as well. Barlow turned over command of his division to Miles in the morning and by the end of the day, Miles' soldiers had killed the livestock and wasted the crops all the way down to Malone's Crossing, about two miles south of Reams Station and about five miles from where the railroad crossed Rowanty Creek. Hancock and Gibbon allowed the soldiers of Gibbon's division to rest in the works though only thirty yards of slashing separated the northwest angle from the woods to the west—twenty yards fewer than the distance that had proven inadequate protection for Wright's Georgia brigade on August 16.

Spear's brigade of cavalry preceded Miles' foot soldiers to Malone's Crossing, covering the approach of the working party. During the day, skirmishing took place between Spear's pickets and Confederate cavalrymen. Miles sent to Spear's aid two regiments from Broady's brigade, the 145th and 148th Pennsylvania. Spear picketed the southern approaches to Reams Station while Gregg picketed from the Jerusalem Plank Road to Warren's left. Late in the afternoon, all of Miles' infantry withdrew to Reams Station, leaving Spear's brigade alone at Malone's Crossing. Miles put Col. Levin Crandell of the 125th New York in charge of the division's picket line. Crandell's face bore a scar from a shell fragment that had wounded him in an assault on Petersburg on June 16. Command of Crandell's New York brigade devolved upon Lt. Col. Joseph Hyde of the 125th New York. Captain Nelson Penfield from Company F of the 125th took command of that regiment.

Given the absence of serious opposition from the Rebels, it appeared that in another couple of days Hancock's force would have the Weldon Railroad wrecked all the way to where the tracks crossed Rowanty Creek—about a third of the way from Globe Tavern to Hicksford. The rest of the way would require around another week.

In the trenches east of the Cockade City, the Secessionists menaced XVIII Corps. During the forenoon, an estimated 5,000 Rebel infantry apparently massed opposite Ord's left division, near the Crater. The Union signal officers actually saw a much smaller number of soldiers from Scales' brigade pulling out

---

16 Kirk, *Heavy Guns and Light*, 336-7.

of the trenches for a march down the Weldon Railroad. By late afternoon, the Federals had come to consider the threat as illusory. Terry departed from Bermuda Hundred with two brigades totaling 1,800 infantry to go to the relief of XVIII Corps. Straggling during what turned into a night march cut this force of exhausted X Corps troops down to 700 soldiers by the time they reached Ord.

More ominous developments took place on the Union left. Before sundown, Federal signal officers reported 8,000 to 10,000 Secessionist infantry hiking southwest on the Vaughan Road. Meade cautioned Hancock to prepare for an attack by this force. Despite the warning, Hancock allowed the night to pass as he and Gibbon had allowed the day to pass—without effecting a single improvement in the breastworks at Reams Station. This would have serious repercussions on the morrow and raises the question of whether, unlike Hancock and his troops, Ord and XVIII Corps would have possessed the willpower and energy to improve the fortifications at Reams Station. Exhaustion from entrenching beat starvation at Andersonville.

The fight by moonlight of August 23 led directly to Second Reams Station. On the night of the fight and on the following morning, Hampton evaluated the reports of his subordinates. The South Carolinian perceived the weakness of the Northern force at Reams Station—according to his information, a single division each of cavalry and infantry without any artillery. In the finest tradition of the Army of Northern Virginia, Lee's best yet least senior current corps chief proposed to the army leader that the infantry join the cavalry in an attack on the Federals at Reams Station. Hampton withdrew his men from the immediate environs of the station but held the junction of the Stage Road and the Depot Road to protect the Monk's Neck Bridge crossing of Rowanty Creek.

Always willing to consider the ideas and initiatives of subordinates, and ever eager to strike at "those people," Lee initially thought it inadvisable to send any portion of his infantry that far from the Petersburg lines. Upon mature consideration, the Virginian accepted the South Carolinian's suggestion. The Federal troops at Reams Station simultaneously threatened Hicksford and Dinwiddie Court House. The Confederates could retain the Cockade City and Richmond despite the destruction of the Weldon Railroad as far south as Hicksford. That would only hamper Rebel supply efforts. Dinwiddie Court House constituted a far more important target. Unionist occupation of Dinwiddie Court House would compel the abandonment of the Petersburg-Richmond position. A Northern force at Dinwiddie Court House would cut off the wagon trains from either Stony Creek or Hicksford on the Weldon Railroad and threaten the South Side Railroad, the Richmond and Danville Railroad, and Lee's line of retreat. Rather than extend his outnumbered forces to guard against a Federal occupation of Dinwiddic Court House or a Union cavalry raid on the South Side Railroad and the Richmond and Danville, still not fully repaired from the June raid that had ended with First Reams Station, the Virginian chose to drive off Hancock's force. Lee also perceived the political benefits that could accrue to the Secessionist cause from a victory. Every defeat inflicted on Grant's forces would tend to discredit the Northern war party, though the Virginian could not rely on Secretary of War Stanton permitting the use of Union telegraph lines to transmit news of such a defeat, and Stanton routinely cut by half or even two thirds the Federal casualty figures he released to the press.[17]

At first Lee responded tentatively to Hampton's idea for an attack on the foe at Reams Station. The Virginian dispatched only Wilcox's division to Hampton's assistance. In response to a communication from the South Carolinian during the mid-afternoon, Lee also sent part of Harry Heth's division and put A. P. Hill in charge of the expedition. Still later, the army leader dispatched part of Mahone's division. This stripped the Petersburg lines to the point where only a single rank occupied them.

Lee did not want to attack as Beauregard and Hill had the first two days at Globe Tavern. The army commander considered those efforts piecemeal and felt they had contributed to defeat there. The arrival at the Cockade City of Anderson's, Bratton's and Law's brigades of Field's division over the past few days made possible the dispatch of a force commensurate with the task at hand. All told, the Virginian sent eight brigades of infantry to attack Hancock. These troops marched lightly armed and equipped because they had to return to the nearly empty Petersburg trenches as soon as possible. Wilcox led Anderson's brigade from Field's division and McGowan's, Scales', and Lane's brigades of Wilcox's division. With Heth went Weisiger's and Sanders' brigades from Mahone's division, and Cooke's and MacRae's brigades from Heth's division. Under Lt. Col. William J. Pegram, the Letcher Artillery and the Purcell Artillery of his own battalion, Battery A of the Sumter Artillery of Cutts' battalion, and sections of Clutter's battery and Hurt's battery of McIntosh's battalion rolled along with Hill's infantry.

---

17 Benjamin P. Thomas, ed., *Three Years with Grant as Recalled by War Correspondent Sylvanus Cadwallader* (New York, 1961), 218-9.

Lee's plan for his offensive resembled the Grant plan that had started August's struggle. The Virginian decided to feint with one wing and strike with the other. The feint would make the strike more effective. He employed an elaborate ruse for August 25 on his left while Hill struck on the far right. Major General George E. Pickett, in command of the Confederates on the Howlett Line, would demonstrate against the Federal works across the base of Bermuda Hundred. Pickett and Beauregard would exchange false signals to deceive the Unionists into thinking an attack imminent along the Bermuda Hundred and Petersburg lines. Lee hoped this would draw or immobilize Northern reserves.

Late on August 24, to avoid the Federals at Globe Tavern, Hill led his troops on a circuitous march by various routes. Second Lieutenant John F. Sale of Company H, the Norfolk Juniors, in the 12th Virginia of Weisiger's brigade, wrote of this hike in his diary:

> Remained quiet until about 1 o'clock when the everlasting order came "prepare to march & leave your baggage." Generally speaking, every one can form some idea or at least imagines he can of where we are going when such orders come but this time they fooled all the knowing ones. We did not start until 3 or 4 o'clock in the evening, and took the line of breastworks, coming out near Battery 41, I believe on the plank road. We did not keep this long but traveled by all sorts of blind roads. . . .[18]

Many soldiers left Petersburg under the impression that they would escort one of the wagon trains that had just started hauling supplies around the break in the Weldon Railroad from Stony Creek to the Cockade City by way of Dinwiddie Court House.

Wilcox's troops swung wide, taking the Boydton Plank and then the Duncan Road. They crossed Hatcher's Run, a tributary of Rowanty Creek, at Armstrong's Mill. The Duncan Road then led Wilcox's soldiers into the Vaughan Road, and they camped three or four miles beyond Armstrong's Mill, near Holly Church and the intersection of the Vaughan Road with the Monk's Neck Road. Some of Heth's troops tramped south on the Squirrel Level Road. A safe distance beyond Globe Tavern, they switched over to the more easterly Vaughan Road, still heading south. Others followed in the steps of Wilcox's soldiers. Heth's troops encamped a short distance downstream from Armstrong's Mill. Stragglers from the other infantry brigades up ahead recuperated along the roadside. "From the troops along our expedition is not

---

18 John F. Sale Diary, August 24, 1864, John F. Sale Papers.

that of guarding a wagon train," observed Private Bernard of the 12th Virginia's Petersburg Riflemen.[19]

Around sunset, Hill and Hampton conferred near Monk's Neck Bridge. Though Hill had command of the operation, he did not know the ground around Reams Station. The Virginian acquiesced in the battle plan that the South Carolinian proposed. Hampton wanted part of the Rebel cavalry to cover Hill's approach from the west on the Depot Road while the main force of Confederate horsemen took up a position on the Weldon Railroad that would threaten the southern flank of the Federals at Reams Station. The Secessionist infantry and cavalry would attack early and simultaneously, putting the Unionists in a vise. The troops bedded down with orders to march at 4:00 a.m. next morning.

---

19 George S. Bernard Diary, August 24, 1864, George S. Bernard Papers, Alderman Library, University of Virginia, Charlottesville, Virginia.

Chapter 11

The Second Battle of Reams Station, August 25, 1864

The men in Hancock's corps had enjoyed several days of unmolested demolition. The Weldon Railroad from Globe Tavern all the way south to Malone's Crossing lay in clumps of twisted iron and charred wood by the side of the grade. August 25 would prove a much different experience for the II Corps chief and his troops.

At about 3:00 a.m. on August 25, Hampton left Dunovant's brigade and the 7th Virginia Cavalry to screen Hill's approach. The South Carolinian set out with Barringer's brigade of Rooney Lee's division and the remainder of Butler's division to join Chambliss' brigade at Malone's Bridge. The Cavalry Corps leader ordered Barringer, in command of Rooney Lee's Division, to send Chambliss' brigade up Malone's Road, across Malone's Bridge, and toward Malone's Crossing from the southwest. Rosser's brigade—the Laurel Brigade—now back under the command of Brig. Gen. Thomas L. Rosser, and Young's brigade, led by Col. Gilbert J. "Gib" Wright of the 7th Georgia Cavalry, a Mexican War veteran, would support Chambliss' brigade. Hampton accompanied this column. He also directed Barringer to take Barringer's brigade, under the command of Col. William H. Cheek, up the Halifax Road toward Malone's Crossing from the southeast.

While Hampton and his cavalry approached Hancock's left south of Reams Station, Pickett staged the demonstration Lee had suggested. Near Ware Bottom Church a strong Rebel skirmish line from Hunton's brigade charged the Union pickets of X Corps. The Confederates pressed back the Federals and took a portion of the entrenched picket line. Before long, the Northern pickets counterattacked and retook the ground lost. This affair cost each side approximately fifty casualties.[1] It paid the Rebels rich dividends by drawing the attention of the Unionist high command to the right while Lee's blow neared from the left.

At Reams Station, the objective of the Virginian's blow, Hancock finally began to display concern for the security of his position. At daylight, Barlow's division of II Corps relieved Gibbon's division in the earthworks and on the picket line around Reams Station. Miles' brigade occupied the stretch of works on the right from Jones Hole Swamp to the railroad. The 140th Pennsylvania held the extreme right of the earthworks. To the 140th's left, Colonel Lynch respectively positioned the 61st New York, the 2nd New York heavies, the 12th Battery, New York light artillery, the 3rd Battery New Jersey Light Artillery, the 183rd Pennsylvania, the 5th New Hampshire, the 26th Michigan, the 28th Massachusetts, and the 81st Pennsylvania. This last regiment had its left resting on the railroad. The two batteries stood about a third of a mile east of the roadbed. To the left of Lynch's brigade, Crandell's brigade held the works from the railway to the traverse. The 4th New York heavies occupied the earthworks from the traverse back to the tracks. Someone strung telegraph wire in front of the southwestern face of the fortifications. East of the roadbed, on the left of the 4th New York heavies, Broady's brigade began constructing a light line of rifle pits that ran northeast for about 150 yards at the same angle as the works held by Miles' brigade. The refused left of the line of rifle pits ran parallel to the western face of the fortifications. As soon as Miles' brigade occupied the works, General Miles employed the entire pioneer corps of Barlow's division and an additional detail of fifty ax men in slashing the timber in front of his line. This detail also cut roads for the movement of troops and artillery behind the line.

Hancock also went on the lookout for the Secessionists. Shortly after 6:00 a.m., he directed his cavalry to undertake a reconnaissance of his front and right and promised David Gregg a brigade of infantry for support. The II Corps chief had decided not to send out Gibbon's division to wreck the Weldon Railroad down to Rowanty Creek as planned until he had assured himself of the inaccuracy of the report of Southerners headed in his direction. Before the brigade of infantry reached Gregg, his horsemen drove in the Confederate cavalry pickets at two points on the Vaughan Road west of Reams Station and

---

1   Benj. F. Butler to Lieutenant-General Grant, August 25, 1864-12:30 o'clock, in *OR* 42, pt. 2, 498; D. B. Birney to Major-General Butler, August 25, 1864, ibid., 502.

found no evidence of Rebels heading Hancock's way. The II Corps leader rode about constantly, conveying his anxiety to his troops.

Exhausted from the previous day's hot ten-mile march, Hill's foot soldiers did not rise until about 7:00 a.m. Wilcox's troops, the vanguard, crossed Monk's Neck Bridge about an hour later. Gregg's cavalry probes made Hill cautious. The prospect of a meeting engagement such as that of August 23 forced the Third Corps chief to deploy Wilcox's soldiers in line of battle. Turning off to the south, Wilcox's troops formed at right angles to the Depot Road. This threw off the timing of Hampton's plan, which called for the Rebel infantry to arrive in front of Reams Station about 9:00 a.m. Instead, after marching for around a mile cross-country, Wilcox's soldiers halted at that time. Two miles still separated them from Reams Station.

Hill's delay gave Hancock a false sense of security. Reports from Gregg's squadrons assured the II Corps leader that no large body of Secessionists had arrived in his vicinity. At about the same time as Wilcox's battle line halted, Hancock decided to send Gibbon's division out to work on the destruction of the railroad. Gibbon's division had hardly gotten out of the earthworks before Spear, as usual on outpost duty, reported the Southern cavalry advancing on him in force at Malone's Crossing.

After trotting across Malone's Bridge over Rowanty Creek, the 9th Virginia Cavalry of Chambliss' brigade dismounted and plodded to a small stream about half a mile southwest of Malone's Crossing—the Brick Kiln Branch of Warren Swamp, a tributary of Rowanty Creek. The Virginians drove in the Federal pickets and found Spear's troopers occupying a cut of the railroad on the right and left of the old brick kiln that gave the branch its name. The Union line outflanked the Virginian right. The left of the Virginians overlapped the Federal right.

The 10th Virginia Cavalry received instructions to advance and extend the 9th's line to the right. Observing the arrival of the 10th, the 9th's soldiers raised a yell and charged. They carried the Union line before the 10th could form. As the Northerners fled, they received an enfilading fire on the left and threw away their repeating rifles in their haste to retreat. A section of the 2nd Battery Jeb Stuart Light Artillery soon unlimbered and contributed to the confusion of the Federals by a rapid and well-directed fire. A few stray shots from this battery fell with unnerving effect among the Union troops along the western face of the works at Reams Station.

Chambliss' brigade and its supports followed Spear's troopers up the Halifax Road toward Reams Station for about half a mile. There the Virginians

Lt. Gen. Ambrose Powell Hill, C.S.A. *Library of Congress*

saw a large body of Federal cavalry and led-horses occupying a field. The Unionist horsemen retreated before the Confederates could take advantage of the opportunity for a charge. Spear's horse soldiers joined Gregg back at Reams Station.

While Chambliss' brigade drove Spear's men from Malone's Crossing, Barringer's brigade veered away from the Halifax Road and thrust between Reams Station and the Jerusalem Plank Road. Near the Haddon house, where the railroad and the Halifax Road swung west, Barringer's North Carolinians kept going along a lane that went northeast between the Shands and J. Parham farms and then turned northwest until, near the Tucker farm, the lane reached the road that ran from Reams Station to the Temple house on the Jerusalem Plank Road. While the 3rd North Carolina Cavalry protected Barringer's rear, the 1st North Carolina Cavalry dismounted and attacked at Tucker's farm about 9:30 a.m. Supported by the 2nd and 5th North Carolina Cavalry, the 1st broke through the 16th Pennsylvania Cavalry, which formed Gregg's picket line from Reams Station east to the Jerusalem Plank Road. The Tarheels drove the Pennsylvanians across a creek, through a wide swamp and up to within a short distance of the Federal infantry. Barringer's attack at Tucker's farm seriously affected Meade's use of the Army of the Potomac's reserves, which in turn led to a critical misunderstanding between Meade and Hancock.

As the main body of Hampton's cavalry advanced from the south, the 6th South Carolina Cavalry of Dunovant's brigade screening Hill's infantry drove in the cavalry pickets of the 13th Pennsylvania Cavalry on the Depot Road to the west of Reams Station. The 6th dismounted and pursued the Pennsylvanians to the swamp and ice pond about 400 yards northwest of the main Federal earthworks. Here the South Carolinians ran into Colonel Crandell's infantry pickets, who along with the 4th Pennsylvania Cavalry forced the 6th to withdraw several hundred yards and restored the Union cavalry picket line.

Massed in the corn and sorghum fields behind Oak Grove Church, where some of the soldiers had feasted on green corn and sweet potatoes, Gibbon's division received directions to move out to meet the Confederates advancing up the railroad from the south. Smyth's brigade, followed by Macy's brigade and then Murphy's New York brigade, double-quicked down the Halifax Road.

About three quarters of a mile down the road, near the Lanier farm, Gibbon ordered Smyth to halt and deploy skirmishers to the right of the railroad to recover the entrenching tools left by Barlow's division the previous day. Gibbon also wanted Smyth to try to capture the Rebel force confronting the Federals. Smyth's vanguard halted to the left of the railway about 400 yards from the Secessionists and opened an ineffective fire from beyond a barricade of fence rails. Colonel Thomas Alfred Smyth, a former wood carver and carriage maker from Ireland who had filibustered with William Walker in Nicaragua, deployed the 1st Delaware as skirmishers to the right of the roadbed with the 12th New Jersey in support. Advancing this line, Smyth made a left wheel in his approach and engaged the Confederates. Smyth found both of his flanks exposed and deployed two companies of the 12th New Jersey to protect his left. On the right he posted the 108th New York at nearly right angles to the skirmish line. This formation advanced about half a mile against stiff resistance, including clubbed muskets.

Smyth directed the right wing of the 12th New Jersey to deploy in single rank and to charge the Rebel cavalry skirmishers with the 1st Delaware. He also brought the rest of his brigade to a position a short distance behind his skirmish line. Smyth's skirmishers pushed the Secessionists through a corn field into an open field and then into a wood. As the Southern skirmishers disappeared into the trees, a battle line of dismounted Confederate horse soldiers emerged and forced Smyth's skirmish line back to the position it had occupied before its charge. Private William P. Haines of the 12th New Jersey's Company F, a carpenter wounded at Chancellorsville, the Wilderness, and Spotsylvania, remembered:

> We were close enough to the enemy to hear their guns snap and hear the officers giving their commands. Captain F. M. Acton and the writer lay low among the corn, as close to the ground as we could lie, the cornstalks near and around us being cut off by the bullets of the enemy, as though knives were cutting them, the balls striking in the sand threw it in our faces.[2]

The Rebels repulsed Smyth's skirmish line and then withdrew into the timber.

Threatened on both flanks by Smyth's maneuvers and perplexed by Hill's inaction, Hampton notified Hill of the Secessionist cavalry's situation. The South Carolinian tactfully suggested that the Virginian attack. Hill responded with a modification of the plan agreed upon at the previous evening's conference. The Virginian promised an attack and urged Hampton to try to draw the Federals down the railroad in order that the Confederate infantry might strike the rear of Hancock's force. Still in line of battle where they had halted two hours earlier, Wilcox's infantry returned to the Depot Road and then headed along that road toward Reams Station.

---

2 William P. Haines, *History of the Men of Co. F, with Description of the Marches and Battles of the 12th New Jersey Vols.* (Camden NJ, 1892), 80.

Upon receipt of Hill's response, Hampton complied with the Virginian's recommendation and attempted to draw the Unionists down the railway. The South Carolinian ordered Barringer to picket the road strongly from Reams Station to the Temple house and, with the rest of his command, to join the main body of the Rebel cavalry at Malone's Crossing. Barringer left Company H of the 5th North Carolina Cavalry to picket the road. The Tarheels arrived at Malone's Crossing just as Hampton's battle line withdrew about 400 yards down the roadbed. The South Carolinian directed the 2nd North Carolina Cavalry to dismount, take position on the right of the line and try to turn the flank of the Federals if an opportunity arose.

When Smyth reported the withdrawal of the Secessionist line of battle to Gibbon, the latter ordered Smyth to press the Southerners and ascertain their force and position. Smyth deployed in double line the 7th West Virginia Battalion, the 4th Ohio Battalion and the 14th Connecticut. A battalion of the 12th New Jersey took position in echelon on the left flank of this line. A battalion of the 14th Connecticut bore well to the right and rear to protect the line's right. Smyth supported the line with the 69th and 106th Pennsylvania. Advancing, Smyth's troops drove the Confederates until the Federal right flank reached a swamp. Smyth discovered the Rebels on the other side. Subjected to a severe fire, Smyth's soldiers could not advance.

As Smyth's brigade deployed to the right of the railroad, Macy's brigade took the place of Smyth's troops on the railway's left and Murphy's New Yorkers crossed the roadbed into Smyth's rear. Macy's brigade, under the command of Lieutenant Colonel Rugg of the 59th New York, deployed on the left of and at right angles to the railway. The 59th New York and the 7th Michigan advanced as skirmishers to feel the enemy on the left and kept up with Smyth's advance. Behind the New Yorkers and Michiganders, the rest of Rugg's soldiers formed in line of battle. A section of the 10th Battery Massachusetts Light Artillery unlimbered on the left front of Macy's brigade and silenced an opposing Secessionist battery. Rugg's skirmishers pressed forward about a mile and found Southern cavalry, part mounted, part dismounted.

While Gibbon followed Hampton's force back toward Malone's Crossing, the 16th Pennsylvania Cavalry and two small regiments from Broady's brigade of Barlow's division, the 116th and 145th Pennsylvania, reestablished the Unionist picket line between the Halifax Road and the Jerusalem Plank Road about 11:00 a.m. To prevent the Confederates from getting possession of the roads leading from Reams Station to the Jerusalem Plank Road, Gregg gave the roads the additional protection of the 4th and 8th Pennsylvania Cavalry. To repel any further attacks from the left and rear, the 3rd battery, New Jersey Light Artillery moved from its position on the northern return to the corn field behind the church. One section unlimbered on the knoll near the end of what would become the southern return and faced south. The other section unlimbered between the knoll and the road to Shay's Tavern and faced east. Hancock shifted his field hospitals to Oak Grove Church from the Emmons house, about a mile east of the railroad on the road to Shay's Tavern. The 140th Pennsylvania of Miles' brigade trudged eastward about three quarters of a mile on the road to Shay's Tavern and established a road block.

Back at II Corps headquarters, Hancock learned from prisoners that Rebel infantry would soon join in the attack on his force. The Pennsylvanian prepared for battle. Hancock began by directing the section of the 10th Battery, Massachusetts Light Artillery and the better part of Gibbon's division to return to Reams Station. The guns returned to their parent unit, stationed between the traverse and the Depot Road. Murphy's New Yorkers relieved that portion of Broady's brigade still in the newly constructed rifle pits that formed the beginning of the southern return. Miles ordered the 116th and 145th Pennsylvania of Broady's brigade back from the vicinity of the Tucker farm.

Broady's brigade relieved the part of Crandell's brigade occupying the earthworks between the 10th Battery, Massachusetts Light Artillery and the Depot Road. From left to right, the 7th New York heavies, the 145th Pennsylvania and the 66th New York occupied this stretch of the works. The 64th New York and the 116th Pennsylvania tramped out to the west of the earthworks as skirmishers. The 53rd and 148th Pennsylvania plodded into reserve except for Company E of the 148th, which took position as sharpshooters in the Heath house, near the picket line.

Crandell's brigade contracted its line to extend from the Depot Road to the left of Miles' brigade. The former Third Brigade, consisting of the 7th, 39th, 52nd, 57th, 111th, 125th and 126th New York, formed the left of Crandell's brigade. The former Second Brigade, the 63rd, 69th and 88th New York—the remnant of the Irish Brigade—constituted the right of Crandell's brigade.

Macy's brigade of Gibbon's division withdrew to Reams Station and took up a position on the left of Murphy's New Yorkers, except for the 7th Michigan and the 59th New York. After exchanging shots with the Rebels, these two regiments also received orders to withdraw. They halted in the woods north of the Lanier farm and functioned as a picket line there.

Smyth's brigade remained on the right of the railroad. Discovering dismounted Secessionist cavalry moving to his right in considerable force, Smyth deployed the 10th New York Battalion to meet this threat. The 10th proved insufficient to guard the rear of the brigade, and Smyth subsequently shifted the 108th New York and the 1st Delaware to his right rear, connecting with the 10th on their left and covering a lane to the railway on their right.

Macy's and Murphy's brigades, along with the accompanying section of the 10th Battery, Massachusetts Light Artillery, arrived back at Reams Station around noon, just as the Confederate infantry drove in the Union cavalry pickets on the Depot Road. In the midst of preparing lunch, Private Billings of the 10th Battery, Massachusetts Light Artillery heard the crash of small arms and looked up to see the Northern horsemen dash through the road's nearby opening in the earthworks, "raising a great dust, and riding as recklessly as if the whole Rebel army was at their heels."[3]

Cadmus Wilcox's division, the vanguard of Hill's infantry, had finally reached the battlefield. Riding eastward toward Reams Station along the Depot Road to reconnoiter in person, Wilcox found between the head of his column and the Federal infantry's rifle pits an uncultivated field broken by clumps of trees. This field stretched between thick pine woods for about 100 yards on each side of the Depot Road. Behind the Unionist rifle pits on the left of the road, a similar open field extended for several hundred yards to another pine forest, which hid the main Federal works. On the right of the road, the Union rifle pits extended to a field of corn which stretched back beyond the wall of pines on the road's left side. In this corn field stood the buildings of the Heath farm. Wilcox could see the smoke of the Federal artillery rising beyond these houses as the Union guns swept the Depot Road with shot and shell. Hill's artillery unlimbered under heavy fire 400 yards south of the Depot Road and about 1600 yards from the Unionist works, opposite the Federal left. As soon as the Confederate gunners opened fire, the Northern artillerists ceased.

Several hundred yards farther back and out of sight of the Northerners, Wilcox deployed his brigades as they arrived. Scales' brigade trudged into the thick pines on the left side of the road. Into the dense woods on the right of the road plodded McGowan's brigade, now back under Brig. Gen. Samuel McGowan, a lawyer, Mexican War Veteran, and politician who had just returned from a furlough for his fourth wound of the war. Lane's brigade, now

3 Billings, *Tenth Massachusetts Battery*, 243.

under General Conner, followed Scales' brigade into the pine forest on the road's left side.

At the same time, Wilcox deployed the sharpshooter battalions of these three brigades across the road. He then directed them to advance. The lead battalion of marksmen, from Scales' brigade, engaged the Federal pickets before McGowan's brigade had gotten into position. McGowan's sharpshooters covered and supported Scales' marksmen, following at a distance of from seventy-five to 100 yards. The sharpshooters of Lane's brigade covered and supported McGowan's marksmen, following at a similar distance.

As the marksmen of Scales' brigade advanced eastward toward the Union position at Reams Station, they found themselves in the presence of a large force of Northerners which overlapped them on both flanks. McGowan's sharpshooters therefore moved up on the right of Scales' marksmen and the sharpshooters of Lane's brigade supported the left. The three sharpshooter battalions stalked slowly through the woods and drove in the Unionist skirmishers. At the edge of the corn field beyond, the Secessionists struck the entrenched Federal picket line. With a yell, the Southern marksmen charged. The Union pickets held their position until the Confederates threatened to overwhelm them. Then the Federals broke and fled across the corn field to the cover of their main line on the railroad. The Rebel sharpshooters gave chase. As the Northern skirmishers driven in by the Secessionist sharpshooters reformed behind the breastworks, a hasty barricade of logs and brush went up across the gap where the Depot Road passed through the fortifications.

While the sharpshooters advanced, Wilcox instructed Scales' and Lane's brigades to keep under cover of the woods and pass into the pines behind the Unionist rifle pits. The division commander accompanied McGowan's brigade forward through the trees on the right of the woods as the Federal gunners shelled the timber. Wilcox's foot soldiers passed the Rebel gunners, who limbered up, advanced 300 yards, and went into battery again.

Observing the relatively unimpeded advance of his sharpshooters through the woods west of the entrenched Unionist picket line and hearing no fire from any line of battle, Wilcox thought the Northerners in the process of retiring. As a result, he sent Anderson's brigade into the woods north of the Depot Road. Meanwhile, McGowan's brigade reached the corn field south of the Depot Road and halted behind the crest. Ordering this brigade to advance no farther, Wilcox entered the woods north of the Depot Road and positioned Anderson's and Scales' brigades for an attack on the Federals.

Anderson's brigade formed in the woods about 400 yards across an open field from the Unionists. Scales' brigade deployed in the trees on the left of Anderson's brigade. The right regiment of Scales' brigade faced the same open field as Anderson's brigade. Thick woods intervened between Brig. Gen. Alfred Scales' other three regiments and the Federal earthworks.

Wilcox's charging marksmen found the earthworks along the railroad occupied not by a small force of cavalry as expected but by the better part of Hancock's two divisions of infantry. Major William S. Dunlop, the commander of McGowan's sharpshooters, remembered: "They received us with a blizzard as we cleared the field of their skirmishers."[4] The Southern marksmen engaged the Federal main line for a few minutes at short range. Developing the full strength of the Unionist line, obviously too great for them, the sharpshooters dropped back about 400 yards. This put about half the Confederate marksmen in the pine forest north of the Depot Road and the other half just behind the crest that ran north and south through the corn field on the south side of the road. The Federals mistook the advance of the sharpshooters for an assault.

Hancock reacted to the advance of the Rebel marksmen by shifting more of his troops to the western face of the earthworks. The Pennsylvanian ordered Macy's brigade from the left of Murphy's New Yorkers to the support of Crandell's brigade. Macy's brigade took position in the railroad cut. Hancock also directed Smyth's brigade to return to the works and fill the void that the departure of Macy's brigade had created on Murphy's left. David Gregg called in the videttes of the 16th Pennsylvania Cavalry from their line stretching to the Jerusalem Plank Road and put this regiment on the left of the southern return, behind Reams Station.

The II Corps leader ordered the restoration of his picket line. The task of implementing this command fell to Lt. Col. Knut Oscar Broady of the 61st New York and his brigade. Broady dispatched the 116th and 148th Pennsylvania into the corn field south of the Depot Road. At the same time, he took charge of Crandell's brigade from Lieutenant Colonel Hyde and sent Captain Penfield forward into the woods with the 111th, 125th and 126th New York. Broady ordered Penfield to link up with the 116th and 148th Pennsylvania on the left and the pickets of Miles' brigade on the right.

The advance of Penfield's force caused General Scales to report that the Union line extended beyond his left. Wilcox dispatched two regiments of

4 Dunlop, *Lee's Sharpshooters*, 192.

Lane's brigade to protect Scales' left flank. The 116th and 148th Pennsylvania pursued the Secessionist sharpshooters back to the crest in the corn field, taking a few prisoners along the way. There the Keystoners encountered McGowan's line of battle and fell back to their own works. Penfield, finding his left exposed and unable to link his right to the skirmishers of Miles' brigade, also retreated to the fortifications.

Ill that day, Hill found the heat of the day aggravating his condition. The corps commander dismounted and lay down on the ground, leaving the direction of the fighting to Wilcox. Having deployed and felt the enemy, Wilcox decided on his own initiative that an attack could not wait for the arrival of Heth's troops. The apparently withdrawing Federals might escape.

The North Carolina-born Wilcox ordered McGowan to create a diversion to prevent the Northerners from reinforcing the point where Wilcox intended to strike. At the sound of McGowan's gunfire, shortly after Penfield's and Broady's skirmishers had fallen back to the earthworks, Scales' and Anderson's brigades advanced. Scales' brigade charged with an impetus that carried it through the clutching underbrush to within a few yards of the Federal earthworks. Present with Anderson's brigade, Wilcox observed in that formation, "an evident indisposition to advance."[5] The Georgians, used up in the fighting north of the James and fatigued by long marches from there to Petersburg and from the Cockade City to Reams Station, at length entered the open field, cheered, and dashed toward the main Unionist works.

Anderson's brigade charged unscathed to within 200 yards of the earthworks. The Northerners delivered a volley that inflicted a relative handful of casualties. That handful included the brigade's only field officer, Colonel Little, and Anderson's brigade retreated. The soldiers in the right regiment of Scales' brigade saw Anderson's brigade retire and themselves fell back. One by one, from right to left, Scales' other regiments also withdrew.

The feebleness of this attack displeased Wilcox. He and Hill commended Scales' brigade and blamed Anderson's brigade. Wilcox determined to renew the assault at once with his two unused formations, Lane's and McGowan's brigades. He withdrew the two regiments of Lane's brigade from the left of Scales' brigade and began to send for McGowan's brigade, which would have to come by an awkward route that would expose the South Carolinians to artillery

---

5 Cadmus M. Wilcox, Reports, 1863-1865, Lee's Headquarters Collection, Virginia Historical Society, Richmond, Virginia.

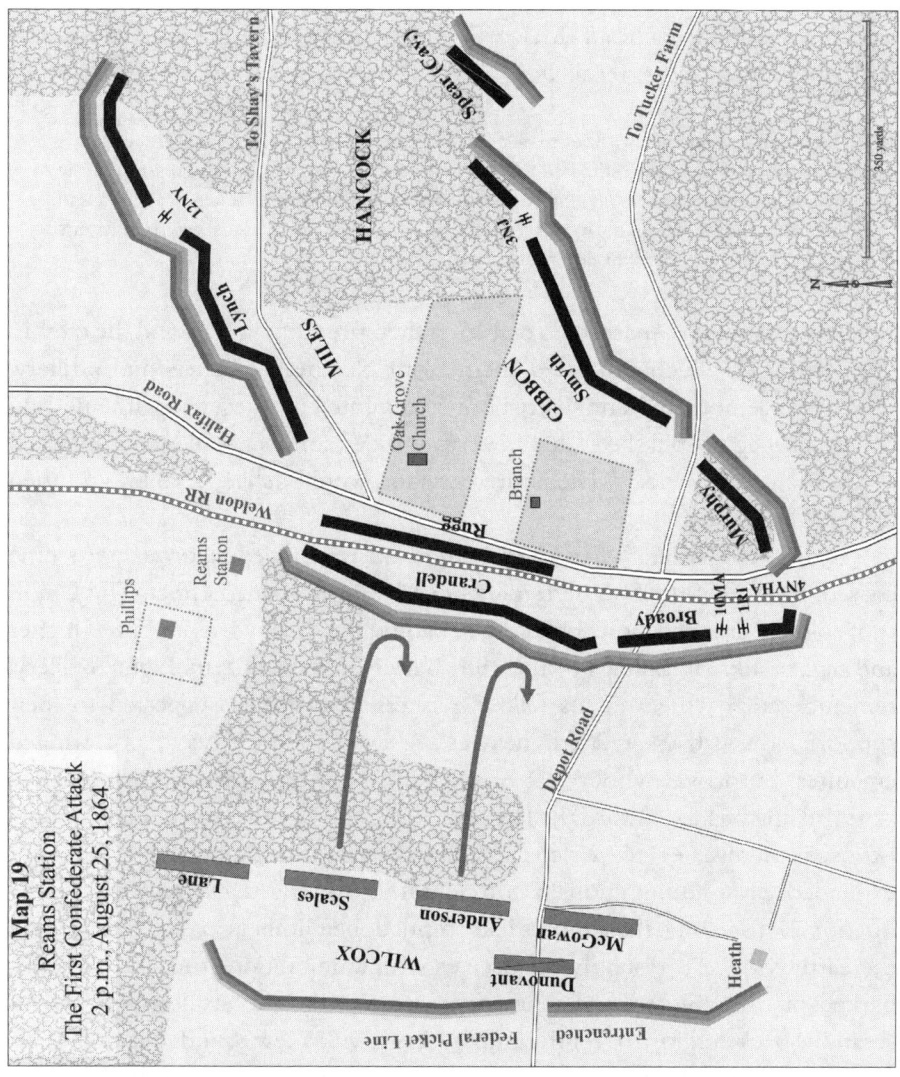

fire and leave unengaged Federals in the portion of the earthworks south of the Depot Road. The Confederate artillerists limbered up and galloped about 500 yards to the right oblique. Clearing the right of McGowan's infantry by 400 yards, the guns went into battery again within 700 yards of the enemy. Wilcox suspended his attempt to renew the attack and reported in person to Hill at 3 p.m., when Heth's command began arriving.

As the assaulting Rebel brigades retired through Wilcox's sharpshooters, nearly three hours of hell began for the Unionist soldiers and horses in the works west of the railroad. Major Dunlop, the commander of McGowan's sharpshooter battalion, recalled:

> Here, deliberately, but without malice, planning the destruction of their enemies, the sharpshooters carefully estimated the distance between the lines, the depression of the ground where the enemy lay, the course the ball would take in its trajectory flight, and the exact point where it would cut the line of fire; then adjusting their sights accordingly, they entered upon the work in hand.[6]

The Secessionist marksmen delivered their fire from just behind the crest in the corn field, which protected them from Northern muskets and artillery. Dunlop remembered: "The sharpshooters mounted the crest and with unerring aim proceeded to split the scalp of every mother's son that dared to lift his head above the breastworks."[7] The entire battalion would deliver a volley and then drop back to reload.

At first the Federal infantry and artillerists responded vigorously. As time passed, the fire of the Southern marksmen had its intended effect. The Union foot soldiers crouched lower and lower behind the earthworks and fired higher and higher. Private Billings of the 10th Battery, Massachusetts Light Artillery, remembered that he and his fellow gunners sarcastically suggested to their supports, the 7th New York heavies, "that the Rebels were not winged creatures, but it was wholly lost on them."[8] Each time that the Confederate skirmish line pushed toward the Federal works, the Union artillerymen not only exposed themselves to Wilcox's sharpshooters by firing their guns but expended extra ammunition in compensating for the slackening fire of the infantry. Before long, the gunners had emptied their limbers, parked just behind the earthworks. To resupply themselves with ammunition from the caissons, parked on the railroad embankment's eastern side, the artillerymen had to scramble back and forth over the embankment with a few rounds at a time. This further exposed the gunners to the Rebel marksmen. Southern bullets took such a significant toll of the Northern artillerists that, to man its guns, the 10th Massachusetts Battery began to draw upon volunteers from its supporting infantry, the 7th New York heavies. The 4th New York heavies supported

---

6 Dunlop, *Lee's Sharpshooters*, 192.

7 Ibid., 193.

8 Billings, *Tenth Massachusetts Battery*, 247.

Batteries A and B of the 1st Rhode Island Artillery and supplied volunteers to man those guns.

The Secessionist sharpshooters put more lead into the artillery horses than into the gunners. Private Billings recalled the terrible ordeal of these animals:

> Standing out in bold relief above the slight earthwork, in teams of six, they were naturally a prominent target for Rebel bullets, and the peculiar dull thud of these, at short intervals, told either that another animal had fallen a victim to the enemy's fire, or, what was frequently the case, that one already hit was further wounded. Some of the horses would fall when struck by the first bullet, lie quiet awhile, then struggle to their feet again to receive additional injuries. Frequently a ball would enter a horse's neck, with the effect only of causing him to shake his head a few times as if pestered by a fly, and then he would stand as quietly as if nothing had happened. I remember seeing one pole-horse shot in the leg—the bone evidently fractured—go down in a heap, then, all encumbered as he was with harness and limber, scramble up and stand on three legs. It was a sad sight to see a single horse left standing, with his five associates lying dead or dying around him, himself the centre of a concentrated fire, until he, too, was laid low. I saw one such struck by seven bullets ere he fell for the last time. Several received as many as five, and it was thought by some that they would average that number apiece. They were certainly thoroughly riddled, and long before the serious fighting of the day occurred, but two, out of the thirty plainly visible to the enemy, were left standing. These two had been struck, but not vitally, and survived some time longer. This statement does not include the horses on the caissons, most of which also fell.[9]

The slaughter of the artillery horses signified that the Confederates intended to capture the guns. "We knew it was fight or Andersonville," recalled Private Roback of the 152nd New York in Macy's brigade.[10]

The gunners of Batteries A and B, 1st Rhode Island Light Artillery, shelled the Rebel sharpshooters for a short time, but then received orders to cease fire from a staff officer who accused the artillerists of firing on their own soldiers. The 10th Battery, Massachusetts Light Artillery, bombarded the woods, the corn field and the buildings of the Heath farm. Shells riddled the house, and one of the dependencies took fire. The barrage drove the sharpshooters from the buildings, but could not drive them from their work.

While Wilcox's command locked horns with Miles' division, events elsewhere affected the outcome of the battle. These events all involved the creation and employment of reserves.

---

9 Ibid., 245-6.

10 Roback, *152d New York*, 119.

Maj. Gen. George G. Meade, U.S.A. *Library of Congress*

Instead of relieving XVIII Corps with part of the substantially larger X Corps, as Grant had desired, Benjamin Butler merely ordered the two corps to exchange places. In the middle of this exchange, Butler began preparing to depart for New York. The politician-general turned over command of the Army of the James to Ord, its senior corps commander. Ostensibly, Butler departed to probate his brother's will. Actually, this presidential hopeful left to keep a closer watch on the Democratic convention. On top of all this, Pickett's dawn demonstration, erroneous intelligence that Mahone's division had reinforced Pickett, and the concocted signals of a Rebel mine ruse sufficed to keep the 3,000 man reserve of the Army of the James occupied until early evening, far too late for its availability to assist Meade in meeting the contingencies that he faced.

Just before noon, Meade left his headquarters with the intention of conferring with Hancock at Reams Station. On the way, the Army of the Potomac's leader arrived at Mott's command post near the Jones house around 12:20 p.m. There Meade received a report, based on information from Rebel deserters, that Lee had stripped the Confederate lines at Petersburg to drive the Federals from the Weldon Railroad. Only one rank, weaker than a picket line, occupied the Southern trenches in front of Mott's division. The cautious Meade told Mott to ready his reserves to send to Hancock or Warren if necessary. The more aggressive Grant, who might well have directed Mott to attack the thinly occupied Secessionist fortifications, felt too unwell to go to the front that day and contemplated a boat trip from City Point to Fortress Monroe at 4:00 p.m.

By 1:00 p.m., Meade had made his way to Warren's headquarters at Globe Tavern. The army commander proceeded no farther. At Globe Tavern, Meade read an 11:40 a.m. dispatch from Hancock reporting Barringer's breakthrough into the rear of II Corps. Hancock's telegraph line to Army of the Potomac headquarters had not yet opened at 11:40 a.m., and the II Corps chief had sent the message to Warren's headquarters, five miles away, for transmission.

Meade interpreted Hancock's report in accordance with his own preconceptions. These rested only in part on the Confederate movements reported by the signal officers on the previous evening and the statements of the Rebels who had deserted to Mott that morning. Still earlier that morning, City Point had received a report of the imminent return of Fitzhugh Lee's division of cavalry from the Shenandoah Valley. On August 23, two Northern born boys had fled Petersburg and told the Unionists of the rumor circulating in the city about Early returning from the Shenandoah, presumably with his entire corps and Kershaw's division of Anderson's Corps. Back in June of 1862, such a shift of Secessionist forces from the Valley had preceded the Seven Days Battles on the Peninsula, just east of Richmond between the York and James

Rivers. The leader of a brigade at the time, Meade had suffered a wound at the battle of Glendale, one of the Seven Days Battles near Fussell's Mill.

Grant had begun the fourth offensive—Hancock's attacks north of James River, the advance of V Corps to the Weldon Railroad, Hancock's move to Reams Station, and the contemplated advance to Hicksford—to force the Confederates to withdraw troops from the Shenandoah Valley. Such a shift in Rebel manpower now threatened to hoist the Federals on their own petard. The prospect of troops from the Valley joining Lee for a descent upon the Army of the Potomac's unprotected rear alarmed Meade.

By 2:00 p.m. on August 25, he had concluded that Lee would try to maneuver the Army of the Potomac off the Weldon Railroad by thrusting around the Federal left on the Jerusalem Plank Road with troops withdrawn from the Shenandoah. In Barringer's attack on Gregg's picket line, Meade discerned the beginning of just such a maneuver. A single brigade of horsemen screened the Union left from the Jerusalem Plank Road to the James River. The weakness of this force rendered the Federal rear vulnerable all the way back to the army's cattle pens at Coggins Point, twenty-five miles northeast of Reams Station on the James. Just over three weeks later, Hampton's raid on those cattle pens would demonstrate this vulnerability beyond question. In his mind's eye, Meade may have seen Lee again driving the Army of the Potomac all the way back to the James and the protection of the Union gunboats as in 1862.

To prevent such a disaster, Meade pushed forward men to guard his army's left. He sent two forces to Shay's Tavern at the junction of the Jerusalem Plank Road with the lane to Reams Station. Shortly after 2:00 p.m., McAllister's brigade and part of Pulford's brigade of Mott's division pulled out of the Federal works near the Jones house. This force marched under Col. Robert McAllister of the 11th New Jersey, the victim of a severe Gettysburg wound. McAllister's command comprised about 2,000 soldiers. To replace McAllister's troops, Humphreys filled the trenches with about 1,000 engineers and the army's headquarters infantry. After a detachment of around forty cavalrymen from the Army of the Potomac's provost guard joined McAllister's force, the column headed south on the Jerusalem Plank Road toward Shay's Tavern.

Meade also looked to IX Corps to protect his army's left. About 3:00 p.m., Orlando Willcox's division, about 2,000 strong, pulled out of the breastworks near Globe Tavern and hiked five miles southeastward mostly cross-country to Shay's Tavern. Three batteries of artillery accompanied this division. Meade ordered Willcox and McAllister to report to Hancock upon their arrival at the Shay's Tavern intersection, which Meade considered crucial to the defense of the Army of the Potomac's rear. In case the Confederates interposed between V Corps and Hancock, which Hancock also feared, Meade held in reserve at Globe Tavern the remnant of Crawford's division of V Corps and White's small division of IX Corps—around 2,000 soldiers more.

Instead of concentrating his reserves and taking the offensive, Meade frittered them away trying to defend everything. The commitment of engineers, headquarters infantry and the provost guard emphasized his passivity. Concentrated for a single blow, they and McAllister's detachment of Mott's II Corps division, Crawford's division of V Corps, and Willcox's and White's divisions of IX Corps might well have penetrated Lee's Petersburg lines if held as thinly as reports suggested. They at least could have mounted a daunting demonstration.

Again with the intent of guarding his army's left and rear, Meade at 1:00 p.m. authorized Hancock to withdraw from Reams Station but left the matter to Hancock's discretion. This authorization traveled down the railroad by messenger from Warren's headquarters and did not reach Hancock until almost 2:45 p.m., after Cadmus Wilcox's assault. Hancock considered his force too closely engaged to withdraw before dark. He declined to retreat. Just after 4:00 p.m., he received another message from Meade by courier from the headquarters of V Corps. This message informed Hancock that Meade had also sent to the Federal left Orlando Willcox's division of IX Corps and authorized Hancock to call upon the division.

The misunderstanding between Meade and Hancock arose over the route assigned to Willcox's division. Hancock saw this unit solely as a reinforcement for his troops at Reams Station. By 4:15 p.m., he had already complained to Meade that because Meade had not directed Willcox straight down the Weldon Railroad from Globe Tavern to Reams Station, a distance of five miles, Willcox would not arrive in time to help. Willcox's actual line of march, from Globe Tavern to Reams Station by way of Shay's Tavern on the Jerusalem Plank Road, involved a distance of at least eight miles.

Hancock did not see the big picture. He failed to grasp that Meade intended to use Willcox's division primarily to guard the Army of the Potomac's left rear and only secondarily as a reinforcement for Hancock. After complaining to Meade, the II Corps leader dispatched a staff officer to conduct Willcox's division to Reams Station.

The Confederates roaming around the Union left posed as many threats to the Army of the Potomac as the Federal force at Reams Station posed to Petersburg and Richmond. Beyond the Jerusalem Plank Road lay City Point, the source of supply for Grant's whole army group. Farther east stood Fort Powhatan, where Secessionist guns might interdict the ships that supplied City Point. Unlike Lee, Meade chose to guard against the threats instead of eliminating their source or posing further threats of his own. By committing all of the army group's reserves to the line or earmarking them for local contingencies, Meade thought he had managed to deal with all of the potential problems that he faced. As events would show, a possibility existed which he had overlooked.

The ailing Grant gradually lost his characteristic aggressiveness. At noon, he still wanted Hancock's force to execute a day's march toward Weldon, rip up a few more miles of track, and return by a road farther east than the one on which it had ventured forth. By a little after 2:00 p.m., Grant decided that he must consolidate and leave such a raid to the future.

Harry Heth arrived on the battlefield with Cooke's and MacRae's North Carolina brigades of his division at about 3:00 p.m. When Wilcox reported the feebleness of his first assault to Hill, the Third Corps chief roused himself from his illness and considered withdrawing despite Wilcox's determination to renew the attack. Hill feared a repetition of the costly repulse suffered in the Confederate assault on Warren's fortifications at Globe Tavern only four days earlier. Heth conferred with Brigadier Generals John Rogers Cooke and William MacRae, two of Lee's finest brigadiers, both excellent disciplinarians. Cooke, the son of Brig. Gen. Phillip St. George Cooke of the United States Army and brother-in-law of the late Maj. Gen. James Ewell Brown "Jeb" Stuart, commander of Lee's Cavalry Corps, had graduated from Harvard and worked as a railway engineer before joining the United States Army and then resigning upon Virginia's secession. He bore the scars of seven wounds. MacRae, another engineer, had risen from a private in the Monroe Light Infantry, Company B of the 15th North Carolina, and had served under Cooke. After the conference with Cooke and MacRae, Heth sent word to Hill that Cooke's and MacRae's brigades could take the works if supported by Wilcox's troops. This convinced Hill to reconsider. The Third Corps leader ordered a renewal of the attack.

Hill and Wilcox realized that Heth's soldiers could deploy for the attack much more quickly and less awkwardly than McGowan's men could reposition themselves. The Third Corps leader directed Wilcox to tell Heth to attack with Cooke's and MacRae's brigades. Though Wilcox conveyed the order to Heth, Hill's subordinates modified the order. Wilcox proposed to make the attack with one of his own brigades and one of Heth's brigades. After the two major generals examined the Federal position together, they decided to attack with

Lane's brigade on the left and Cooke's brigade on the right. Instructed to support these units, Scales' brigade took position behind and to the left of Lane's brigade, and MacRae's brigade formed line of battle behind and to the right of Cooke's brigade. Hill posted Weisiger's and Sanders' brigades to prevent any attack on his left flank by the Unionists at Globe Tavern. He positioned Anderson's brigade behind MacRae's right and McGowan's brigade behind Anderson's right. Hill then fell ill again, leaving Heth in command.

While the infantry deployed for the assault, Heth left to reposition Pegram's guns. The Rebel artillerymen of Brander's and Cayce's batteries manhandled their eight Napoleons into place behind the crest of the corn field south of the Depot Road, near the Heath house and 300 yards closer to the Unionist earthworks. The eight Napoleons now stood to the right of the assault column and within 400 yards of the enemy's fortifications. During Heth's absence, Wilcox shifted the attack force farther to the left, so that only the right half of Cooke's brigade had an open field to cross. The other half, like Lane's brigade, had to negotiate dense woods and then an abatis. Anderson's brigade reformed behind MacRae's right, but the Georgians did not form part of the attack force. MacRae's sharpshooters joined those of McGowan and Scales, adding to the discomfiture of man and beast in the Federal earthworks.

The preparations for the attack took until almost 5:00 p.m. When Wilcox had deployed the infantry to his satisfaction, he reported to Heth. The Virginian had stationed himself with Pegram and the guns. At such short range, the artillerists cut their fuses to one second for the first time in the war.

The plan devised by Hill and Hampton the previous evening had failed, primarily due to the time required for the tired Secessionist infantry to reach the field. Now the Southerners abandoned subtlety and staked everything on a frontal assault. The new plan of attack simply called for the infantry to advance on the works after an artillery barrage. No time remained for further maneuvering or for another assault if this one failed.

While the Rebels prepared to strike again, the Federals also redeployed their forces. Smyth's brigade had not arrived back at Reams Station until after the repulse of the first Confederate assault. This brigade took up a line east of the railroad embankment. The line followed a crest through the corn field across the road that led past the Tucker farm. Smyth's brigade immediately began building breastworks along this line. Smyth deployed the 4th Ohio Battalion as skirmishers beyond the road. Detached from the rest of the brigade, the 12th New Jersey went to the support of the 3rd Battery, New Jersey Light Artillery.

Gregg placed the 1st District of Columbia Cavalry of Spear's brigade in a hastily constructed work atop a hillock slightly advanced and to the left of Smyth's troops. A squadron of the 11th Pennsylvania Cavalry of Spear's brigade advanced as videttes in front of this earthwork with orders to alert Gregg if Rebels emerged from the woods southeast of Reams Station. The 16th Pennsylvania Cavalry of Gregg's Second Brigade, now under Col. Charles H. Smith, remained mounted on the left of this earthwork. Gregg dismounted the 1st Maine Cavalry of Smith's brigade in the swamp on the left of the 11th Pennsylvania Cavalry. The ravine that ran south of and roughly parallel to the road to Shay's Tavern debouched into this swamp. The Federals now had a southern return parallel to their northern return. Unknown to them, the Confederate artillery enfiladed the southern return.

The 19th Maine and 19th Massachusetts of Macy's brigade received instructions to position themselves at the junction of Murphy's and Smyth's brigades. North of the Depot Road, in the railroad cut behind Crandell's brigade, the 20th Massachusetts, 1st Minnesota, and the 184th Pennsylvania remained on the right, while the 152nd New York, the 36th Wisconsin, and the 20th Massachusetts stayed on the left.

General Miles sensed an attack coming at his right, and he made use of the time afforded him to prepare to meet that assault. He directed Captain Penfield to picket the front of the right of Crandell's brigade again. Penfield found a strong Secessionist line in front of him and while swinging to the left captured pickets of the 13th North Carolina of Scales' brigade. Penfield's picket line covered the right of Crandell's brigade, but not the left. No connection existed between Penfield and the skirmishers of Miles' brigade. The nearest picket force of Miles' brigade occupied the Phillips house, just west of the railway.

The withdrawal of Penfield's force from the sector of the earthworks occupied by Crandell's brigade left the works filled by only a single line of soldiers, in some places a pace apart. No troops stood in the gaps to the right of the brigade for the Halifax Road and the railway, and to the left of the brigade for the Depot Road. To repair this situation, Broady detached the 53rd and 148th Pennsylvania from his own brigade and stationed them behind Crandell's brigade and in front of the railroad cut, which held most of Macy's brigade. The 53rd and 148th took position behind the former Irish Brigade, which formed the right of Crandell's brigade. The 53rd stood to the rear of the 69th New York, and the 148th lined up on the 53rd's right.

Miles prepared a warm reception for any Rebels assaulting the northwest angle of the fortifications. He detached the 152nd New York from Macy's command and sent it up the railroad to the vicinity of the Phillips house, where the tracks ran along an embankment again. Miles gave the 152nd orders to strike the flank and rear of a Confederate force attacking the northwest angle. In case of an attempt to turn the Union right, the 152nd had instructions to deploy behind the embankment and fight a delaying action. Miles also placed a Napoleon of the 12th Battery, New York Light Artillery east of the railroad cut and north of the church. This gun raked the opening where the railroad and the Halifax Road entered the northern face of the earthworks.

Like Meade, Hancock feared that the Southerners would interpose between II Corps at Reams Station and V Corps at Globe Tavern. By 4:30 p.m., it had become apparent to Hancock that insufficient time remained for the Secessionists to flank the northern return on his right, anchored on Jones Hole Swamp and screened by Stedman's cavalry brigade. The II Corps chief thought it would require "vigorous use" of the hours of daylight remaining for the Rebels to work their way around the southern return on his left, strongly posted on another swamp and picketed by Spear's brigade of horsemen.[11]

Fifteen minutes later, pickets to the south of the Depot Road reported the Confederates moving artillery into position. This indicated another attack, almost certainly against the western face of the earthworks again. North of the Depot Road, twenty-five soldiers of Penfield's force advanced farther west in the pines with instructions to give notice of the approach of the Rebels. Penfield received warning of a large force of Southerners heading his way. He did not credit the warning, and he gave no order for the pickets to fall back so that in a hasty retreat they would not screen the Secessionists from Federal fire.

McAllister arrived at Shay's Tavern about this time. Massing his soldiers to the right and left of the plank road, he dispatched a staff officer to report to Hancock. Before the staff officer's return, Meade in person arrived and directed McAllister to deploy his men in a good position across the Jerusalem Plank Road. After reconnoitering, McAllister found a position to his satisfaction about a mile south of the intersection with the road to Shay's Tavern. He threw his cavalry out in a screen still farther south. Battery D, Pennsylvania Light Artillery soon arrived. McAllister posted two of its cannon on the left of the road and four on the right. The guns afforded a complete sweep of both roads. McAllister's troops began fortifying this position.

---

11 Winf'd S. Hancock to Major-General Humphreys, August 25, 1864, in *OR* 42 pt 2, 484.

Telegraph Wagon *Library of Congress*

Shortly before 5:00 p.m., the staff officer sent by McAllister reported to Hancock the arrival of McAllister's force at Shay's Tavern. Because Orlando Willcox's division would turn off the Jerusalem Plank road there for Reams Station before the staffer could return with similar orders for McAllister, Hancock sent instructions to McAllister to hold well down the plank road in anticipation of any attempt by the Confederates to turn the left of II Corps and reach the Federal rear. Hancock also sent a separate dispatch directing McAllister to arrest all stragglers and form them into regiments.

As of 5:00 p.m., the fight seemed a Union victory. A reporter who traveled with Hancock described it as a triumph in the dispatch that he hurried to send off in time to make the deadline for the following day's paper.

The dispatch went out a little too soon. A contingency that Meade had not foreseen would soon come to pass.

Chapter 12

The Second Battle of Reams Station, August 25, 1864: The Second Confederate Assault

The first Confederate attack on Hancock's position had failed. Now, with corps commander Hill still sick, Harry Heth and his subordinates coiled for another attempt. Cadmus Wilcox had positioned his infantry brigades and reported to Heth. Wilcox declared the assault force ready for action. The two major generals and Lieutenant Colonel Pegram synchronized their watches. Heth ordered Pegram's batteries to fire as rapidly as possible for thirty minutes. Then Pegram's guns would cease fire and the infantry would advance.

Toward five o'clock, Pegram's batteries opened up on the Union earthworks. Seventeen guns fired about three rounds per minute. A shell burst in and around the Federal works almost every second. Captain William B. Hurt had to remind the gunners in the section of his Alabama battery present not to fire too rapidly lest they burst their gun. The Rebel guns inflicted few casualties on the Unionists in the works west of the railroad but disabled the leftmost gun of the 10th Battery, Massachusetts Light Artillery, blew up one of this battery's caissons, and shattered the wheels of another. The guns of the 3rd Battery, New Jersey Light Artillery, in a sorghum field about 300 yards behind the railway, occupied high ground in full view of the Rebel batteries. The Secessionist fire became so severe that the New Jersey artillerists could not stand to their guns but had to lie on their faces. The barrage demoralized many green Northerners—particularly among Gibbon's troops, whom the Confederate guns enfiladed.

The peculiar sound of the solitary Whitworth in the section of Hurt's Alabama battery proved unusually unnerving. Imported by both sides during the war, the Whitworth fired an elongated 12-pound shell. A breechloader, it could fire a solid shot beyond 2,800 yards. The shot made a distinctive shrill sound as the Whitworth flew overhead. A reporter for the New York Sun remembered that

> the man who hears the scream of a Whitworth shell will never forget the sound to the day of his death. It is a concentration of the war whoop of an Indian, the snarl of a tiger, and the scream of a woman in mortal terror. It begins afar off with a muttered threat of vengeance; it grows upon the ear with a howl as of wolves in pursuit of the lone traveler; it comes nearer with shrieks of baffled rage; it is at hand with a scream which can be likened to nothing but the cries of a mob mad for death and destruction.[1]

During the Southern bombardment, the 12th Battery, New York Light Artillery pounded the woods in front of Crandell's brigade. Projectiles from the New Yorkers overshot the North Carolinians in Lane's brigade and Cooke's left and landed among the Confederate reserves—the Virginians of Weisiger's brigade and the Alabamians of Sanders' brigade.

After about fifteen minutes, General Conner led Lane's brigade forward on Cooke's left through the undergrowth toward the abatis. General Cooke sent forward the left half of his line, the 27th and 48th North Carolina, along with Lane's brigade, but held back the right, the 46th and 15th North Carolina, which had to cross only the open field in front of them. Cooke did not want the right to outstrip the left and suffer a repulse for lack of support. Pegram's guns continued to hammer the Federal works upon and south of the Depot Road, facing the open field Cooke's right would have to cross.

The North Carolina infantrymen advanced with a thunderstorm bearing down on them from behind and Rebel cannon balls screeching over their heads. They faced the enemy's canister and minie bullets. The brigades of Lane on the left, Cooke in the center, and MacRae on the right totaled about 1,750 soldiers. Captain John H. Thorp of Company A in the 47th North Carolina of MacRae's brigade, facing the open field from behind Cooke's right, imagined that, "the heretofore triumphant Federals must have smiled as they beheld the small force

---

1 James M. Aubery, *The Thirty-Sixth Wisconsin Volunteer Infantry 1st Brigade 2nd Div. 2nd Army Corps* (Milwaukee, 1900), 126. Mechanical difficulties with the breech mechanism made the Whitworth unpopular with gunners and a rarity on the battlefield.

advancing against them, and intended to withhold their fire until we should reach a point from which we might be unable to escape."[2]

The Northerners now paid the price for Captain Penfield's failure to heed the warning that he had received about the approach of the Secessionist infantry and order his pickets to withdraw to the fortifications. Lane's brigade and Cooke's left advanced with "the utmost silence," remembered Lt. Col. William Wilson of the 81st Pennsylvania in Crandell's brigade.[3] The Tarheels refused to answer the fire of the Unionist skirmishers. The North Carolinian battle lines struck the Federal pickets with full force. Penfield's skirmishers became mingled with the pursuing Tarheels. The 12th Battery, New York Light Artillery could not open fire on the North Carolinians until Penfield's pickets had cleared. The gunners then opened a rapid fire of canister upon the Tarheels. Crandell's brigade also reserved its fire for a time to allow Penfield's skirmishers to retire, but then poured heavy volleys on the North Carolinians. The 53rd and 148th Pennsylvania, as they rushed forward to join in the firing, caused confusion in the former Irish Brigade in the right of the line of Crandell's brigade.

The Tarheel attackers neared the Union breastworks in the face of a deadly musketry and artillery fire. The left of Lane's brigade encountered only the railway cut but faced the most severe hail of minnies and canister. The soldiers of the brigade's center and right picked their way in squads and individually through the thirty yards of slashing. Some men literally had to crawl through the abatis. To the right of Lane's brigade, Cooke's left faced thinner timber and fifty to seventy-five yards of slashing. Pushing aside the underbrush and destroying the abatis in front of the Federal fortifications, Cooke's troops reached the works in small squads. The 48th North Carolina, the right regiment of Cooke's left, reached the fortifications first. As the Tarheels gathered in front of the earthworks, Crandell's brigade stood firm. Hand-to-hand fighting started and spread along the face of the fortifications. Many North Carolinians fell back. Those who remained at the works struggled to survive. Captain Thorpe of the 27th North Carolina on the extreme left of Cooke's brigade remembered, "Three times Captain Shade Wooten, Company C, finding one of the enemy

---

2 Clark, *North Carolina Regiments*, 3:97.

3 Report of Lieut. Col. William Wilson, Eighty-first Pennsylvania Infantry, commanding Consolidated Brigade, of operations August 22-26, in OR 42, pt. 1, 289.

Brig. Gen. William MacRae, C.S.A.
Library of Congress

poking his gun up to shoot him, grabbed a handful of dirt from the embankment and dashed it in the eyes of his opponent and thus saved his life."[4]

General MacRae struggled to gauge the assault's progress. He could tell from the firing that Lane's right and Cooke's left had advanced, though the woods hid these soldiers from him. As MacRae's own brigade waited in a pine thicket about 300 yards from the earthworks, MacRae issued his orders. He wanted his soldiers to advance in silence through the timber in front of them. When they reached the open field, MacRae enjoined that, "Every man must yell as if he were a division in himself, dash for the enemy's works, and not fire until there."[5] In high spirits, his troops joked and laughed. "All right, General, we will go there," the soldiers responded.[6]

MacRae heard the sound of firing from the direction of Lane's brigade increase. The visible portion of Cooke's line remained still. Five or ten minutes passed. MacRae sensed that the decisive moment had arrived. "I shall wait no longer for orders," he told his Assistant Adjutant General, Capt. Louis G. Young. "Lane is drawing the entire fire of the enemy; give the order to advance at once."[7] Young ordered the troops forward. The advance of MacRae's brigade nudged Cooke's right into motion. The 46th and 15th North Carolina charged across the same field that Anderson's brigade and Scales' right had crossed more than three hours earlier. Pegram's guns stopped bombarding the

4   Clark, *North Carolina Regiments*, 2:447-8.

5   Ibid., 4:565.

6   Ibid., 5:209.

7   Ibid.

earthworks in front of Cooke's right and MacRae's brigade. Corporal Daniel Chisholm of Company K of the 116th Pennsylvania in Broady's brigade in those works recalled, "Suddenly the firing ceased, and with low yells and without firing a gun they sprang forward, hats pulled down over their eyes and guns on a trail."[8]

Cooke's right hit the Union line. It struck the left of Crandell's brigade. Fire from Crandell's brigade, Broady's brigade, the 4th New York heavies, and the 10th Battery, Massachusetts Light Artillery, nearly annihilated Cooke's right. The 46th North Carolina, the left regiment of Cooke's right, lost seventy-three soldiers.[9] The 15th North Carolina, Cooke's farthest right, closer to the remaining guns of the 10th Battery, Massachusetts Light Artillery and the guns that Batteries A and B, 1st Rhode Island Light Artillery, could bring to bear, lost 114.[10] North Carolinian dead and wounded covered the field. Corporal Chisholm recalled, "When they would drop wounded they would haul out an old dirty handkerchief and wave it while they lay on their backs."[11] Had not the Rebel sharpshooters and Pegram's barrage cowed the Union infantry into firing high, the troops of Cooke's right would have suffered even more. A few soldiers of the 15th and 46th North Carolina reached the works. The opposing regiments of Crandell's and Broady's brigades remained steady. Farther to the Federal left, some troops of the 7th New York heavies stampeded but quickly rallied. With the aid of canister from the 10th Battery, Massachusetts Light Artillery, Crandell's and Broady's brigades drove back the opposing Tarheels.

As soldiers of Cooke's right recoiled in confusion, MacRae's brigade ran into them and carried them back toward the Union earthworks. Now the efforts of the Confederate sharpshooters paid their richest dividends. The 10th Battery, Massachusetts Light Artillery, had used up almost the last of its canister west of the embankment in blasting Cooke's right. The gunners of this battery found themselves with only one or two rounds of canister per gun as MacRae's brigade advanced, and the artillerists reserved these rounds for short range work. The 12th Battery, New York Light Artillery and 3rd Battery, New Jersey

---

8 W. Springer Menge and J. August Shimrak, eds., *The Civil War Notebook of Daniel Chisholm, A Chronicle of Daily Life in the Union Army 1864-1865* (New York, 1969), 36.

9 Clark, *North Carolina Regiments*, 3:78.

10 Ibid., 1:747.

11 Menge and Shimrak, eds., *The Civil War Notebook of Daniel Chisholm*, 36.

Light Artillery could not fire without fear of hitting their own troops. The leftmost gun of Batteries A and B, 1st Rhode Island Light Artillery, on low ground on the Halifax Road, could not fire over the railroad embankment. The other three guns of this consolidated battery could bear on the charging North Carolinians only when the Tarheels crossed the open field. Once the North Carolinians reached the earthworks, these guns could not fire for fear of hitting Lieutenant Colonel Broady's infantry and the 10th Battery, Massachusetts Light Artilllery.

MacRae's soldiers advanced at the double-quick, "in a line almost as straight and unbroken as they presented when on parade," remembered Maj. Charles M. Stedman of the 44th North Carolina in the center of MacRae's brigade.[12] MacRae's men did not fire until they reached the earthworks. Mounting the fortifications, MacRae's troops and the survivors of Cooke's right landed among the Federal infantry on the other side.

These Tarheels burst through the inadequate barricade across the gap where the Depot Road passed through the fortifications. The North Carolinians hurdled the earthworks on either side. MacRae's right overlapped the left of the 66th New York, the northernmost regiment of Broady's brigade, just south of the road. The main impact of Cooke's right and MacRae's brigade fell on the left of Crandell's brigade—the 7th, 39th and 52nd New York. In his official report of the battle, Hancock wrote of these regiments:

> The Seventh, Fifty-second, and Thirty-ninth New York are largely made up of recruits and substitutes. The first-named regiment in particular is entirely new, companies being formed in New York and sent down here, some officers being unable to speak English. The material compares very unfavorably with the veterans absent.[13]

Demoralized by the hours of sharpshooter fire, as well as by Pegram's barrage, these green troops, "sent their shots into the tops of the trees," recalled Captain Young.[14] The Federal infantry, "did not show the determination which had generally marked the conduct of Hancock's Corps," remembered Major Stedman.[15] He thought that the Union foot soldiers, "seemed to be dazed by

---

12 Clark, *North Carolina Regiments*, 3:31.

13 OR 42, pt, 1, 227.

14 Clark, *North Carolina Regiments*, 4:565.

15 Ibid., 5:210.

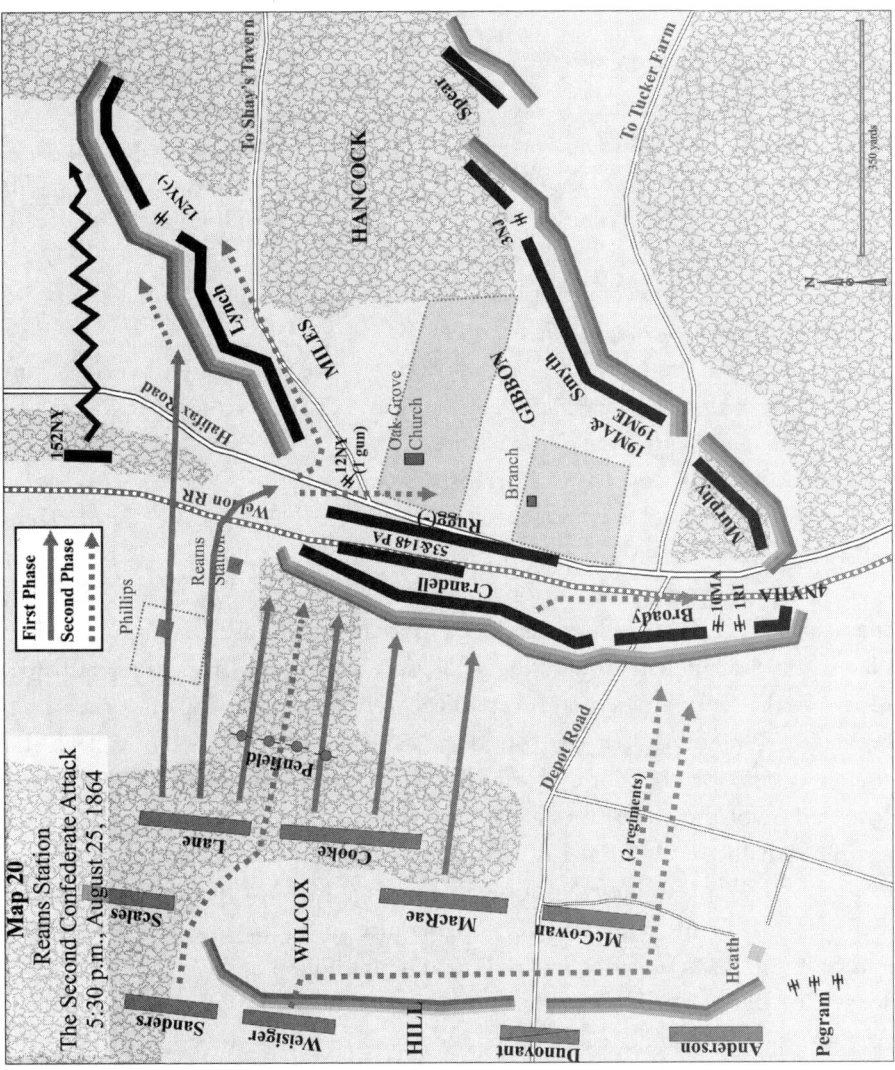

the vehemence of the attack and made a very feeble resistance after their ranks were reached."[16] MacRae's right encountered stiffer resistance. The 66th New York, on the right of Broady's brigade, initially withstood MacRae's onslaught. The 47th North Carolina lost heavily, including a disproportionate number of its best soldiers. Captain Thorp of the 47th, which suffered a permanent weakening, remembered, "Men who seemed to have possessed charmed lives;

16 Ibid., 3:30.

who struck so quick, and were so cool and daring to pass the danger line, were struck down in a body."[17] The rest of MacRae's brigade suffered lighter losses in its dash toward the works.

Hancock's position began to unravel. The New York conscripts north of the Depot Road broke as MacRae's left and the survivors of Cooke's right scaled the earthworks. Some of the New Yorkers fled and others surrendered. Lieutenant Colonel Rugg's left regiments, the 36th Wisconsin and the 20th Massachusetts, advanced and received the North Carolinians with a sharp fire that momentarily checked their progress.

Seeing the green New Yorkers on their left give way, the Tarheels in front of the 66th New York renewed their attack and drove the 66th back from the earthworks to the railroad embankment. MacRae's right drove down the earthworks into Broady's brigade in three columns, one outside, one inside and one along the fortifications' crest. Flanked, the regiments of Broady's brigade fell back one by one. A column of the 7th New York heavies on Broady's left filed off like sheep into captivity. The gunners of the 10th Battery, Massachusetts Light Artillery who stuck to their guns refused to surrender. The North Carolinians had to take the artillerists captive by sheer physical force. Most of the gunners retired from piece to piece. One by one, the three remaining guns fired their last rounds of canister. Trained to use artillery, the sharpshooters of the 44th North Carolina turned the cannons they had captured upon the line of retreat of Crandell's brigade and Rugg's troops.

The advance of MacRae's right stopped at the traverse, where a battalion of the brigade-sized 4th New York heavies changed front to face the oncoming Tarheels. The Confederates artillery opened fire again, this time on the Federals south of MacRae's brigade. Second Lieutenant Gideon Spencer of the western section of Battery B, 1st Rhode Island Light Artillery, urged Lt. Col. Thomas Allcock, the commander of the heavies, to counterattack and cut off the North Carolinians by closing the opening for the Depot Road, Allcock replied that he lacked the appropriate orders. "To hell with orders," said Spencer. "March your men in there and cut off the enemy from getting back!"[18] Allcock refused to budge.

---

17 Ibid., 97.

18 Thomas M. Aldritch, *The History of Battery A First Regiment Rhode Island Light Artillery in the War to Preserve the Union, 1861-1865* (Providence, 1904), 379.

A few hundred yards to the north, in front of the center of Crandell's brigade, some Tarheels in Cooke's left and Lane's right had begun throwing down their arms as a preliminary to surrendering, while others had started to withdraw. Now, stimulated by the shouts of MacRae's brigade and Cooke's right, the retreating soldiers of Cooke's left and Lane's right reversed course through the fallen timber to rejoin their comrades close under the earthworks and all redoubled their efforts to break into the Federal position. Panic from the left of Crandell's brigade spread to the remainder and the brigade started to crumble. Chaplain Ezra D. Simons of the 125th New York recalled, "This was the turning point of the fight, and here we failed."[19]

Lane's brigade punched another hole in the Union line. The 37th North Carolina in the center of Lane's brigade drove through the gap for the railway and the Halifax Road in the earthworks between Crandell's and Miles' brigades, where Penfield's pickets had regrouped. Penfield's troops broke again. His panic-stricken soldiers fled through the ranks of the two regiments of Lieutenant Colonel Rugg's right, the 1st Minnesota and the 184th Pennsylvania. The New Yorkers created confusion among Rugg's troops and made it impossible for them to fire on the North Carolinians. The panic of Penfield's soldiers then spread to Rugg's men. When the color bearer of the 37th North Carolina leapt into the railroad cut and landed at General Miles' feet, Miles ordered the right of Rugg's soldiers to counterattack and plug the gap. The troops of Rugg's right either lay on their faces or got up and ran to the rear. The Napoleon from the 12th Battery, New York Light Artillery sited to rake the opening in the fortifications for the railroad fired canister until Lane's brigade came over the earthworks. The gunners then attempted to limber up and escape, but the North Carolinians shot a wheel horse. Lane's brigade captured the gun and began infiltrating into the rear of Crandell's brigade. Like MacRae's troops, the soldiers of Lane's brigade turned the captured gun on the line of retreat of Crandell's brigade.

Because of the angle at which the left of Lane's brigade approached the earthworks, it lagged behind the rest of the brigade. The angle of approach exposed the brigade's left to an enfilade fire from Miles' brigade and the 152nd New York. The trap that Miles had prepared for such a Confederate assault failed to spring. The 152nd changed front and advanced to within 200 yards of

---

19 Ezra D. Simons, *A Regimental History of the One Hundred And Twenty-Fifth New York State Volunteers* (New York, 1888), 242.

Lane's flank and rear, then bolted for the Federal rear without having fired more than a few shots at the North Carolinians.

The 28th North Carolina encountered "dense obstructions" and charged at an angle that left it "terably exposed," according to its commander, Maj. Samuel N. Stowe, who added that the regiment, "for a short time did fail to advance as rapidly as our friends on the right."[20] The 28th quickly caught up with the 37th after that regiment had penetrated the Federal earthworks at the railroad cut. Captain Gold G. Holland of the 28th's Company H outdistanced his company and became one of the first of his regiment to mount the works. Finding the works still well-manned and himself unsupported, he bluffed the Unionists and yelled out, "Yanks, if you know what is best for you, you will make a blue streak toward sunset."[21] The Northerners in front of Captain Holland made the streak. The 7th North Carolina, on the extreme left of Lane's brigade, fell into confusion from the fire it took in front and flank from Miles' brigade and the 12th Battery, New York Light Artillery. The 7th's officers restored order but the regiment could not negotiate the abatis in front of the northern return. "The men stood firmly and returned the fire of the enemy…exposed to the most galling they had ever been under," recalled the regiment's commander, Capt. James G. Harris of Company H.[22]

The penetration of Lane's brigade into the railroad cut precipitated the first of several pockets that developed during the fighting. Engaged with the Tarheels in their immediate front, the soldiers of the right and center of Crandell's brigade and Rugg's left failed to notice the North Carolinians infiltrating their rear. Tarheels from Lane's brigade worked their way down the railroad cut behind these Federals while MacRae's left drove the 66th New York from behind the railroad embankment on the left of Rugg's detachment. Within five minutes, the North Carolinians had surrounded the soldiers of Crandell's brigade and Rugg's force who had not fled.

The center of Crandell's brigade finally collapsed. Enough of Lane's right and Cooke's left had reached the works to scale them successfully. Private Roback of the 152nd New York remembered that the North Carolinians, "arose like demons from the bowels of the earth, and with one prolonged yell

---

20 Report of Maj. Samuel N. Stowe, August 28th, 1864, James H. Lane Papers, Auburn University, Auburn, Alabama.

21 Clark, *North Carolina Regiments*, 2:480.

22 Report of Capt. James G. Harris, August 28th, James H. Lane Papers.

they vaulted over the works and with the bayonet drove the men, capturing many and cutting the line in two parts."[23] With the captured cannon playing on their line of retreat, the New Yorkers failed to rally and counterattack. Many soldiers from the center of Crandell's brigade surrendered. Major Jackson Lafayette Bost, a bachelor physician captured at Hanover Court House and wounded at Chancellorsville and Gettysburg, led the 37th North Carolina that day and remembered, "The prisoners, were with a few exceptions, only directed which way to go."[24]

Engaged by Tarheels in front, with others advancing on both flanks, Rugg's troops attempted to withdraw. Then, for the first time, Rugg's soldiers saw the North Carolinians and the captured guns cutting off their line of retreat. Like Hartshorne's soldiers at Globe Tavern, only a handful ran the gauntlet. The rest threw down their arms and filed off into captivity.

Scattered groups from Cooke's and Lane's brigades began working their way out toward the 12th Battery, New York Light Artillery along the outside of the northern return and through the woods in the return's rear. Captain George F. McNight, the battery commander, pulled out his left gun and sited it to the west on the road from Shay's Tavern to Reams Station. This gun kept the Tarheels off the road, but the North Carolinians broke the line that Miles attempted to form in the woods to the battery's left. The gunners fired double-shotted canister until the Tarheels had almost reached the battery under cover of the woods. McNight ordered a retreat, but the North Carolinians shot the teams of the two westernmost guns before they could limber up and flee. The New Yorkers succeeded in limbering up the third cannon, but it did not get far before the Tarheels brought down its horses. A handful of North Carolinians representing each of the three brigades in the assault briefly took possession of the battery's three easternmost guns.

Though Confederate units had overrun the Union line at multiple locations, the assault appeared a failure to Wilcox and Heth, who observed from a distance. The smoke obscured their vision. From their vantage point, they saw only what seemed large numbers of their soldiers retiring. In fact, the two major generals witnessed large numbers of Unionists marching unescorted into captivity. Wilcox dispatched an aide who quickly ascertained that the

---

23 Roback, *152d New York*, 119.

24 Report of Major J. L. Bost, August 29th, 1864, James H. Lane Papers.

assault had succeeded in capturing the Federal works and many prisoners. Wilcox went forward to see for himself.

Heth ordered two regiments of McGowan's brigade and the brigade's sharpshooters to advance under Capt. Langdon Hascall, the Assistant Adjutant General of the brigade. The brigade's remaining three regiments stayed put to guard the Confederate right. The gunners of Batteries A and B, 1st Rhode Island Light Artillery, ran out of ammunition and abandoned their horseless pieces. MacRae's soldiers engaged the infantry support of the battery. Langdon's two regiments and McGowan's sharpshooters took the guns of the consolidated Rhode Island battery and around 500 prisoners, mostly from a battalion of the 4th New York heavies that did not receive orders to fall back in time. First Lieutenant Thomas C. Parkhurst of Company H, a graduate of Oberlin College, recalled that when surrounded and called upon to surrender,

> I at once shouted to the men, "Fire and get out quick!" and suited the action to the command by setting such an example of racing and hurdle-jumping as would have secured an engagement in a Wild West show. I escaped with six bullet-holes through my clothing, but not a scratch except as made by brush and brier. The men wisely deemed discretion the better part of valor and, in company with their newly found escorts, started for that goal of their ambition—Petersburg.[25]

Like the soldiers of Lane's and MacRae's brigades, McGowan's troops turned the captured field pieces on the retreating foe.

To secure the initial success and occupy the captured earthworks, Heth called up his reserve brigades. He ordered forward Sanders' brigade on the left and shifted Weisiger's brigade to the right. Sanders' brigade hastened to reinforce the Rebels in the captured works west of the railroad and north of the Depot Road. Weisiger's Virginians double-quicked towards the right for 700 yards across a flat, muddy field behind McGowan's sharpshooters. Private Birdie Bird—back with the Petersburg New Grays of the 12th Virginia Infantry after his stint with the color guard—found himself headed toward an enemy cannon. "The muzzle looked as large as an ordinary flour barrel," he remembered.[26] A bullet struck and killed the New Gray next to Bird—Sgt. Joseph R. Bell, who had just returned to the ranks from a wound suffered in the Wilderness.

---

25 Kirk, *Heavy Guns and Light*, 348.

26 Letter, Bird to Randolph, October 15, 1864, Bird Family Papers.

When within 200 yards of the earthworks, the Virginians saw hundreds of Federals crossing the encompassing ditch and coming in as prisoners. A few ran southward along the ditch, seemingly attempting to escape. The Virginians thought the fugitives might sweep around the right flank of the Confederates in the captured earthworks. Weisiger's soldiers hastened toward the works, which consisted of railroad iron and cross-ties protected by telegraph wire. The wire remained invisible until the troops came within a few feet of it. "We were too tired to mind trifles and it was laughable even in the midst of the fire to see men catch their feet in the wire and plunge headlong against the works," Bird recalled.[27]

Weisiger's brigade assisted McGowan's soldiers in securing the works against counterattack. The Northerners running southward did not appear to have anything in mind other than saving their hides. "They did not fire a gun at us as well as I could see as we charged upon them," recalled Private Bernard of the 12th Virginia's Petersburg Riflemen. Like other Rebel infantrymen on this part of the field, Bird and about a dozen more of the Kid Glove Boys jumped over the works, dropped their rifles, turned a captured Napoleon on the Unionists, and fired double charges of canister. Bird and his comrades, "did perhaps some of the wildest shooting of the war," Bernard observed.[28] Their first shot cut off the top of a nearby pine. The wild cannonade that followed did more than the Federals to delay the Southern cavalry bearing down on the Unionist left flank.

With the captured earthworks secured, the Confederate artillerists limbered up yet again and unlimbered in front of the fortifications. Lieutenant Colonel Pegram ordered the gunners to reserve fire in case of a Federal counterattack. A Unionist shell exploded a limber chest, killing four horses. Some Rebel artillerists hopped over the breastworks and helped Weisiger's and McGowan's amateur gunners serve the captured pieces more accurately.

As Hancock's position fell apart, he joined many of his officers in trying to rally his troops.

"Men, will you leave me?" he cried.[29]

---

27 Letter, Bird to Randolph, August 28, 1864, Bird Family Papers.

28 George S. Bernard Diary, August 27, 1864, George S. Bernard Papers, Alderman Library, University of Virginia, Charlottesville, Virginia.

29 Simons, *One Hundred And Twenty-Fifth New York*, 243.

To ascertain the damage, the corps commander sent forward his chief of staff, Lieutenant Colonel Walker. Acting as an orderly that day, Pvt. Patrick Ginley of the 12th Battery, New York Light Artillery accompanied Walker. Riding the customary short distance behind the chief of staff, Ginley saw him captured by the Rebels as Walker entered the railroad cut. Ginley reversed course and headed for the rear but had his horse shot out from under him. Scrambling to an abandoned gun of his battery, he loaded it and fired a blast of canister into the advancing Confederates, then fled on foot. On the way back to Federal lines, he seized the flag of a Massachusetts regiment from its color bearer's dead hands and carried it to safety. These exploits helped earn Ginley a Medal of Honor.

Captain Joseph Egolf, left in command of the 125th New York of Crandell's brigade, succeeded in rallying some of his soldiers behind an old ice house east of the railway. He led them in a counterattack that disintegrated when a Secessionist bullet wounded him as he crossed the railroad cut. An attempt to reform just east of the roadbed what remained of the 4th New York heavies failed. Fugitives from Barlow's division retreated to Gibbon's line in the southern return, sowing confusion. The fire of the captured cannon and the Confederate musketry enfiladed Gibbon's troops and forced them to relocate themselves to the reverse side of the southern return. The right of Murphy's brigade retreated to a traverse, abandoning the stretch of the southern return adjacent to the railroad. Rebel fire commanded the inside of both returns for 200 or 300 yards back from the roadbed. The Union line between the returns now ran parallel to the railway halfway between the railroad and the woods to the east, with the 3rd Battery, New Jersey Light Artillery in its center. The line ran through a corn field.

McGowan's South Carolinians soon had to face a counterthrust ordered by Col. Matthew Murphy of the 182nd New York. This officer, on his own initiative, sent two small regiments of the Corcoran Legion amounting to fewer than 150 soldiers to reoccupy the stretch of the southern return adjacent to the railway. Murphy personally led these men of the 155th and 170th New York. They accomplished the task tardily because of the heavy fire they met. Murphy then headed back toward the 182nd New York in the center of his brigade. Exhausted, unable to attack, unwilling to retreat, the two New York regiments and McGowan's South Carolinians fired intermittently at one another.

Weisiger's Virginians reinforced McGowan's troops during this stalemate and soon "out-Yankeed the Yankees," recalled Capt. Frank M. Myers in Company A of the 35th Battalion Cavalry, the Comanches, in the Laurel

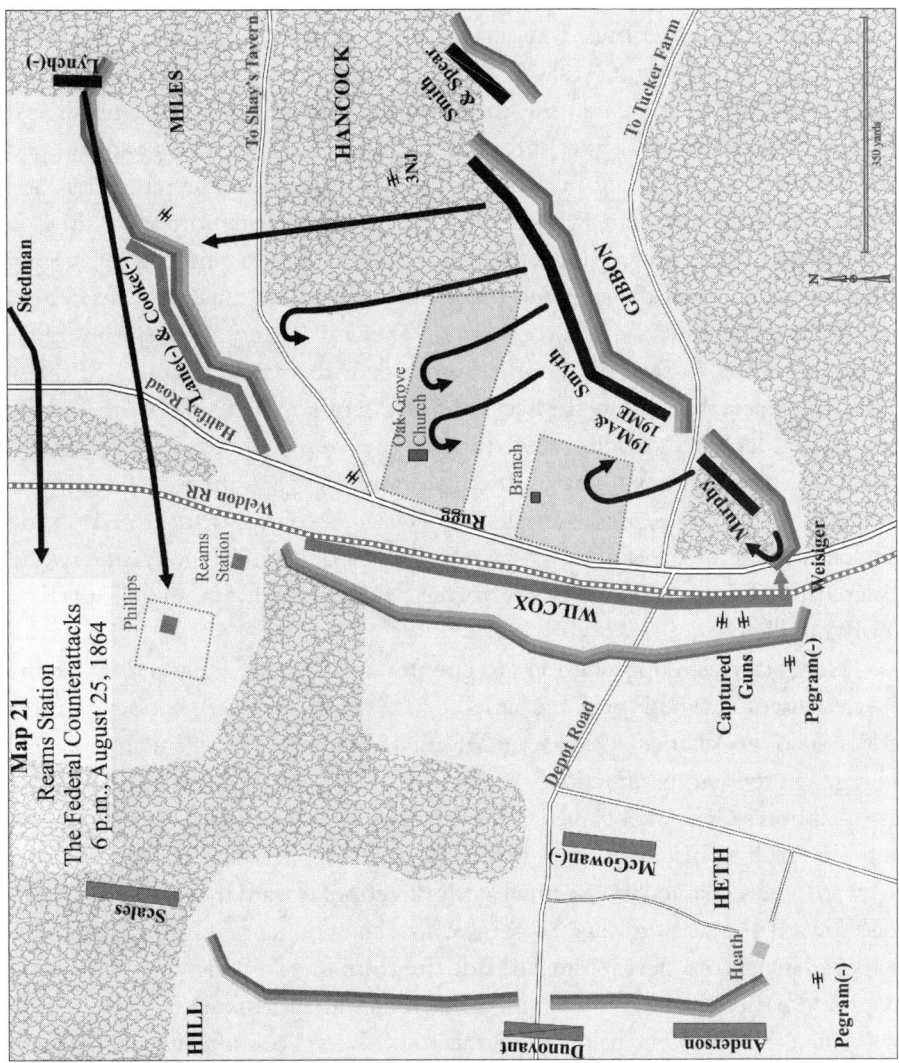

Brigade approaching from the south.[30] Teams of soldiers from Weisiger's brigade tossed cross-ties and rails over the embankment onto the heads of the New Yorkers, driving them from the east side of the embankment.

The impetus of the assaulting Confederate infantry had now spent itself. On the far left, the 7th North Carolina withdrew to the railroad. A handful of

---

30 Frank M. Myers, *The Comanches: A History of White's Battalion, Virginia Cavalry, Laurel Brig., Hampton Div., A.N.V., C.S.A.* (Baltimore, 1871), 327-8.

disorganized Tarheels milled about the three easternmost guns of the 12th Battery, New York Light Artillery. Some of the soldiers of Lane's brigade had turned on the Federal line in the corn field the captured gun at the northwest angle of the earthworks. Except for part of Miles' brigade, which had stopped the Tarheel advance along the northern return near where the return reached Jones Hole Swamp, Barlow's division and the attached portion of Macy's brigade had disintegrated. Groups of Rebels attempted to pursue the fleeing Federals of Barlow's division and Macy's brigade across the corn field behind the church and into the woods beyond. The 3rd Battery, New Jersey Light Artillery turned to face the Southerners and, with the aid of the 12th New Jersey, succeeded in halting the Secessionists. Between the Depot Road and the traverse, MacRae's troops had turned the guns of the 10th Battery, Massachusetts Light Artillery on the Unionists. Between the traverse and the acute southern angle, McGowan's and Weisiger's soldiers had turned on the Federals the guns of Batteries A and B, 1st Rhode Island Light Artillery and cleared the southern return to the traverse where the 155th and 170th New York huddled.

Hancock called upon Gibbon to counterattack immediately and retake the lost earthworks. The North Carolina-born Gibbon hastened to obey, but his thrust had no chance whatsoever of retaking the lost entrenchments. He charged in the wrong direction.

Gibbon's division occupied the reverse side of the southern return. Gibbon did not realign his division before attacking. He just ordered his soldiers forward. They charged in a northwesterly direction, toward the northern return, not toward the western face of the works. The course of Gibbon's division exposed its left to a devastating enfilade fire from the Confederate infantry and captured batteries on the other side of the railroad embankment.

The 8th New York heavies and the 164th New York of Murphy's brigade formed the left of Gibbon's attack force. The 19th Maine and 19th Massachusetts, a detachment from Macy's brigade, comprised the center. Smyth's brigade charged on the right. Demoralized by the enfilade fire from the railway embankment, disordered by the fugitives of Barlow's division, exhausted by the morning's marching, countermarching, digging, and fighting, Gibbon's troops responded sluggishly to the order to charge.

Gibbon's exposed left faltered first. The raking fire from the railroad embankment proved unendurable to the participating portion of Murphy's brigade. Led by Gibbon's acting assistant adjutant general, Capt. A. Henry Embler, the 8th New York heavies and the 164th New York, closest to the enfilade fire, quickly disintegrated and fell back to the southern return in confusion.

The detachment from Macy's brigade advanced at the double-quick despite the galling crossfire. These Federals proceeded farther than the detachment from Murphy's brigade, nearly to the church and the nearby Branch house north of the junction of the Depot and Halifax Roads. The 19th Maine and 19th Massachusetts still failed to retake any of the lost earthworks. Perceiving the troops on both their flanks falling back, they reformed behind the church and the Branch house and then withdrew to the southern return.

Smyth's left consisted of the 1st Delaware and the 2nd Delaware Battalion, the 69th and 106th Pennsylvania, the 108th New York, the 7th West Virginia Battalion, and three companies of the 10th New York Battalion. This force crossed open ground and fell apart under the enfilade fire from the Confederates and the captured guns on the other side of the railway embankment before the soldiers from Macy's brigade reached the church.

The right of Smyth's brigade achieved some success. It consisted of the 12th New Jersey, the 14th Connecticut and the other three companies of the 10th New York Battalion. Hancock and Smyth led this force in a charge through timber rather than over open ground. The left of the 14th Connecticut, "suddenly broke and retreated, overwhelmed by the terrific fire that was raining down upon us," recalled Sgt. Henry Lydall of the 14th's Company F.[31] Lydall took cover in a deserted rifle pit. Sergeant James White of the 12th New Jersey's Company F, a store clerk, remembered that the rest of this force, "swept through that timber just like a whirlwind," and recaptured part of the northern return.[32]

The successful portion of Smyth's brigade halted and remained in the recaptured earthworks. The rest of Gibbon's counterattackers retreated to the reverse side of the southern return, the detachment from Macy's brigade in relatively good condition, the other survivors in a state of profound disorganization. Smyth had difficulty restoring order to the part of his command that the Confederates had repulsed. Murphy had just returned to the 182nd New York when the right of his brigade came streaming back slightly to the east of where it had begun its charge. He only partially restored order to the

---

31 Charles D. Page, *History of the Fourteenth Regiment, Connecticut Volunteer Infantry* (Meriden CT, 1906), 305.

32 Haines, *The Men of Company F, 12th New Jersey*, 78.

8th New York heavies and the 164th New York. Gibbon rode along his line with his horse at a walk, the picture of despair, casting frequent and anxious glances toward the position lost by Barlow's division in anticipation of an attack against his own completely demoralized soldiers.

A motley force that included representatives from Miles' and Smyth's brigades drove off the handful of Rebels milling around the guns of the 12th Battery, New York Light Artillery. Repossessing the guns, this force almost completely reoccupied the northern return. General Miles directed Colonel Lynch to cross the railroad and attack the Secessionist left flank to recapture the works lost by Crandell's brigade. With a force of about 200 officers and men from nearly every Federal infantry regiment on the field, Lynch had difficulty advancing. Friendly fire from the Unionists occupying the northern return hindered this counterattack, as did the force's lack of organization.

Lynch's troops eventually reached the Phillips house, west of the railway and about 200 yards from the left flank of the Southerners. From there the Federal infantrymen enfiladed the Confederates along the roadbed. The fire from Lynch's soldiers proved no more than annoying to the Rebels.

The horsemen of Stedman's brigade joined Lynch's troops in this counterattack. Stedman's brigade threatened Hill's left flank, which the 7th Virginia Cavalry screened. Partially armed with Henry repeaters captured from Federal cavalry at First Reams Station, the 7th fired so noisily that Hill roused himself and sent to the assistance of the Virginian horsemen his personal staff couriers, a pair of howitzers from Brander's battery, and all mounted and dismounted men in reach, as well as the three regiments of McGowan's brigade guarding the right. Stedman's troopers withdrew.

The 13th and 16th North Carolina of Scales' brigade drove back Lynch and his 200 soldiers from the Phillips house. Lynch's troops retreated to the earthworks east of the railroad.

At about 6:15 p.m., Hancock directed Gibbon to renew his counterattack across the open field toward the church. The II Corps chief wanted Gibbon's soldiers to converge with Miles' counterthrust. Still in the process of reforming his routed units, Gibbon could do no more than push forward a skirmish line.

Hancock strained to reverse matters. He personally urged Gibbon's troops forward again. Bareheaded and with loosened sleeves, his bridle rein cut by a bullet, the corps leader administered a string of the horrible oaths that his admirers considered his most serious fault. Private William Hyndman of Company A of the 4th Pennsylvania Cavalry recalled that Hancock, "looked more like a wild man or a soldier possessed with a restless and demoniac spirit,

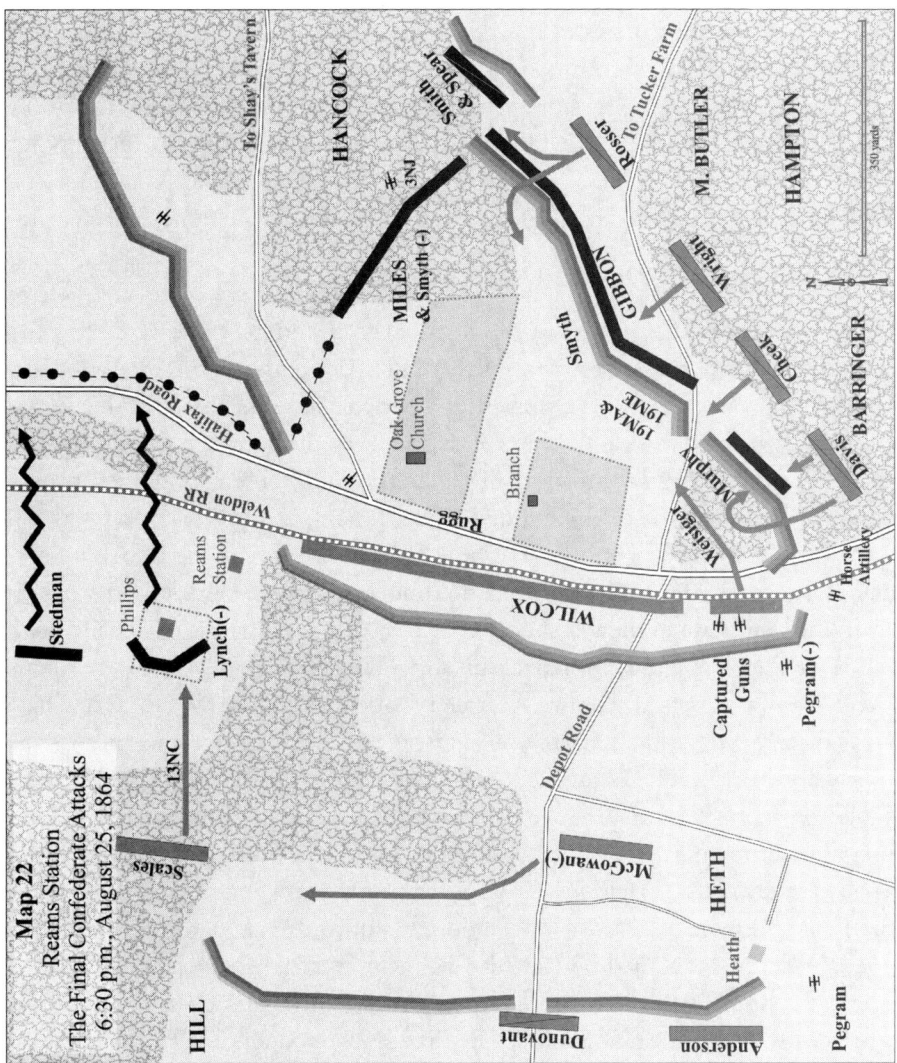

than a general commanding in a good cause."³³ Followed by two or three of his personal staff, the II Corps chief rode up to the northern return, waived his cap and shouted, "Come on! We can beat them yet. Don't leave me for God's sake."³⁴ Not half a dozen soldiers responded to his appeal. At this point, a bullet

33 William Hyndman, *History of a Cavalry Company, A Complete Record of Company 'A', 4th Penn'a Cavalry* (Philadelphia, 1872), 226-7.

34 Billings, *10th Massachusetts Battery*, 253.

wounded Hancock's horse in the neck. The animal fell forward, temporarily dismounting the corps commander. The wounded horse recovered in a few minutes. Hancock remounted the animal and rode up to one of his staff at the 3rd Battery, New Jersey Light Artillery. Begrimed with powder and smoke, covered with dust, Hancock put his hand on the staff officer's shoulder and said, "Colonel, I do not care to die, but I pray God I may never leave this field!"[35]

Gibbon's division had still not completely reformed on the reverse side of the earthworks when, around 6:45 p.m., it again found itself subjected to a fire from its rear. In response to this fire, which Gibbon remembered as "very feeble," the soldiers of his division shifted back again to the inside of the works, some changing from side to side for as much as the fourth time.[36] Gibbon's troops suffered a heavy enfilading fire from the Confederates and the captured guns on the other side of the railroad embankment.

Hampton's cavalry, joining the fight from the south as the Rebel infantry gained success from the west, fired the bullets that came at Gibbon's troops from the rear. Late in the afternoon, a courier reached Malone's Crossing with the news that Hill had commenced his long-awaited advance. A few moments later, Hampton heard Pegram's artillery open fire. The South Carolinian immediately ordered an advance of his whole line, which stretched across the railroad at Malone's Crossing. Mounted, the 2nd North Carolina Cavalry and a squadron from the 9th Virginia Cavalry led the advance. Immediately behind these horsemen tramped the remainder of the 9th on foot. At the Lanier farm, about a mile north of Malone's Crossing and only a few hundred yards south of the Federal earthworks at Reams Station, Hampton's vanguard encountered a line of rifle pits occupied by the 7th Michigan and 59th New York of Macy's brigade. The mounted Virginians and North Carolinians charged, leapt the works with their horses, and took more than sixty prisoners.[37] The Tarheels and Virginians waited at the Lanier farm until the dismounted Virginians behind them reached this line.

---

35 Walker, *General Hancock*, 275.

36 Report of Maj. Gen. John Gibbon, U.S. Army, commanding Second Division, of operations August 25, in *OR* 42, pt. 1, 294.

37 Report of Maj. Gen. Wade Hampton, C.S. Army, commanding Cavalry Corps, Army of Northern Virginia, of operations August 25, ibid., 943; Beale, *Ninth Virginia Cavalry*, 142.

By the time Hampton and the dismounted Virginians arrived at the Lanier farm, Hill's infantry had driven the Unionists from the earthworks west of the railroad at Reams Station. Seeing this, the South Carolininian double-quicked Butler's division from the west side of the railway to the right and formed a new line. Chambliss' brigade, with its left on the railroad, formed the new line's left. Barringer's brigade constituted the center. Young's brigade advanced on the right. Behind this line, the Laurel Brigade deployed in support. The two batteries of horse artillery took the place of Butler's division west of the roadbed. Hampton had most of his troopers dismount, but kept some mounted soldiers in reserve. Once he had rearranged his forces, Hampton issued orders that his troopers should advance slowly with their left on the railroad while their right swung around to strike the rear of the Federals at the refused left of the southern return.

The Secessionist formation wheeled into the belt of woods north of the Lanier farm. The Rebel cavalrymen advanced steadily over this difficult terrain. They encountered only enemy picket fire. A short distance into the trees, the Confederates reached a line of rifle pits. There, without offering much resistance, about fifty videttes from Company F of the 4th New York heavies surrendered.[38]

Hampton's troopers continued to wheel through the woods. The Secessionists slogged to a slashing south of the main Unionist earthworks. The going became even more difficult. Due to the configuration of the Federal trenches, the right of Hampton's line had to advance more rapidly than the center or the left. The Laurel Brigade veered more and more to the right until the 12th Virginia Cavalry moved up from the supporting line and formed the extreme right of the main battle line. The 11th Virginia Cavalry and some of the Comanches found themselves behind Young's brigade. As the dismounted Rebel cavalrymen emerged from the trees, they saw before them a gentle slope leading up to the southern return, which extended along the crest of the slope. On their left, slashing intervened between the timber and the return. On the right, the trees naturally receded from the fortifications. Gibbon's division, which occupied the southern return, shifted back to the original inside of the earthworks and opened a heavy fire on the Confederate troopers emerging from the woods. The Confederate infantry and the captured guns west of the railroad reopened their severe enfilading fire on Gibbon's soldiers.

38 Ibid., 143; Kirk, *Heavy Guns and Light*, 340.

Hampton directed the troopers of Chambliss' brigade to lie down until support came up on their right. Due to the exertions of Weisiger's Virginians, the New Yorkers of Murphy's brigade had abandoned for good the short stretch of the southern return adjacent to the railroad embankment. The western flank of the Union troops in the southern return now rested behind a traverse. As the Federal bullets pattered against the foliage, Hampton instructed a squadron of the 9th Virginia Cavalry to scale the vacant section of the southern return. The attention of Gibbon's troops focused on the Rebels in front of them. The squadron of the 9th Virginian Cavalry advanced undetected. At the other end of the line, Young's brigade appeared about 200 yards in the left rear of the Unionists and discharged a volley followed by a rush. When the squadron of Virginians reached the traverse and gave the Federals a galling volley in flank and rear, fire from all directions pinned down the Unionists. All along the southern return, Federals began surrendering. A handful of Confederates started leading hundreds of Gibbon's soldiers into captivity.

Private Robert Laird Stewart of Company G, 140th Pennsylvania, in Miles' brigade, had recovered enough from a Gettysburg wound to return to his unit, but not to the ranks. He remembered the dislocating effect of Hampton's attack on the Unionist position:

> The writer, who was on detached service in the Adjutant-General's office of the Division at this time, was seated on a log at the temporary Headquarters, preparing a report, which had been ordered from the several brigades, when this fusillade broke out from the rear. With the line breaking up in our front and a force of the enemy of unknown strength directly in our rear, it seemed for a few moments as if we were all in a fair way to be escorted directly to Richmond. It was a position in which, for the time, there was no rear and no place which was not swept by artillery fire or musketry or both.[39]

Some Northerners, as they surrendered, discovered the weakness of the Southern force. Running into the sorghum field behind the earthworks, these escaped prisoners started firing again. The dismounted Southern cavalrymen pursued these Federals. From behind a hasty breastwork of fence rails on the wooded knoll opposite the right of Hampton's troopers, Union cavalry opened fire on the advancing Rebels. The Secessionist cavalrymen also found themselves subjected to friendly fire from the captured batteries west of the

---

39 Robert L. Stewart, *History of the One Hundred and Fortieth Regiment Pennsylvania Volunteers* (Philadelphia, 1912), 236.

railroad embankment. Caught in this crossfire and faced by fire from the 3rd Battery, New Jersey Light Artillery, the Confederates recoiled. "A rusher in any sort of a fight," according to one of his troopers, Lt. Wiley C. Howard of Company C in the Cobb Legion Cavalry, the impetuous Col. Gib Wright incurred the wrath of the soldiers of Young's brigade when he castigated them for falling back.[40]

As Hampton's advance slowed, Weisiger's foot soldiers helped Hampton's momentarily stymied cavalrymen by advancing against feeble resistance. As darkness fell, the 12th Virginia Infantry of Weisiger's brigade and the 12th Virginia Cavalry of the Laurel Brigade charged side by side and drove the dismounted Federal horsemen back from the wooded knoll into the woods that harbored the fugitives from Gibbon's division.

Union prisoners passed Weisiger's acting ordnance officer, Sgt. Westwood A. Todd, a Norfolk native and former member of the Petersburg Riflemen who had lost a finger at Second Bull Run. Todd, who had never before seen so many prisoners taken in a battle, recalled:

> Among them was a full regiment of Pennsylvania "Bucktails," so-called from each man wearing a buck's tail in his hat. Our men were very much pleased with the buck tails and asked the prisoners for them. Some of our men took the buck tails without saying "by your leave."[41]

Gibbon reorganized his routed soldiers. Smyth dispatched the 69th and 106th Pennsylvania to link up with his troops in the northern return. The Unionist cavalry reformed on Gibbon's left facing south. Miles' brigade, Smyth's brigade, the 3rd Battery, New Jersey Light Artillery, and the horse soldiers kept open the route of retreat—the road to Shay's Tavern.

The Confederates having by this time driven Lynch's force back across the railroad, Miles established a picket line running from the northern return northward along the Halifax Road. While inspecting this line, Miles heard enemy officers and color bearers calling out their regiments. This led Miles to believe—very mistakenly—that the Rebels had suffered heavier losses than his men and an equal degree of disorganization. Though his routed and totally shattered command had little prospect of retaking anything, the commander of

---

40 Wiley C. Howard, *Sketch of Cobb Legion Cavalry* (Suffolk VA, 1986), 12.

41 Westwood Todd Reminiscences, Southern Historical Collection, Wilson Library, University of North Carolina at Chapel Hill, Chapel Hill, North Carolina.

Barlow's division determined that he could retake his entire line. Miles forwarded his wildly optimistic assessment to Hancock.

The II Corps chief consulted his other divisional commanders. Gregg, whose command may actually have had the capacity for successful offensive action, like Miles offered to retake the entire position from which the Secessionists had driven his men. Gibbon bluntly admitted the obvious. He confessed that his routed and disorganized division could not retake any part of its previous position. Without reinforcements and unable to keep open the only line of retreat without reoccupying the lost southern return, Hancock ordered a withdrawal. Miles' soldiers covered the retreat, with the provost guard and the 61st New York acting as rear guard.

At about 7:00 p.m., Hancock's force met Orlando Willcox's division, still a mile and a half from the battlefield. Hancock's order to McAllister to arrest stragglers had instead reached Willcox shortly after 6:00 p.m. Willcox, who had performed capably at Globe Tavern on August 19 but unsatisfactorily at the Crater on July 30, failed to observe that Hancock had addressed the order to McAllister. The erratic Willcox deployed Humphrey's brigade across the road to arrest the stragglers already coming back in droves. That the stragglers included officers disturbed Willcox. Not only stragglers, but wagons and ambulances filled the road and impeded the progress of Willcox's division. While engaged in stopping and reorganizing the fugitives, Willcox received from Hancock an urgent call for reinforcements. Throwing off their knapsacks, Willcox's men started for the battlefield at a double-quick only to receive from Lieutenant Colonel Morgan, Hancock's chief of staff, instructions to cover the withdrawal of Hancock's troops. As Hancock's force abandoned the battlefield, night came on and a violent rain poured down.

After dark, the Rebels fired blindly along the inside of the northern return. The Federals there returned the fire at gunflashes, voices, and clinking, rattling canteens. The battlefield took on a different aspect as needy Secessionists gathered small arms and otherwise equipped themselves at the expense of the Unionist casualties. Sergeant Lydall of the 14th Connecticut lay flat in his rifle pit until, he recalled, "the shadows of night concealed me from the view of the enemy, when peering forth I could see the flickering lights of many lanterns, and I know that the human vultures were at their unholy work of robbing the dead and wounded."[42] Creeping forth from his hiding place, he heard the cry of

---

42 Page, *Fourteenth Connecticut*, 305.

a wounded comrade, Captain James R. Nickels of Company I, hit in the leg. Lydall assisted Nickels to safety.

At 9:00 p.m. that night, Meade directed the divisions of Crawford and White at Globe Tavern to join Hancock near the junction of the Jerusalem Plank Road with the road to Shay's Tavern. In a telegram to Hancock at 11:00 p.m., Meade explained the concerns that had governed his use of the Army of the Potomac's reserves, but Hancock remained convinced that Meade ought to have sent reinforcements straight down the railroad from Globe Tavern to Reams Station.

Willcox's troops took over the duties of a rear guard around 11:00 p.m., after Miles' division finished passing. At 11:30 p.m., learning of Hancock's abandonment of the field, Meade authorized Warren to retain Crawford's and White's divisions. About midnight, Hancock's soldiers encamped by the Williams house, near where the Jerusalem Plank Road crossed Second Swamp. Willcox's division began its return to the Jerusalem Plank Road. On the way, this command aroused and collected hundreds of stragglers asleep and exhausted along the lane and in the woods. McAllister's force remained in position until after 1 a.m., when Willcox's division passed the junction at Shay's Tavern and turned toward Dr. Gurley's house. McAllister's soldiers then marched to their old position near the Jones house, arriving at 5:00 a.m. This left Gregg's cavalry holding the Jerusalem Plank Road and the country between that road and Warren's position at Globe Tavern.

The Confederates did not pursue that night. They removed the wounded, buried the dead and secured the captured small arms and artillery. Around midnight, when the rain stopped, the Rebel infantry withdrew from the captured earthworks. Seven regiments of Hampton's cavalry remained on the battlefield. Marching almost until day, the Southern foot soldiers bivouacked for a few hours about five miles west of Rowanty Creek.

In the morning, while other Secessionist horsemen continued burying the dead and removing the wounded, Company B of the 12th Virginia Cavalry followed Hancock's path of retreat toward Shay's Tavern and took prisoner a great many stragglers. Encountering Stedman's brigade of horsemen about two miles from the battlefield around 10 a.m., the Southern cavalrymen skirmished briefly and then withdrew. The Confederate infantrymen staggered into the thinly held Petersburg trenches that evening, leaving a trail of stragglers many miles long. "We got back after sunset to camp, after one of the most weary and hot marches I ever had," recalled Master Sergeant Fielding of the 9th Alabama in Sanders' brigade. "Some 8 or 10 of the reg't came with us, the rest broke down on the way."[43]

Union killed, wounded, and captured at Second Reams Station totaled 2,727, and the Rebels took more than 2,000 prisoners.[44] For some time after the battle, the soldiers of the 28th North Carolina in Lane's brigade joked among themselves that Grant would have to send Hancock back north to recruit a new command. The Secessionists took twelve colors, nine guns, and 3,100 stands of arms.[45] The color bearer of the 33rd North Carolina in Lane's brigade claimed to have captured Hancock's coat tail. Though probably untrue in fact, the claim had some basis in figure. If true in fact, it provided another instance of Hancock's extraordinary personal courage.

Secessionist losses at Second Reams Station numbered about 750, most of them in the infantry, and included around twenty-five captives.[46] The Southern

---

43 Axford, *"To Lochaber Na Mair,"* 130.

44 Return of Casualties in the Union Forces, Reams Station, August 25, 1864, in *OR* 42, pt. 1, 131. These numbers purportedly included the losses during the skirmishes of the preceding three days. Ibid. The 115 lost by the Federal cavalry on August 23 do not seem included because their inclusion would mean the Unionist horsemen suffered virtually no losses at Second Reams Station. Ibid., 608; see Chapter 10, note 10. The Return of Casualties appears to include from August 23 only the fifteen soldiers lost by the Fourth New York Heavy Artillery. *OR* 42, pt. 1, 269-70. Hill reported 2,150 prisoners. A. P. Hill to Col. W. H. Taylor, August 31, 1864, ibid., 940.

45 Ibid.

46 Estimates of Rebel losses at Second Reams Station ranged as high as 1,000. Macon *Daily Telegraph*, September 3, 1864, p. 1, col. 2-3. A more conservative estimate put Confederate casualties at between 600 and 700 killed and wounded. *The Southern Recorder* (Milledgeville, Ga.) September 13, 1864, p. 1, col. 3. Special Correspondent J. W. W. estimated the Southern killed, wounded, and missing as not less than 500 and not over 800. Augusta *Chronicle & Sentinel*, September 9, 1864, p. 1, col. 2. Officially, Confederate losses totaled 720. *OR* 42, pt. 1, 940. This figure did not include the losses during the skirmishes of the preceding three days.

Lane's brigade of Wilcox's command lost twelve killed, ninety-seven wounded and six missing. James H. Lane, "History of Lane's N. C. Brigade—Campaign of 1864—Anecdote about Captain G. G. Holland, 28th N. C. Troops," *SHSP*, vol. 9 (1881), 357. McGowan's brigade lost two killed and twenty wounded. Caldwell, *McGowan's Brigade*, 181. Anderson's brigade lost four killed, thirty-three wounded, one missing. Record Group 109, Compiled Service Records, National Archives; Persons, "Unpublished Study of Anderson's Brigade," Persons Private Collection. "Anderson's brigade did not lose over fifty men." Augusta *Chronicle & Sentinel*, Sept. 9, p. 1, col. 2. The 13th North Carolina of Scales' brigade lost one killed, sixteen wounded and six missing. Raleigh Daily *Confederate*, September 28, 1864, p. 2, col. 3.

Initially, Wilcox stated: "My entire loss was 200, in McGowan, slight, 22 total, Lane's the most, Scales but little, Anderson not much. . . ." Wilcox Report. If Lane's Brigade lost the most, a total loss for Wilcox's command of more than 300 does not make sense because it would have

cavalry lost ninety-four troopers.[47] Private Edward Laight Wells of the Charleston Light Dragoons, Company K of the 4th South Carolina Cavalry in

---

had to occur principally in Scales' brigade, for which the fewest figures exist, but which Wilcox still said had lost "little." Ibid.

Accepting Wilcox's initial estimate as his closest to the mark and taking the other available figures into account yields by process of elimination twenty-five as the number of soldiers lost by Scales' brigade at Second Reams Station. In light of the loss of twenty-three suffered by the 13th North Carolina and Wilcox's feeling that he had initially underestimated his losses, it seems likely that Wilcox's command lost about 250 at Second Reams Station. This assumes that the 16th North Carolina lost as many soldiers as the 13th and that the other two regiments of Scales' brigade each lost about half as many.

Wilcox's tendency to revise his reports, sometimes years after their preparation, detracted from his reliability. Douglas Southall Freeman, *Lee's Lieutenants: A Study in Command*, (3 vols.) (New York, 1944), 1:258, note 86.

In Heth's command, Cooke's brigade suffered the most. The 15th North Carolina on Cooke's far right lost twenty-three killed and ninety-one wounded. Clark, *North Carolina Regiments*, 1:747. The 46th North Carolina on the 15th's left but still crossing the open field, lost seventy-three killed and wounded. Ibid., 3:78. Assuming that the two regiments of Cooke's left lost as many soldiers as the similarly circumstanced two regiments of Lane's right yields seventeen as the approximate number of soldiers lost by Cooke's left. (The 7th North Carolina on the left of Lane's brigade lost four killed and twenty-eight wounded. Ibid., 1:385. On the 7th's right, the 28th North Carolina lost six killed and thirty-one wounded. Report of Maj. Samuel N. Stowe, August 28th, 1864, James H. Lane Papers. In the brigade's center, the 37th North Carolina lost twenty-four wounded and five missing. Report of Major J. L. Bost, August 29th, 1864, James H. Lane Papers. On the brigade's far right, the 18th North Carolina—which took just twenty-five men into action—lost one killed and five wounded. Report of Captain B. F. Rinaldi, August 28th, 1864, James H. Lane Papers. By process of elimination, the 33rd North Carolina, to the 18th's left, must have suffered eleven casualties. Wilcox Report.) Company G of the 27th North Carolina, one of the regiments on Cooke's left, alone lost one killed and seven wounded of eleven taken into action. Wagstaff, H. M., ed., The Jas. A. Graham Papers, 1861-1864, The Jas. Sprunt Historical Studies, vol. 20, No. 2 (1928), 313. In view of the few soldiers taken into action by the 18th North Carolina of Lane's brigade providing comparison and the losses of Company G of the 27th North Carolina, it appears that Cooke's left lost approximately fifty soldiers, and that Cooke's brigade lost around 240.

In MacRae's brigade, the 26th North Carolina lost three killed and twenty-two wounded. Raleigh *Daily Confederate*, September 2, 1864, p. 2, col. 5. The 47th North Carolina lost three killed and thirty-four wounded. Ibid., September 28, 1864, p. 2, col. 5. These figures indicate that MacRae's brigade lost approximately 150 soldiers.

Sanders' brigade lost seven wounded and two captured. Richmond *Sentinel*, October 29, 1864, p. 1, col. 6. The 11th Alabama in Sanders' brigade suffered one killed, six wounded at Second Reams Station. Griffin, *11th Alabama*, 209. (Sanders' brigade may have lost more heavily than reported in the Richmond *Sentinel*.) The 12th Virginia of Weisiger's brigade lost one killed and one wounded. Macon *Daily Telegraph*, September 3, 1864, p. 1, col. 3. Company I, 61st Virginia lost none. McAlpine, "Sketch of Company I, 61st Virginia Infantry, Mahone's brigade, C. S. A.," 103. The losses of Weisiger's brigade probably numbered around ten.

Heth's command thus suffered about 400 casualties at Second Reams Station.

47 Butler's division lost six killed, twenty-five wounded and two missing, while W. H. F. Lee's division lost ten killed, fifty wounded and one missing. OR 42, pt. 1, 944.

Dunovant's brigade, considered the official loss of 720 soldiers "surprisingly small in proportion to the fire sustained, the shooting of the Federals being unusually wild, the bullets ranging very high, a sure sign of want of skill or nerve."[48]

From Hancock's point of view, according to Lieutenant Colonel Walker, "Reams Station was but a nightmare and a hideous dream."[49] The debacle eliminated whatever prospects the budding politician had of obtaining the Democratic Party's presidential or vice presidential nomination in 1864. As a general, Hancock had never before suffered such a defeat. He had seen his troops fail to carry enemy fortifications but, Walker recalled, Hancock

> had never before had the mortification of seeing them driven and his lines and guns taken, as on this occasion; and never before had he seen his men fail to respond to the utmost when he called upon them personally for a supreme effort; nor had he ever before ridden toward the enemy followed by a beggarly army of a few hundred stragglers who had been gathered together and pushed toward the enemy.[50]

To make matters worse, the Northern newspapers picked up the dispatch written by Hancock's reporter before the final Confederate assault and proclaimed on the following day, "Another great victory by Gen. Hancock!"[51] Secretary of War Stanton went along with the newspapers and began issuing press releases about the victory. Because Hancock could not publicly contradict Stanton, the II Corps chief had to endure this embarrassing false propaganda for a number of days.

Hancock suffered still another humiliation stemming from the disaster. On August 30, Gibbon sought authority to deprive the 8th New York heavies, the 164th New York and the 36th Wisconsin of the right to carry colors because these regiments had lost their banners at Second Reams Station. Referring the matter to Meade on September 3, Hancock recommended that Meade deprive all regiments which had lost their flags of the right to carry colors. On September 23, the Army of the Potomac's leader adopted Hancock's recommendation prospectively but otherwise sustained Gibbon. This made

---

48 Wells, *Hampton and His Cavalry in '64*, 283.

49 Walker, *Second Army Corps*, 606.

50 Walker, *General Hancock*, 275.

51 Glenn Tucker, *Hancock the Superb* (Dayton OH, 1980), 255.

Hancock's men the only ones deprived of the right to carry colors. Meade published in all the daily newspapers received in the Army of the Potomac the order depriving the three regiments of this right.

As a result of this controversy, Hancock's already strained relationship with Gibbon became positively poisonous. When Gibbon suggested a reorganization of II Corps, Hancock suggested that Gibbon resign. Hancock's friendship with Meade also suffered, and Hancock took his leave of II Corps and the Army of the Potomac on November 26—to go on recruiting duty, as soldiers of the 28th North Carolina had joked. Not for nothing did Lieutenant Colonel Walker write in regard to Reams Station:

> The agony of that day never passed away from that proud soldier....So one who was gifted to discern the real forces which in us make for life or death, looking down on the cold and pallid form of Hancock as he lay at rest beneath the drooping flag of his country on Governor's Island, in February, 1886, would have seen Reams's Station written on brow or brain and heart as palpable as, to the common eye, were the scars of Gettysburg.[52]

After the catastrophe, the officers and men of II Corps sought to exonerate themselves of responsibility for the loss at Second Reams Station. Hancock and his apologists blamed the defeat on a Confederate superiority in numbers of two or three to one, on the poor location of the earthworks, on Gibbon's thumbs down on a second counterattack, on Meade's failure to withdraw Hancock from Reams Station on the morning of August 25, on Meade's failure to send reinforcements straight down the Weldon Railroad from Globe Tavern, and on the unwillingness of the Federal foot soldiers to fight. These excuses all lack merit.

That the Rebels outnumbered Hancock's force at Second Reams Station by a factor of two or three to one amounted to a myth.[53] In fact, the Unionists faced a roughly equal number of Rebels. Hill left Petersburg with no more than 6,500 muskets and probably fewer.[54] Of this number, no more than 4,500 or

---

52 Walker, *General Hancock*, 275-6.

53 Tucker, *Hancock the Superb*, 275-6. A historian of the Irish Brigade and the Corcoran Legion claimed that Hancock's force faced three-to-one odds. Conyngham, *The Irish Brigade*, 479. The historian of the 12th New Jersey claimed that the Confederate had 30,000 soldiers at Second Reams Station. Haines, *Company F, 12th New Jersey*, 80-81.

54 Hill estimated the strength of his infantry force at 8,000. David Cardwell, "The Battle of Five Forks," *Confederate Veteran*, vol. 22 (1914), 117. This must have represented an estimate of

5,000 arrived at Reams Station before the battle ended and in all likelihood not that many.⁵⁵ As for the Secessionist cavalry, Hampton had about 3,000

> his infantry's strength on paper because Hill also concurred in an estimate of Hancock's strength at 20,000. Ibid. Two brigades of Heth's division numbered about 2,200 soldiers on paper. Two brigades of Mahone's division numbered around 1,200 troops on paper. Three brigades of Wilcox's division numbered approximately 3,500 men on paper. One brigade of Field's division numbered about 900 soldiers on paper. These figures, based on dividing the number of a division's brigades into the abstract of the division's returns from a date after the end of the August fighting, yield an overall estimate of around 7,800 infantry with Hill at Second Reams Station. Abstract from field return of the Army of Northern Virginia, General Robert E. Lee commanding, for September 10, 1864, in OR 42, pt. 2, 1243.
>
> Employing the same method, dividing the number of II Corps' divisions into the abstract of the corps' returns from a date after the end of August's fighting, yields an estimate of 8,800 infantry with Hancock. Abstract from the return of the Army of the Potomac, Maj. Gen. George G. Meade commanding, for the month of August, 1864, ibid., 611. This method does not even take into account the terrible Federal losses at Second Reams Station. Factored in, they suggest that Hancock had more than 11,000 foot soldiers. Ibid., pt. 1, 131. That this method results in an obvious overestimate of Hancock's force renders suspect the results obtained by the application of the method to Hill's command.
>
> During late August and early September, 1864, 800 soldiers represented the highest estimate of the actual strength of the average infantry brigade in the Third Corps of the Army of Northern Virginia. J. McEntee to Major-General Humphreys, September 4, 1864, ibid., pt. 2, 683-684. The average infantry brigade in Hill's force had marched somewhat less but fought much more in the fourth offensive than the average infantry brigade in Hancock's force. It seems reasonable to allow for at least as great a reduction in Hill's force as in Hancock's for the effects of marching and fighting. Accepting Federal estimates of Hancock's actual infantry force as from 6,000 to 6,500 soldiers requires acquiescence in 6,500 as the largest possible number of infantrymen with which Hill could have begun the march from Petersburg to Reams Station.
>
> 55 The route taken by the Confederate infantry from Petersburg to Reams Station measured about fifteen miles. Terry's two-brigade force of 1,800 troops had dwindled to 700 on a much shorter march on the previous day. E. O. C. Ord to General Birney, August 25, 1864, ibid., 502. While the Confederates almost certainly did not lose as high a percentage of soldiers as Terry's force, the effects of straggling must account in part for Hill's failure to arrive at Reams Station at the appointed time in that his troops could not move until 7:00 a.m. on August 25.
>
> Anderson's brigade had 600 or 700 soldiers on the battlefield at Second Reams Station. Wilcox Report. Cooke's, MacRae's and Lane's brigades had no more than 1,750 troops between them. Clark, *North Carolina Regiments*, 1:747; ibid., 2:448. (This almost certainly meant the effective strength, or "muskets." Effective strength meant all privates and non-commissioned officers present for duty. Total strength meant all privates and non-commissioned officers present, including sick, in arrest and on extra duty. Aggregate strength meant all officers and men present. Real strength meant effective strength plus officers present for duty. William Allan, "History of the Campaign of Gen T. J. (Stonewall) Jackson in the Shenandoah Valley of Virginia, from November 4, 1861, to June 17, 1862," *SHSP*, vol. 43 (1920), 206n. Only twenty-five soldiers of the 18th North Carolina in Lane's Brigade saw combat at Second Reams Station. Report of Captain B. F. Rinaldi, August 28th, 1864, James H. Lane Papers. Only eleven infantrymen of Company G of the 27th North Carolina fought at

sabers.⁵⁶ The Southerners thus fielded 1,000 fewer infantry and 1,000 more cavalry than their opponents. They outnumbered Hancock's force in guns, twenty-five to sixteen.⁵⁷

Reams Station. Wagstaff, ed., Graham Papers, 313. Anderson's and Lane's brigades had fought at Second Deep Bottom. Cooke's and MacRae's brigades had fought at Globe Tavern.

Prior to Second Deep Bottom, Federal intelligence officers had estimated the strength of McGowan's brigade at 1,250 soldiers, equal to their estimate of Lane's brigade at that time. List of the rebel forces now on the north side of the James River, in OR 42, pt. 2, 159. Lane's brigade had lost more heavily than McGowan's brigade at Second Deep Bottom. Lane, "History of Lane's N. C. Brigade—Campaign of 1864—Anecdote about Captain G. G. Holland, 28th N. C. Troops," 357; Caldwell, *McGowan's Brigade*, 178, 180. Lane's brigade fielded no more than 600 troops at Second Reams Station. Clark, *North Carolina Regiments*, 1:747; ibid., 2:448. McGowan's brigade probably fielded the same number.

Scales' brigade, one of the freshest of the Confederate infantry brigades at Second Reams Station, numbered around 700 soldiers on September 6, and the 38th North Carolina, the largest regiment in the brigade, had 200 troops on that date. J. McEntee to Major-General Humphreys, September 6, 1864, in OR 42, pt. 2, 718. Scales' brigade had fought at Globe Tavern.

Sanders' brigade, which fought in all three of August's battles, numbered no more than 500 men as of September 1st. J. McEntee to Major-General Humphreys, September 1, 1864, ibid., 628. The 9th Alabama had eighty-eight muskets as of September 4, and the brigade had no more than 600. On July 30, the brigade had fielded only about 630 soldiers at the battle of the Crater. George Clark, "Alabamians in the Crater Battle," *Confederate Veteran*, vol. 3 (1895), 68; John C. Featherston, "Brilliant Page in History Of War," *SHSP*, vol. 36 (1908), 165.

Weisiger's brigade had only fielded "over 500 muskets" at Globe Tavern on August 19. George S. Bernard Papers, Southern Historical Collection. On that date, the 12th Virginia Infantry had taken into action between ninety and ninety-four soldiers. Ibid.; Petersburg *Daily Register*, August 22, 1864, p. 2, col. 2-3. The 61st Virginia had taken into action 150 "muskets," nineteen officers and fifteen ambulance men on August 19, and this regiment's Company I took twenty soldiers into action at Second Reams Station. McAlpine, "Sketch of Company I, 61st Virginia Infantry, Mahone's brigade, C. S. A.," 103. Estimates of the average brigade in Mahone's division varied from 500 soldiers as of September 1 to fewer than 800 as of September 4. OR, 42, pt. 2, 628, 683-684. The brigade marched to Reams Station without the 41st Virginia, which remained in the Petersburg trenches and probably reduced the brigade's strength by twenty percent to around 400 troops. A. A. Humphreys to Major-General Meade, August 25, 1864, ibid., 475-476.

56 Hill concurred in this estimate of Hampton's strength. Cardwell, "The Battle of Five Forks," 117. Cf. Letter, Wade Hampton to Francis A. Walker, March 29, 1884, Sessler Collection, Civil War Library and Museum, Philadelphia, Pennsylvania; Walker, *Second Army Corps*, 603; George K. Dauchy, "The Battle of Reams Station," Papers read before the Commandery of the State of Illinois, Military Order of the Loyal Legion of the United States, vol. 3 (1899), 133. Hampton's entire mounted force numbered no more than 4,500 as of September 5. J. McEntee to Major-General Humphreys, September 5, 1864, in OR 42, pt. 2, 698.

57 The Southerners had the four Napoleons of Brander's battery (Letcher Artillery), the four Napoleons of Cayce's battery (Purcell Artillery), the four Napoleons and two ten pound Parrott rifles of Ross' battery (Battery A, Sumter Artillery), the sole Whitworth of a section of Hurt's

The poor location of the earthworks may have contributed to the disaster, but Hancock had forgone the opportunity to improve them on August 24. Only thirty yards of slashing separated the northwest angle from the woods when fifty yards of slashing had proven insufficient on August 16 in front of the Confederate earthworks above Fussell's Mill. Gaps remained in the fortifications where the railway and the Depot Road entered and Hancock had done little to remedy this situation. If the II Corps chief on August 24 faced the question of, to paraphrase Private Roback of the 152nd New York, "Dig or Andersonville," Hancock answered, "Andersonville," whereas on August 20 Warren had answered, "Dig." That Grant and Meade overlooked Hancock's dereliction and held against Warren his correct assessment suggests a degree of irrationality in their relationships with these corps commanders. One can say nothing in defense of how Grant and Meade held against Warren the way he won at Globe Tavern except that his two superiors believed they must take Richmond, not just another railroad, to justify the casualties incurred in the Virginia campaign of 1864 and get Lincoln reelected. Even after Atlanta's capture Grant and Meade kept lunging at the Confederate capital.[58]

Hancock displayed a similar irrationality in the different ways he treated Miles and Gibbon. The collapse of Miles' command lost the battle. Miles counterattacked with a single brigade, Gibbon with almost his entire division. Both forces participated in recapturing the northern return and three guns of the 12th Battery, New York Light Artillery. Because Miles misrepresented that his troops could counterattack again and retake the rest of their original position while Gibbon accurately assessed that his soldiers could do no such thing, Hancock exonerated Miles and never forgave Gibbon.

Complaining about the late hour at which he received authorization to withdraw reflected badly on Hancock. He had a responsibility to hold his position until relieved. Meade's permission to withdraw at all departed from

---

battery, and a two gun section, either Napoleons or three inch rifles, of Clutter's battery. Report of Brig. Gen. William N. Pendleton, C.S.A., Chief of Artillery, Army of Northern Virginia, of operations August 10-December 31, ibid., pt. 1, 858; Tabular report of field artillery serving with Army of Northern Virginia, Brig. Gen. William N. Pendleton, chief of artillery, commanding, ibid., pt. 3, 1341; Aubery, *Thirty-Sixth Wisconsin*, 126.

58 For an account of the siege of Petersburg from the end of August, 1864, until the November election, see Horn, *The Petersburg Campaign*, 155-89.

Grant's policy of encouraging costly Secessionist counterattacks.[59] The assaults against the Federal fortifications at Second Reams Station ought to have resulted in a Confederate defeat approaching the proportions of the repulse at Globe Tavern four days earlier.

Meade had valid reasons not to route reinforcements straight down the railroad. He placed a higher priority on guarding the Union rear than on reinforcing a reputedly crack command that occupied fortifications. Unknown to Hancock and his apologists, the Confederate brigades of Scales, Weisiger, and Sanders guarded against Federal reinforcements routed down the roadbed.

Hancock's apologists came closer to the truth when they blamed the fiasco on the unwillingness of the troops to fight. Lieutenant Colonel Walker, captured by the Rebels at Second Reams Station, remembered:

> Worn out by excessive exertions, cut up in a score of charges against intrenched positions, their better officers and braver sergeants and men nearly all killed or in hospital, regiments reduced to a captain's command, companies often to a corporal's guard—this was the state to which four months of continuous campaigning upon the avowed policy of "hammering" had brought the old divisions of Richardson and Sedgwick. Already twenty-seven officers had fallen in command of brigades, one hundred and twenty-five in command of regiments. Could the killed and wounded of but half an hour's fighting at Cold Harbor have been called back to the Second Corps on the 25th of August, Heth and Wilcox might have charged till the sun went down, and all to no purpose. Had Tyler, Brooke, McKeen, Haskell, McMahon, Byrnes, Morris, and Porter stood over the skeleton regiments at Ream's, the northwest angle would not have been carried, and Hill would have gone back in his intrenchments that night with none but his own colors and guns.[60]

Despite Meade's failure to withdraw Hancock's force on the morning of the 25th, despite Meade's failure to route reinforcements straight down the railroad from Globe Tavern, despite the inability of Gibbon's division to counterattack a second time, despite the unsatisfactory location of the earthworks, despite Hancock's failure to take prompt action to improve them, Hancock would have won at Second Reams Station if his troops had possessed the will to fight. The Federal conscripts had none of the coolness and determination that evoked Heth's admiration when he wrote of the soldiers who participated in the charge that determined the outcome of the battle: "This

---

59 Hampton Newsome, *Richmond Must Fall: The Richmond-Petersburg Campaign, October 1864* (Kent OH: The Kent State University Press), 277.

60 Walker, *General Hancock*, 269-70.

charge and its results has proved to me that nothing is impossible to men determined to win."[61] By the end of Grant's fourth offensive at Petersburg, natural selection in the Army of the Potomac had produced a soldier who would not fight. Chaplain Simon of the 125th New York responded to these questions far more forthrightly than Hancock:

> The works might have been held. To be sure, our line was quite narrow, and the centre of it presented but a narrow front; true, that in rear of the front of the centre, only a few feet, was the railroad cut, at least twelve feet deep, to be crossed with great difficulty; true, that it would have been the part of wisdom to have had our front on the near instead of the far side of the railroad; yet the works, which were old ones, constructed by the cavalry some time before, ought to have been held by our men. There is no excuse to offer that they were not held.[62]

If the troops ought to have held the works, some responsibility for the loss of the battle rested with the officer who had sent used up soldiers to Reams Station. Walker's analysis implies that responsibility lay primarily with Grant because of his hammering tactics, but Grant had not wanted to send II Corps to wreck the railroad. Grant had wanted to send XVIII Corps. Meade had incrementally committed the exhausted II Corps divisions to the task of demolishing the Weldon Railroad even though Grant had repeatedly signified that he wanted the task assigned to the albeit sickly XVIII Corps. No one can ever know if XVIII Corps would have performed better than II Corps on August 25, but employing XVIII Corps represented what Brig. Gen. Edward Porter Alexander would have called, "the safest game."[63] Meade's poor personnel management, his failure to rotate his troops, contributed to the disaster at Second reams Station.

The rank and file disagreed with Hancock about where blame belonged. Quartermaster Sergeant James M. Hudnut of Company D, 8th New York Heavy Artillery, wounded on June 5, recalled:

> The fact was—at Ream's Station, the blundering of those higher up placed the regiment in a position where those who did not run were taken prisoners. Those of the regiment who ran away at Ream's Station lived to fight again, but of those who were

---

61 Heth, *Report of December 7th*, 1864.

62 Simons, *One Hundred And Twenty-Fifth New York*, 242. VI Corps, not the cavalry, had constructed the earthworks at Reams Station.

63 Gallagher, ed., *Fighting for the Confederacy*, 276.

taken prisoner over one-half died during their imprisonment, and comparatively few ever returned to the ranks to fight again.[64]

News of the Rebel victory at Second Reams Station caused rejoicing throughout the Confederacy during the few days that remained before the fall of Atlanta. Major Stowe of the 28th North Carolina in Lane's brigade considered Second Reams Station "the greatest victory of the war."[65] Though Stowe may have overstated the matter, frontal assaults against breastworks defended by artillery as well as infantry rarely succeeded.

On August 29, 1864, Lee in a letter to Governor Zebulon B. Vance of North Carolina singled out for praise the brigades of Cooke, MacRae, Lane and Barringer, writing, "I have frequently been called upon to mention the services of the North Carolina soldiers in this army, but their gallantry and conduct were never more deserving of admiration than in the engagement at Reams Station, on the 25th instant."[66]

To Brig. Gen. James H. Lane, who had missed the August battles because of a Cold Harbor wound, Lee said that, "the three North Carolina brigades, Lane's, Cooke's and MacRae's, which made the second assault, after the failure of the first by other troops, had by their gallantry not only placed North Carolina, but the whole Confederacy, under a debt of gratitude, which could never be repaid."[67]

Had Hill failed to drive Hancock's soldiers from Reams Station and had the Federals pressed on to occupy Dinwiddie Court House, the Rebels would have had to evacuate Richmond.[68] The commander of the Army of Northern Virginia probably had this possibility in mind when he spoke to Lane.[69] Lee could not know that occupying Dinwiddie Court House had not even occurred to Grant.

---

64 James M. Hudnut, *Casualties By Battle And By Name In The Eighth New York Heavy Artillery August 22, 1862-June 5, 1865 Together With A Review Of The Service Of The Regiment Fifty Years After Muster-In* (New York, 1913), 53-54.

65 Report of Maj. Samuel N. Stowe, August 28th, 1864, James H. Lane Papers.

66 R. E. Lee to His Excellency Z. B. Vance, in OR 42, pt. 2, 1207.

67 Clark, *North Carolina Regiments*, 2:575.

68 Dowdey and Manarin, eds., *The Wartime Papers of R. E. Lee*, 922.

69 Winf'd S. Hancock to General Humphreys, in OR 42, pt. 2, 448.

The Army of Northern Virginia's leader certainly had in mind the possibility of a cavalry raid on the South Side Railroad and the Richmond and Danville Railroad when he spoke to Lane, and the opportunity for such a raid did occur to at least some in the Unionist high command.[70] The countryside around Richmond and Petersburg afforded sufficient subsistence that mere disruption of the capital's supply lines could not force its evacuation, but the effects of privation had already made clear to Lee that each interruption of the flow of provisions and forage would hasten the day when lack of men and mounts reduced his force to where it could no longer successfully resist the opposing Northerners.

---

70 Rufus Ingalls to M. C. Meigs, August 24, ibid., 443; R. E. Lee to Maj. Gen. Wade Hampton, August 26, 1864, ibid., 1205.

Chapter 13

Had Not Success Come Elsewhere

The Battle of Second Reams Station brought to an end the major fighting of the siege of Petersburg for the month of August, 1864. Casualties continued to mount from sniping, shelling and skirmishing. This attritional warfare resulted in about a thousand killed, wounded and captured during August for the Federals beyond the 9,922 casualties incurred at Second Deep Bottom, Globe Tavern, and Second Reams Station.[1] The Confederates lost a similar number in the month's lesser known fights beyond the approximately 4,500 in the month's three battles.[2] Unionist

---

1 General summary of Casualties in the Union Forces operating against Richmond, Va., under Lieut. Gen. U. S. Grant, during the month of August, 1864, in OR 42, pt. 1, 132. These casualties included Private Hardenbergh in the Preacher's Company of the 39th Illinois in the Western Brigade of Terry's division. Confederate fire killed him on the Bermuda Hundred front on August 28 before the arrival of his Medal of Honor and a commission as a lieutenant in the 36th United States Colored Troops. He lies in Poplar Grove National Cemetery, about a mile and a half west of Globe Tavern.

2 The losses of Johnson's division in the Petersburg trenches from August 1st to August 19th, 1864, 150 men killed and wounded, give rise to this inference. Reports of Maj. Gen. Bushrod R. Johnson, C. S. Army, commanding Johnson's division, ibid., 884-9. Hoke's division also held Petersburg trenches in close proximity to the Federals. Pickett's division and Thomas' and Scales' brigades of Wilcox's division held the Howlett Line close to the Federals at Bermuda Hundred. On the right of the Petersburg trenches, greater distances separated Heth's and Mahone's divisions from the opposing Unionists.

Lt. Gen. Ulysses S. Grant, U.S.A. *Library of Congress*

casualties for the month totaled 10,999.³ The Rebels lost around 5,500 soldiers.⁴ Of all the months of the Petersburg campaign, only June surpassed August in bloodiness, and Grant launched two offensives in June.

During the August battles around the Cockade City and Richmond, a number of military leaders distinguished themselves—some for better, some for worse.

The High Command

Grant performed masterfully on the strategic plane. The general-in-chief believed that his plan of pressuring the Confederacy on all fronts would produce victory, and he had the character to stick to his plan despite pressure from friend and foe. Grant's unification of Federal commands in the Shenandoah Valley laid the foundation for Sheridan's future victories.

Operationally, the general-in-chief's plan to cut the Weldon Railroad, employed for the second time in three weeks, finally succeeded. His plan exhibited his predilection for maneuver. His critics tagged him as a hammerer for his many assaults during the Overland Campaign, but the Fort Donelson and Vicksburg campaigns as well as his original plan for a sea-borne approach to Richmond in 1864 invite comparison with the wide enveloping maneuvers of Napoleon I in the Ulm campaign and von Moltke the Elder in the opening campaign of the Franco-Prussian War. Neither Napoleon nor Moltke faced the likes of Lee and Beauregard, who made the course of the Petersburg campaign so unlike Donelson, Vicksburg, Metz, or Sedan, where the victors enveloped and compelled the surrender of their victims, sometimes after a siege.⁵

---

3   Ibid., 132.

4   Ibid. 884-9.
    For Confederate losses at Second Deep Bottom, see Chapter 5, note 8.
    For Confederate losses at Globe Tavern, see Chapter 9, note 36.
    For Confederate losses in the "fight by moonlight" of August 23, see Chapter 10, note 11.
    For Confederate losses at Second Reams Station, see Chapter 12, note 46.

5   At Ulm in 1805, Napoleon I enveloped and compelled the surrender of an Austrian army. At Fort Donelson, Grant enveloped and compelled the surrender of a Confederate army in 1862. At Vicksburg, Grant enveloped and compelled the surrender of a Rebel army after a siege in 1863. At Metz, Moltke enveloped, besieged, and compelled the surrender of a French army in 1870. At Sedan, Moltke enveloped and compelled the surrender of a French army attempting to relieve the siege of Metz.

The scheme that Grant employed in his third, fourth and fifth offensives at Petersburg provides a textbook example of a many-branched plan. In executing the plan, Grant displayed a tendency to issue orders in ignorance of readily ascertainable facts. He failed to apprise himself of the difficulties of landing troops at Deep Bottom. Ignoring the power of the combination of the strategic offensive with the tactical defensive and without knowing the ground, he meddled unjustifiably in Warren's handling of the fighting at Globe Tavern. Not content with severing the Weldon Railroad, Grant pushed his subordinate into terrain that negated the numerical advantage of V Corps in soldiers and cannon. The general-in-chief thus bore much of the responsibility for the disaster of August 19. Grant also failed to appreciate the importance of occupying Dinwiddie Court House, which would have compelled the evacuation of Petersburg and Richmond. Illness mitigated his failure to demand that Meade follow orders and send XVIII Corps rather than the exhausted soldiers of II Corps to wreck the Weldon Railroad. Illness mitigated Grant's failure to strike the nearly empty Rebel trenches at Petersburg on August 25.

President Davis, Grant's opponent on the strategic level, showed the danger inherent in the combination of a strong will and a bad plan. That Davis failed to consider the possibility of shifting forces from Virginia to Georgia demonstrated the wisdom and effectiveness of Grant's design as well as the defects of Davis' judgment. Unlike Meade during the autumn of Chickamauga, Grant kept the Confederates in Virginia so occupied that their high command did not even think of such a shift. Davis' folly displayed itself in his rigid adherence to his departmental system of defense, which caused him to refrain from transferring to Georgia forces from less important departments, such as Mississippi.

Lee, Grant's opponent within the Virginia theater, wisely attempted to shift the scene of hostilities to the vicinity of Washington. The Virginian's will did not equal that of the Federal general-in-chief. Just as in July, Lee overreacted to Hancock's movement north of the James. During the battle of Globe Tavern, the Secessionists suffered from Lee's failure to develop a counter to the maneuver that resulted in First Deep Bottom—a Unionist thrust north of James River. The Rebels also suffered from his failure to develop a proper staff that could mount a counterattack with as many soldiers as possible as quickly as possible. Sensitive to the political consequences of casualties in the North, Lee had the good sense to approve the initiatives and adopt the plans of subordinates such as Mahone and Hampton. Lee's audacity led him to disregard the danger of a Unionist thrust at the Petersburg trenches and to launch nine brigades and part of a tenth at Warren, but the lack of a much-needed sense of urgency allowed Warren to render his position nearly impregnable. Second Reams Station showed that the Virginian remained as bold as at the beginning of the Seven Days. That he adopted Hampton's plan after a acheme of the South Carolinian had failed north of the James reflected especially well on Lee. After Second Reams Station, he failed to push the advantage his troops held in morale—unlike an increasing proportion of Federal soldiers, Lee's Miserables remained willing to fight. His failure to leave adequate forces north of the James led to the loss of Fort Harrison in September, but the Beefsteak Raid of that month probably signified that he harbored an unrecorded design against the Unionist left rear—something akin to the seizure of Fort Powhatan that Beauregard had contemplated in May, or perhaps even a thrust against the Federal supply base at City Point.

Like Frederick the Great, Lee preferred battle to maneuver and favored narrow turning movements. The advent of the rifled musket required the Virginian to swing more widely at Chancellorsville, his masterpiece, than the Prussian had at Leuthen, the soldier-king's quintessential triumph.[6] Unlike Frederick, Lee never appears to have realized that he fought too much and expended too many soldiers. His taste for attacking "those people" often got the better of him. No need to take the offensive existed at Deep Bottom on August 18. The time had passed for attacking at Globe Tavern on August 21. Lee's assault on the Northern force at Reams Station ought not to have succeeded, but the threat to Dinwiddie Court House required an immediate and violent response—a Unionist force at Dinwiddie Court House would have had the inside track to cut off any Confederate army trying to retreat from Petersburg and Richmond to North Carolina. The British military historian Fuller considered the campaign as Lee's "most skilful, masterful and heroic."[7]

Meade functioned better as a staff officer than as a commander. The notoriously irascible Pennsylvanian very capably shifted forces to reinforce Warren, but failed to perceive the weakness of V Corps' position on August 19. The Army of the Potomac's leader reacted too passively during Second Reams Station, when he ought to have at least feinted against the nearly empty Confederate trenches at Petersburg. Meade bore some of the responsibility for

---

6   At Leuthen in 1757, Frederick defeated a much larger Austrian army by striking its flank with almost his entire force.

7   Fuller, *The Generalship of Ulysses S. Grant*, 381.

Gen. Robert E. Lee, C.S.A. *Library of Congress*

the disaster at Second Reams Station in that he saw but disregarded the terrible condition of Barlow's and Gibbon's divisions of II Corps and ignored Grant's repeated directives to employ XVIII Corps in demolishing the Weldon Railroad.

Responsibility for the retention of a political general such as Benjamin Butler ultimately rested with President Lincoln. Of the political advantages that Butler's retention brought to the administration in smoke filled rooms, Butler in the field negated fewer in August than in May and June, when Petersburg and Richmond had slipped through his fingers. His misunderstanding of Grant's orders led to insufficient reserves on August 25, but Meade defended too passively for such reserves to have changed the outcome. That an army leader would leave his troops during a crisis to probate a will ought ordinarily at least to have raised an eyebrow. That such a commander would use the probate of a will to conceal his real purpose—attending the political convention of a party opposed to the administration which he served—would seem shameful if done by anyone else. That Butler's departure during the crisis of that day provoked no protest from Grant, Meade, or their staffs suggests that they felt entirely at ease in his absence. Different rules applied to the leader of the Army of the James than to an ordinary officer. All concerned probably believed that Butler would serve more effectively at the Democratic Convention than in the field. Butler would call this judgment into question by his surprisingly good performance in Grant's fifth offensive, when the Beast finally forced the Secessionists from the New Market Heights position.

Despite carping from within the Davis administration, Gus Beauregard made the most of his situation on August 18 and 19. On the 18th, the Louisianan kept no more men in the trenches than did Lee on August 21. On the 19th, Beauregard might have called out the militia and thus spared another brigade for the attack, but even Mahone contended he needed two more to drive the Federals from the Weldon Railroad. Beauregard's principal shortcoming lay in failing to muster on August 20 the troops mustered on August 21, almost all of them available to him then. The Louisianan could have complied on the 20th with Lee's insistence on concentration.

Humphreys, the chief of staff of the Army of the Potomac, had no real counterpart in the Army of Northern Virginia or Lee's army group. The Army of Northern Virginia had no official chief of staff. The post of Lee's personal chief of staff stood vacant at the time. Beauregard had volunteered to serve as an unofficial chief of staff when outranked by Gen. Joe Johnston at First Bull Run and by Gen. Albert Sidney Johnston at Shiloh, and the Louisianan would serve Joe Johnston again in this capacity while unassigned during the closing days of the war in North Carolina.[8] Sometimes a divisional officer between

---

8 That Beauregard did not serve Lee as an unofficial chief of staff during the Petersburg campaign suggests cooler relations between the Army of Northern Virginia's chief and the Louisianan than between Gus and the Johnstons.

assignments would act as an aide-de-camp, as Maj. Gen. Daniel Harvey Hill did for Beauregard at Second Drewry's Bluff in May, 1864, but such an officer could not issue orders. The Southerners just could not spare from field command an officer of Humphreys' caliber—like David Birney, Humphreys had led with distinction a III Corps division destroyed through no fault of his own at Gettysburg. His efforts and Meade's in shifting reserves to provide reinforcements for Warren may have saved the day on August 19. A perceptive historian as well, he learned from the disaster of August 19 and tried to apply the lesson on October 1 when he ordered Warren to refuse his right to prevent history from repeating itself.

At Second Deep Bottom, in command of a small army of five divisions of infantry and one of cavalry, Hancock exercised an autonomy matching that of Meade or Butler. The II Corps leader had the good fortune to capture prisoners, flags and guns at Deep Bottom for the second time in three weeks, but his overall performance showed that as an independent commander he had begun to rise above his level of maximum competence. On August 13, he and his staff gamely attempted to make up for Grant's carelessness about the details of landing at Deep Bottom. From there, Hancock's performance went downhill. On August 14, cavalry ought to have preceded Barlow's foot soldiers to Bailey's Creek—Hancock's failure to employ horsemen to seize a crossing suggests he placed Barlow's craving for a second star above accomplishing the mission. The II Corps chief inexcusably neglected to inform David Birney about the existence of Fussell's mill pond before transferring Birney and his men to the Federal right on August 15. On the following day, Hancock failed to give Birney's attack above the pond sufficient support, whether directly through reinforcement or indirectly by an attack below the pond. On the critical days of the operation, August 14 and 16, Hancock failed to concentrate his effort.

Corps Command

When Hancock returned to corps command, his performance deteriorated still further. His failure to prepare adequately the defensive position at Reams Station on August 24 amounted to an unequivocal dereliction of duty. Wider slashing at the northwest angle and more formidable barriers at the openings in the works for the Weldon Railroad and the Halifax Road on the north side and the Depot Road on the west side might have prevented disaster on August 25. He embarrassed himself by the depth of his denial over his responsibility for the fiasco at Second Reams Station.

David Birney's corps captured guns and prisoners on August 14 at Deep Bottom. The terrible condition of his troops on August 15 after their march in the previous night's rain made it impossible for him to attack until late that day above Fussell's mill pond. His failure to reconnoiter to the west and find the mill pond resulted in Terry's failure to attack at dawn on August 16, which reduced the prospects the Federals had of outflanking Field's position on New Market Heights. Birney forfeited whatever chance he had of exploiting Terry's breakthrough by failing to reinforce it immediately.

An engineer like Meade, Warren defended as passively as did the leader of the Army of the Potomac, but Warren's situation at Globe Tavern called for a passive defense. Pushing up to the Petersburg fortifications through uncharted terrain might well have led V Corps into ambushes that could have loosened its hold on the Weldon Railroad. Warren's complicated artillery arrangements with Wainwright backfired on V Corps on August 19. The V Corps chief's inability to get his infantry subordinates to position their pickets as he intended contributed to the catastrophe that day, as did the posting of a picket line so extended that those charged with supporting it could not hear its firing. Left to his own devices on August 21, the V Corps leader showed that his eye for ground remained as good as when he saved the Union left at Gettysburg. The Federal artillery dominated the field on August 21, just as Warren intended.

A. P. Hill deserved some of the credit for the damage inflicted on the Unionists at Globe Tavern on August 18 and 19. His rejection of the ad hoc brigade from Johnson's division on August 20 contributed to the failure of the Secessionists to attack at Globe Tavern on that critical day. Hill's failure to reconnoiter properly for the attack on August 21, as well as his failure to halt the attack once he had seen that the Unionists had retired to a new position, led to unacceptable casualties. Straggling prevented his force from arriving at Reams Station in accordance with Hampton's plan. Illness compelled Hill to relinquish field command after he mounted one inadequate two-brigade assault and acquiesced in another. His untimely death may have allowed others to shift blame to him and take credit that belonged to him.

Field failed even to consider a flank attack against David Birney's vulnerable right north of Fussell's mill pond on August 15 or 16. The Kentuckian's instant response to the break in his line on August 16 may have saved New Market Heights and Richmond.

In ill health and beset with personal tragedy, Barlow proved a bust as a corps commander. He dispersed his effort on August 14 when sheer weight of numbers ought to have allowed him to capture the enemy earthworks across

Bailey's Creek. He failed to position Macy's brigade properly for the final attack of that day. As a result, Macy's right struck Fussell's mill pond.

One corps commander stood head and shoulders above all others in regard to his performance during August, 1864. Hampton more than justified his appointment to command the Army of Northern Virginia's Cavalry Corps. Unsuccessful in his attack of August 18 at Deep Bottom because of an unfortunate failure to get into position on time, the South Carolinian a week later showed himself the war's best leader of a cavalry corps attached to an army and the best corps commander in Virginia on either side. Hampton's initiative led to the Confederate triumph at Second Reams Station, where he had to stand by and watch victory nearly elude a committee of less capable infantry chieftains senior to him in rank.

Division Command

Terry captured guns and prisoners at Deep Bottom on August 14. He took prisoners and flags on August 16 at Fussell's Mill. That he placed a different brigade of his division in the lead each time he deployed to attack on August 16 showed that at least one eastern general did not invariably deploy his western soldiers as shock troops.

William Birney demonstrated his incompetence on August 15, when his soldiers fired on one another north of Fussell's mill pond. He displayed ineptitude again on August 16 when, disregarding the Confederates gathering on the flank of Osborn's brigade, he launched that brigade into a crossfire.

David Gregg failed to coordinate well with Spear near Reams Station on August 23. Under Gregg's command, Spear drew more than his fair share of hazardous assignments. On August 25, Gregg's division left Reams Station in better condition than any of the other Unionist divisions that participated in the battle.

Crawford bore much of the responsibility for the disaster that befell V Corps on August 19 at Globe Tavern. He failed to attend properly to the execution of Warren's orders for the placement of Bragg's picket line.

Orlando Willcox's error on August 25 ensured that his division would not reach Reams Station in time to change the outcome.

White arrived in the nick of time on August 19 at Globe Tavern. His prompt deployment and advance contained Weisiger's brigade and ensured that Mahone would inflict no more damage that day.

Miles, a future general-in-chief of the United States Army, proved unable to command Barlow's division on August 25 at Second Reams Station. Retaining command of his own brigade, the three New York regiments of the former Irish Brigade in Crandell's brigade, and a detachment from Macy's brigade of Gibbon's division, Miles split off the 152nd New York from the rest of the detachment from Macy's brigade. This left Miles with four units under his command. He allowed Broady to exercise command over the rest of Barlow's division. Broady divided his own brigade and the remainder of Crandell's brigade. Broady thus led an ad hoc division of five subordinate units: the 4th New York heavies, the 53rd and 148th Pennsylvania, the rest of Broady's brigade, the three regiments of Penfield's force from Crandell's brigade, and the balance of Crandell's brigade. The fragmentation effected by Miles and Broady contributed to the collapse of Barlow's division. Miles exaggerated the effect of his counterattack, which nonetheless contributed to the recapture of the three guns of the 12th Battery, New York Light Artillery and the northern return, and he unrealistically proposed another counterstroke.

Gibbon inexcusably failed to improve the earthworks at Reams Station on his own initiative on August 24. He counterattacked too hastily to align his forces properly on August 25, but his counterstroke also contributed to the recapture of the three guns of the 12th Battery, New York Light Artillery and the northern return. His bluntness about the inability of his troops to counterattack again provided Hancock's partisans with yet another excuse for the loss of the battle but did Gibbon credit—not for nothing did he end the war in command of a corps. Gibbon failed to investigate fully before depriving three of his regiments of the right to carry colors—a majority of the soldiers in those regiments had not abandoned their flags but had followed them into captivity.

Conner performed admirably in command of the two-brigade detachment from Wilcox's division on August 16 above Fussell's mill pond, counterattacking the northern flank of the Federal infantry's breakthrough on his own initiative. Sanders rallied the broken Rebels south and west of the Federal breakthrough that day and kept panic from spreading to his men.

Harry Heth, heavily outnumbered on August 18 at Globe Tavern, inflicted disproportionate damage on the Unionists with two brigades but wisely held Colquitt's brigade in reserve. The senior major general of Hill's Corps deserved some of the credit for such success as the Rebels achieved August 19. He distinguished himself as an artillerist as well as an infantry commander by positioning the Confederate guns on August 18 and 19 at Globe Tavern and on

August 25 at Second Reams Station. Pegram's death at Five Forks insured that Heth, an old-fashioned Virginia gentleman, would never claim the credit actually due him. The Secessionist guns helped keep Federal heads down at Second Reams Station.

The former president of the Norfolk and Petersburg Railroad, Mahone brilliantly conceived and executed the devastating Southern ambush of August 19 at Globe Tavern. His acquiescence in the inadequate reconnaissance of August 20 and failure to call off the attack of the next day, when it became clear that the Northerners had withdrawn to a new position, contributed to the costly Confederate repulse that day.

The actual commander of the Rebel infantry at Second Reams Station, Wilcox followed one piecemeal assault with another. But for MacRae's initiative, the Federals might well have repelled the final Secessionist attack. Wilcox also positioned himself poorly to ascertain the results of the final assault. A prompter commitment of the supporting brigades could only have increased the magnitude of the Southern victory.

Brigadiers

Osborn and Shaw shared with William Birney some of the blame for the fiasco on August 15 in which their brigades fired on one another above Fussell's mill pond.

At Globe Tavern on August 19, Bragg shared with Crawford, Warren, Meade, and Grant responsibility for the disaster. Bragg willfully failed to position his troops as Warren desired and deployed his reserve regiment where it could not hear the "dropping shots" fired when Mahone pierced the 19th Indiana's picket line. Wheelock skillfully extricated Coulter's brigade from its perilous position in the midst of Old Porte's onslaught.

In the cavalry skirmishes preceding Second Reams Station, Spear led his brigade with unusual aggressiveness for a Unionist, nearly routing Matthew Butler's division on August 23 in the "fight by moonlight."

On August 16 Tige Anderson knew what to do—his instant response to Field's request for reinforcements halted Hawley's brigade and prevented it from exploiting the Unionist breaktthroough. Oates' prompt response and skillful flank attack stopped Craig's brigade and ended any chance of its flanking or enveloping The Bastion. DuBose performed outstandingly well. The effective commander of the detachments from Field's division south and west of the Federal breakthrough above Fussell's mill pond in the final phase of the counterattack, DuBose drove the Unionists from the captured works with a scratch force. Barbour executed the difficult task of withdrawing Lane's brigade when Wright's brigade broke, helping rally his troops, and then leading them in the less successful counterattack from the left.

On August 19 at Globe Tavern, Weisiger's astuteness saved his Virginians from walking into a Federal envelopment similar to the one that swallowed most of Hagood's brigade two days later.

Hagood kept his head at Globe Tavern on August 21 and at least extricated a remnant of his South Carolinians from the encircling Northerners.

In the second Rebel assault on August 25 at Reams Station, Cooke committed his brigade with admirable skill. MacRae saved the day for the Rebels by advancing on his own initiative in support of Cooke's right.

Field Officers

Colonel Haskell, Colonel Robins, Captain Barham, and Lieutenant Carter saved New Market Heights and possibly Richmond on August 14 by their defense of Bailey's Creek below Fussell's millpond. No other regiment or battery had as much influence on the outcome of the fourth offensive as Haskell's 7th South Carolina Cavalry, Robins' and then Barham's 24th Virginia Cavalry, both of Gary's brigade of the Department of Richmond, and Carter's right section of the 3rd Richmond Howitzers. These units barred the door to Barlow's command at the critical moments of Grant's fourth offensive.

Individuals

Two individuals affected the August fighting to an extraordinary degree.

Lieutenant Colonel Lyman recognized the defect in Warren's dispositions on August 19 at Globe Tavern yet said nothing, mistakenly deferring to the misjudgment of the military professionals around him, including Meade. Little if any time remained to rectify the weakness in the deployment of V Corps, but Lyman had a duty to speak. A staff officer and graduate of Harvard ought not to have allowed the knocking of West Point class rings on table tops to intimidate him.[9] The defect in Warren's dispositions resulted in the loss of about 3,000 soldiers.

---

9 A way West Pointers remind those who have not graduated from the Military Academy of their inferior status.

Private Pryor's inadequate reconnaissance of Warren's left at Globe Tavern on August 20 led to the unnecessary loss of about 1,400 Rebels the next day. This fiasco rendered the adjective "Pyrrhic" inapplicable to the Federal victory at Globe Tavern. Pryor proved as incompetent a private soldier as he had a brigadier.

The Rank and File

The performance of the troops around Petersburg during August, 1864, varied as widely as the behavior of their leaders. Some performed extraordinarily, while others behaved abysmally. More Southerners performed extraordinarily than Northerners, and more Northerners behaved abysmally than Southerners.

Federals

On the whole, Unionist troops performed worse than in any other month during the Petersburg campaign.

The soldiers of Terry's division demonstrated that they had more fight in them than any other troops in Grant's army group. They had more fight in them because, except for the men of Foster's brigade, which had fought in First Deep Bottom at the end of July, they had not fought since Ware Bottom Church in June. Foster's brigade had an exceptional day on August 14 at Deep Bottom, capturing prisoners and cannon. The brigade's New Yorkers and Marylanders did not behave as well as its stalwart New Englanders above Fussell's mill pond on August 16 and 18, but the brigade still lost only one prisoner for every seven soldiers killed and wounded.[10] Terry's division as a whole lost but a single prisoner for every eight soldiers killed or wounded, a showing unmatched by any other Federal division heavily engaged during August, 1864.[11]

Used up in the fighting at the Crater, Coan's and Osborn's brigades of William Birney's division did not perform as well above Fussell's mill pond as

---

10 Foster's brigade lost 71 killed, 423 wounded and 69 missing for a total of 563 casualties. *OR* 42, pt. 1, 119.

11 Terry's division lost 160 killed, 802 wounded and 138 missing for a total of 1,100 casualties. Ibid.

Terry's troops. Coan's brigade lost four prisoners for every five soldiers killed or wounded while on the defensive.[12] Osborn's brigade did much better, losing almost two men killed or wounded for every prisoner, and Osborn's troops suffered their casualties on the attack.[13]

Extraordinary motivation not to surrender resulted in the Colored Brigade of William Birney's division losing only one prisoner for every fifteen soldiers killed or wounded.[14] The 7th and 9th United States Colored Troops performed with distinction at Deep Bottom on August 14 and the 9th did so again above Fussell's mill pond on August 16.

The ratio of killed and wounded to prisoners in X Corps as a whole, approximately four and a half to one, far surpassed that of any other corps, Union or Confederate.[15] That X Corps yielded these prisoners during the course of an attack above Fussell's mill pond reflected still more favorably upon this formation. Attackers who surrendered when pinned down or counterattacked differed substantially from defenders who failed to fight.

The statistical performance of Macy's brigade contradicts Barlow's complaints about the vigor with which the sleepless, heat-sick II Corps troops attacked near the Darbytown Road and at Fussell's Mill on August 14. Poorly positioned, with its right blocked by Fussell's mill pond, Macy's brigade gamely charged toward breastworks across a steep-sided, vine-choked ravine. Macy's soldiers had an honorable ratio of killed and wounded to prisoners, more than three to one, and that on the offensive.[16] Craig's brigade above Fussell's mill pond and Miles' brigade along the Charles City Road did not perform as well on August 16, losing almost as many prisoners as killed and wounded—but these prisoners had attacked and fallen prey to sunstroke and powerful Rebel

---

12 Coan's brigade lost 16 killed, 94 wounded and 84 missing for a total of 194 casualties at Deep Bottom. Ibid., 120.

13 Osborn's brigade lost 22 killed, 118 wounded and 83 missing for a total of 223 casualties at Deep Bottom. Ibid.

14 The Colored Brigade lost 14 killed, 117 wounded and 5 missing for a total of 136 casualties at Deep Bottom. Ibid.

15 X Corps lost 213 killed, 1,154 wounded and 311 missing for a total of 1,678 casualties at Deep Bottom. Ibid.

16 Macy's brigade lost 14 killed, 132 wounded and 45 missing for a total of 191 casualties at Deep Bottom. Ibid., 117.

counterattacks.[17] Overall, II Corps at Deep Bottom achieved a ratio of killed and wounded to prisoners of approximately two to one—very respectable in light of the fact that the corps yielded the prisoners on the attack.[18]

Exhausted at the beginning of Second Deep Bottom, beyond exhaustion after the muddy night marches that followed the battle, the once elite II Corps performed abysmally at Second Reams Station on August 25. More than three of its soldiers surrendered for every one who suffered death or a wound, and prisoners accounted for seventy percent of the corps' casualties.[19] Contrary to the impression left by the official reports of Hancock and Miles, Barlow's division performed as poorly as Gibbon's troops, losing 965 prisoners as opposed to 1,005, seventy-eight percent of its casualties as opposed to eighty percent—and but for the collapse of Miles' division, Gibbon's division would not have suffered such heavy casualties.[20] Smyth's brigade, with 140 prisoners, fifty-nine percent of its casualties, did not get the credit that it deserved for its participation in the counterattack that retook the northern face of the earthworks and the three guns of the 12th Battery, New York Light Artillery.[21] Miles' brigade, with 156 prisoners, sixty-four percent of its losses, has received more credit than it deserved.[22]

---

17 Miles' brigade lost 21 killed, 122 wounded and 131 missing for a total of 274 casualties at Deep Bottom. Ibid., 116. Craig's brigade lost 7 killed, 109 wounded and 118 prisoners for a total of 234 casualties at Deep Bottom. Ibid., 118.

18 II Corps lost 82 killed, 561 wounded and 321 missing for a total of 964 casualties at Deep Bottom. Ibid., 119.

19 II Corps lost 117 killed, 439 wounded and 2,046 missing for a total of 2,602 casualties at Second Reams Station and in skirmishes August 22 to 24, inclusive. Ibid., 129, 131. All but fifteen of these casualties, which the Fourth New York Heavy Artillery lost on August 23, appear to have occurred at Second Reams Station. Ibid., 269-70. The Fourth New York Heavy Artillery suffered four killed, six wounded, two missing, and three sunstruck on August 23. Ibid.

20 Barlow's division lost 63 killed, 221 wounded and 967 missing for a total of 1,251 casualties at Second Reams Station and in skirmishes August 22 to 24, inclusive. Ibid., 129. Fifteen of these casualties occurred August 23. Ibid., 269-70. Gibbon's division lost 42 killed, 215 wounded and 1,005 missing for a total of 1,244 casualties at Second Reams Station. Ibid., 130.

21 Smyth's brigade lost 16 killed, 81 wounded and 140 missing for a total of 237 casualties at Second Reams Station. Ibid.

22 Miles' brigade lost 25 killed, 64 wounded and 156 missing for a total of 245 casualties at Second Reams Station. Ibid., 129.

David Gregg's cavalry division fought admirably at Second Deep Bottom, losing nearly two soldiers killed or wounded per prisoner yielded.[23] At Second Reams Station, Gregg's division lost only nine missing out of sixty-nine total casualties, a ratio of one prisoner to almost every seven men killed and wounded.[24] To Stedman's brigade alone belongs the distinction of having participated in all three of August's major battles plus the "fight by moonlight" near Monk's Neck Bridge.

Statistically, V Corps fought almost as feebly at Globe Tavern as II Corps at Second Reams Station.[25] The figures by themselves deceive and look better than reality. Warren lost only two prisoners for every three killed or wounded along the Weldon Railroad on August 18, but this occurred as a result of a frontal attack by two Confederate brigades upon an initially equal number of Federals.[26] The Rebels had some advantage from surprise, but reinforcements increased the odds to three to one in favor of the Unionists before they brought the Secessionists to a halt. The circumstances of this attack reflect far worse on Warren's soldiers than the ratio of prisoners to killed or wounded among the casualties.

The figures for August 19 at Globe Tavern show V Corps performing even worse than II Corps at Second Reams Station. Prisoners outnumbered killed or wounded by approximately eight to one.[27] The unusual circumstances of this attack mitigated in favor of V Corps. The troops of II Corps experienced the unpleasantness of concentric fire at Second Reams Station, but neither a barrage directed at them by their own artillery nor—except to some degree for the soldiers of Gibbon's division—a force of Confederates appearing in their immediate rear with little or no warning.

---

23 Gregg's cavalry division lost 28 killed, 117 wounded and 80 missing for a total of 225 casualties at Deep Bottom. Ibid., 121.

24 Gregg's cavalry division lost 15 killed, 45 wounded and 9 missing for a total of 69 casualties at Second Reams Station and supposedly in the skirmishes of August 22 to 24. Ibid., 131. It appears that these figures omit up to seventy-five killed and wounded suffered on August 23. Ibid., pt. 2, 436.

25 V Corps lost 188 killed, 821 wounded and 2,660 missing for a total of 3,669 casualties. Ibid., pt 1, 125.

26 V Corps lost about 66 killed, 478 wounded and 392 missing for an approximate total of 936 casualties. Ibid., 429.

27 V Corps lost around 46 killed, 218 wounded and 2,457 missing for a total of about 2,721 casualties. Ibid., 430.

V Corps lost one prisoner for every two killed and wounded on August 21 at Globe Tavern.²⁸ Pickets accounted for most of the captives, and no disgrace accrued to a captured picket—such duty by its very nature carried with it a strong risk of capture. The main body of V Corps occupied a nearly impregnable position on August 21 and had such overwhelming artillery support that the Rebels inflicted relatively few killed and wounded, further skewing the casualty figures to understate the performance of V Corps that day.

Engaged on August 19 and 21 at Globe Tavern, IX Corps lost almost two killed and wounded for every prisoner.²⁹ Because pickets captured on August 21 accounted for many of the captives, IX Corps like V Corps fought better than the cold numbers indicate for that day. At Globe Tavern, IX Corps fought better than any other infantry corps in the Army of the Potomac during August.

At Second Reams Station, Spear's brigade of Kautz's cavalry division of the Army of the James achieved a very honorable ratio of killed and wounded to prisoners of about three to one.³⁰

Despite the frequency of mitigating circumstances, the overall Union ratio for August of six prisoners for every five soldiers killed or wounded reflected very poorly on the will to fight of the troops in Grant's army group during the month of August, 1864.³¹ In no other month of the Petersburg campaign did such an unfavorable ratio of prisoners to killed and wounded prevail. The figures reflect the nadir of morale in Grant's army group during 1864. In the campaign of that year, Grant's refusal to exchange prisoners made them the equivalent of the dead—neither class of casualty would return to the ranks during the campaign. Assuming that half the wounded would not return during the campaign, in August, 1864, the Federals lost about 8,922, while the Secessionists, assuming they had the same ratio of dead to wounded as the

---

28 V Corps lost approximately 37 killed, 162 wounded and 103 missing for a total of around 302 casualties. Ibid., 431.

29 IX Corps lost 60 killed, 315 wounded and 218 missing for a total of 593 casualties. Ibid., 127.

30 Spear's brigade lost 8 killed, 45 wounded and 18 missing for a total of 71 casualties at Second Reams Station and supposedly in the skirmishes of August 22 to 24. Ibid., 131. It appears that these figures omit the eight killed and thirty-two wounded suffered by Spear's brigade August 23. Ibid., pt. 2, 427.

31 Grant's army group lost 877 killed, 4,153 wounded and 5,969 missing for a total of 10,999 casualties in August, 1864. Ibid.

Unionists, lost around 3,831.[32] The difference in losses approached the proportions of Fredericksburg. The Northerners could not long afford such casualties. They might replace the bodies, but they could not replace the men willing to fight.

Confederates

Rebel units generally performed better than their opponents around Petersburg and Richmond during August, 1864.

At Second Deep Bottom, Field's division suffered about 500 killed or wounded as opposed to about 100 captured, and most of the prisoners represented captured pickets.[33] Conner's detachment of Wilcox's division also had an honorable ratio of killed and wounded to prisoners, losing thirty-five missing out of 215 casualties, also about five to one.[34] The detachment from Mahone's division behaved badly, losing approximately five prisoners for every three killed and wounded—mainly in Wright's Georgia brigade.[35] Sanders' brigade received an accolade from Surgeon Trueheart of the 8th Alabama, a native of Virginia who called Sanders' soldiers "bull dog Alabamians" and praised them for their contribution to the victory at Fussell's Mill.[36] Among the approximately 300 casualties in the Secessionist cavalry, killed and wounded probably outnumbered prisoners by about five to one, which reflected well on the horsemen.[37]

Davis' and Walker's brigades of Heth's Division performed an outstanding feat of arms on August 18 when they attacked and inflicted about 936 casualties on a Federal force at least three times their size at a cost of around 300 soldiers.[38] Assuming that each of the two Southern and six Unionist brigades had about 1,000 troops engaged, the Confederates inflicted more than 450

---

32 See Table 3: Casualties.

33 For Confederate casualties at Second Deep Bottom, see Chapter 5, note 11.

34 Ibid.

35 Ibid.

36 Williams, ed., *Rebel Brothers*, 111.

37 See Chapter 5, note 11.

38 *OR* 42, pt. 1, 429. For Confederate casualties in Davis' and Walker's brigades on August 18, see Chapter 6, note 24.

casualties per 1,000 soldiers engaged while the Northerners inflicted about fifty per 1,000. This represented a nine to one advantage in combat efficiency without factoring in the advantage to the Federals of a defensive posture and the advantage to the Secessionists of surprise.[39]

On August 19, this less disciplined half of Heth's division assisted Mahone's three-brigade force of about 2,000 soldiers in capturing around 2,700 Unionists. On August 18 and 19 together, Davis' brigade had an outstanding ten to one ratio of killed and wounded to prisoners.[40] Walker's brigade could not equal that ratio, losing about sixty prisoners among fewer than 200 casualties, but about thirty of the captures occurred during a picket affair on August 20.[41] Each of these two brigades lost a flag on August 19, but each faced more than twice its number of the enemy who stood on the defensive at the beginning of the action.

Cooke's and MacRae's brigades of Heth's division lost a total of about 200 soldiers while attacking on August 21, including almost no prisoners.[42] During its attack on August 21, Ransom's brigade lost almost three soldiers killed and wounded for every man taken prisoner.[43] The terrible prisoner losses of Harris' brigade of Mahone's division and Hagood's brigade of Hoke's division in their attacks of August 21 occurred as a result of attackers pinned down by overwhelming fire and gobbled up by counterattacks.[44] These circumstances bespoke a willingness to fight.

The victorious Rebels at Second Reams Station on August 25 lost practically no prisoners, in part because they recaptured some soldiers taken by the enemy earlier in the day.[45] The troops of Cooke's, MacRae's and Lane's brigades conducted themselves heroically. The sharpshooters had a spectacular day, their best of the war. Only Anderson's brigade drew criticism, and the criticism originated with Wilcox, who did not commit Anderson's and Scales' brigades as skillfully as Cooke committed the halves of his brigade later that

---

39 Dupuy, *The Evolution of Weapons and Warfare*, 336.

40 Petersburg *Register*, August 22, 1864, p. 2, col. 3.

41 See Chapter 8, note 4.

42 See Chapter 9, note 34.

43 Ibid.

44 Ibid.

45 "George Nash Truss." *Confederate Veteran*, vol. 20 (1912), 481.

day—with the soldiers facing woods and underbrush advancing earlier than those who confronted only an open field. The loss of the only remaining field officer of Anderson's brigade in the attack doubtlessly contributed to the brigade's disappointing performance. Tige Anderson censured his brigade but took the name of every man who participated in the charge, complimented them, and put their names in the brigade's archives.[46]

Prisoners accounted for no more than a quarter of the approximately 5,500 casualties suffered by the Secessionists around Petersburg and Richmond in August of 1864, and three quarters of the Southern missing lay among attackers or pickets.[47] Such circumstances attended the capture of no more than one quarter of the almost 6,000 Federals taken during the month. A far greater willingness to fight prevailed among the Confederates than among the Northerners, who usually required overwhelming artillery support and extensive fortifications to withstand attack. Among the Rebels, only Wright's brigade performed poorly, losing almost two soldiers captured for every man killed or wounded.

Effects of Attrition

The campaign of attrition that Lee had launched in May had succeeded to a greater degree than Army of Northern Virginia's chief realized.[48] The formation of sharpshooter battalions in April contributed heavily to this end. Every time the armies touched, first contact occurred between the best Confederate

---

46 Letter, James Alexander Daniel to Teresa Augusta Cobb, September 27, 1864, private collection of Marvin Giddings, Americus, Georgia.

47 For Confederate losses at Second Deep Bottom, see Chapter 5, note 11.
  For Confederate losses at Globe Tavern, see Chapter 9, note 36.
  For Confederate losses at the "fight by moonlight, see Chapter 10, note 11.
  For Confederate losses at Second Reams Station, see Chapter 12, note 46.

48 James M. McPherson, *Battle Cry of Freedom: The Civil War Era* (New York, 1988), 732.
  For a discussion of the difference between a strategy of annihilation and a strategy of attrition, see Hans Delbruck, *History of the Art of War*, translated by Walter J. Renfroe, Jr., (4 vols) (Lincoln: University of Nebraska Press, 1975), vol. 1, *Warfare in Antiquity*, 135-136, 338. Lee, though he may have—as Fuller thought—sought to annihilate Grant's army in the Wilderness, nonetheless pursued a strategy of attrition because he did not seek to subjugate the United States of America to the Confederate States of America. Ibid.; Fuller, *The Generalship of U. S. Grant*, 237. Grant pursued a strategy of annihilation because he sought to subjugate the Confederate States of America to the United States of America. Delbruck, *Warfare in Antiquity*, 1:135-6, 338.

marksmen and mere rank and file Federals except for a few shrunken regiments of sharpshooters. Casualties and expiring enlistments had resulted in the inability of Grant's army group to hold even earthworks. The general-in-chief received such poor replacements that Lieutenant Colonel Lyman of Meade's staff wrote:

> By the Lord! I wish these gentlemen who would overwhelm us with Germans, negroes, and the offscourings of great cities, could only see—only see—a Rebel regiment, in all their rags and squalor. If they had eyes they would know that these men are like wolf-hounds, and not to be beaten by turnspits.[49]

At the end of August, Lee held the greatest advantage that he had ever before held or would ever again hold in the battle of attrition. His army group's morale had reached its zenith, while Grant's army group's morale had sunk to its nadir. During Grant's fourth offensive at Petersburg, the Secessionists displayed 350 percent of the combat effectiveness of the Federals, inflicting 9,922 casualties at Second Deep Bottom, Globe Tavern, and Second Reams Station, while the Unionists fought at twenty-eight and a half percent of the combat effectiveness of the Southerners, inflicting about 4,500 losses upon their foes.[50]

By the end of the fourth offensive, the pendulum had swung even further in favor of the Confederates. Second Reams Station provides the offensive's best illustration of the disparity in combat efficiency between Northerners and the Rebels because of the relatively easily ascertainable numbers involved and the relatively easily ascertainable casualties. At Second Reams Station, about 8,000 Unionists faced about 8,000 Secessionists. The 8,000 Federals inflicted around 750 casualties. The 8,000 Southerners inflicted 2,727 casualties. Every 100 Unionists inflicted nine and three-eighths casualties. Every 100 Rebels inflicted thirty-four casualties. Without adjusting for the advantage given the Northerners by their defensive posture, they fought at twenty-seven and a half percent the efficiency of the Rebels, who fought at 363 percent of the efficiency of their foes. Adjusting further for the prepared defense of the Federals, they fought at eighteen and four-tenths percent the efficiency of the attacking

---

49 Agassiz, *Meade's Headquarters*, 208. Lyman ought to have seen the 7th and 9th United States Colored Troops along the Kingsland Road on August 14 or the 9th above Fussell's mill pond on August 16.

50 See Table 4: Combat Efficiency.

Secessionists, while the Southerners fought at 544 percent the combat efficiency of the Unionists. The Confederates had attained a level of combat efficiency over the Northerners of a degree greater than that of World War I Germans over the French but still not approaching the lopsided superiority in combat efficiency of World War I Germans over the Russians.[51]

William Swinton, a war correspondent for the New York Times and later a historian of the Army of the Potomac, recalled:

> Had not success come elsewhere to brighten the horizon, it would have been difficult to have raised new forces to recruit the Army of the Potomac, which, shaken in its structure, its valor quenched in blood, and thousands of its ablest officers killed and wounded, was the Army of the Potomac no more.[52]

Perspectives on Grant's fourth offensive at Petersburg

Terms such as victory or defeat do not adequately describe the results of Grant's fourth offensive, which included the battles and skirmishes of August, 1864. Certain advantages or disadvantages accrued to both sides.

Like a complex painting, the outcome of Grant's fourth offensive appears different when viewed from different perspectives.

Viewed in the narrowest context, that of the Petersburg campaign, the fourth offensive began and ended in stalemate.

On the one hand, the Federals had inflicted about 4,500 casualties upon the Rebels and had captured four guns and thirteen colors. Grant made progress toward completing the investment of Petersburg. The Union armies had taken one more step toward severing all of Richmond's supply lines.

The interruption of the Weldon Railroad aggravated the already dire Secessionist meat and forage shortages in Virginia. Resumption of service by the poorly run Richmond and Danville Railroad took place just as the fall of Atlanta cut off Lee's forces from their sources of supply in southwest Georgia and central Alabama. Though the Southerners ran corn and Nassau bacon

---

51 T. N. Dupuy, *A Genius for War: The German Army and General Staff, 1807-1945* (London, 1977), 328-32. See also Table 4: Combat Efficiency.

52 William Swinton, *Campaigns of the Army of the Potomac* (New York, 1866), 495. That X Corps performed better than any of the Army of the Potomac's corps suggests all the more strongly that Meade ought to have complied with Grant's instruction to employ XVIII Corps on the mission that took II Corps to Reams Station.

through the blockade into Wilmington, North Carolina, wagons on a thirty-mile haul from Stony Creek to Petersburg could not adequately replace railroad trains even in the dilapidated state which the Confederate track and rolling stock had reached by this time. The increasingly short supply of meat played a role in September's Beefsteak Raid.

The consequence of the absence of forage reached further. The horseflesh of the Army of Northern Virginia never recovered from the corn shortage that began in August of 1864. The number of dismounted cavalrymen grew until the Rebel high command detached Hampton and two brigades of horseless horsemen to South Carolina in early 1864, partially to procure new mounts. The disgrace at Five Forks would never have happened with Hampton present.

The artillery horses and transport animals fared as poorly as the cavalry mounts. Lee delayed his contemplated departure from Petersburg in early 1865 in the hope that the strength of his command's horses and mules might improve. The abandoned guns, caissons, limbers, ambulances and forage wagons that littered the road to Appomattox testified to the effects of the lack of forage that began with the losses of Atlanta and the Weldon Railroad in August, 1864.

The fall of Atlanta probably contributed more than the loss of the Weldon Railroad to the lack of forage. Lieutenant Colonel Walter Herron Taylor, a graduate of Virginia Military Institute and a member of Lee's personal staff, recalled about the loss of the Weldon Railroad, probably accurately, that, "whilst we are inconvenienced by it, no material harm is done us."[53]

On the other hand, Grant had paid a high price for the progress that he made—9,922 soldiers, more than two casualties for every one that his troops inflicted. The Federals had also lost nine guns and twenty flags. The casualties had serious repercussions. The demoralization of Grant's soldiers relative to their foes increased. The likelihood of President Lincoln's reelection in November decreased.

The general-in-chief did not have forever to capture Richmond. He had only until November 8, 1864. For Grant's Petersburg campaign alone to have provided the results required to justify the year's terrible casualties, the general-in-chief needed to capture the Secessionist capital before the November election. This Grant failed to accomplish in August, 1864. The

---

53 R. Lockwood Tower, *Lee's Adjutant: The Wartime Letters of Colonel Walter Herron Taylor, 1862-1865* (Columbia SC, 1995), 186.

fighting of that month left his army group in such poor condition that the general-in-chief could not undertake another offensive for nearly five weeks. Not only Richmond but Petersburg remained in Southern hands for the decisive November election.

The results of Grant's fourth offensive look differently when viewed in the context of the war's eastern theater. The Federal general-in-chief prevented Lee from shifting the scene of conflict to the vicinity of the Union capital. Regardless of Lee's specific intent, the presence near Washington of three of the Army of Northern Virginia's four corps commanders—Anderson, Early and Hampton—would soon have necessitated the army leader's own presence there. Grant forced Lee to recall forces en route to the Shenandoah Valley and to retain troops under orders to march to the Valley.

Just as in the case of the Petersburg campaign itself, for operations within the Eastern theater alone to have had a decisive outcome, they would have had to result in the capture of Richmond before the election. This did not happen. If preservation of the Union had depended on the capture of the Confederate capital before the election, the Union would not have survived the war.

Only on the next level, the strategic level, did Grant's fourth offensive pay dividends that justified its cost. If Lee could not reinforce Early in the Shenandoah Valley, Lee's government could not send soldiers from Virginia to reinforce Hood at Atlanta. Grant's fourth offensive foreclosed the possibility of a feared last ditch Rebel concentration against Sherman. The fourth offensive thus contributed to the decisive military event of the war—the capture of Atlanta.

As Grant's fourth offensive ground to a halt, another thrust got underway in distant Georgia that redeemed the sacrifices made by Grant's army group. Within a week of Second Reams Station, Sherman's army group outflanked Hood's vastly outnumbered forces and cut the last railroad into Atlanta. Though gold briefly rose during Hood's desperate struggle to defend the railroad, Sherman emerged the victor at Jonesboro and compelled Atlanta's evacuation.

The capture of Atlanta provided the success necessary to justify the administration's hard war policy and 1864's heavy casualties. As Grant later wrote:

> The news of Sherman's success reached the North instantaneously, and set the country all aglow. This was the first great political campaign for the Republicans in their canvass of 1864. It was followed later by Sheridan's campaign in the Shenandoah Valley, and these two campaigns probably had more effect in settling the election of

the following November than all the speeches, all the bonfires, and all the parading with banners and bands of music in the North.[54]

Atlanta's capture effected a dramatic reversal of fortune. Second Deep Bottom and Second Reams Station became truly lost victories for the Secessionists.

The Democratic Party fell prey to dissention. On August 29, their Chicago convention had nominated McClellan for president on a platform that called for an unconditional armistice that would necessarily result in Confederate independence. McClellan concurred in the platform in the first three drafts of his letter accepting the Democratic nomination. By the time he released his final draft on September 8, War Democrats and the fall of Atlanta had persuaded him to repudiate his party's precondition of peace. This stance alternated many Peace Democrats, who felt that McClellan had betrayed them.

The Republicans closed ranks. Calls for a new convention to replace Lincoln with another candidate ceased. The initially uninspiring victory at Mobile Bay took on new luster with the capture of Atlanta. Secretary of State William H. Seward proclaimed, "Sherman and Farragut have knocked the bottom out of the Chicago platform."[55] Two weeks after McClellan's divisive letter of acceptance, Fremont withdrew his splinter candidacy and left the Republican Party united behind its incumbent president.

Some Rebels did not consider the fall of Atlanta a fatal blow. These included Brig. Gen. Josiah Gorgas, a Northern born West Pointer and Mexican War Veteran who served as the Confederate Chief of Ordnance, and Lieutenant Colonel Taylor, Lee's Assistant Adjutant General.

Other Southerners, such as John Beauchamp Jones, a clerk in the Confederate War Department in Richmond, considered news of Atlanta's fall, "a stunning blow."[56] Neither the loss of Vicksburg nor the defeat at Gettysburg produced such a painful impression. Mary Boykin Chesnut, a member of Columbia, South Carolina's planter elite, despaired. She wrote in her diary:

---

54 Grant, *Personal Memoirs of U. S. Grant*, 439.

55 McPherson, *Battle Cry of Freedom*, 772, 775-6. Significantly, Seward said nothing about severing the Weldon Railroad.

56 Jones, *A Rebel War Clerk's Diary*, 2:276-7.

Atlanta gone. Well—that agony is over. Like David when the child was dead, I will get up from my knees, will wash my face and comb my hair. No hope. We will try to have no fear.[57]

Northern morale soared. Sherman's victory transformed defeatism into determination to fight to the last. Volunteers appeared instead of draft rioters.

The opinion prevailed prior to the November election that for Lincoln to win, Federal forces had to capture Richmond or Atlanta. With Sherman's capture of Atlanta, the burden of persuading the Northern electorate shifted to the Secessionists. The Southerners failed to meet this burden. By October 17, Hood had abandoned his attempt to maneuver Sherman out of Atlanta. On October 19, at the battle of Cedar Creek, Early failed to drive Sheridan from the Shenandoah and mount yet another threat to Washington. Grant, by calling his sixth offensive of the Petersburg campaign a "reconnaissance," easily swept under the rug its failure on October 27 to force the Rebels out of Richmond.[58]

Less than two weeks later, Lincoln's margin of victory confirmed the accuracy of the opinion prevailing prior to the election. The President swayed fifty-five percent of the voters, a percentage which signified that in other circumstances the election could well have gone the other way.

In the spring of 1864 Lincoln had said of Grant's grand design to pin down the Confederacy's armies so that they could not reinforce one another, "Those not skinning can hold a leg."[59] During August of 1864, Grant held a leg while Sherman skinned.

---

57 C. Van Woodward, *Mary Chesnut's Civil War* (New Haven CT, 1981), 642. Mrs. Chesnut alluded to 2 Samuel 12: 15-23.

58 U. S. Grant to Hon. E. M. Stanton, October 27, 1864, in *OR* 42, pt. 1, 22-23.

59 McPherson, *Battle Cry of Freedom*, 722.

Table 1

Federal Strength, July 31, 1864

TABLE 1
FEDERAL STRENGTH, JULY 31, 1864

Army of the Potomac	Officers	Enlisted	Total
General headquarters	35		35
Provost Guard	58	895	953
Engineer Brigade	43	1,710	1,753
Battalion United States Engineers	7	282	289
Artillery (Hunt)	66	1,607	1,673
Guards and Orderlies (Ingalls)	3	80	83
Signal Corps	13	186	199
Second Army Corps (Hancock)	876	13,981	14,857
Fifth Army Corps (Warren)	862	15,882	16,744
Ninth Army Corps (Parke)	499	10,741	11,240
Second Cavalry Division (Gregg)	182	4,033	4,215
Present for duty	2,664	49,397	52,061[1]
Army of the James			
General headquarters	28		28
Signal Corps (Norton)	24	155	179
Naval Brigade (Graham)	20	621	641
1st New York Engineers (Graaf)	7	104	111
Siege Artillery (Abbot)	37	762	799
Unattached troops	150	3,638	3,788
Tenth Army Corps (Birney)	638	13,191	13,829
Eighteenth Army Corps (Ord)	457	11,574	12,031
Cavalry Division (Kautz)	87	2,323	2,410
Present for duty	1,448	32,368	33,816[2]
Grand total, Grant's army group	4,112	81,765	85,877

1 Abstract from return of the Army of the Potomac, Maj. Gen. George G. Meade, U.S. Army, commanding, for the month of July, 1864, in OR 40, pt. 3, 728.

2 Abstract from returns of the Department of Virginia and North Carolina, Maj. Gen. Benjamin F. Butler, U.S. Army, commanding, for the month of July, 1864, ibid., 737.

Table 2

Confederate Strength, July-August, 1864

TABLE 2
CONFEDERATE STRENGTH, JULY-AUGUST, 1864

	Officers	Enlisted	Total
Department of North Carolina and Southern Virginia			
Infantry, July 10, 1864	892	11,069	11,961[1]
Cavalry, September 1, 1864 (Dearing)	84	1,407	1,491[2]
Artillery, July 10, 1864	54	953	1,007
Present for duty	1,030	13,429	14,459
Army of Northern Virginia			
First Army Corps (Anderson)	874	8,756	9,630
Third Army Corps (Hill)	1,422	15,253	16,675
Cavalry Corps (Hampton)	464	6,845	7,309
Artillery	222	4,340	4,562
Present for duty, July 10, 1864	2,982	35,194	38,176[3]
Department of Richmond	12		12
Infantry	45	712	757
Cavalry Brigade (Gary)	54	984	1,039
Artillery Defenses	121	2,231	2,352
Present for duty, July 31, 1864	232	3,928	4,160[4]
Grand total, Lee's army group	4,244	52,551	56,795

1 Abstract from field return of the Army of Northern Virginia, General Robert E. Lee commanding, for July 10, 1864, in OR 40, pt. 3, 761.

2 Abstract from return of the troops in the Department of North Carolina and Southern Virginia, General G. T. Beauregard, commanding, for September 1, 1864, ibid., 42, pt. 2, 1224.

3 Abstract from field return of the Army of Northern Virginia, General Robert E. Lee commanding, for July 10, 1864, ibid., 40, pt. 3, 761.

4 Abstract from tri-monthly return of the Department of Richmond, Lieut. Gen. R. S. Ewell commanding, for July 31, 1864, ibid., 822.

Table 3

Casualties

**TABLE 3
CASUALTIES
Federal**

Battle	Killed & Wounded (total)	Captured & Missing	Aggregate
Deep Bottom	328 & 1,852 (2,180)	721	2,901[1]
Globe Tavern	251 & 1,149 (1,400)	2,809	4,279[2]
Reams Station	140 & 529 (669)	2,073	2,742[3]
All August Battles	719 & 3,530 (4,249)	5,603	9,922[4]
All August	877 & 4,153 (5,030)	5,969	10,999[5]

1 OR 42, pt. 1, 121.

2 Ibid., 128.

3 Ibid., 131. Not including the casualties from August 23rd's "fight by moonlight" except for four killed, six wounded, two missing, and three sunstruck in the 4th New York Heavy Artillery. See Chapter 10, note 10.

4 Ibid., 121, 128, 131.

5 OR 42, pt. 1, 132. This row includes the casualties from August 23rd's "fight by moonlight" except for four killed, six wounded, two missing, and three sunstruck in the 4th New York Heavy Artillery. See Chapter 10, note 10.

| | Confederate | | |
Battle	Killed & Wounded (total)	Captured & Missing	Aggregate
Deep Bottom	(900)	350	1,250[6]
Globe Tavern	(1,525)	875	2,400[7]
Reams Station	(725)	25	750[8]
All August Battles	(3,150)	1,250	4,400[9]
All August	(3,800)	1,600	5,400[10]

6   See Chapter 5, note 11.

7   See Chapter 9, note 36.

8   See Chapter 12, note 46. Not including the casualties from August 23rd's "fight by moonlight." See Chapter 10, note 11.

9   See Chapter 5, note 11; Chapter 9, note 36; and Chapter 12, note 46. Ibid., 121, 128, 131.

10   I assume the Confederates lost as many soldiers in trench warfare and picket affairs as the Federals. OR, 42, pt. 1, 132. This row includes the casualties from August 23rd's "fight by moonlight." See Chapter 10, note 11.

Table 4

Combat Efficiency

TABLE 4
COMBAT EFFICIENCY
Grant's Fourth Offensive at Petersburg

	Number of Battles	Total Engaged	Total Casualties	Average Casualties Per Day (12)	Percent Casualties Per Day	Casualties Inflicted Per Day Per 100 Men[1]	Score Eff.[2]
U.S.A.	3	85,877	9,933	827	0.96	0.4 (28.5%)	0.33
C.S.A.	3	56,795	4,500	375	0.66	1.4 (350%)	1.16

Second Reams Station

	Total Engaged	Total Casualties	Percent Casualties	Casualties Per 100 Men	Score Effectiveness[3]
U.S.A.	8,000	2,727	34.0	9.375 (27.5%)	6.25 (18.4)
C.S.A.	8,000	750	9.375	34.0 (363%)	34.0 (544%)

1 This column corresponds to Dupuy's "Score" and represents "the casualties per day as a percentage of the force inflicting the casualties, derived by applying the casualties of one side to the starting or overall strength of the other side." Dupuy, *A Genius for War*, 328. The figure in parenthesis represents one side's "Score" or combat efficiency as a percentage of the "Score" of the other side. The Unionists (at 28.5% of the Confederates) had fallen a long way from the combat efficiency displayed at Antietam (61% of the defending Rebels), while the Confederates (at 350% of the Federals) performed better than at Gettysburg (100% of the defending Northerners). Beringer, Hattaway, Jones, and Still, *Why The South Lost The Civil War*, 472. Dupuy displays an alternate "Score" excluding prisoners. Dupuy, *A Genius for War*, 330-331. I have not shown an alternate "Score" excluding prisoners because in the campaign of 1864 a prisoner amounted to a dead man due to Grant's refusal to exchange prisoners.

2 "This last column, 'Score Effectiveness,' adjusts the Score value to approximately reflect the known operational advantage ... conferred by defensive posture." Ibid., 328. Because both sides attacked and at least partially engaged also in hasty defense during Grant's Fourth Offensive, I have applied the operational advantage of 1.2 estimated by Dupuy for such situations. Ibid. Looking at Dupuy's Figure C-1/Aggregated Statistics of Fifteen World War I Battles, the results of Grant's Fourth Offensive most resemble 1915's 45-day Champaign II battle, where with the benefit of machine guns and modern artillery the defending Germans attained a score effectiveness of 1.06 and the attacking French had a score effectiveness of 0.27. Ibid., 330-331. The 15-day Aisne II (Nivelle offensive) where the defending Germans had a score effectiveness of 1.03 and the attacking French attained a score effectiveness of 0.27, may provide a better example because of a length similar to Grant's Fourth Offensive and the tendency of score effectiveness to drop as battles drag on. Ibid., 328-331.

3 This column adjusts score effectiveness at Second Reams Station by 1.5 for the Prepared Defense of the Federals. Ibid., 328. It did not amount to a Fortified Defense which would have required an adjustment by 1.6 because the Unionists failed to improve the Reams Station earthworks significantly. Id. Even giving the

Federals every benefit of the doubt and adjusting by 1.3 for a Hasty Defense, they attained a Score Effectiveness of 7.21. Either way, the Unionists scored surprisingly well at Second Reams Station—just not very well in relation to the Confederates. Whether the Federals attained a score effectiveness of 6.25 or 7.21, their score effectiveness resembles that of the victorious Germans in 1914's battle of the Masurian Lakes. Ibid., 330-331. Unfortunately for the Northerners at Second Reams Station, the victorious Rebels attained a far higher score effectiveness of 34.0, approaching the 38.1 of the victorious Germans in 1915's battle of Gorlice-Tarnow. Ibid. Dupuy's chart does not list a battle where the defeated attained a score effectiveness above the 3.86 of the Germans in 1914's Marne battle. Ibid. The score effectiveness of the armies for the entire fourth offensive gives a better idea of their capacities compared to WWI troops than the score effectiveness for the single day's combat at Second Reams Station. Ibid., 329-331.

Appendix A

Orders of Battle, Second Deep Bottom

FEDERAL
SECOND ARMY CORPS
Maj. Gen. Winfield S. Hancock
(also in charge of the cavalry and X Corps troops engaged)

ESCORT
1st Vermont Cav., Co. M

FIRST DIVISION
Brig. Gen. Francis C. Barlow
(*sick from August 17*)
Brig. Gen. Nelson A. Miles

FIRST BRIGADE
Brig. Gen. Nelson A. Miles
Col. James C. Lynch

28th Massachusetts
26th Michigan
5th New Hampshire
2nd New York Heavy Artillery
4th New York Heavy Artillery
61st New York
81st Pennsylvania
140th Pennsylvania
183rd Pennsylvania

FOURTH BRIGADE
Lt. Col. K. Oscar Broady

7th New York Heavy Artillery
64th New York
66th New York
53rd Pennsylvania
116th Pennsylvania
145th Pennsylvania
148th Pennsylvania

CONSOLIDATED BRIGADE
Col. Levin Crandell

7th New York (five cos.)
39th New York (six cos.)
52nd New York (six cos.)
57th New York
63rd New York (six cos.)
69th New York (six cos.)
88th New York (five cos.)
111th New York
125th New York
126th New York

ARTILLERY

New York Light, 11th Battery
4th United States, Battery K

SECOND DIVISION
Col. Thomas A. Smyth
PROVOST GUARD
2nd Co. Minnesota Sharpshooters

FIRST BRIGADE
Col. George N. Macy
(*disabled August 14*)
Lt. Col. Horace P. Rugg

19th Maine
19th Massachusetts
20th Massachusetts
1st Co. Massachusetts Sharpshooters
7th Michigan
1st Minnesota (two cos.)
59th New York
152nd New York
184th Pennsylvania
36th Wisconsin

SECOND BRIGADE
Col. Matthew Murphy

8th New York Heavy Artillery
155th New York
164th New York
170th New York
182nd New York (*69th New York National Guard Artillery*)

THIRD BRIGADE
Lt. Col. Francis E. Pierce

14th Connecticut
1st Delaware
2nd Delaware (two cos.)
12th New Jersey
10th New York (six cos.)
108th New York
4th Ohio (four cos.)
69th Pennsylvania
106th Pennsylvania (three cos.)
7th West Virginia (four cos.)

ARTILLERY

Maine Light, Sixth Battery (F)
1st New York Light, Battery G

THIRD DIVISION
Brig. Gen. Gershom Mott

FIRST BRIGADE
Brig. Gen. P. Regis de Trobriand

SECOND BRIGADE
Col. Calvin A. Craig
(*killed August 16*)
Col. John Pulford

20th Indiana
1st Maine Heavy Artillery
17th Maine
40th New York
73rd New York
86th New York
124th New York
63rd Pennsylvania (three cos.)
99th Pennsylvania
110th Pennsylvania
2nd United States Sharpshooters

1st Massachusetts Heavy Artillery
5th Michigan
93rd New York
57th Pennsylvania
84th Pennsylvania
105th Pennsylvania
141st Pennsylvania
1st United States Sharpshooters

THIRD BRIGADE
11th Massachusetts (seven cos.)
5th New Jersey (three cos.)
6th New Jersey (three cos.)
7th New Jersey
8th New Jersey
11th New Jersey
72nd New York (one co.)
120th New York

ARTILLERY
1st New Jersey Light, Battery B
1st Pennsylvania Light, Battery F

TENTH ARMY CORPS
Maj. Gen. David B. Birney
FIRST DIVISION
Brig. Gen. Alfred H. Terry

FIRST BRIGADE
Col. Francis B. Pond
(*prostrated by heat August 16*)
Col. Alvin C. Voris
(*outranked August 18*)
Col. Joshua B. Howell
(*assumed command August 18*)

39th Illinois
62nd Ohio
67th Ohio (four cos.)
85th Pennsylvania

SECOND BRIGADE
Col. Joseph R. Hawley
(*prostrated by heat August 16*)
Col. Joseph C. Abbott

6th Connecticut
7th Connecticut
3rd New Hampshire
7th New Hampshire

THIRD BRIGADE
Brig. Gen. Robert S. Foster

10th Connecticut
10th Connecticut
1st Maryland Cavalry (dismounted)
24th Massachusetts
100th New York

PROVISIONAL DIVISION
Brig. Gen. William Birney

SECOND BRIGADE
Lt. Col. William B. Coan

47th New York
48th New York
11th Maine
97th Pennsylvania

COLORED BRIGADE
Col. James Shaw
29th Connecticut Colored Infantry
7th United States Colored Troops
8th United States Colored Troops
9th United States Colored Troops

THIRD BRIGADE
Col. Francis A. Osborn
(*wounded August 16*)
Lt. Col. Nathan J. Johnson
(*wounded August 16*)
Maj. Ezra L. Walrath
(*wounded August 16*)
Capt. Francis W. Parker
(*wounded August 16*)
Capt. Robert J. Gray

13th Indiana (three cos.)
9th Maine
4th New Hampshire
115th New York

ARTILLERY BRIGADE
Lt. Col. Freeman McGilvery

Connecticut Light, 1st Battery
3rd Rhode Island Light, Battery C

New Jersey Light, 4th Battery
1st United States, Batteries C and D

UNASSIGNED

4th Massachusetts Cavalry, 1st and 3rd Battalions

DETACHMENT DUNCAN'S BRIGADE, CARR'S DIVISION, EIGHTEENTH ARMY CORPS
Maj. Benjamin C. Ludlow

4th United States Colored Troops

6th United States Colored Troops

CAVALRY

SECOND DIVISION, ARMY OF THE POTOMAC
Brig. Gen. David McM. Gregg

FIRST BRIGADE
Col. William Stedman

SECOND BRIGADE
Col. J. Irvin Gregg
(*wounded August 16*)
Col. Michael Kerwin
(*outranked August 20*)
Col. Charles H. Smith
(*assumed command August 20*)

1st Massachusetts
1st New Jersey
10th New York
6th Ohio
1st Pennsylvania

1st Maine
2nd Pennsylvania
4th Pennsylvania
8th Pennsylvania
13th Pennsylvania
16th Pennsylvania

HORSE ARTILLERY
2nd United States, Battery A

CONFEDERATE
FIELD'S PROVISIONAL ARMY CORPS
Maj. Gen. Charles W. Field
FIELD'S DIVISION
Brig. Gen. John Gregg

ANDERSON'S BRIGADE
Brig. Gen. George T. Anderson

7th Georgia
8th Georgia
9th Georgia
11th Georgia
59th Georgia

LAW'S BRIGADE
Col. Pinckney D. Bowles

4th Alabama
15th Alabama
44th Alabama
47th Alabama
48th Georgia

BENNING'S BRIGADE
Col. Dudley M. DuBose

2nd Georgia
15th Georgia
17th Georgia
20th Georgia

BRATTON'S PROVISIONAL DIVISION
Brig. Gen. John Bratton

BRATTON'S BRIGADE
Brig. Gen. John Bratton

1st South Carolina Volunteers
2nd South Carolina Rifles
5th South Carolina
6th South Carolina
Palmetto Sharpshooters

JOHNSON'S BRIGADE
Col. John M. Hughs

17th/23rd Tennessee
25th/44th Tennessee
63rd Tennessee

DETACH. PICKETT'S DIVISION
Lt. Col. Frank H. Langley

1st Virginia
11th Virginia
19th Virginia

25th Virginia Battalion

DETACH. THOMAS' BRIGADE

DETACH. SCALES' BRIGADE

DETACHMENT, WILCOX'S DIVISION
Brig. Gen. James Conner

MCGOWAN'S BRIGADE	**LANE'S BRIGADE**
Col. Isaac F. Hunt	Col. William M. Barbour
1st South Carolina Rifles	7th North Carolina
12th South Carolina	18th North Carolina
13th South Carolina	28th North Carolina
14th South Carolina	33rd North Carolina
Orr's Rifles	37th North Carolina

DETACHMENT, MAHONE'S DIVISION
Brig. Gen. John C. C. Sanders
(outranked August 17)
Brig. Gen. Nathaniel H. Harris
(assumed command August 17)

HARRIS' BRIGADE	**SANDERS' BRIGADE**
Col. Joseph M. Jayne	Col. J. Horace King
	(outranked August 17)
	Brig. Gen. John C. C. Sanders
	(assumed command August 17)
12th Mississippi	8th Alabama
16th Mississippi	9th Alabama
19th Mississippi	10th Alabama
48th Mississippi	11th Alabama
	14th Alabama

WRIGHT'S BRIGADE
Brig. Gen. Victor J. B. Girardey
(killed August 16)
Col. William Gibson

2nd Georgian Battalion
10th Georgia Battalion
3rd Georgia
22nd Georgia
48th Georgia
64th Georgia

ARTILLERY
BROWNS' BATTALION
Lt. Col. Robert A. Hardaway

Powhatan Artillery	3rd Company Richmond Howitzers
Rockbridge Artillery	Salem Flying Artillery

CAVALRY
CAVALRY CORPS, ARMY OF NORTHERN VIRGINIA
Maj. Gen. Wade Hampton
BUTLER'S DIVISION
Maj. Gen. Matthew C. Butler

BUTLER'S BRIGADE
Col. Hugh K. Aiken

3rd South Carolina
4th South Carolina
5th South Carolina
6th South Carolina

YOUNG'S BRIGADE
Col. Gilbert J. Wright

Cobb's Georgia Legion
Phillips Georgia Legion
Jeff Davis Legion
Millen's Georgia Battalion
Love's Alabama Battalion
7th Georgia Cavalry

ROSSER'S BRIGADE
Col. Richard H. Dulany

7th Virginia
11th Virginia
12th Virginia
35th Virginia Battalion

W. H. F. LEE'S DIVISION
Maj. Gen. William H. F. "Rooney" Lee

BARRINGER'S BRIGADE
Brig. Gen. Rufus Barringer

1st North Carolina
2nd North Carolina
3rd North Carolina
5th North Carolina

CHAMBLISS' BRIGADE
Brig. Gen. John R. Chambliss
(*killed August 16*)
Col. J. Lucius Davis

9th Virginia
10th Virginia
13th Virginia

HORSE ARTILLERY
Maj. R. Preston Chew

Washington (S.C.) Artillery

2nd Jeb Stuart Horse Artillery

GARY'S PROVISIONAL DIVISION
Brig. Gen. Martin W. Gary

GARY'S BRIGADE (Cavalry)	**GREGG'S BRIGADE (Infantry)**
Col. Alexander C. Haskell	Col. Frederick S. Bass
7th Georgia	3rd Arkansas
(detached from Young's Brigade)	1st Texas
Hampton Legion	4th Texas
7th South Carolina	5th Texas
24th Virginia	

Appendix B

Orders of Battle, Globe Tavern

FEDERAL
FIFTH ARMY CORPS
Maj. Gen. Gouverneur K. Warren
(also in charge of the cavalry and X Corps troops engaged)

PROVOST GUARD
5th New York (battalion)

FIRST DIVISION
Brig. Gen. Charles Griffin

FIRST BRIGADE	**SECOND BRIGADE**
Col. William S. Tilton	Col. Edgar M. Gregory
121st Pennsylvania	32nd Massachusetts
142nd Pennsylvania	21st Pennsylvania Cavalry (dismounted)
143rd Pennsylvania	91st Pennsylvania
149th Pennsylvania	155th Pennsylvania
150th Pennsylvania	
187th Pennsylvania	

THIRD BRIGADE
Col. James Gwyn

20th Maine	44th New York
18th Massachusetts	83rd Pennsylvania
1st Michigan	118th Pennsylvania
16th Michigan	

SECOND DIVISION
Brig. Gen. Romeyn B. Ayres

FIRST BRIGADE
Brig. Gen. Joseph Hayes
(*captured August 19*)
Col. Frederick Winthrop

5th New York
140th New York
146th New York
10th United States (three cos.)
11th United States
12th United States
14th United States
17th United States

SECOND BRIGADE
Col. Nathan T. Dushane
(*killed August 21*)
Col. Samuel A. Graham

1st Maryland
4th Maryland
7th Maryland
8th Maryland
Purnell (Maryland) Legion

THIRD BRIGADE
Lt. Col. Michael Wiedrich

15th New York Heavy Artillery

THIRD DIVISION
Brig. Gen. Samuel W. Crawford

FIRST BRIGADE
Col. Peter Lyle

16th Maine
39th Massachusetts
104th New York
90th Pennsylvania
107th Pennsylvania

SECOND BRIGADE
Col. Richard Coulter
(*sick from August 18*)
Col. Charles Wheelock

94th New York
97th New York
11th Pennsylvania
88th Pennsylvania

THIRD BRIGADE
Col. William R. Hartshorne
(*captured August 19*)

190th Pennsylvania
191st Pennsylvania

FOURTH DIVISION
Brig. Gen. Lysander Cutler
(wounded August 21)

PROVOST GUARD
Independent (Wisconsin) Battalion

FIRST BRIGADE
Brig. Gen. Edward S. Bragg

7th Indiana
19th Indiana
24th Michigan
1st Battalion New York Sharpshooters
6th Wisconsin
7th Wisconsin

SECOND BRIGADE
Col. J. William Hofmann

3rd Delaware
4th Delaware
76th New York
95th New York
147th New York
56th Pennsylvania
157th Pennsylvania (battalion)

ARTILLERY BRIGADE
Col. Charles S. Wainwright

Massachusetts Light, 3rd Battery (C)
Massachusetts Light, 5th Battery (E)
Massachusetts Light, 9th Battery
1st New York Light, Battery B
1st New York Light, Battery C
1st New York Light, Battery D

1st New York Light, Battery H
1st New York Light, Battery L
New York Light, 15th Battery
1st Pennsylvania Light, Battery B
5th United States, Battery D

NINTH ARMY CORPS
FIRST DIVISION
Brig. Gen. Julius White

FIRST BRIGADE
Lt. Col. Joseph R. Barnes

21st Massachusetts (three cos.)
29th Massachusetts
35th Massachusetts
56th Massachusetts
57th Massachusetts
59th Massachusetts
100th Pennsylvania

SECOND BRIGADE
Lt. Col. Gilbert P. Robinson

3rd Maryland (battalion)
14th New York Heavy Artillery
179th New York
2nd Pennsylvania Provisional Hvy Artillery

ARTILLERY
Massachusetts Light, 14th Battery

SECOND DIVISION
Brig. Gen. Robert B. Potter

FIRST BRIGADE
Col. Zenas R. Bliss
(*outranked August 21*)
Col. John I. Curtin
(*assumed command August 21*)

36th Massachusetts
58th Massachusetts
2nd New York Mounted Rifles (*dismounted*)
51st New York
45th Pennsylvania
48th Pennsylvania
4th Rhode Island

SECOND BRIGADE
Brig. Gen. Simon G. Griffin

31st Maine
32nd Maine
2nd Maryland
6th New Hampshire
9th New Hampshire
11th New Hampshire
17th Vermont

ACTING ENGINEERS
Lt. Col. Percy Daniels

7th Rhode Island

ARTILLERY

Massachusetts Light, 11th Battery
New York Light, 19th Battery

THIRD DIVISION
Brig. Gen. Orlando B. Willcox

FIRST BRIGADE
Brig. Gen. John F. Hartranft

8th Michigan
27th Michigan (*1st and 2nd cos.*
Michigan Sharpshooters attached)
109th New York
13th Ohio Cavalry (*dismounted*)
51st Pennsylvania
37th Wisconsin
38th Wisconsin

SECOND BRIGADE
Col. William Humphrey

1st Michigan Sharpshooters
2nd Michigan
20th Michigan
24th New York Cavalry (dismounted)
46th New York
60th Ohio (9th and 10th Cos. Ohio
Sharpshooters attached)
50th Pennsylvania

ACTING ENGINEERS
Capt. Joseph A. Sudsborough

17th Michigan

CAVALRY

FIRST BRIGADE, SECOND DIV., ARMY OF THE POTOMAC
Col. William Stedman

1st Massachusetts
1st New Jersey
10th New York
6th Ohio
1st Pennsylvania

SECOND BRIGADE, CAVALRY DIV., ARMY OF THE JAMES
Col. Samuel P. Spear

1st District of Columbia
11th Pennsylvania

CONFEDERATE

AUGUST 18

DEPARTMENT OF NORTH CAROLINA AND SOUTHERN VIRGINIA
Gen. P. G. T. Beauregard

THIRD ARMY CORPS
Lt. Gen. A. P. Hill

HETH'S PROVISIONAL DIVISION
Maj. Gen. Henry Heth

DAVIS' BRIGADE
Brig. Gen. Joseph R. Davis

1st Confederate Battalion
2nd Mississippi
11th Mississippi
26th Mississippi
42nd Mississippi
55th North Carolina

WALKER'S BRIGADE
Col. Robert M. Mayo

13th Alabama
2nd Maryland Battalion
1st Tennessee
7th Tennessee
14th Tennessee
22nd Virginia Battalion
40th Virginia
47th Virginia
55th Virginia

COLQUITT'S BRIGADE
Brig. Gen. Alfred H. Colquitt

6th Georgia	27th Georgia
19th Georgia	28th Georgia
23rd Georgia	

ARTILLERY
PEGRAM'S BATTALION
Lt. Col. William J. Pegram

Letcher Artillery

CAVALRY
DEARING'S BRIGADE
Brig. Gen. James Dearing

7th Confederate	62nd Georgia
4th North Carolina	6th North Carolina
Petersburg Artillery	

AUGUST 19

DEPARTMENT OF NORTH CAROLINA AND SOUTHERN VIRGINIA
Gen. P. G. T. Beauregard

THIRD ARMY CORPS
Lt. Gen. A. P. Hill

DETACHMENT, HETH'S DIVISION
Maj. Gen. Henry Heth

DAVIS' BRIGADE	WALKER'S BRIGADE
Brig. Gen. Joseph R. Davis	Col. Robert M. Mayo
	(*ill August 19*)
	Col. William S. Christian
1st Confederate Battalion	13th Alabama
2nd Mississippi	2nd Maryland Battalion
11th Mississippi	1st Tennessee
26th Mississippi	7th Tennessee
42nd Mississippi	14th Tennessee
55th North Carolina	22nd Virginia Battalion
	40th Virginia
	47th Virginia
	55th Virginia

MAHONE'S PROVISIONAL DIVISION
Maj. Gen. William Mahone

COLQUITT'S BRIGADE	CLINGMAN'S BRIGADE
Brig. Gen. Alfred H. Colquitt	Brig. Gen. Thomas L. Clingman
	(*wounded August 19*)
	Col. Hector McKethan
6th Georgia	8th North Carolina
19th Georgia	31st North Carolina
23rd Georgia	51st North Carolina
27th Georgia	61st North Carolina
28th Georgia	

WEISIGER'S BRIGADE
Col. David A. Weisiger

6th Virginia	41st Virginia
12th Virginia	61st Virginia
16th Virginia	

ARTILLERY
PEGRAM'S BATTALION
Lt. Col. William J. Pegram

Pee Dee Artillery	Fredericksburg Artillery
Letcher Artillery	Purcell Artillery
Crenshaw's Battery	

CAVALRY
DEARING'S BRIGADE
Brig. Gen. James Dearing

7th Confederate	62nd Georgia
4th North Carolina	6th North Carolina
Petersburg Artillery	

AUGUST 21

ARMY OF NORTHERN VIRGINIA
Gen. Robert E. Lee
THIRD ARMY CORPS
Lt. Gen. A. P. Hill
HETH'S PROVISIONAL DIVISION
Maj. Gen. Henry Heth

COOKE'S BRIGADE
Brig. Gen. John R. Cooke

15th North Carolina
27th North Carolina
46th North Carolina
48th North Carolina

MACRAE'S BRIGADE
Brig. Gen. William MacRae

11th North Carolina
26th North Carolina
44th North Carolina
47th North Carolina
52nd North Carolina

RANSOM'S BRIGADE
Lt. Col. John L. Harris

24th North Carolina
25th North Carolina
35th North Carolina

49th North Carolina
56th North Carolina

MAHONE'S PROVISIONAL DIVISION
Maj. Gen. William Mahone

HARRIS' BRIGADE
Col. Joseph M. Jayne

12th Mississippi
16th Mississippi
19th Mississippi
48th Mississippi

WRIGHT'S BRIGADE
Col. William Gibson

2nd Georgia Battalion
3rd Georgia
10th Georgia Battalion
22nd Georgia
48th Georgia
64th Georgia

SANDERS' BRIGADE
Brig. Gen. John C. C. Sanders (killed)
Col. J. Horace King

    8th Alabama
    9th Alabama
    10th Alabama
    11th Alabama
    14th Alabama

FINEGAN'S BRIGADE
Brig. Gen. Joseph Finegan

    2nd Florida
    5th Florida
    8th Florida
    9th Florida
    10th Florida
    11th Florida

Appendix C

Orders of Battle, Second Reams Station

FEDERAL
SECOND ARMY CORPS
Maj. Gen. Winfield S. Hancock
(also in charge of the cavalry engaged)

FIRST DIVISION
Brig. Gen. Nelson A. Miles

FIRST BRIGADE
Col. James C. Lynch

28th Massachusetts
26th Michigan
5th New Hampshire
2nd New York Heavy Artillery
61st New York
81st Pennsylvania
140th Pennsylvania
183rd Pennsylvania

CONSOLIDATED BRIGADE
Col. Levin Crandell (*in charge of picket line*)
Lt. Col. Joseph Hyde

7th New York (five cos.)
39th New York (six cos.)
52nd New York (six cos.)
57th New York
63rd New York (six cos.)
69th New York (six cos.)
88th New York (five cos.)
111th New York
125th New York
126th New York

FOURTH BRIGADE
Lt. Col. K. Oscar Broady
(*wounded*)
Lt. Col. William Glenny

7th New York Heavy Artillery
64th New York
66th New York
53rd Pennsylvania
116th Pennsylvania
145th Pennsylvania
148th Pennsylvania

UNATTACHED
Lt. Col. Thomas Allcock
(*wounded*)
Capt. John B. Vande Weile

4th New York Heavy Artillery

SECOND DIVISION
Brig. Gen. John Gibbon
PROVOST GUARD
2nd Co. Minnesota Sharpshooters

FIRST BRIGADE	SECOND BRIGADE
Lt. Col. Horace P. Rugg	Col. Matthew Murphy
19th Maine	8th New York Heavy Artillery
19th Massachusetts	155th New York
20th Massachusetts	164th New York
1st Co. Massachusetts Sharpshooters	170th New York
7th Michigan	182nd New York (69th New York
1st Minnesota (two cos.)	National Guard Artillery)
59th New York	
152nd New York	
184th Pennsylvania	
36th Wisconsin	

THIRD BRIGADE
Col. Thomas A. Smyth

14th Connecticut	108th New York
1st Delaware	4th Ohio (four cos.)
2nd Delaware (two cos.)	69th Pennsylvania
12th New Jersey	106th Pennsylvania (three cos.)
10th New York (six cos.)	7th West Virginia (four cos.)

ARTILLERY BRIGADE
Capt. A. Judson Clark

Massachusetts Light, 10th Battery	New Jersey Light, 3rd Battery
New York Light, 12th Battery	1st Rhode Island Light, Batteries A and B

CAVALRY
SECOND DIVISION, ARMY OF THE POTOMAC
Brig. Gen. David McM. Gregg

FIRST BRIGADE	SECOND BRIGADE
Col. William Stedman	Col. Charles H. Smith
1st Massachusetts	1st Maine
1st New Jersey	2nd Pennsylvania
10th New York	4th Pennsylvania
6th Ohio	8th Pennsylvania
1st Pennsylvania	13th Pennsylvania
	16th Pennsylvania

SECOND BRIGADE, CAVALRY DIVISION, ARMY OF THE JAMES
Col. Samuel P. Spear

1st District of Columbia

11th Pennsylvania

CONFEDERATE
THIRD ARMY CORPS
Lt. Gen. A. P. Hill

WILCOX'S PROVISIONAL DIVISION
Maj. Gen. Cadmus M. Wilcox

ANDERSON'S BRIGADE
Col. Francis H. Little
(*wounded*)

7th Georgia
8th Georgia
9th Georgia
11th Georgia
59th Georgia

SCALES' BRIGADE
Brig. Gen. Alfred M. Scales

13th North Carolina
16th North Carolina
22nd North Carolina
34th North Carolina
38th North Carolina

MCGOWAN'S BRIGADE
Col. Isaac F. Hunt

1st South Carolina Rifles
12th South Carolina
13th South Carolina
14th South Carolina
Orr's Rifles

LANE'S BRIGADE
Col. William M. Barbour

7th North Carolina
18th North Carolina
28th North Carolina
33rd North Carolina
37th North Carolina

HETH'S PROVISIONAL DIVISION
Maj. Gen. Henry Heth

COOKE'S BRIGADE
Brig. Gen. John R. Cooke

15th North Carolina
27th North Carolina
46th North Carolina
48th North Carolina

MACRAE'S BRIGADE
Brig. Gen. William MacRae

11th North Carolina
26th North Carolina
44th North Carolina
47th North Carolina
52nd North Carolina

SANDERS' BRIGADE
Col. J. Horace King

8th Alabama
9th Alabama
10th Alabama
11th Alabama
14th Alabama

WEISIGER'S BRIGADE
Brig. Gen. David A. Weisiger

6th Virginia
12th Virginia
16th Virginia
61st Virginia

ARTILLERY
PEGRAM'S PROVISIONAL BATTALION
Lt. Col. William J. Pegram

Clutter's Battery (section)
Letcher Artillery
Battery A, Sumter Artillery

Hardaway Artillery (section)
Purcell Artillery

CAVALRY
CAVALRY CORPS, ARMY OF NORTHERN VIRGINIA
Maj. Gen. Wade Hampton

BUTLER'S DIVISION
Maj. Gen. Matthew C. Butler

DUNOVANT'S BRIGADE
Brig. Gen. John Dunovant

3rd South Carolina
4th South Carolina
5th South Carolina
6th South Carolina

YOUNG'S BRIGADE
Col. Gilbert J. Wright

Cobb's Georgia Legion
Phillips Georgia Legion
Jeff Davis Legion
Millen's Georgia Battalion
Love's Alabama Battalion
7th Georgia

ROSSER'S BRIGADE
Col. Richard H. Dulany

7th Virginia
11th Virginia

12th Virginia
35th Virginia Battalion

W. H. F. LEE'S DIVISION
Maj. Gen. William H. F. "Rooney" Lee

BARRINGER'S BRIGADE	**CHAMBLISS' BRIGADE**
Col. William H. Cheek	Col. J. Lucius Davis
1st North Carolina	9th Virginia
2nd North Carolina	10th Virginia
3rd North Carolina	13th Virginia
5th North Carolina	

HORSE ARTILLERY
Maj. R. Preston Chew

Washington (S.C.) Artillery	2nd Jeb Stuart Horse Artillery

Bibliography

Primary Manuscript Sources

T. G. Barham, Compiled Service Record, Record Group 109, National Archives, Washington, D.C.;
Ransom Bedell Letters, Illinois State Historical Library, Springfield, Illinois.
George S. Bernard Papers, Alderman Library, University of Virginia, Charlottesville, Virginia.
George S. Bernard Papers, Perkins Library, Duke University, Durham, North Carolina.
George S. Bernard Papers, Southern Historical Collection, Wilson Library, University of North Carolina, Chapel Hill, North Carolina.
Henry Van Leuvenigh Bird Letters, Bird Family Papers, Virginia Historical Society, Richmond, Virginia.
Octave Bruso August 1864 Diary Entries, Tom Bauerle, ed., The Siege of Petersburg Online.
John Bryden Letter, August 30, 1864, Letters of John Bryden, The Siege of Petersburg Online.
Cornelius H. Carlton Diary, Virginia State Library, Richmond, Virginia.
Civil War Diary of John Kennedy Coleman, Manuscripts Division, South Caroliniana Library, University of South Carolina, Columbia, South Carolina.
David Coon Papers, Elwyn B. Robinson Department of Special Collections, Chester Fritz Library, University of North Dakota, Grand Forks, North Dakota.Letter, Robert Crump to mother and sister, August 26, 1864, Petersburg National Battlefield, Petersburg, Virginia.
Letter, James Alexander Daniel to Teresa Augusta Cobb, September 27, 1864, Marvin Giddings Private Collection, Americus, Georgia.Nicholas Degraff Memoir, 1862-1865, "Civil War Times Illustrated," Collection of Civil War Papers, United States Army Military History Institute, Carlisle Barracks, Pennsylvania.
Washington L. Dunn Diary, United Daughters of the Confederacy Collection, Georgia Department of Archives and History, Atlanta, Georgia.

Franklin M. Fleming Correspondence, Hargrett Rare Book and Manuscript Library, University of Georgia, Athens, Georgia.
Isaac Foskett August 1864 Diary Entries, The Siege of Petersburg Online.
George S. Gove Letter, August 28, 1864, Parsons Family Papers, Milne Special Collections and Archives, University of New Hampshire, Durham, New Hampshire.
Letter, Wade Hampton to Francis A. Walker, March 29, 1884, Sessler Collection, Civil War Library and Museum, Philadelphia, Pennsylvania.
Henry M. Hardenbergh, Compiled Service Record, Record Group 109, National Archives, Washington, D.C.William Henry Harder Memoir, Richmond National Battlefield, Richmond, Virginia.Joseph Hayes, "Report of November 26, 1867," Petersburg National Battlefield, Petersburg, Virginia.
Henry Heth, "Report of December 7th, 1864," Heth Papers, Eleanor S. Brockenbrough Library, Museum of the Confederacy, Richmond, Virginia.
James H. Lane Papers, Auburn University Archives and Manuscripts Department, Auburn University, Auburn, Alabama.
William Mahone Papers, Preston Library, Virginia Military Institute, Lexington, Virginia.
John D. McConnell, "Recollections of the Civil War," Richmond National Battlefield, Richmond, Virginia.
Joseph Mullen, Jr. Diary, Elizabeth S. Brockenbrough Library, Museum of the Confederacy, Richmond, Virginia.
Records Group 109, War Department Collection of Confederate Records, National Archives, Washington, D.C.
John Reed Memoir, Alabama State Archives, Montgomery, Alabama.
Washington A. Roebling, Report of the Operations of the 5th Corps, A. P. in Genl. Grant's Campaign from Culpeper to Petersburg, as seen by W.A. Roebling, Maj. A.D.C. 1864. Gouverneur K. Warren Collection, New York State Library and Archives, Albany, New York.
John F. Sale Diary, John F. Sale Papers, Virginia State Library, Richmond, Virginia.
Terry Family Papers, Yale University, New Haven, Connecticut.
Letter of John W. Thomas, Petersburg National Battlefield, Petersburg, Virginia.
Westwood Todd Reminiscences, Southern Historical Collection, Wilson Library, University of North Carolina at Chapel Hill, Chapel Hill, North Carolina.
James E. Whitehorne Papers, Virginia State Library, Richmond, Virginia.
Cadmus M. Wilcox, Reports, 1863-1865, Lee's Headquarters Collection, Virginia Historical Society, Richmond, Virginia.
Byrd C. Willis Diary, Virginia State Library, Richmond, Virginia.

Other Manuscript Sources

Bearss, Edwin C. "Battle of the Weldon Railroad," Petersburg National Battlefield, Petersburg, Virginia.
———, "The Battle of Ream's Station" (1964), Petersburg National Battleveild, Petersburg, Virginia.
Persons, Henry W, Jr. Unpublished study of Anderson's Brigade, Army of Northern Virginia. Henry W. Persons, Jr., Private Collection, Severn, Maryland.
Suderow, Bryce C. "Confederate Casualties during the Siege of Petersburg, June 13-August 25, 1864," Bryce A. Suderow Private Collection, Washington, D.C.

———, "Target Richmond: The Civil War North of the James June 21-August 21 1864," Bryce A. Suderow Private Collection, Washington, D.C.

Newspaper Sources

Augusta *Chronicle and Sentinel*
Augusta *Daily Constitutionalist*
Charleston *Daily Courier*
Charleston Mercury
Columbia *Daily South Carolinian*
Columbus (Ga.) *Times*
Columbus (Ga.) *Daily Sun*
Harris County (Georgia) *Enterprise*
Macon Daily Telegraph
Montgomery (Ala.) *Daily Mail*
North Carolinian (Fayetteville)
Petersburg Daily *Register*
Petersburg *Express*
Raleigh *Daily Confederate*
(Raleigh) Semi-Weekly *North Carolina Standard*
Richmond *Dispatch*
Richmond *Enquirer*
Richmond *Examiner*
Richmond *Sentinel*
Richmond *Whig*
Savannah Republican
Southern Recorder (Milledgeville, Ga.)
Southern Watchman (Athens, Ga.)
Weekly Catawba Journal

Periodical Sources

Allan, William. "History of the Campaign of Gen T. J. (Stonewall) Jackson in the Shenandoah Valley of Virginia, from November 4, 1861, to June 17, 1862." *Southern Historical Society Papers*, vol. 43 (1920): 111-294.
    Cardwell, David. "The Battle of Five Forks." *Confederate Veteran*, vol. 22 (1914): 117-120.
    Clark, George. "Alabamians in the Crater Battle." *Confederate Veteran*, vol. 3 (1895): 68-69.
    Dauchy, George K. "The Battle of Reams Station." *Papers read before the Commandery of the State of Illinois, Military Order of the Loyal Legion of the United States*, vol. 3 (1899): 125-140.
    Letter, John E. Davis to Charles Marshall, n.d., *Southern Historical Society Papers*, vol. 17 (1889).Day, W. A. "Life Among Bullets—In The Rifle Pits." *Confederate Veteran*, vol. 29 (1921): 216-219.
    De Peyster, J. Watts. "A Military Memoir of William Mahone, Major-General in the Confederate Army." *The Historical Magazine*, vol. 7, Second Series, No. 6 (June, 1870): 390-406.

Featherston, John C. "Brilliant Page in History Of War." *Southern Historical Society Papers*, vol. 36 (1908): 161-173.

Field, Charles W. "The Campaign of 1864 and 1865: The Narrative of Major-General C. W. Field." *Southern Historical Society Papers*, vol. 14 (1886): 542-563.

Fortin, Maurice S., ed. "Colonel Hilary A. Herbert's History of the Eighth Alabama volunteer regiment, C. S. A." *Alabama Historical Quarterly*, vol. 39 (1977): 5-321.

"Capt. M. C. House, Company H, Eighth North Carolina Regiment, writes . . . .." *Confederate Veteran*, vol. 7 (1899): 217.

Lane, James H. "History of Lane's N. C. Brigade—Campaign of 1864—Anecdote about Captain G. G. Holland, 28th N. C. Troops." *Southern Historical Society Papers*, vol. 9 (1881): 353-361.

Larkin, James E. "Regarding Battle of Reams Station." *Confederate Veteran*, vol. 18 (1910): 26.

———. "Fight at Reams Station." *Confederate Veteran*, vol. 19 (1911): 231-232.

Lokey, J. W. "The Battle Near Deep Bottom, Va." *Confederate Veteran*, vol. 33 (1925): 127-128.

"Col. T. B. Massie." *Confederate Veteran*, vol. 16 (1908): 472.

McAlpine, Charles R. "Sketch of Company I, 61st Virginia Infantry, Mahone's brigade, C. S. A." *Southern Historical Society Papers*, vol. 24 (1896): 98-108.

McCabe, W. Gordon. "Defense of Petersburg." *Southern Historical Society Papers*, vol. 2 (1876): 257-306.

McDavid, Peter A. "With the Palmetto Riflemen." *Confederate Veteran*, vol. 37 (1929): 298-300.

Pomfret, John E., ed. "Letters of Fred Lockley, Union Soldier 1864-1865." *Huntington Library Quarterly*, vol. 16 (1952): 75-112.

Porter, Charles H. "Operations Against the Weldon Railroad, August 18, 19, 21, 1864." *Papers Read before the Military Historical Society of Massachusetts*, vol. 5 (1906): 241-266.

Powell, Junius L. "A Memory of Our Great War," *Journal of the Military Service Institute of the United States*, vol. 48 (1911): 87-99.

Rogers, George T. "Retaking Railroad at Reams Station." *Confederate Veteran*, vol. 5 (1897): 580-581.

Seyburn, Stephen Young. *"Tenth regiment of infantry." Journal of the Military Service Institute of the United States*, vol. 13 (1892): 415-428.

Steuart, Richard D. "How Johnny Got His Gun." *Confederate Veteran*, vol. 32 (1924): 166-169.

Stewart, William H., and White, Whitman V. "The No Name Battle." *Blue and Gray*, vol, 5, No. 1 (Jan., 1895): 29-35.

"George Nash Truss." *Confederate Veteran*, vol. 22 (1912): 481.

Wagstaff, H. M., ed. "The Jas. A. Graham Papers, 1861-1864." *The Jas. Sprunt Historical Studies*, vol. 20, No. 2 (1928): 87-324.

Waring, Joseph Ioor, ed. "The Diary of William G. Hinson during the War of Secession." *The South Carolina Historical Magazine*, vol. 75, No. 1 (January, 1974): 111-120.

Primary Book Sources

Agassiz, George, ed. *Meade's Headquarters, 1863-1865: Letters of Colonel Theodore Lyman from the Wilderness to Appomattox.* Boston: Massachusetts Historical Society, 1922.

Aldritch, Thomas M. *The History of Battery A. First Regiment Rhode Island Light Artillery in the War to Preserve the Union, 1861-1865.* Providence: Snow & Farnham, 1904.

Alexander, Edward Porter. *Military Memoirs of a Confederate.* Bloomington: Indiana University Press, 1962.

Anderson, John. *The Fifty-Seventh Regiment of Massachusetts Volunteers in the War of the Rebellion, Army of the Potomac.* Boston: E. B. Stillings & Co., Printers, 1896.

Aston, Howard. *History and Roster of the Fourth and Fifth Independent Battalions and Thirteenth Regiment Ohio Cavalry Volunteers Their Battles Skirmishes Rosters of the Dead etc.* Columbus, Oh.: Press of Fred J. Heer, 1902.

Aubery, James M. *The Thirty-Sixth Wisconsin Volunteer Infantry 1st Brigade 2nd Div. 2nd Army Corps.* Milwaukee: Evening Wisconsin Company, 1900.

Axford, Faye Acton. *"To Lochaber Na Mair": Southerners View the Civil War, Eyewitness Accounts of Soldiers on the Field of Battle and the Loved Ones They Left Behind Beginning with the War in Virginia and the Occupation of Athens, Alabama, the Sense of the Impermanence of "A Way Of Life" and Ending with an Account of Return to a Modicum of Normalcy a Year after Appomattox.* Athens, Alabama: Athens Publishing Company, 1987.

Baker, Levi W. *History of the Ninth Mass. Battery Recruited July, 1862; Mustered in Aug. 10, 1862; Mustered out June 9, 1865, at the Close of the Rebellion.* South Framingham, Ma.: Lakeview Press, 1888.

Barham, Theophilus G. *The War Record of T. G. Barham.* Gray, Va.: n. p., 1885.

Baylor, George. *Bull Run to Bull Run: Four Years in the Army of Northern Virginia.* Richmond: B. F. Johnson Publishing Co., 1900.

Beale, Richard L. T. *History of the Ninth Virginia Cavalry In The War Between the States.* Richmond: B. F. Johnson Publishing Co., 1899.

Beecher, Herbert W. *History of the First Light Battery Connecticut Volunteers, 1861-1865.* New York: A. T. De La Mare Ptg. and Pub. Co., Ltd., 1901.

Billings, John D. Billings. *The History of the Tenth Massachusetts Battery of Light Artillery in the War of the Rebellion Formerly of the Third Corps and Afterward of Hancock's Second Corps, Army of the Potomac. 1862-1865.* Boston: Hall & Whiting, Publishers, 1881.

Birney, William Birney. *General William Birney's Answer To Libels Clandestinely Circulated By James Shaw, Jr.* Washington, D.C.: Stanley Snodgrass, Printer, 1878.

Board of Commissioners. *Minnesota in the Civil and Indian Wars.* 2 Volumes. St. Paul: Pioneer Press, 1890.

Board of State Institutions. *Soldiers of Florida in the Seminole Indian, Civil and Spanish-American Wars.* Live Oak, Fla.: Democrat book and job print, 1903.

Bond, Natalie Jenkins, and Coward, Osman Latrobe, eds. *The South Carolinians: Colonel Asbury Coward's Memoirs.* New York: Vantage Press, 1968.

Brady, Robert. *The Story of One Regiment: The Eleventh Maine Infantry Volunteers in the War of the Rebellion.* New York: J. J. Little & Company, 1896.

Brainard, Mary G. *Campaigns of the One Hundred and Forty-sixth Regiment New York State Volunteers, Also Known as Halleck's Infantry, the Fifth Oneida, and Garrard's Tigers.* New York: G. P. Putnam's Sons, 1915.

Brooks, U. R. *Butler and His Cavalry in the War of Secession, 1861-1865.* Columbia: The State Company, 1909.

Brown, J. Willard. *The Signal Corps, U.S.A. in the War of the Rebellion.* Boston: U. S. Veteran Signal Corps Association, 1896.

Bruce, George A. *The Twentieth Regiment of Massachusetts Volunteer Infantry, 1861-1865.* Boston: Houghton, Mifflin Co., 1906.

Cadwell, Charles K. *The Old Sixth Regiment, Its War Record, 1861-65.* New Haven, Conn.: Tuttle, Morehouse & Taylor, Printers, 1875.

Caldwell, James F. J. *The History of a Brigade of South Carolinians, Known First as "Gregg's" and Subsequently as "McGowan's" Brigade.* Philadelphia: King & Baird Printers, 1866.

Calhoun, Charles M. *Liberty dethroned, A Concise History of Some of the Most Startling Events Before, During, and Since the Civil War.* Greenwood, S.C., n. p., 1903.

Califf, Joseph. *Record of the Services of the Seventh Regiment, U.S. Colored Troops from September, 1863, to November, 1866.* Providence: E. L. Freeman & Company, 1878.

Camper, Charles, and Kirkley, J. W. *Historical Record of the First Regiment Maryland Infantry, with an Appendix containing a Register of the Officers and Enlisted Men, Biographies of Deceased Officers, etc., War of the Rebellion.* Washington: Gibson Brothers, Printers, 1871.

Cheek, Phillip, and Pointon, Mair. *History of the Sauk County Riflemen Known as Company 'A', Sixth Wisconsin Veteran Volunteer Infantry, 1861-1865.* Madison: Democratic Printing Company, 1909.

Child, William. *A History of the Fifth Regiment New Hampshire Volunteers in the American Civil War, 1861-1865.* Bristol, N.H.: R. W. Musgrove, Printer, 1893.

Clark, Charles M. *The History of the Thirty-Ninth Regiment Illinois Volunteer Veteran Infantry (Yates Phalanx) in the War of the Rebellion, 1861-1865.* Chicago: Veterans Association, 1889.

Clark, James H. *The Iron Hearted Regiment: Being an Account of the Battles, Marches and Gallant Deeds Performed by the 115th Regiment N. Y. Vols.* Albany, N. Y.: J. Munsell, 1865.

Clark, Walter, ed. *Histories of the Several Regiments and Battalions from North Carolina in the Great War, 1861-'65.* 5 Volumes. Goldsboro, N.C.: Nash Brothers, Book and Job Printers, 1901.

Cockrell, Thomas D., and Ballard, Michael B. *A Mississippi Rebel in the Army of Northern Virginia: The Civil War Memoirs of Private David Holt.* Baton Rouge: Louisiana State University Press, 2001.

Committee. *History of the Fifth Massachusetts Battery, Organized October 3, 1861, Mustered Out June 12, 1865.* Boston: Luther E. Cowles, Publisher, 1902.

Committee of the Regimental Association. *History of the Thirty-Fifth Regiment Massachusetts Volunteers, 1862-1865.* Boston: Mills, Knight & Co, 1884.

Conyngham, Capt. D. P. *The Irish Brigade and Its Campaigns.* New York: William McSorley & Co., Publishers, 1867.

Copp, Elbridge J. *Reminiscences of the War of the Rebellion.* Nashua, N. H.: The Telegraph Publishing Company, 1911.

Corbin, Richard W. *Letters of a Confederate Officer to His Family in Europe During the Last Year of the War of Secession.* Paris: Neale's English Library, 1913.

Cowtan, Charles W. *Services of the Tenth New York Volunteers (National Zouaves) in the War of the Rebellion.* New York: C. H. Ludwig, 1882.

Crater, Lewis. *History of the Fiftieth Regiment, Penna. Vet. Vols., 1861-1865.* Reading, Pa.: Coleman Printing House, 1884.

Croom, Wendell D. *The War History of Company 'C', (Beauregard Volunteers) Sixth Georgia Regiment, (Infantry)*. Fort Valley, Ga.: Advertiser, 1879.

Curtis, O. B. *History of the Twenty-Fourth Michigan, of the Iron Brigade, Known as the Detroit and Wayne County Regiment*. Detroit: Winn & Hammond, 1891.

Daly, Louise Haskell. *Alexander Cheves Haskell: the Portrait of a Man*. Norwood, Mass.: The Plimpton Press, 1934.

Davis, Oliver W. *Life of David Bell Birney, Major-General United States Volunteers*. Philadelphia: King & Baird, 1867.

Dennett, George M. *History of the Ninth U. S. C. Troops from Its Organization till Mustered Out*. Philadelphia: King & Baird, 1866.

Dowdey, Clifford, and Manarin, Louis, eds. *The Wartime Papers of R. E. Lee*. Boston: Little, Brown and Company, 1961.

Dunlop, William S. *Lee's Sharpshooters; or, the Forefront of Battle: A Story of Southern Valor that Never Has Been Told*. Little Rock: Tunnah & Pittard, 1899.

Eden, R. C. *The Sword and Gun, a History of the 37th Wis. Volunteer Infantry*. Madison: Atwood & Rublee, 1865.

Eldredge, Daniel. *The Third New Hampshire and All About It*. Boston: E. B. Stillings and Company, 1893.

Fox, William F. *Regimental Losses in the American Civil War, 1861-1865*. Albany, N.Y.: Albany Publishing Company, 1889.

Gallagher, Gary, ed., *Fighting for the Confederacy: The Personal Recollections of General Edward Porter Alexander*. Chapel Hill: The University of North Carolina Press, 1989.

Gibbon, John. *Personal Recollections of the Civil War*. New York: G. P. Putnam's Sons, 1928.

Goldsborough, W. W. *The Maryland Line in the Confederate Army, 1861-1865*. Baltimore: Press of Guggenheimer, Weil & Co., 1900.

Grant, Ulysses S. *Personal Memoirs of U. S. Grant*. New York: Charles L. Webster & Company, 1894.

Griffin, Ronald C. *The 11th Alabama Volunteer Regiment in the Civil War*. Jefferson, N.C.: McFarland & Company, 2008.

Hagood, Johnson. *Memoirs of the War of Secession*. Columbia, S.C.: The State Company, 1909.

Haines, William P. Haines. *History of the Men of Co. F, with Description of the Marches and Battles of the 12th New Jersey Vols*. Camden, N. J.: C. S. McGrath, 1892.

Hall, Isaac. *History of the Ninety-Seventh Regiment New York Volunteers ("Conkling rifles") in the War for the Union*. Utica, N.Y.: 1890.

Hamil, John W. *The Story of a Confederate Soldier: 1862-1865*. Cragford, Ala.: n. p., 1973.

Hardee, William J. *Hardee's Light Infantry Tactics Complete In One Book*. Memphis: E. C. Kirk & Co., 1861.

Harris, J. S. *Historical Sketches of the Seventh Regiment North Carolina Troops*. Mooresville, N.C.: Mooresville Printing Co., 1893.

Harris, W. H., comp. *Movements of the Confederate army in Virginia and the part taken therein by the Nineteenth Mississippi regiment from the diary of Gen. Nat. H. Harris*. Duncansby, Miss., n. p., 1901.

History Committee. *History of the Eleventh Pennsylvania Volunteer Cavalry*. Philadelphia: Franklin Print Co., 1902.

Howard, Wiley C. *Sketch of Cobb Legion Cavalry*. Suffolk, Va.: Robert Hardy Publications, 1986).

Hudnut, James M. *Casualties By Battle And By Name In The Eighth New York Heavy Artillery August 22, 1862-June 5, 1865 Together With A Review Of The Service Of The Regiment Fifty Years After Muster-In.* New York: n. p., 1913.

Humphreys, Andrew A. *The Virginia Campaign of '64 and '65: the Army of the Potomac and the Army of the James.* 2 Volumes. Reprint Edition. New York: Thomas Yoseloff, 1963.

Hyndman, William. *History of a Cavalry Company, A Complete Record of Company 'A', 4th Penn'a Cavalry.* Philadelphia: Jas. B. Rodgers Co., Printers, 1872.

Izlar, William V. *A Sketch of the War Record of the Edisto Rifles, 1861-1865* (cited hereinafter as Edisto Rifles. Columbia, S. C.: The State Company, 1914.

Jewett, Albert H. C. *A Boy Goes to War.* Bloomington, Ill.: Grace Jewett Austin, 1944.

Johnson, Robert U., and Buel, Clarence C., eds. *Battles and Leaders of the Civil War.* 4 Volumes. New York: The Century Company, 1884, 1888.

Jones, John Beauchamp. *A Rebel War Clerk's Diary at the Confederate States Capital.* 2 Volumes. Philadelphia: J. B. Lippincott, 1866.

Jordan, William C. *Some Events and Incidents During the Civil War.* Montgomery, Ala.: The Paragon Press, 1909.

Judson, A. M. *History of the Eighty-Third Regiment Pennsylvania Volunteers.* Erie, Pa.: B. F. H. Lynn, 1865.

Kirk, Hyland C. *Heavy Guns and Light of the 4th New York Heavy Artillery.* New York: C. T. Dillingham, Publisher, 1890.

Laine, J. Gary, and Penny, Morris M. *Law's Alabama Brigade in the War Between the Union and the Confederacy.* Shippensburg, Pa.: White Mane Pub., 1996.

Lee, Susan P. *Memoirs of William Nelson Pendleton, D. D.* Philadelphia: J. B. Lippincott, 1983.

Little, Henry F. W. *The Seventh Regiment New Hampshire Volunteers in the War of the Rebellion.* Concord, N. H.: Ira C. Evans, Printer, 1896.

Locke, William H. *The Story of the Regiment.* Philadelphia: J. B. Lippincott & Co., 1868.

Loehr, Charles T. War *History of the Old First Virginia Infantry Regiment, Army of Northern Virginia.* Richmond, Va.: William Ellis Jones, 1884.

Maine Gettysburg Commission. *Maine at Gettysburg.* Portland, Me.: The Lakeside Press, 1898.

Maxfield, Albert. *Roster and statistical record of Company D, of the Eleventh Maine Infantry volunteers.* New York: Press of Thomas Humphrey, 1890.

M'Bride, R. E. *In the Ranks from the Wilderness to Appomattox Court House.* Cincinatti: Walden & Stowe, 1881.

McCarthy, Carlton, ed. *Contributions to a History of the Richmond Howitzer Battalion.* Richmond, 1883-1886.

McDonald, William N. *A History of the Laurel Brigade Originally the Ashby Cavalry of the Army of Northern Virginia and Chew's Battery.* Baltimore: Sun Job Printing Office, 1907.

Meade, George. *The Life and Letters of George Gordon Meade, Major-General United States Army.* 2 Volumes. New York: Charles Scribner's Sons, 1913.

Menge, W. Springer, and Shimrak, J. August. *The Civil War Notebook of Daniel Chisholm, A Chronicle of Daily Life in the Union Army 1864-1865.* New York: Orion Books, 1989.

Minnesota Board of Commissioners on Publication of History of Minnesota in Civil and Indian Wars. *Minnesota in the Civil and Indian Wars, 1861-1865.* St. Paul: Pioneer Press Co., 1890.

Morrison, James L., ed. *The Memoirs of Henry Heth.* Westport, Conn: Greenwood Press, 1974.

Mulholland, St. Clair A. *The Story of the 116th Regiment, Pennsylvania Volunteer Infantry.* Philadelphia: F. McManus, Jr. and Co., 1899.

Murphey, Thomas G. *Four Years in the War.* Philadelphia: J. S. Claxton, 1866.

Myers, Frank M. *The Comanches: A History of White's Battalion, Virginia Cavalry, Laurel Brig., Hampton Div., A.N.V., C.S.A.* Baltimore: Kelly, Piet & Co., 1871.

Nevins, Alan, ed. *A Diary of Battle: The Personal Journals of Colonel Charles S. Wainwright, 1861-1865.* New York: Harcourt, Brace & World, 1962.

Newsome, Hampton, Horn, John, and Selby, John G., eds., *Civil War Talks: Further Reminiscences Of George S. Bernard & His Fellow Veterans.* Charlottesville, Va.: University Press of Virginia, 2012.

Nichols, James M. *Perry's Saints or the Fighting Parson's Regiment in the War of the Rebellion.* Boston: D. Lothrop and Company, 1886.

Oates, William C. *The War between the Union and the Confederacy and its lost opportunities, with a history of the 15th Alabama regiment (cited hereinafter as The War between the Union and the Confederacy.* New York: The Neale Publishing Company, 1905.

Peck, Hiram T. *Army Journal.* New Haven, Conn.: O. A. Dorman, 1874.

Polley, Joseph B. *A Soldier's Letters to Charming Nellie.* New York: The Neal Publishing Company, 1908.

———. *Hood's Texas Brigade: It's Marches, Its Battles, Its Achievements.* New York: The Neale Publishing Company, 1910.

Porter, Horace. *Campaigning with Grant.* New York: The Century Co., 1897.

Powell, William H. *The Fifth Army Corps (Army of the Potomac) A Record of Operations during the Civil War in the United States of American, 1861-1865.* New York: G. P. Putnam's Sons, 1896.

Powelson, B.F. *History of Company K of the 140th Regiment Pennsylvania Volunteers (1862-'65).* Steubenville, Oh.: The Carnahan Printing Company, 1906)

Preston, Noble D. *History of the Tenth Regiment of Cavalry, New York State Volunteers.* New York: D. Appleton and Company, 1892.

Price, Isaiah. *History of the Ninety-Seventh Regiment Pennsylvania Volunteer Infantry During the War of the Rebellion 1861-1865, With Biographical Sketches of Its Field and Staff and a Complete Service Record of Each Officer and Enlisted Man.* Philadelphia: B & E, Printers, 1875.

Proceedings, Findings and Opinions of the [Warren] Court of Inquiry. Washington, D.C.: Government Printing Office, 1883.

Publishing Committee. *A Brief History of the Fourth Veteran Pennsylvania Cavalry.* Pittsburgh: Ewens & Eberle, Book and Job Printers, 1891.

Pyne, Henry R. *The History of the First New Jersey Cavalry (Sixteenth Regiment, New Jersey Volunteers.* Trenton, N. J.: J. A. Beecher, Publisher, 1871.

Rhodes, John H. *The History of Battery B, First Regiment, Rhode Island Light Artillery, in the War to Preserve the Union, 1861-1865.* Providence: Snow & Farnham, 1894.

Roback, Henry. *The Veteran Volunteers of Herkimer and Otsego Counties in the War of the Rebellion, being a History of the 152d New York Volunteers.* Little Falls, N.Y.: Press of L. C. Childs & son, 1888.

Roe, Alfred S. *The Twenty-Fourth Regiment Massachusetts Volunteers, 1861-1866.* Worcester, Mass.: The Blanchard Press, 1907.

———. *The Thirty-Ninth Regiment Massachusetts Volunteers 1862-1865* (Worcester, Ma.: Commonwealth Press, 1914).

Rowland, Dunbar. *Military History of Mississippi, 1803-1898.* Nashville: State of Mississippi, 1908.

Scott, Kate M. *History of the One Hundred and Fifth Regiment of Pennsylvania Volunteers.* Philadelphia: New World Pub. Co., 1877.

Simons, Ezra D. *A Regimental History of the One Hundred And Twenty-Fifth New York State Volunteers.* New York: Press of the Judson Printing Co., 1888.

Simpson, Harold. *Hood's Texas Brigade: A Compendium.* Hillsboro, Texas: Hill Jr. College Press, 1977.

Small, Abner R. *The Sixteenth Maine Regiment in the War of the Rebellion, 1861-1865.* Portland, Me.: B. Thurston & Co., 1886.

Smith, John D. *The History of the Nineteenth Regiment of Maine Volunteer Infantry.* Minneapolis: Great Western Printing Co., 1909.

Sparks, David, ed. *Inside Lincoln's Army: The Diary of Marsena Rudolph Patrick, Provost Marshal General, Army of the Potomac.* New York: Thomas Yoseloff, 1964.

Stevens, C. A. *Berdan's United States Sharpshooters in the Army of the Potomac, 1861-1865.* St. Paul: The Price-McGill Company, 1892.

Stewart, Robert L. *History of the One Hundred and Fortieth Regiment Pennsylvania Volunteers.* Philadelphia: The Franklin Bindery, 1912.

Stewart, William H. *A Pair of Blankets: War-Time History In Letters To The Young People Of The South.* New York: Broadway Publishing Company, 1911.

Stowits, George H. *History of the One Hundreth Regiment of New York State Volunteers.* Buffalo: Matthews & Warren, 1870.

Survivors' Association. *History of the Corn Exchange Regiment, the 118th Pennsylvania Volunteers.* Philadelphia: J. L. Smith, 1888.

Survivors' Association. *History of the 121st Regiment Pennsylvania Volunteers, "An Account from the Ranks."* Revised Edition. Philadelphia, Pa.: Press of Catholic Standard and Times, 1906.

Swinton, William. *Campaigns of the Army of the Potomac.* New York: Charles B. Richardson, 1866.

Talbot, Edith Armstrong. *Samuel Chapman Armstrong, A Biographical Study.* New York: Doubleday, Page & Company, 1904.

Taylor, Walter H. *General Lee: His Campaigns in Virginia, 1861-1865.* Norfolk: Press of Braunworth & Company, 1906.

Thomas, Benjamin P., ed. *Three Years with Grant as Recalled by War Correspondent Sylvanus Cadwallader.* New York: Alfred A. Knopf, 1961.

Tobie, Edward P. *History of the First Maine Cavalry, 1861-1865.* Boston: Emery & Hughes, 1887.

Tower, R. Lockwood, ed. *Lee's Adjutant: The Wartime Letters of Colonel Walter Herron Taylor, 1862-1865.* Columbia, S.C.: University of South Carolina Press, 1995.

Trobriand, P. Regis d. *Four Years with the Army of the Potomac.* Boston: Ticknor and Company, 1889.

Trumbull, H. Clay. *The Knightly Soldier, A Biography of Major Henry Ward Camp.* Boston: Nichols And Noyes, 1865.

United States War Department. *The War of the Rebellion: A Compilation of the Official Records of the Union and Confederate Armies.* 128 Volumes. Washington, D.C.: U. S. Government Printing Office, 1880-1901.

Vandiver, Frank E., ed. *The Civil War Diary of General Josiah Gorgas.* Tuscaloosa: University of Alabama Press, 1947.

Vautier, John D. *History of the 88th Pennsylvania Volunteers in the War for the Union, 1861-1865.* Philadelphia: J. B. Lippincott Company, 1894.

Walker, Francis A. *History of the Second Army Corps in the Army of the Potomac.* New York: Charles Scribner's Sons, 1886.

———. *General Hancock.* New York: D. Appleton and Co., 1895.

Walkley, Stephen, comp. *History of the Seventh Connecticut Volunteer Infantry: Hawley's Brigade, Terry's Division, Tenth Army Corps, 1861-1865.* Stonington, Conn.: n. p., 1905.

Wallace, Lew, et al. *The Story of American Heroism, Thrilling Narratives of Personal Adventures during the Great Civil War as Told by the Medal Winners and Roll of Honor Men.* New York: Western W. Wilson, 1896.

Warren, Horatio N. *The Declarations of Independence and War History, Bull Run to Appomattox.* Buffalo: The Courier Company, Printers, 1894.

Washburn, George H. *A Complete Military History and Record of the 108th Regiment, N. Y. Vols.* Rochester: Press of E. R. Andrews, 1894.

Webb, Alexander S. *The Peninsula.* New York: Charles Scribner's Sons, 1881.

Welch, Spencer G. *A Confederate Surgeon's Letters to his Wife.* New York: The Neale Publishing Company, 1911.

Wells, Edward L. *Hampton and his Cavalry in '64.* Richmond, Va.: B. F. Johnson Publishing Company, 1899.

Weygant, Charles H. *History of the One Hundred and Twenty-Fourth Regiment, N.Y.S.V.* Newburgh, N.Y.: Journal Printing House, 1877.

Williams, Edward B., ed. *Rebel Brothers: The Civil War Letters of the Truehearts.* College Station: 1995.

Williams, T. P. *The Mississippi Brigade of Brig. Gen. Joseph R. Davis: A Geographical Account of Its Campaigns and a Biographical Account of Its Personalities, 1861-1865.* Dayton, Oh.: Morningside House, Inc., 1999.

Woodward, C. Vann, ed. *Mary Chesnut's Civil War.* New Haven, Conn.: Yale University Press, 1981.

Other Book Sources

Balfour, Daniel T. *13th Virginia Cavalry.* Lynchburg, Va.: H. E. Howard, Inc., 1986.

Beringer, Richard E., Hattaway, Herman, Jones, Archer, and Still, William N., Jr. *Why The South Lost The Civil War.* Athens, Ga., 1986.

Bearss, Edwin C., with Suderow, Bryce. *The Petersburg Campaign: The Eastern Front Battles, June–August 1864.* El Dorado Hills, Ca.: Savas Beatie, 2012.

Castel, Albert. *Decision in the West: The Atlanta Campaign of 1864.* Lawrence, Ks.: University Press of Kansas, 1992.

Catton, Bruce. *A Stillness at Appomattox.* Garden City, N. Y.: Doubleday, 1953.

———. *Never Call Retreat.* Garden City, N. Y.: Doubleday, 1965.

———. *Grant Takes Command.* Boston: Little, Brown 1969.

Chandler, David G. *The Campaigns of Napoleon: The Mind and Method of History's Greatest Soldier.* New York: Simon & Schuster, 1966.

Cullen, Joseph P. *The Siege of Petersburg.* Harrisburg, Pa.: Historical Times, Inc. 1970.

Delbruck, Hans. *History of the Art of War.* Translated by Walter J. Renfroe, Jr. 4 Volumes. Lincoln: University of Nebraska Press, 1975.

Dupuy, T. N. *A Genius for War: The German Army and General Staff, 1807-1945*. London: MacDonald and Jane's, 1977.

———. *The Evolution of Weapons and Warfare*. Indianapolis: The Bobbs-Merrill Company, Inc., 1980.

Evans. Clement, ed. *Confederate Military History*. 11 Volumes. Atlanta: Confederate Publishing Co., 1899.

Freeman, Douglas Southall. *R. E. Lee: A Biography*. 4 Volumes. New York: Charles Scribner's Sons, 1935.

———. *Lee's Lieutenants: A Study in Command*. 3 Volumes. New York: Charles Scribner's Sons, 1944.

Fuller, J. F. C. *The Generalship of Ulysses S. Grant*. Reprint Edition. Boston: Da Capo Press, 1991.

Horn, John. *The Petersburg Campaign: June 1864-April 1865*. Conshohocken, Pa.: Combined Books, 1993.

Jones, Richard L. *Dinwiddie County: Carrefour of the Commonwealth*. Richmond, Va.: Whittet & Shepperson, 1976.

Krick, Robert K. *9th Virginia Cavalry*. Lynchburg, Va.: H. E. Howard, Inc., 1982.

Livermore, Thomas L. *Numbers and Losses in the Civil War in America: 1861-1865*. Bloomington, In.: Indiana University Press, 1957.

Long, E. B. *The Civil War Day by Day: An Almanac, 1861-1865*. Garden City, N. Y.: Doubleday & Co., 1871.

Manarin, Louis H. *Henrico County Field of Honor*. Richmond, Va.: Carter Printing Company, 2004.

Manstein, Field Marshal Erich von. *Lost Victories: The War Memoirs of Hitler's Most Brilliant General*. Novato, Ca.: Presidio Press, 1982.

McFeely, William S. *Grant: A Biography*. New York: W. W. Norton & Company, 1981.

McPherson, James M. *Battle Cry of Freedom: The Civil War Era*. New York: Oxford University Press, 1988.

Mellenthin, F. W. von. *Panzer Battles: A Study of the Employment of Armor in the Second World War*. New York: Ballantine Books, 1971.

Montgomery of Alamein, Field Marshal Viscount. *A History of Warfare*. Cleveland: The World Publishing Company, 1968.

Newsome, Hampton. *Richmond Must Fall: The Richmond Petersburg Campaign, October 1864*. Kent, Oh.: The Kent State University Press, 2013.

Robertson, James I., Jr. *General A. P. Hill: The Story of a Confederate Warrior*. New York: Random House, Inc. 1987.

Scott, James G., and Wyatt, Edward A. *Petersburg's Story: A History*. Petersburg: Titmus Optical Co., 1960.

Silo, Mark. *The 115th New York in the Civil War: A Regimental History*. Jefferson, N.C.: McFarland & Company, Inc., 2013).

Sommers, Richard J. *Richmond Redeemed: The Siege at Petersburg*. Garden City, N. Y.: Doubleday & Company, Inc., 1981.

Taylor, Emerson G. *Gouverneur Kemble Warren: The Life and Letters of an American Soldier, 1830-1882*. Boston: Houghton Mifflin Co., 1932.

Trask, Benjamin H. *Sixteenth Virginia Infantry*. Lynchburg, Va.: H. E. Howard, Inc., 1986.

Trudeau, Noah Andre. *The Last Citadel: Petersburg, Virginia, June 1864–April 1865.* Boston: Little, Brown and Company, 1991.

Tucker, Glenn. *Hancock the Superb.* Dayton, Oh.: Morningside, Press, 1980.

Wallace, Lee A., Jr. *1st Virginia Infantry.* Lynchburg, Va.: H. E. Howard, Inc., 1984.

Warner, Ezra J. *Generals in Blue: Lives of the Union Commanders.* Baton Rouge: Louisiana State University Press, 1964.

———. *Generals in Gray: Lives of the Confederate Commanders.* Baton Rouge: Louisiana State University Press, 1959.

Williams, T. Harry. *Lincoln and his Generals.* New York: Albert A. Knopf, 1952.

———. *P. G. T. Beauregard: Napoleon in Gray.* Baton Rouge: Louisiana State University Press, 1955.

Map Sources

Cowles, Calvin D., ed. *Atlas to Accompany the Official Records of the Union and Confederate Armies.* Reprint Edition. New York: Thomas Yoseloff, Inc., 1958.

Records Group 77, Office of the Chief of Engineers, National Archives, Washington, D. C.

United States Geological Survey. Virginia 7.5 Minute Series. Carson, Dutch Gap, and Petersburg Quadrangles.

Index

Abbott, Joseph C., 88, 324
abolition, abandonment of, 3
Adams, Henry, 63
Adams, Richard H. T., 148-149
USS *Agawam*, 35
Aiken house, 142, 144-145, 150, 152, 161, 170, 181
Aiken, Hugh K., 328
Aiken's Landing, 102, 105-106
Alabama Units
4th Infantry, 93, 326
8th Infantry, 73, 75, 93, 191, 305, 327 338, 342
9th Infantry, 52, 73, 181, 275, 281n, 327, 338, 342
10th Infantry, 73, 78-79 327, 338, 342
11th Infantry, 72-73, 78-78n, 79, 103, 104n, 204n, 277n, 327, 338, 342
13th Infantry, 172n, 334-335
14th Infantry, 73, 327, 338, 342
15th Infantry, 35, 84-85, 97, 103, 113n, 326
44th Infantry, 326
47th Infantry, 326
48th Infantry, 84-85, 113n, 326
Love's Battalion, 328, 342
Alexander, Edward P., 176, 284
Allcock, Thomas, 258, 339
Anderson, Fred C., 201
Anderson, George T. "Tige," and his brigade, 298, 326; Second Deep Bottom, 38, 46n, 72-73, 82-83, 85-86, 88, 91-92, 103n, 112; casualties at Second Deep Bottom, 113n; Battle of Globe Tavern, 203-204; wrecking the Weldon Railroad, 224; Second Reams Station, 237-238, 247, 276n, 280n, 306-307
Anderson, Richard H., 5, 9, 13, 33, 311; Second Deep Bottom, 23, 32; Battle of Globe Tavern, 148; Second Reams Station, 243
Antietam, battle of, 29, 103
Appomattox River, 119, 143, 210
Armstrong, Samuel C., 98, 106
Arkansas Unit, 3rd Cavalry, 329
Arthur Swamp, 212
Aston, Howard, 166
Ayres, Romeyn B. and his division, 171, 181, 331; Battle of Globe Tavern, 122, 124-126, 129, 131-132, 134-135, 145, 147, 158, 160-161, 170, 174-175, 184-185; calls for reinforcements, 132-133

Babcock, Orville E., 8
Bailey's Creek, 10, 18, 20, 27-33, 36, 38, 40, 45, 49, 52, 82, 93, 107, 299
Baldwin, Leonard, 29
Barbour, William M., 92, 98, 299, 327, 341
Barham, Theophilus G., 43, 299
Barlow, Francis C. and his division, 46, 90, 212, 321; Second Deep Bottom, 20, 27, 29-30, 32-33, 38, 40, 43-44, 53, 65, 111, 301; strict march disciplinarian, 29; relinquishes command to Miles, 107; Battle of Globe Tavern, 203; wrecking the Weldon Railroad, 213, 217, 218-219, 292; Second Reams Station, 228, 231, 233, 264, 266, 268, 274, 295, 297, 302, 302n; *photo*, 16
Barnes, Joseph R., 161-162, 167, 332
Barringer, Rufus and his brigade, 328; Second Deep Bottom, 51, 53, 55, 63-64, 67, 101; casualties at Second Deep Bottom, 114; Battle of Globe Tavern, 202-203; wrecking the Weldon Railroad, 213; Second Reams Station, 227, 231, 233, 243, 271, 285
Bass, Frederick S., 329
"The Bastion," 79,82-83, 85-86, 91-92, 94-95, 97
Beals, Richard L. T., 66
Beauregard, Pierre G. T., 111, 119, 126-128, 137, 147, 150, 173, 182, 225, 291, 293-294, 334, 335; Battle of Globe Tavern, 171, 174, 178, 180, 183-184, 186; *photo*, 179
Beefsteak Raid, 310
Bell, Joseph R., 262
Benning, Henry L., 23-24, 72, 91, 93, 113n, 115
Bermuda Hundred, 6-7, 9-10, 21-22, 38, 104, 112, 115, 210, 212, 223, 225, 287n
Bernard, George S., 171, 226, 263
Billings, John D., 221, 235, 240-241
Bird, Henry Van Leuvenigh, 168-171, 262-263
Birney, David B. and his corps, 16, 49, 324; Second Deep Bottom, 20, 22, 33-36, 38, 44-45, 48, 52-53, 56, 58, 64-65, 67, 69, 71, 88, 90, 93-94, 96, 102, 104, 295; Battle of Globe Tavern, 136, 176, 210; wrecking the Weldon Railroad, 212; Second Reams Station, 294-295; *photo*, 34
Birney, William and his division, 56, 296, 298, 324; Second Deep Bottom, 33, 35, 44-45, 53, 55, 57n, 65, 88, 90-91, 111, 300; *photo*, 54

Index

Blick house, 124, 132, 134-135, 145, 153, 169-170, 185
Bliss, Zenas R., 173, 333
Bost, Jackson L., 261, 277n
Bottom's Bridge, 18
Bounty And Furlough Act, 11n
Bowles, Pinckney D., 326
Boydton Plank Road, 128, 207, 225
Bradshaw, Elbridge, 131
Brady, George K., 158
Brady, Jr., Robert, 21, 23, 26, 43, 52, 69, 72
Bragg, Edward S. and his brigade, 133, 332; Battle of Globe Tavern, 135, 140-143, 145-147, 150, 152-155, 159-160, 173n, 174-176, 181, 183, 185, 188-189, 191-193, 298
Branch house, 147, 149, 180, 267
Brandy Station, battle of, 108
Bratton, John and his brigade, 326; Second Deep Bottom, 23-24, 46n, 57, 86, 90, 93, 102-103, 108, 112; casualties at Second Deep Bottom, 113n; Battle of Globe Tavern, 203-204; wrecking the Weldon Railroad, 224
Broady, K. Oscar and his brigade, 257, 90, 297, 321, 339; Second Deep Bottom, 27, 38, 40, 47, 101-102, 104; wrecking the Weldon Railroad, 222; Second Reams Station, 228, 233, 237-238, 248, 255-256, 258
Brooks, Ulysses R., 218
Brown, Charles E., 170
Bruce, George A., 10
Burgwyn, William H. S., 195
Burton, John E., 45n
Butler, Benjamin F., 9, 12, 17, 18n, 38, 51, 64, 102, 106, 210, 212, 219n, 242-243, 293
Butler, Matthew C. and his division, 9-10, 13, 298, 328, 342; casualties at Second Deep Bottom, 114; Second Deep Bottom, 47, 65, 108, 111-112; Second Reams Station, 227, 271, 277n; wrecking the Weldon Railroad, 213-214, 217, 219
Calhoun, Charles M., 217
Califf, Joseph, 49
Camp Holly, 35, 84
Camp, Henry W., 96, 109
Campbell, Edward, 24n, 76, 78-79
Carr, Eugene A., 10
Carter, Henry C., 32-33, 38, 40, 299
Cayer, Ovila, 158, 247
Chaffin's Bluff, 10, 15, 18, 20, 28, 48, 64, 82, 102-103, 107, 128, 144, 196
Chambersburg, Pennsylvania, 4, 5n
Chambliss, John R. and his brigade, 328; Second Deep Bottom, 55, 62-65, 67; body returned to Confederate lines, 106; casualties at Second Deep Bottom, 114; Battle of Globe Tavern, 164; wrecking the Weldon Railroad, 212; Second Reams Station, 227, 229, 231, 271-272
Chancellorsville, battle of, 27, 53, 55, 86, 98, 133, 153, 169, 232, 261
Charles City Road, 18, 20, 42-44, 48, 50-53, 55, 57-59, 61-67, 71, 73, 100-101, 104, 107, 30
Cheek, William H., 227, 337
Chesnut, Mary B., 312
Chester, Walter T., 140-142
Chew, R. Preston, 328, 343
Chieves house, 122, 142, 145
Child, William, 62
Chisholm, Daniel, 255
Christian, William S., 153-154
Citadel Military Academy, 57
City Point explosion, 7, 9
City Point, Virginia, 3, 9-10, 17, 116, 120, 213, 243, 245-246, 291
Clark, A. Judson, 340
Clingman, Thomas L. and his brigade, 171, 336; Battle of Globe Tavern, 150-153, 158-160, 162-163, 175, 182, 191
Coan, William B., and his brigade, 324; Second Deep Bottom, 22, 38, 88, 90-91, 95, 97- 98, 300, 301-301n
Cold Harbor, battle of, 84, 154
Coleman, John Kennedy, 105
Coleman, Mike, 153
Colquitt, Alfred H., and his brigade, 171, 297, 335, 336; Battle of Globe Tavern, 128, 135, 137, 139, 150-151, 153, 155-158, 160-164, 166-167, 169, 173-173n, 175, 182, 191
Confederate Units
1st Battalion, 334-335
7th Cavalry, 335-336
Connecticut Units
1st Battery, 35, 325
6th Infantry, 24, 36, 70, 80, 83-84, 92, 324
7th Infantry, 45n, 70-71, 80, 82, 84, 88, 324
10th Infantry, 22-24, 26, 45n, 67, 71, 79, 84, 96, 108-109, 324
14th Infantry, 233, 267, 274, 322, 340
20th Infantry, 35
29th Colored Infantry, 49, 90, 102-103
Conner, James, and his detachment, 236, 327; Second Deep Bottom, 18, 23, 73, 91-92, 95, 97-98, 108, 305; Second Reams Station, 252
Conyngham, D. P., 32
Cook, John E., 134
Cooke, Charles M., 129
Cooke, John R., and his brigade, 337, 341; Battle of Globe Tavern, 182-183, 193, 195, 197, 204n,

306; wrecking the Weldon Railroad, 224; Second Reams Station, 246-247, 252-256, 258-259, 261, 277n, 280n, 285, 306
Cooke, Phillip St. George, 246
Coon, David, 42
Cope, Emmor B., 141-144
Copp, Elbridge J., 80
Corbin, Richard, 38, 74, 114
Corps, Army of the Potomac
II Corps, 15-17, 20-21, 26-28, 33, 36 38, 43, 48-49, 52, 58, 64, 67-69, 72, 82, 90, 92- 93, 104, 112-113, 116, 143, 145, 148-149, 172, 176, 181-182, 203, 207, 209, 212, 219-219n, 220, 227-229, 234, 237, 243, 245, 249-250, 268-269, 274, 278-279, 280n, 282, 284, 294, 301, 302-302n, 303, 309n, 321, 339
III Corps, 294
V Corps, 104, 106, 112, 117, 119-120, 122-124, 132-133, 135-137, 139, 141, 143-144, 146- 147, 149, 154, 160, 163, 170, 173-176, 181-182, 185-186, 202, 207, 209, 213, 219, 244-245, 249, 290-291, 295, 299, 303-303n, 304-304n, 330
VI Corps, 73, 148, 220
IX Corps, 111, 117, 119, 122, 135, 136-136n, 137, 140-145, 160-163, 168-170, 174, 181- 182, 203, 210, 219, 244-245, 304-304n, 332
X Corps, 16-17, 19-23, 26-28, 32, 35-36, 38, 43-44, 48-53, 56, 60, 71, 88, 90, 93, 95, 101, 104, 111-113, 115, 117, 119, 210, 212-213, 219, 223, 227, 242, 301-301n, 309n, 324
XVIII Corps, 10, 117, 119, 122, 128, 137, 140, 143, 176, 207, 210, 212-213, 219-219n, 222-223, 242, 284, 290, 309n, 325
Coulter, Richard, and his brigade, 298, 331; Battle of Globe Tavern, 117, 125, 131, 135, 141, 144, 146, 154-155, 159, 170, 173n, 175
Coward, Asbury, 57-58, 86, 88, 94
Craig, Calvin A., and his brigade, 88, 298, 323; Second Deep Bottom, 53-56, 68-69, 71, 83-86, 88, 90, 102, 104, 301, 302n
Crandell, Levin, and his brigade, 297, 321, 339; Second Deep Bottom, 32, 228, 231, 234, 237, 248, 252-253, 255-256, 259-261, 268, 275; wrecking the Weldon Railroad, 222
Crater, battle of the, 1, 7, 15, 24, 73, 100, 103, 119, 149, 164, 168, 191, 222, 281n, 300
Crater, Lewis, 144
Crawford, Samuel W., and his division, 296, 133, 331; Battle of Globe Tavern, 117, 122, 125-125n, 126, 131, 134-135, 140-142, 145-147, 150n, 153, 155, 159-160, 170, 174-176, 182, 188, 195, 197; Second Reams Station, 245, 275
Culpeper Court House, 5, 9, 12-13, 47
Culpepper, James M., 157-158

Curtin, John I., 333
Cutler, Lysander, 122, 132-134, 185, 199, 331
Dailey, Dennis B., 199-201
Daniels, Percy, 333
Darbytown Road, 28, 30, 32-33, 38, 58, 67, 72-72n, 73, 75, 80, 82-82n, 85, 92-93, 107
Davenport, John I., 17
Davis farm and house, 125-126, 128-129, 132, 134-135, 137, 144-145, 153-154, 160, 180, 183-184, 186, 188, 193, 195-196, 203
Davis, J. Lucius, 328, 343
Davis, James L., 63
Davis, James T., 197
Davis, Jefferson, President, 3, 6, 13, 63, 107, 129, 205, 290
Davis, John E., 100
Davis, Joseph R. and his brigade, 149, 172n, 334-335; Battle of Globe Tavern, 128, 130, 138n, 139, 153, 82, 306; Second Deep Bottom, 305
Day, William A., 196
De Graff, Nicholas, 106, 109
de Trobriand, P. Regis, 323
Dearing, James, and his brigade, 335-336; Battle of Globe Tavern, 119, 123, 126-129, 138n, 149, 171
Deep Bottom Road, 18, 22-23
Defnal, W. I., 97
Delaware Units
1st Infantry, 231-232, 235, 267, 322, 340
2nd Battalion, 267
2nd Infantry, 322, 340
3rd Infantry, 199-200, 332
4th Infantry, 332
Department of North Carolina and Southern Virginia, 13n, 119
Department of Richmond, 7, 13n, 18-8n, 72, 114
Department of South Carolina, George and Florida, 13n
Department of Virginia, 18n
Depot Road, 214, 217, 220-221, 223, 226, 229, 231-232, 234-237, 239, 247-249, 252, 256, 258, 262, 266-267, 282
Deserted House, 203
Dillard, R. K., 9
Dimmock Line, 149, 180
Dinwiddie Court House, 126, 207, 223-225, 285, 290-291
District of Columbia Unit
1st Cavalry, 248, 334, 341
Doty, Albert, 167-168
Douglas, Stephen A., 133
Draper, A. H., 78
Drewry's Bluff, 47-48, 147
DuBose, Dudley M., and his brigade, 86, 88, 91, 94, 298-299, 326

Index 361

Dulany, Richard H., and his brigade, 108, 111, 214, 328, 342
Duncan, R. P., 163
Dunlop house, 142, 155, 170, 182
Dunlop, William S., 237, 240
Dunn, Washington L., 173
Dunovant, John, and his brigade, 217, 227 342
Dushane, Nathan T., and his brigade, 129, 175, 188, 331
Dusseault, John H., 131, 159
Dutch Gap, 9-10, 18, 64, 102, 105-106
Early, Jubal A., 1, 3-5, 10, 17, 28, 47, 112, 311
Eastern revine, 68, 71, 84, 100
Edwards, Albert M., 192
Egolf, Joseph, 264, 270
Eldredge, Daniel, 80
Ellis, Horace A., 193
Embler, A. Henry, 266
Evans, Andrew W., 46n
Ewell, Richard S., 13n, 18n
Fagan, W. L., 191
Farwell, James C., 40
Field, Charles W., and his division, 13-14, 72, 108, 298, 326; Second Deep Bottom, 18, 28, 32-33, 35, 39, 47-48, 57, 73-75, 82, 112, 305; casualties at Second Deep Bottom, 113-113n, 114-115; Battle of Globe Tavern, 180, 184, 203-204; wrecking the Weldon Railroad, 224
Fielding, William E., 52, 181, 275, 280n, 295
Finegan, Joseph, 182-183, 187, 192, 204n, 338
First Bull Run, battle of, 140
First Deep Bottom, 290, 300
First Reams Station, 220, 224, 268
Fisher farm, 44, 51, 61
Fisher, Adoniram J., 95
Fisher's Run, 51, 55, 62, 67, 101-102, 107
Fitch, D. B., 29
Five Forks, battle of, 209, 298
Fleming, James, 45n
Florida Units
2nd Infantry, 204n, 338
5th Infantry, 204n, 338
8th Infantry, 204n, 338
9th Infantry, 204n, 338
10th Infantry, 204n, 338
11th Infantry, 204n, 338
Florida Brigade, 73
Flowers, Thomas, and his house, 134, 188, 190
Fort Harrison, 291
Fort Powatan, 213, 246, 291
Fort Sedgwick, 149
Fortress Monroe, 4

Foster, Robert S. and his brigade, 6, 300, 324; Second Deep Bottom, 19, 22-24, 36, 44-45, 49, 51-52, 67-70, 79, 90, 96-98, 100, 108; casualties at Second Deep Bottom, 114-115
Four Mile Creek, 6, 18, 20, 22-23, 26, 33, 35-36, 38, 44-45, 48-49, 102
Fourth Offensive, 207, 244, 283, 308-309, 311
Fowle, George E., 157
Frayser's Farm, battle of, 108
Fredericksburg, battle of, 305
Fremont, John C., 3
Fussell's Mill, 18, 20, 28, 32-33, 40, 43, 46, 48, 52, 57, 64-65, 67, 70, 72, 90, 93 101, 111, 282, 301
Fussell's Mill Pond, 45, 51-53, 56, 58, 60, 64, 67-69, 72-73, 90, 92, 102, 104, 106-108, 119, 180, 294-301
Galloway, John M., 202
Gary, Martin W., 28, 42-43, 57, 65, 101, 114-115, 329
Georgia Units
2nd Battalion, 77, 327, 337
2nd Infantry, 173n, 326
3rd Infantry, 327, 337
6th Cavalry, 157
6th Infantry, 335-336
7th Cavalry, 65, 114, 227, 328-329, 342
7th Infantry, 72, 82, 91, 93, 326, 341
8th Infantry, 72, 82, 86, 88, 91, 94, 326, 341
9th Infantry, 38, 48, 73, 74, 82, 326, 341
10th Battalion, 77, 78n, 327, 337
11th Infantry, 73, 326, 341
15th Infantry, 86, 326
17th Infantry, 93, 326
19th Infantry, 335-336
20th Infantry, 86, 326
22nd Infantry, 327, 337
23rd Infantry, 173n, 335-336
27th Infantry, 173-173n, 335-336
28th Infantry, 335-336
48th Infantry, 78, 113n, 327, 337
59th Infantry, 25, 72, 82, 86, 88, 91, 94, 113n, 326, 341
62nd Infantry, 335-336
64th Infantry, 77-78, 327, 337
Cobb's Legion, 108, 328, 342
Millen's Battalion, 328, 342
Phillips Legion, 328, 342
Gettysburg, battle of, 29, 86, 98, 103, 131, 153, 261
Gibbon, John, and his corps, Second Deep Bottom, 20, 27, 29, 40, 43, 46, 92, 111; Battle of Globe Tavern, 203; wrecking the Weldon Railroad, 219-222, 292; Second Reams Station, 228-229, 231, 233-234, 251, 266-267, 268, 270-274, 278, 282, 297, 302-302n, 303; bad blood with Hancock, 279; *photo*, 16

Gibson, William, 78, 327, 337, 340
Ginley, Patrick, 264
Girardey, Victor J. B., 73, 77-78, 180, 327
Glendale, battle of, 108
Glenny, William, 339
Globe Tavern, battle of, 116, 122, 124, 126-129, 131-133, 135, 141, 143, 149, 152, 154-158, 160-164, 166-167, 170-171, 172-172n, 175-176, 182, 185, 188, 193, 196, 202-203, 205, 211, 224-225, 227, 245-247, 261, 274-275, 279, 282-283, 287, 290-291, 295-296, 298-300, 303- 306, 308
Goodman's farm, 44
Gorgas, Josiah, 312
Gosse, Albert, 45n
Graham, Robert D., 195-196
Graham, Samuel A., 188, 331
Grant, Ulysses S., 9n, 14, 28, 112, 224, 308, 313; appalling casualies in the Overland Campaign, 1; believed in overwhelming numbers, 2; criticized by Halleck, 3-4; never lost sight of the overall view, 4; lays out foundation for victory, 5; City Point explosion, 7, 9; Vicksburg, 7; issues new directives, 10; decides to take offensive, 15; Hancock's expedition to the north side of the James, 16; third offensive ends, 16; Fourth Offensive, 17, 207, 244, 283, 290, 308-309, 311; tries to force Lee to withdraw Early, 17; Second Deep Bottom, 21, 35-36, 38, 64, 102, 104-105; steamboat scheme, 27; August 14 a disappointing day, 47; fears Lee is reinforcing Early, 47; orders a raid on the Weldon Railroad, 106; orders Hancock to attack with entire force, 111; orders Warren to desroy the Weldon Railroad, 120, 122; intends to reinforce Warren, 136; Globe Tavern, 139, 172, 298; Battle of Globe Tavern, 144, 146-147, 174, 176, 205, 209; opinion of Warren, 209; sacks Warren, 210; wants Weldon Railroad wrecked, 211; suspends X Corps attack on Bermuda Hundred, 212; orders X corps to relieve XVIII Corps, 213; V Corps disaster on Aug. 19, 213; wrecking the Weldon Railroad, 219, 225; misunderstanding with Meade, 231; Second Reams Station, 242-243, 246, 276, 282, 284, 292, 304; August casualties, 287n, 289; Ben Butler, 293; casualties, 310; forces Lee to recall forces, 311; *photo*, 288
Gravelly Run, engagement at, 213
Gray, Robert J. and his brigade, 91, 299, 324
Gregg, David McM., and his division, 16, 296, 325, 340; Second Deep Bottom, 19, 42, 44, 58, 62-65, 67, 71, 100-101, 104, 108, 111, 303-303n; casualties at Second Deep Bottom, 113; Battle of Globe Tavern, 116, 182; wrecking the Weldon Railroad, 213, 217-218, 219n, 222; Second Reams Station, 228-231, 233, 237, 244, 248, 274-275, 303;
Gregg, J. Irwin, and his brigade, 325-326; Second Deep Bottom, 18, 44, 50-51, 61-62, 64, 72, 75, 101, 108; casualties at Second Deep Bottom, 113n, 115; Battle of Globe Tavern, 204
Gregory, Edgar M., 122-124, 134, 160, 330
Griffin, Charles, 122, 181, 330; Battle of Globe Tavern, 117, 122, 124, 133-134, 155, 160, 170, 173, 175-176, 184, 190, 194, 198-199, 202
Griffin, Simon G., 333
Griswold, Edward, 35
Groner, Virginius, 169
Gurley house, 120, 122, 143, 148, 204, 275
Gwyn, James, and his brigade, 330; Battle of Globe Tavern, 117, 124, 133-134, 160, 170, 176, 194, 198, 201
Haddon house, 231
Hagood, James R., 299
Hagood, Johnson and his brigade, Second Deep Bottom, 46n; Battle of Globe Tavern, 178-180, 183, 187-188, 190-191, 197-200, 201, 203, 205n; wrecking the Weldon Railroad, 219; Globe Tavern, 306
Haines, Benjamin F., 150n
Haines, William P., 232
Halfway House, 47
Halifax Road, 126, 135, 160, 178, 183, 186, 188, 227, 229, 231, 248-249, 256, 259, 267, 273, 294
Hall, Delos E., 125n
Hall, Isaac, 177
Halleck, Henry W. "Old Brains," 3-5, 106
Hamil, John W., 38, 48, 74
Hamlin, James H., 45n
Hampton, Wade, and his corps, 9-10, 107, 310-311, 328, 342; wrecking the Weldon Railroad, 223-224, 226; Second Reams Station, 227, 231-233, 247, 270, 271-273, 275, 280n, 281n, 291, 295-296; cattle raid, 244; August casualties, 290; *photo*, 215
Hancock, Winfield S., 15-16, 90, 321, 339; Second Deep Bottom, 18, 26-29, 34, 44, 46, 48, 51-53, 57, 60, 64-65, 73, 92-93, 102, 104, 107-108, 112; Gettysburg, 29; August 14 a disappointing day, 47; disgusted with Birney, 58 Grant orders a raid on the Weldon Railroad, 106, 111; forces don't take Richmond, 112; Battle of Globe Tavern, 136, 144, 209; wrecking the Weldon Railroad, 220, 222, 223, 224; Second Reams Station, 227-229, 232, 234, 237, 243, 244-246, 249-251,

Index 363

256, 258, 263, 266-268, 270, 274-276, 278, 279n, 281-284, 302; misunderstatding with Meade, 245; bad blood with Gibbon, 279, *photo*, 16
Hanover Court House, 261
Hardaway, Robert A., 327
Hardenbeergh, Henry M., 76, 78-78n
Harney, George, 133-135, 185
Harris, James G., 260
Harris, John L., and his brigade, 337; Second Deep Bottom, 104, 107-109; casualties at Second Deep Bottom, 114n; Battle of Globe Tavern, 137, 147, 180, 183, 187, 192- 194, 204n; Globe Tavern, 306
Harris, Nathaniel H., and his detachment, 107, 327
Hartranft, John F., and his brigade, 333; Battle of Globe Tavern, 160-162, 164, 166, 170, 173n, 176
Hartshorne, William R., and his brigade, 146, 331; Battle of Globe Tavern, 125, 134-135, 141, 144, 147, 150n, 153, 159, 170, 164; Second Reams Station, 261
Hascall, Langdon, 262
Haskell, Alexander C., 30, 101, 299, 329
Hatcher's Run, 225
Hawley, Joseph R., and his brigade, 324; Second Deep Bottom, 22, 24, 33, 35, 37, 44, 67, 70-71, 80, 82-84, 86, 88, 90, 98, 107n
Hayes, Joseph, and his brigade, 171, 331; Battle of Globe Tavern, 124, 126, 129-130, 132-133, 144-146 153-154, 158-159, 170, 174-175, 181, 185, 188, 193, 195, 157
Henry, Robert R., 163-164
Heth, Henry, and his division, 171, 172n, 334-335, 337, 341; Battle of Globe Tavern, 119, 128-129, 132-135, 137, 138-138n, 139, 151-154, 163, 176, 182, 184, 193-194, 204n; Globe Tavern, 149, 170, 306; wrecking the Weldon Railroad, 224-225; Second Reams Station, 238-239, 246-247, 251, 261-262, 277n, 280n, 297; August casualties, 287n; Second Deep Bottom, 305
Hill, Ambrose P., 128, 148-149, 163, 334-335, 337, 341; Battle of Globe Tavern, 119, 176, 178-180, 182-184, 188, 190, 192-193, 202; Globe Tavern, 171, 295; wrecking the Weldon Railroad, 224-226; Second Reams Station, 227, 229, 232-233, 235, 238-239, 246-247, 251, 268, 270-271, 276n, 280n, 281n, 297; *photo*, 230
Hill, Daniel H., 294
Hill, Jonathan A., 97
Hofmann, J. William, and his brigade, 133, 332; Battle of Globe Tavern, 122n, 132, 134, 145, 153-154, 158, 185, 192, 199
Hogg, George, 30, 30n, 31-32

Hoke, Robert F. and his division, 119, 150, 178, 182, 287n, 306
Holland, Gold G., 260, 276n, 281n
Holt, David E., 109
Hood, John Bell, 2, 10
Hottenstine, Soloman J., 159
House, M. C., 159
Howard, Wiley C., 273
Howell, Joshua B., 324
Howlett Line, 112, 115, 225
Hudnut, James M., 45n, 284
Hughs, John M., 102-103, 326
Hulser, Oscar F., 45n
Humphrey, William, and his brigade, 333; Battle of Globe Tavern, 161, 166, 170, 173n; Second Reams Station, 274, 280n
Humphreys, Andrew A., 117, 120, 122, 137, 139-140, 143-144, 174, 176-177, 244, 281n, 293-294; *photo*, 118
Hunt, Isaac F., 327, 341
Hunter, David, 3, 5
Hurt, William B., 251-252
Hyde, Joseph, 222, 237, 339
Hyndman, William, 268
Illinois Units
37th Infantry, 143
39th Infantry, 24, 49, 70, 72n, 76, 78, 84, 287n, 324
Indiana Units
7th Infantry, 141, 152, 332
11th Infantry, 22
13th Infantry, 79, 324
19th Infantry, 146-147, 150, 152, 181, 298, 332;
20th Infantry, 323
Izlar, William V., 190, 200
Jackson, Thomas J. "Stonewall," 2
James River Flotilla, 9
Jayne, Joseph M., 107, 187, 327, 337
Jennings, James T., 154
Jerusalem Plank Road, 47, 52, 57-58, 73, 117, 119, 122-123, 136, 138-138n, 140, 142, 147-149, 152, 163, 204, 220, 231, 233, 237, 244-245, 249-250, 275
Jewett, Albert H. C., 91
Johnson farm and road, 82, 85, 125, 136, 141, 146, 148-150, 161, 169
Johnson, Bushrod R., and his brigade, Second Deep Bottom, 18, 72, 102, 109-111; casualties at Second Deep Bottom, 115; Battle of Globe Tavern, 119-120, 128, 178, 182, 193; August casualties, 287n
Johnson, Nathan, 90, 324
Johnston, Joseph E., 13

Jones Hole Swamp, 220, 228, 249, 266
Jones house, 142-143
Jones' Neck, 10, 49, 143; *photo*, 50
Jones, George W., 138n
Jones, John B., 312
Jones, Willis F., 74
Jordan, Willliam C., 35, 103
Judson, Amos M., 117, 198
Kahler, Francis M., 45n
Kautz, August V., and his division, 117, 119-120, 137, 141, 304
Kershaw, Joseph B., 5, 13, 243
Kerwin, Michael, 62, 65, 325
King, J. Horace, 327, 338, 342
Kingsland Road, 18, 20, 23, 33, 36, 44-45, 55, 102
Kinsley, Willard C., 131
Knower, William B., 214
Lane, James H., and his brigade, 44, 259-260, 281n, 299; Second Deep Bottom, 23, 52, 73-75, 81-82, 92, 94, 98, 104, 108; casualties at Second Deep Bottom, 113n; Battle of Globe Tavern, 184; wrecking the Weldon Railroad, 224; Second Reams Station, 235-236, 238, 247, 252-254, 259-261, 266, 276, 276n, 277n, 280n, 285, 306
Langley, Frank H., 104, 107, 111, 326
Lanier farm and house, 163, 182, 231, 234, 270-271
Law, Evander M., and his brigade, 84, 104n; Second Deep Bottom, 23-24, 35, 72, 90, 93, 112; casualties at Second Deep Bottom, 113n; Battle of Globe Tavern, 203-204; wrecking the Weldon Railroad, 224
Lead Works, 178, 183-184, 187
Lee, Robert E., 2, 5n, 17, 47, 75, 86, 100, 102, 104-105, 107, 119-120, 182, 184, 196, 203, 223-225, 228, 245, 285, 291, 308, 311, 337; indirect strategy, 3; Grant's reinforcements to the Shenandoah, 5; sends troops to Early, 9, 28; moves to Chaffin's Bluff, 52; visits New Market Heights, 57-58; looking for wounded men, 93-94; moves to Petersburg, 112; orders Wilcox's division to Petersburg, 112; Weldon Railroad, 128; writes off Weldon Railroad as indefensible, 137-138; Battle of Globe Tavern, 147, 173, 183, 204-205; feels Grant will settle for a siege, 205; feels Grant will settle for a siege, 206; loss of the Weldon Railroad, 207; wrecking the Weldon Railroad, 225; Second Reams Station, 227, 243, 246; Second Reams Station, 286; August casualties, 290; *photo*, 292
Lee, W. H. F. "Rooney," and his division, 5, 13-14, 63, 171, 328, 343; Second Deep Bottom, 47, 51, 57, 64-65, 107-108, 111-112; Battle of Globe Tavern, 137, 180; wrecking the Weldon Railroad, 211; Second Reams Station, 227, 243; 277n
Leonard, William E., 78
Lincoln, Abraham, President, 3-4, 5-5n, 207, 212, 282, 293, 310, 312-313
Little, Francis H., 73, 341; Second Deep Bottom, 74, 92, 94, 104; Second Reams Station, 238
Locke, F. T., 219n
Locke, William H., 117
Lockley, Frederck E., 47
Long Bridge Road, 18, 20, 22, 29-30, 44, 53, 82n, 108
Longstreet, James, 5, 148
Lowther, Alexander A., 84
Ludlow, Benjamin C., 102, 325
Lydall, Henry, 267-268, 274-275
Lyle, Peter, and his brigade, 331; Battle of Globe Tavern, 122, 125-126, 129, 131-132, 134-135, 141, 144, 146, 153-157, 159, 170, 175, 177
Lyman III, Theodore, 138, 145-146, 174-175, 203, 299, 308, 308n
Lynch, James C., and his brigade, 30, 213, 228, 321, 339
MacRae, William, and his brigade, 299, 337, 341; Battle of Globe Tavern, 182-183, 193-197, 204n; wrecking the Weldon Railroad, 224; Second Reams Station, 246-247, 252, 254-259, 262, 266, 277n, 280n, 285, 298, 306; Globe Tavern, 306; *photo*, 254
Macy, George N., and his brigade, 45n, 297, 322; Second Deep Bottom, 27, 29, 40-41, 45-46, 301-301n; Second Reams Station, 231, 233-235, 237, 241, 248, 266-267, 270, 296
Mahone, William, and his brigade, 296, 336-337; Second Deep Bottom, 47, 52, 73, 104, 107-108, 111-112, 305; Battle of Globe Tavern, 119-120, 137, 145, 147-148, 150-155, 162-164, 168-170, 173-176, 180-184, 187-191, 193-195, 197, 202-203, 204n; casualties at Second Deep Bottom, 113; proposed plan of attack, 148; Globe Tavern, 149, 298, 306; Lee's most effective division commander, 149; Second Reams Station, 224, 243, 280n; August casualties, 287n, 290, 293; *photo*, 148
Maker, J. Crosby, 46n
Maine Units
1st Cavalry, 44, 62-63, 65-66, 213, 248, 325, 340
1st Heavy Artillery, 323
6th Battery, Light Artillery, 40, 92, 322
9th Infantry, 91, 324
11th Infantry, 21-22, 24, 26, 43, 45n, 52, 68-69, 72-73, 79, 84, 91, 94-95, 97-98, 324
16th Infantry, 125-126, 129-130, 132, 331

17th Infantry, 323
19th Infantry, 27, 42, 248, 266-267, 322, 340
20th Infantry, 330
31st Infantry, 333
32nd Infantry, 333
Malone's Crossing, 222, 227, 229, 231, 233, 270
Malvern Hill, battle of, 86
Marshall, Charles, 75
Martin, Benjamin, 199
Martin, William J., 193, 197
Maryland Units
1st Cavalry, 23-24, 46n, 51, 68-69, 79, 84, 96-97, 108, 324
1st Infantry, 22, 129-130, 181, 331
2nd Battalion, 181, 334-335
2nd Infantry, 333
3rd Battalion, 332
3rd Infantry, 162
4th Infantry, 191, 331
7th Infantry, 191, 331
8th Infantry, 331
Maryland Brigade, 124, 126, 129-130, 132-134, 145, 185, 188, 193-194
Purnell Legion, 194, 331
Massachusetts Units
1st Battery, Light Artillery, 126
1st Cavalry, 202, 325, 334, 340
1st Heavy Artillery, 53, 68, 84, 323
1st Light Artillery, Battery C, 124, 130, 171
1st Sharpshooters, 322, 340
2nd Infantry, 161
3rd Battery, Light Artillery, 189, 332
4th Cavalry, 325
5th Battery, Light Artillery, 332
9th Battery, Light Artillery, 143, 221, 233-235, 240-241, 251, 255-256, 258, 266, 332
9th Infantry, 155
10th Battery, Light Artillery, 340
10th Infantry, 167
11th Battery, Light Artillery, 202, 333
11th Infantry, 323
14th Battery, Light Artillery, 332
18th Infantry, 201, 330
19th Infantry, 248, 266-267, 322, 340
20th Infantry, 11n, 29, 40, 248, 258, 322, 340
21st Infantry, 332
22nd Infantry, 53
24th Infantry, 22-24, 26, 46n, 68, 79, 84, 89, 96-97, 324
28th Infantry, 45n, 228, 321, 339
29th Infantry, 169, 332
32nd Infantry, 330, 167, 177, 332
36th Infantry, 333

39th Infantry, 122, 125-126, 131-132, 156-157, 159, 177, 331
56th Infantry, 332
57th Infantry, 167-168, 332-333
59th Infantry, 332
Maxwell, John, 9
Mayo, Robert M., and his brigade, 129, 153, 334-335
McAllister, Robert, 250; Second Reams Station, 244-245, 249, 274-275
McAlpine, Charles R., 173n
McClendon, W. A., 97, 100
McCoull house, 44
McDonald, William N,, 214
McGilvery, Freeman, 325
McGowan, Samuel, and his brigade, 13, 281n; Second Deep Bottom, 23-24, 52, 73, 92, 94, 97, 104, 108; casualties at Second Deep Bottom, 113n; Battle of Globe Tavern, 184; wrecking the Weldon Railroad, 224; Second Reams Station, 235-236, 238-240, 246-247, 262-264, 266, 268
McKethan, A. A., 159
McKethan, Hector, 162, 336
McNight, George F., 261
Mead, James P., 142, 145
Meade, George G., 3, 111, 119, 308; Second Deep Bottom, 18n, 299; orders Hancock to move at short notice, 116; misreads Grant, 120; orders Warren to destroy the Weldon Railroad, 120; V corps must fend for itself, 136; Battle of Globe Tavern, 137-141, 143, 145-147, 174, 176, 181, 185, 207, 209; Globe Tavern, 172, 175, 295, 298; planned to sack Warren, 209; resents Warren, 209; wrecking the Weldon Railroad, 212, 219-220, 223; V Corps disaster on Aug. 19, 213; misunderstanding with Grant, 231; Second Reams Station, 243-246, 249-250, 275, 278-279, 280n, 282-283, 294; misunderstatding with Hancock, 245; failure to withdraw Hancock's force, 283; August casualties, 290; Ben Butler, 293; *photo*, 242
Medal of Honor, 78, 287n; *Charles E. Brown*, 170, *Fred C. Anderson*, 201, *George W. Reed*, 197, *Horace A. Ellis*, 193, *James T. Jennngs*, 154, *John F. Hartranft*, 160, *John Shilling*, 202, *Nelson A. Miles*, 53, *Orlando B. Willcox*, 141, *Ovila Cayer*, 158, *Patrick Ginley*, 264, *Solomon J. Hottenstine*, 159
Merrill, Simeon H., 97
Mexican War, 5, 27, 50, 82, 122, 130-131, 140-141, 162, 184, 227, 235
Michigan Units
1st Infantry, 123n, 330
1st Sharpshooters, 333

2nd Infantry, 333
4th Infantry, 88
5th Infantry, 53, 57n, 68-69, 84-85, 323
7th Cavalry, 270
7th Infantry, 42, 233-234, 322, 340
8th Infantry, 333
16th Infantry, 330
17th Infantry, 333
20th Infantry, 333
24th Infantry, 152, 192, 332
26th Infantry, 61, 64, 228, 321, 339
27th Infantry, 333
Miles, Nelson A., and his division, 53, 63, 100, 203, 212, 234, 297, 321, 339; Second Deep Bottom, 20, 58, 60-61, 64-65, 67, 101-102, 104, 301, 302n; Medal of Honor, 53; Barlow relinquishes division, 107; wrecking the Weldon Railroad, 213, 218, 222; Second Reams Station, 228, 234, 238, 241, 248-249, 259-261, 266, 268, 272-274, 282, 297, 302-302n; *photo*, 16
Miller, Edwin C., 94-96
Minnesota Units
1st Infantry, 40, 42, 248, 259, 322
Mississippi Units
2nd Infantry, 334-335
11th Infantry, 334-335
12th Infantry, 192-193, 327, 337
16th Infantry, 109, 192-193, 327, 337
19th Infantry, 107, 327, 337
26th Infantry, 334-335
42nd Infantry, 334-335
48th Infantry, 107, 187, 327, 337
Jeff Davis Legion, 328, 342
Mitchell, William G., 21, 27
Moloney, P. K., 199
Monk's Neck Bridge, 213-214, 223, 225-226, 229, 303
Monocacy Station, 5
Moore, E. Lewis, 71
Morgan, Charles H., 26, 274
Morrison, Gardner L., 213-214
Mott, Gershom, and his division, 38, 68, 172, 323; Second Deep Bottom, 20, 27, 29, 36, 46, 49, 53, 92, 93, 111-112; casualties at Second Deep Bottom, 115; Battle of Globe Tavern, 136-137, 143-145, 176, 181-182, 207; Second Reams Station, 243, 244, 245
Murphy, Matthew, and his brigade, 264, 322, 340; Second Reams Station, 266-267, 272, 231, 233, 235, 237, 248 264
Myers, Frank M., 264
New Hampshire Units

2nd Heavy Artillery, 65
2nd Infantry, 70
3rd Infantry, 45n, 67, 80, 82-84, 92, 107n, 324
4th Infantry, 91, 324
5th Infantry, 61-62, 64, 228, 321, 339
6th Infantry, 333
7th Infantry, 70, 80, 84, 88, 92, 324
9th Infantry, 333
11th Infantry, 333
13th Infantry, 10, 11n
New Jersey Units
1st Cavalry, 116, 203, 211, 325, 334, 340
1st Infantry, 55
1st Light Artillery, Battery B, 323
3rd Battery, Light Artillery, 228, 234, 247, 251, 255, 264, 266, 270, 273, 340
4th Battery, Light Artillery, 72, 325
5th Infantry, 323
6th Infantry, 323
7th Infantry, 323
8th Infantry, 323
11th Infantry, 244, 323
12th Infantry, 232-233, 247, 266-267, 279n, 322, 340
New Market Heights, 7, 10, 17-18, 23-24, 26, 28, 32-35, 38, 56-59, 64, 82-84, 93, 104-105, 295, 299
New Market Road, 10, 20, 27, 36, 82, 102
New York Stock Exchange, 1
New York Times, 3
New York Units
1st Light Artillery, Battery B, 332
1st Light Artillery, Battery C, 332
1st Light Artillery, Battery D, 332
1st Light Artillery, Battery G, 72, 322
1st Light Artillery, Battery H, 135, 332
1st Light Artillery, Battery L, 332
1st Sharpshooters, 141, 152, 332
2nd Heavy Artillery, 30-30n, 31, 45n, 64, 228, 321, 339
2nd Mounted Rifles, (dismounted), 333
4th Heavy Artillery, 30, 213-214, 219n, 221, 228, 240, 255, 258, 262, 264, 271, 276n, 302n, 321, 339
5th Infantry, 124, 158, 171, 195, 331
7th Heavy Artillery, 47, 234, 240, 258, 321, 339
7th Infantry, 234, 255-256, 321, 339
8th Cavalry, 135
8th Heavy Artillery, 45n, 266, 268, 278, 284, 322, 340
10th Battalion, 235, 267
10th Cavalry, 202, 325, 334, 340
10th Infantry, 322, 340
11th Battery, Light Artillery, 40, 45n, 321
12th Battery, Light Artillery, 228, 340, 249, 252-253, 255, 259-261, 264, 266, 268, 282, 297, 302
12th Infantry, 90

12th Militia, 29
14th Heavy Artillery, 332
15th Battery, Light Artillery, 135, 188-190, 332
15th Heavy Artillery, 124, 132-133, 145, 154, 158, 181, 185, 331
15th Infantry, 153
19th Battery, Light Artillery, 333
24th Cavalry (dismounted), 333
39th Infantry, 234, 256, 321, 339
40th Infantry, 323
44th Infantry, 330
46th Infantry, 333
47th Infantry, 324
48th Infantry, 33, 95, 97, 324
51st Infantry, 333
52nd Infantry, 234, 256, 321, 339
53rd Infantry, 297
57th Infantry, 234, 321, 339
59th Infantry, 42, 45n, 233-234, 270, 321-322, 340
61st Infantry, 45n, 228, 237, 274, 321, 339
63rd Infantry, 32, 234, 321, 339
64th Infantry, 321, 339
66th Infantry, 45n, 256-258, 260, 321, 339
69th Infantry, 32, 234, 248, 339
72nd Infantry, 323
73rd Infantry, 323
76th Infantry, 134, 332
86th Infantry, 323
88th Infantry, 32, 234, 321, 339
93rd Infantry, 53,68, 83-84, 90, 323
94th Infantry, 125n, 154, 331-332
97th Infantry, 125n, 132, 150n, 155, 177, 331
100th Infantry, 22, 36, 38, 46n, 49, 51, 68, 71, 79, 84, 93 96-97, 100, 108, 114, 324
104th Infantry, 132, 331
108th Infantry, 232, 235, 267, 322, 340
109th Infantry, 333
111th Infantry, 234, 237, 321, 339
115th Infantry, 90-91, 106, 109, 324
120th Infantry, 323
124th Infantry, 45n, 323
125th Infantry, 222, 234, 237, 259, 264, 284, 321, 339
126th Infantry, 234, 237, 321, 339
140th Infantry, 124, 171, 195, 331
146th Infantry, 124, 171, 193-194, 331
147th Infantry, 132, 185, 332
148th Infantry, 297
152nd Infantry, 29, 241, 248-249, 259-260, 282, 297, 322, 340
153th Infantry, 42
155th Infantry, 264, 266, 322, 340
164th Infantry, 266, 268, 278, 322, 340

170th Infantry, 264, 266, 340
179th Infantry, 162, 169, 322, 332
182nd Infantry, 264, 267, 322
Newbury, Samuel S., 158
Nichols, James M., 33, 90
Nickels, James R., 275
Norfolk and Petersburg Railroad, 115, 148, 298
North Carolina Units
 1st Cavalry, 203, 231, 328, 343
 2nd Cavalry, 57n, 203, 231, 233, 270, 328, 343
 3rd Infantry, 202
 4th Cavalry, 335-336
 5th Cavalry, 231, 233, 328, 343
 5th Infantry, 202
 6th Cavalry, 335-336
 7th Infantry, 260, 265, 277n, 327, 341
 8th Infantry, 159, 336
 11th Infantry, 193, 197
 13th Infantry, 204n, 337, 341, 248, 268, 276n, 277n, 341
 15th Infantry, 246, 252, 254-255, 277n, 337, 341
 16th Infantry, 268, 277n, 341
 18th Infantry, 159, 277n, 327, 341
 22nd Infantry, 341
 24th Infantry, 194, 197, 337
 25th Infantry, 337
 26th Infantry, 204n, 277n, 337, 341
 27th Infantry, 252-253, 277n, 280n, 337, 341
 28th Infantry, 98, 260, 276, 277n, 279, 281n, 285, 327, 341
 31st Infantry, 336
 33rd Infantry, 276, 277n, 327, 341
 34th Infantry, 341
 35th Infantry, 195-196, 337
 37th Infantry, 259-261, 277n, 327, 341
 38th Infantry, 281n, 341
 44th Infantry, 204n, 256, 258, 337, 341
 46th Infantry, 252, 254-255, 277n, 337, 341
 47th Infantry, 204n,252, 257, 277n, 337, 341
 48th Infantry, 252-253, 337, 341
 49th Infantry, 196-197, 337
 51st Infantry, 159, 162, 336
 52nd Infantry, 204n, 337, 341
 55th Infantry, 129, 154, 334-335
 56th Infantry, 195-196, 204n, 337
 61st Infantry, 336
Oak Grove Church, 231, 234
Oates, William C., 84-86, 94
Ohio Units
 4th Battalion, 233, 247
 4th Infantry, 322, 340
 6th Cavalry, 325, 334, 340

6th Infantry, 182
13th Cavalry (Dismounted), 166, 333
60th Infantry, 333
62th Infantry, 24, 45n, 70, 78, 84, 324
67th Infantry, 24, 51, 70, 78, 88, 324
97th Infantry, 166
Ord, Edward O. C., 137, 219n, 222-223, 243
Osborn, Francis A., and his brigade, 89, 296, 301n, 324; Second Deep Bottom, 22,33, 35, 55-56, 88-91, 106, 109, 300-301; Second Reams Station, 298
Otis, John L., 45n, 79
Outlaw, Edward R., 193, 197
Overland Campaign, 11, 289
Parke, John G., 137, 210
Parker, Francis W., 91, 324
Parkhurst, Thomas C., 262
Pegram, William J., and his battalion, 335-336, 342; Battle of Globe Tavern, 153, 160, 188; wrecking the Weldon Railroad, 224; Second Reams Station, 247, 251-252, 255, 263; death of, 298
Pemberton, John C., 6-7, 23, 26, 33, 38; *photo*, 8
Penfield, Nelson, 222, 237-238, 248, 249, 253, 259
Pennsylvania Units
1st Cavalry, 325, 334, 340
1st Light Artillery, Battery B, 332
1st Light Artillery, Battery D, 249
1st Light Artillery, Battery F, 323
2nd Cavalry, 44, 55, 61, 217, 325, 340
2nd Heavy Artillery, 332
4th Cavalry, 53, 55, 61, 231, 234, 268, 325, 340
8th Cavalry, 44, 51, 54, 62, 234, 325, 340
11th Cavalry, 248, 334, 341
11th Infantry, 117, 131, 150n, 197, 248, 331
13th Cavalry, 51, 62, 231, 325, 340
16th Cavalry, 62, 217, 231, 237, 248, 325, 340
16th Infantry, 233
21st Cavalry (Dismounted), 330
23rd Infantry, 133
25th Infantry, 21
45th Infantry, 333
46th Infantry, 63
48th Infantry, 333
50th Infantry, 144, 170, 177, 333
51st Infantry, 333
53rd Infantry, 45n, 234, 248, 253, 321, 339
56th Infantry, 122n, 132, 154, 332
57th Infantry, 53, 68, 83-84, 323
63rd Infantry, 323
69th Infantry, 233, 267, 273, 322, 340
76th Infantry, 97
81st Infantry, 213, 228, 253, 321, 339
83rd Infantry, 117, 198, 330
84th Infantry, 53, 68, 83-84, 323
85th Infantry, 24, 45n, 70, 75n, 76, 78-79, 84, 88, 92, 97
88th Infantry, 132, 135, 141, 150n, 154, 331
90th Infantry, 125-126, 131-132, 331
91st Infantry, 330
97th Infantry, 98, 324
99th Infantry, 323
100th Infantry, 332
105th Infantry, 53, 68, 83-84, 86, 323
106th Infantry, 233, 267, 273, 322, 340
107th Infantry, 125, 150n, 159, 331
110th Infantry, 323
116th Infantry, 233-234, 237-238, 255, 321, 339
118th Infantry, 133, 194, 330
121st Infantry, 123, 202-203, 330
140th Infantry, 60, 203, 228, 234, 272, 321, 339
141st Infantry, 53, 68, 83-84, 86, 323
142nd Infantry, 123, 330
143rd Infantry, 202, 330
145th Infantry, 45n, 222-234, 321, 339
148th Infantry, 45n, 222, 234, 237-238, 248, 253, 321, 339
149th Infantry, 330
150th Infantry, 138n, 330
155th Infantry, 330
157th Infantry, 134, 332
183rd Infantry, 64, 71, 213, 228, 321, 339
184th Infantry, 248, 259, 322, 340
187th Infantry, 171, 202, 330
190th Infantry, 125, 144, 153, 331
191st Infantry, 125, 134-135, 145, 150n, 153, 331
Pennypacker, Galusha, 98
Petersburg Railroad, 15
Petersburg, siege of, 2, 4, 6, 12, 14, 29
Petersburg, Virginia, 3-4, 10, 47, 52-53, 104-105, 111, 119-120, 124, 127-128, 134-135, 143-144, 147-150
Phillips house, 248-249, 268
Phillips, Rolla O., 79
Pickett, George E., and his division, 10, 115; Second Deep Bottom, 104, 107, 111, 112; Battle of Globe Tavern, 180, 210; wrecking the Weldon Railroad, 225; Second Reams Station, 227, 243; August casualties, 287n
Pierce, Francis E., 322
Pierson, Charles L., 131
Plaisted, Harris M., 45n, 97
Plimpton, Homer A., 76, 106
Plimpton, Josiah H., 107n
Polley, Joseph B., 61, 101

Pond, Francis B., and his brigade, 324; Second Deep Bottom, 22, 70, 76, 88, 90
Poplar Spring Church, 187, 202
Porter, Charles H., 122, 156, 160, 177
Porter, Horace, 7
Potter, Edward F., 137, 143, 145, 167-169, 173, 181
Potter, Robert B., 333
Powell, Junius L., 75
Powell, Richard H., 157
Powell, William H., 174
Powelson, Benjamin F., 60, 203
Prince George Court House, 204
Proctor's Creek, 10
Pryor, Roger A., 184, 186, 188
Pulford, John, 57n, 85, 244, 323
Pyne, Henry R., 116, 211
Quaker Road, 44
Ransom, Robert, and his brigade, 195; Battle of Globe Tavern, 182-183, 193-194, 196-197, 204n; Globe Tavern, 306
Reams Station, 119, 141, 148, 185, 211, 213, 217-220, 222-223, 226
Reed, George W., 197
Reed, John, 82-83, 86, 88, 95
Rheinhart, Alfred A., 45n
Rhode Island Units
1st Light Artillery, 241, 256, 258, 262, 266, 325, 340
4th Infantry, 333
7th Infantry, 333
Richardson, Thomas E., 165-166
CSS *Richmond* , 103
Richmond and Danville Railroad, 137-138, 206, 220, 224, 286, 309
Richmond, Virginia, 1, 3-4, 5-5n, 6, 9, 13, 15, 17-18, 20, 64, 75
Richmond's Exterior Defense line, 20
Riddell's Shop, 44, 107-108, 111
Rinaldi, B. F., 277n, 280n
Roback, Henry, 29, 42, 241, 260, 282
Robins, William T., 43, 299
Robinson farm and house, 83, 88, 91, 95, 73, 78
Robinson, Gilbert P., and his brigade, 162, 167, 332
Robinson, William D., 221
Roebling, Washington A., 146
Rosser, Thomas L., Second Deep Bottom, 108, 111, 227; casualties at Second Deep Bottom, 114; wrecking the Weldon Railroad, 214; Second Reams Station, 227
Ruffin house, 23-24
Rugg, Horace P., and his brigade, 45n, 259, 322, 340; Second Deep Bottom, 42; Second Reams Station, 233, 258, 260-261

Sale, John F., 149-149n, 225
Sanders, John C. C., and his brigade, 69, 85, 276, 297, 327, 338; Second Deep Bottom, 47-48, 52, 57, 72-73, 75, 78, 82, 84, 93-94, 103, 104n, 107-108, 305; casualties at Second Deep Bottom, 113n; Battle of Globe Tavern, 183, 187, 198, 204n; death of, 191-192; wrecking the Weldon Railroad, 224; Second Reams Station, 247, 252, 262, 277n, 281n, 283
Sanders, William H., 103
Scales, Alfred M., and his brigade, 341; Second Deep Bottom, 72, 102, 104, 107, 112; Battle of Globe Tavern, 184, 187, 204n, 210; wrecking the Weldon Railroad, 222, 224; Second Reams Station, 236-238, 247-248, 268, 276n, 277n, 281n, 283, 306; August casualties, 287n
Schellenberger, John S., 78
Schreyer, Phillip H., 45n
Scott, James W., 45n
Seaverns, Henry A., 131
Second Bull Run, battle of, 27-28, 53, 103
Second Deep Bottom, battle of, 6-7, 9-10, 15, 17-21, 23, 26, 28-29, 35, 47, 49, 57, 60, 72, 90, 93, 102-104, 107, 112, 115-117, 191, 193, 204, 219n, 281n, 287, 290, 294-296, 301-301n, 302n, 303-303n, 305-306, 308, 312
Second Drewry's Bluff, battle of, 201
Second Reams Station, battle of, 219n, 223-224, 227-238, 240, 243-250, 258-259, 261, 268, 270-271, 275, 276-276n, 277n, 278, 279, 280-280n, 281-281n, 282, 284-285, 287, 291, 292, 294, 296, 298-299, 302, 303-303n, 304, 306, 308, 309n, 311-312
Seward, William H., 312
Shafer, J. W., 219n
Shands farm, 231
Sharpe, George H., 7
Shaw, Jr., James, and his brigade, 324; Second Deep Bottom, 55-56, 90, 93; Second Reams Station, 298
Shay's Tavern, 220, 234, 244-245, 248-250, 261, 273, 275
Sheafer, Henry J., 150n
Shenandoah Valley, 2-3, 10, 13, 17, 21-22, 28, 120, 244, 289, 311
Sheridan, Philip H., 5-5n, 15, 28, 120, 209, 289
Sherman, William T., 2, 4, 5n, 312-313
Sherrill, J. H., 197
Shilling, John, 202
Signal Hill, 10, 18, 35, 102-103, 105
Simons, Ezra D., 259
"The Slash," 27

Smith, Charles H., 248, 325, 340
Smith, Hugh R., 169
Smith, James J., 32
Smith, John Day, 27
Smith, William C., 168
Smyth, Thomas A., and his brigade, 322, 340; Second Deep Bottom, 20; Second Reams Station, 231-233, 235, 247-248, 266-268, 273, 302-302n
South Carolina Units
1st Rifles, 46n, 327, 341
1st Volunteers, 326
2nd Rifles, 24, 93, 326
3rd Cavalry, 328, 342
4th Cavalry, 277, 328, 342
5th Cavalry, 328, 342
5th Infantry, 57, 86, 91, 326
6th Cavalry, 217-218, 231, 328, 342
6th Infantry, 102, 105, 326
7th Cavalry, 18, 28, 30, 114, 329
7th Infantry, 201
11th Infantry, 199
12th Infantry, 92, 327, 341
13th Infantry, 13, 327 341
14th Infantry, 327, 341
21st Infantry, 198, 199
25th Infantry, 190, 198-200
37th Infantry, 92
Hampton Legion, 18, 44, 114, 329
Orr's Rifles, 327, 341
Palmetto Sharpshooters, 24, 326
Pee Dee Artillery, 336
Sumter Artillery, 224
Washington Artillery, 328, 343
Southside Railroad, 2, 128, 137-138, 206, 220, 224, 286
Spear, Samuel P., and his brigade, 171, 248, 296, 334, 341; Battle of Globe Tavern, 141, 185; Second Reams Station, 229-231, 249, 304-304n; wrecking the Weldon Railroad, 211, 213-214, 217, 219n, 222
Spear, William H. A., 98
Spencer, Gideon, 258
Spotsylvania, battle of, 103, 131, 169, 180, 232
Squirrel Level Road, 187, 225
Stage Road, 214, 223
Stanton, Edwin M., 3
Stedman, Charles M., 256
Starke, William N., and his brigade, 163, 303, 325, 334; Second Deep Bottom, 44, 111; Battle of Globe Tavern, 116, 182, 185, 202; Second Reams Station, 249, 275
Stevens, Charles A., 55

Stewart, Robert L., 272
Stewart, William H., 150, 162, 173
Stoney, J. D., 199-200
Stony Creek, 207, 223, 310
Stowe, Samuel N., 260, 285
Stowits, George H., 22, 36, 46n, 51, 108, 114
Strawberry Plains, 19, 28, 44, 49-50
Strong house, 141-143, 145-147, 176
Stuart, James E. B., 246
Sudsborough, Joseph A., 333
Sweeney's Pottery, 10
Taylor, Samuel B., 45n
Taylor, W. H., 276n
Taylor, Walter H., 310, 312
Taylor, William, 130
Taylor, William J., 201
Temple house, 231, 233
Tennessee
1st Infantry, 172n, 334-335
7th Infantry, 172n, 334-335
14th Infantry, 334-335
15th Infantry, 172n
17th/23rd Infantry, 326
23rd Infantry, 102
25th Infantry, 102
25th/44th Infantry, 326
63rd Infantry, 326
Terry, Alfred H., and his division, 26, 51, 68, 70-71, 83, 86, 295, 300, 324; Second Deep Bottom, 22-24, 36, 38, 44, 47, 49, 55-56, 67, 69, 71, 73, 75, 80, 88, 91, 93, 104, 301; wrecking the Weldon Railroad, 223; Second Reams Station, 287n; *photo*, 68
Texas Units
1st Cavalry, 329
4th Cavalry, 329
4th Infantry, 61, 101
5th Cavalry, 329
Texas Brigade, 48, 57, 61, 65, 101
Thieman, August, 157-158
Thomas, George N. B., and his brigade, Second Deep Bottom, 72, 102, 104, 107, 112; Battle of Globe Tavern, 131, 184, 187, 204n, 210; August casualties, 287n
Thomas, Samuel B., 193
Thompson, John, 45n
Thorp, John H., 252-253, 257
Throop, William A., 123n
Tilghman's Gate, 7
Tilton, William S., and his brigade, 171, 330; Battle of Globe Tavern, 122-124, 134, 160, 170, 176, 181, 202
Tobie, Jr., Edward P., 65, 213, 218

Index

Todd, Westwood A., 273
Trueheart, Charles W., 75, 93, 305
Trumbull, Henry C., 96
Terry, Adrian, 24
Tucker farm, 231, 247
United States Colored Troops
4th Infantry, 103, 325
6th Infantry, 103, 325
7th Infantry, 33, 35, 44, 50, 55, 93, 301, 308n, 324
8th Infantry, 35, 44, 49, 90, 102-103, 324
9th Infantry, 33, 35, 44, 55, 93, 97-98, 100, 106, 301, 308n, 324
United States Regular Units
1st Artillery, Batteries C and D, 325
1st Artillery, Battery D, 71
1st Sharpshooters, 53-55, 68, 84, 323
2nd Artillery, Battery A, 325
4th Artillery, Battery K, 72, 321
5th Artillery Battery D, 123n, 332
10th Infantry, 157, 331
11th Infantry, 157, 174, 331
12th Infantry, 124, 145-146, 157-158, 331
14th Infantry, 145-146, 157-158, 331
17th Infantry, 157, 331
Vance, Zebulon, 285
Vande Wiele, John B., 219n, 339
Varina Road, 20, 33
Vaughan farm, 162
Vaughan road, 119, 122, 126, 128, 134, 141-142, 145, 161, 171, 174, 180, 182-184, 186-188, 190, 192-193, 197-198, 202, 204n, 211, 223, 225, 228
Vautier, John D., 154, 156
Virginia Central Railroad, 15, 17, 20, 112, 137
CSS Virginia II, 103
Virginia Military Institute, 129
Virginia Units
1st Infantry, 104, 326
1st Reserves, 18, 115
2nd Battery Jeb Stuart Light Artilley, 63, 229, 328, 343
3rd Company Richmond Howitzers, 32-33, 38, 46n, 57, 299
6th Infantry, 164, 166, 172n, 336, 342
7th Cavalry, 108, 214, 227, 268, 328, 342
9th Cavalry, 43, 62-63, 65-66, 102, 229, 270, 272, 328, 343
10th Cavalry, 62-63, 66, 229, 328, 343
11th Cavalry, 214, 271, 328, 342
11th Infantry, 104, 148, 326
12th Cavalry, 214, 271, 273, 275, 328, 342
12th Infantry, 149, 163-164, 166-169, 171, 172n, 225-226, 262-263, 273, 277n, 281n, 336, 342
13th Cavalry, 55, 62-63, 66, 328, 343
16th Infantry, 164, 172n, 336, 342
19th Infantry, 104, 326
22nd Battalion, 172n, 334-335
24th Cavalry, 18, 28, 42-43, 299, 329
25th Battalion, 18, 72, 102, 115, 326
35th Cavalry Battalion, 214, 264, 328, 342
40th Infantry, 172n, 334-335
41st Infantry, 164, 166-167, 169, 172n, 281n, 336
47th Infantry, 170, 172n, 334-335
55th Infantry, 153, 172n, 334-335
61st Infantry, 150, 162, 164, 169, 277n, 281n, 336, 342
Crenshaw's Battery, 336
Fredericksburg Artillery, 336
Hardaway Light Artillery, 46, 46n, 342
Laurel Brigade, 214-215, 264, 271, 273
Letcher Artillery, 128, 132, 224, 281n, 335-336, 342
Petersburg Artillery, 128, 335-336
Powhatan Artillery, 46n, 327
Purcell Artillery, 336, 342
Rockbridge Artillery, 327
Salem Flying Artillery, 327
Voris, Alvin C., 88, 324
Wainwright, Charles S., 132, 295, 332; Battle of Globe Tavern, 135, 153-157, 160-161, 182-183, 188, 202
Walker, Francis A., 27
Walker's Brigade (R. L. Walker), 139, 149, 278; Battle of Globe Tavern, 128-130, 132, 134-135, 153, 156, 170, 181-182, 193, 195; Globe Tavern, 306; Second Deep Bottom, 305; Second Reams Station, 279, 283-284
Walker, William, 231
Walrath, Ezra L., 90-91, 324
Ware Bottom Church, 210, 227, 300
Warner, Norman C., 76
Warren, Gouverneur K., 203, 330; orders a raid on the Weldon Railroad, 106; Grant orders a raid on the Weldon Railroad, 111; Battle of Globe Tavern, 117, 134-135, 136-136n, 139-147, 150n, 152, 155, 160-162, 166, 174-176, 180-186, 188, 194, 202, 204, 207, 209; ordered to move to the Weldon Railroad, 119-120, 122; makes lodgment on Weldon Railroad, 124; Weldon Railroad, 126, 303; Ayres requests reinforcements, 132-133; Globe Tavern, 149, 172, 290, 298; Five Forks, 209-210; Grant's opinion of, 209; Meade resents, 209; Meade's plan to sack him, 209; wrecking the Weldon Railroad, 211-212, 222; V Corps disaster on Aug. 19, 213; Second Reams Station, 243, 245-246, 275, 282, 291; *photo*, 208
Warren, Horatio N., 123
Washington, D.C., 1, 3-4, 10

Weisiger, David A., and his brigade, 171, 172n, 296, 299, 336, 342; Battle of Globe Tavern, 149n, 150-151, 162-164, 166-169, 176, 182, 191, 201; wrecking the Weldon Railroad, 224; Second Reams Station, 247, 252, 262-263, 265-266, 272-273, 277n, 281n, 283

Welch, Spencer G., 13

Weldon Railroad, 2, 15-17, 104, 106, 111-112, 115-117, 119-120, 123-124, 128, 137-139, 141, 147-149, 156, 158, 162, 171-173, 178, 180-185, 188, 193, 202-206, 211, 213, 222, 223, 225-228, 243-246, 279, 284, 289, 290, 292-295, 309-310

Weldon Railroad, First battle of, 138n

Wells, Edward L., 277

West Point, 5, 7-8, 16, 26, 28, 62-63, 122-123, 137, 140, 220, 299

West Virginia Unit
7th Battalion, 267, 322, 340

Western Brigade, 23-24, 35, 44, 49, 51, 67, 69-71, 75-76, 79-80, 84, 88, 98, 287n

Western Ravine, 71, 72-72n, 73, 79-80, 83-84, 91, 97

Weygant, Charles H., 45n

Wheelock, Charles, and his brigade, 298, 135, 331; Battle of Globe Tavern, 131-132, 150, 155-156, 160, 175, 177, 197

White Oak Swamp, 44, 101, 107

White, J. Chester, 157, 161

White, James, 267, 275

White, Julius, and his Division, 332; Battle of Globe Tavern, 137, 143, 158, 162-163, 166-168, 170, 173n, 176-177, 181; Second Reams Station, 245

White, William S., 23, 57

White's tavern, 44, 50, 55, 62, 64

Wiedrich, Michael, 331

Wilcox farm, 171

Wilcox, Cadmus M., and his division, 13, 305, 341; Second Deep Bottom, 18, 28, 47, 73, 102, 104, 107-108, 112; casualties at Second Deep Bottom, 113-113n; Battle of Globe Tavern, 176, 184, 210; wrecking the Weldon Railroad, 224-225; Second Reams Station, 229, 232, 235-241, 245-247, 251, 261-262, 276n, 277n, 280n, 298, 306; August casualties, 287n; Deep Bottom, 297

Wilderness, battle of, 5, 28, 46, 53, 58, 72, 86, 138, 148, 157, 168, 232, 262

Willcox, Orlando B., and his division, 333; Battle of Globe Tavern, 140-141, 143-144, 146, 160-162, 166, 175-176, 181; Second Reams Station, 244-245, 250, 274-275; Reams Station, 296

Williams house, 275

Willis Church Road, 108

Wilson, John W., 130

Wilson, William, 253-253n

Wilson-Kautz Raid, 138, 206, 220

Winthrop, Frederick, 158, 171, 195, 331

Winton, William, 309

Wisconsin Units
2nd Infantry, 55
6th Infantry, 133, 146, 153, 175, 191, 332
7th Infantry, 147, 152, 181, 193, 332
36th Infantry, 42, 248, 258, 278, 322, 340
37th Infantry, 333
38th Infantry, 333
Independent Battalion, 331

Wooster, William B., 102

Wooten, Chade, 253

Wright, Gilbert J., and his brigade, 76, 299, 328, 342; Battle of Globe Tavern, 183, 187, 204n; casualties at Second Deep Bottom, 113n; Second Deep Bottom, 47-48, 52, 57, 71-75, 77-78, 82, 108, 111, 305; Second Reams Station, 227, 273, 307

Wyatt house, 211-212

Yarbrough house, 22, 23, 44

Young, Louis G. and his brigade, Second Deep Bottom, 108, 111; casualties at Second Deep Bottom, 114; Battle of Globe Tavern, 195; Second Reams Station, 227, 254, 256, 271-273

About the Author

A native of Illinois, John Horn received a B.A. in English and Latin from New College (Sarasota, Florida) in 1973 and a J.D. from Columbia Law School in 1976. He has practiced law in the Chicago area since graduation, occasionally holding local public office, and living in Oak Forest with his wife and law partner, H. Elizabeth Kelley, a native of Richmond, Virginia. They have three children. He and his wife travel to the Old Dominion each year to visit relatives, battlefields, and various archives.

He has published articles in *Civil War Times, Illustrated* and *America's Civil War*, and his books include *The Destruction of the Weldon Railroad and The Petersburg Campaign*. With Hampton Newsome (author of *Richmond Must Fall*) and Dr. John G. Selby (author of *Virginians at War*), Horn co-edited *Civil War Talks: The Further Reminiscences of George S. Bernard & His Fellow Veterans*.